AMERICAN FEDERALISM
IN PERSPECTIVE

INTRODUCTORY READERS IN AMERICAN POLITICS

AMERICAN FEDERALISM
IN PERSPECTIVE

Readings Selected and Edited
by AARON WILDAVSKY
University of California, Berkeley

LITTLE, BROWN AND COMPANY
Boston

Contents

v

Editor's Introduction

The major purpose of this reader is to place American federalism in a broad analytical context. There is ample material available on contemporary practices; this book, however, introduces the subject of federalism by readings on conceptual analysis, general theory, comparative examples, and historical experience. Special attention is given to the interaction between party and federal systems because prevailing theory points to the critical nature of this relationship. The emphasis throughout is on analysis rather than polemics.

The greatest barrier to an understanding of federalism is a lack of conceptual clarity. No theoretical and empirical progress can be made, no reasonable evaluation suggested, if the student is unclear about the meaning given to the diverse phenomena that come under the name of federalism. The articles by Rufus Davis and William Livingston point out to the student the various applications of this term by scholars in the past. The authors then go on to suggest ways of clarifying the many conceptual muddles. To my knowledge, there are no better attempts to straighten out the subject matter of federalism.

There are few theories of the origins and maintenance of federal systems; nor can it be said that most existing theories are buttressed by convincing evidence. Yet the creation and verification of theory is the major goal of any scholarly study. Students need to know the major prevailing theories and to gauge the extent to which they are tenable when confronted with the actual world situation. The most successful attempt to

formulate a theory of federalism, in my opinion, is found in
William Riker's book on *Federalism: Origin, Operation, Significance*. A. H. Birch reaches a conclusion similar to Riker's in his
article evaluating contemporary theories of federalism in which
these theories are also tested on the basis of recent African and
Asian experience.

A review of recent theory suggests that the party system is a
crucial variable in explaining the maintenance of federal governments. This view of the importance of the party system is held
not only by Riker but also by David Truman and Morton
Grodzins in their now classic writings on the subject. Experiences in Australia and Canada provide a comparative view.
These nations are close enough to America to make comparison
meaningful yet sufficiently different to make the contrast valuable. The Australian experience, for example, illustrates the
difficulties that federal structure places in the path of disciplined
national parties ruled from outside the central legislature. No
doubt a parliamentary form of government encourages disciplined parties within the national legislature. Steven Muller's
perceptive analysis of Canadian experience makes us aware,
however, that the existence of independent and vigorous provincial parties helps create a political system extremely sensitive
to regional demands despite the high degree of party cohesion
in Parliament.

The student of American federalism would be ill-served by
the perpetuation of myths concerning the glorious past. Daniel
Elazar shows that, at least in the policy areas covered, there was
in the nineteenth century a great deal more cooperation between
state and nation than has been supposed. Evidently, there is
also more continuity between the past and the present than we
like to believe. Yet the history of federalism, especially as an
expression of popular feeling, has developed in many different
ways throughout the world. Arnold Brecht's comparison of the
United States and Germany brings vividly to mind the vast gulf
that separates a federal union of popularly elected state governments and a federation of princes.

The distinctive character of contemporary American practices
in the operation of federal government is clearly revealed in
Brecht's comparative view. No mere enumeration of the division
of powers in the United States has the force achieved through

contrast with the German example. By focusing on actual behavior rather than on rhetoric, Edward Weidner is able to distinguish conflict over specific policies from disagreement over the structure of the federal system. Students should find these two articles a valuable antidote to extreme statements about the demise of federalism, whether couched in the form of handwringing about the encroachments of the "federal octopus" or moans about reactionary state officials standing in the way of a good life for all. The multiple ways by which federalism is woven into government practices are highlighted in Morton Grodzins' famous analogy—a federal form of government as a marble cake whose layers interpenetrate rather than dominate one another.

Although brief appraisals of federalism are implicit in several of the articles in this collection and explicit in Morton Grodzins' work, I have deliberately avoided the usual polemical literature on states' rights, central control, and the rest. Not that I always dislike polemics; rather, I find the debate on federalism shopworn and less and less meaningful as time goes on. It seemed desirable, therefore, to concentrate on analysis, instructive both in its own right and as a better preparation for those interested in political dispute. Hence, the emphasis here is on conceptual clarity, empirical theory, and comparative analysis. Life is changing; it seems only right that the perennial debate over federalism should be better informed that it may also change.

I would like to thank Steven Muller for his original contribution on federalism in Canada and to express my gratitude to William Riker for reminding me of Arnold Brecht's valuable comparison of German and American federalism. Bryson Collins and Terry Hubbard effectively performed various clerical chores.

SECTION

I

CONCEPTS

1   *The "Federal Principle" Reconsidered*

RUFUS DAVIS

SOME IDEAS CONCERNING THE DIVISION OF FUNCTIONS

The most common idea—sometimes described as the "inescapable federal principle" of distributing functions—is this:[1] That those matters of a "national," "general," or "common" interest should be vested in the central government, while matters of a "local" or "particular" interest should be left in the hands of the regional governments. There are at least two things to be noticed about this so-called "principle." First, it prescribes what is necessarily implicit in the act of federation. It would be absurd, for instance, to reverse the principle so that it enjoined federating states to vest all "local" and "particular" matters in the general government, and all "national" or "common" matters in the regional governments. But aside from this, what one must note is that this "inescapable federal principle of distributing functions" is only a meaningful directive if there is a mode of knowing what is a "national," "common," "local," or "particular" matter. If, for example, we advise an expedition to move in the direction of East or West, there are a number of ways by which this direction can be explained, and whichever of these ways we employ the true test will be that the expedition will in fact move in the desired direction, East or West. Can we, however, formulate an objective test to denote which are and which are not "national" and "local" functions?[2] Sometimes the geo-

From *Australian Journal of Politics and History*, I (May 1956), pp. 223-244. Reprinted by permission of the editors of *The Australian Journal of Politics and History* and the author.

  [1] See McGregor Dawson, *The Government of Canada*, Toronto, 1949, p. 96.

  [2] See generally the suggestive analysis of this problem by William Anderson in *Federalism and Inter-governmental Relations. A Budget of Suggestions for Research.* Mimeographed. Public Administration Service, Chicago, 1946, pp. 18-29. This "Budget of Suggestions" is a mine of valuable research ideas on federalism, and this is the only source, to my knowledge, which has posed the difficulties of designating "national" and "local" functions in any detail.

graphical dichotomy of "external" and "internal" is used to indicate the sort of matters which are appropriately "national" and "local." However, this is of small value as a guide since—as Sidgwick points out—"it leaves doubtful how matters external to the parts but not to the whole are to be determined . . . secondly, matters *prima facie* internal may be of serious common interest to the whole . . ."[3] More commonly the notion of "national" functions is illustrated by such examples as defence, foreign affairs, overseas trade, and "local" functions by such examples as education, health, police, etc. But what is the differentiating property of these activities which characterises them as "national" or "local"? Is it in the nature of the need or the purpose they are intended to satisfy; the nature of the organisation required to administer these needs, or is the identification of "national" or "local" matters a purely subjective preference for centralised or decentralised government in one field of activity or another? There is nowhere a clear answer.

In an issue which came before the United States Supreme Court in 1851 a Mr. Justice Curtis formulated some "tests" to decide whether a matter was appropriate for "national" or "local" regulation. He distinguished four situations:[4] (1) situations in which the nature of the thing to be regulated, or the end to be achieved, imperatively demands a single, nation-wide uniform rule; (2) situations in which a national uniform rule would be desirable, but in which local variations are not intolerable; (3) situations in which there would be a "superior fitness and propriety" to local rules adapted to the needs of the locality and circumstances; and (4) situations in which the conditions "imperatively demand" or require as an "absolute necessity" a diversity of rules.

Attractive as this classification is, it scarcely leaves us in possession of anything even remotely approaching unambiguous or objective criteria. It is, presumably, in the very nature of the "defence" and "foreign affairs" activities which "imperatively demand" a single nation-wide uniform rule, but to which of the categories (2), (3), and (4) should we assign the activities of health, education, banking, agriculture, social insurance, in-

---

[3] See H. Sidgwick, *Elements of Politics*, London, 1891, p. 508.
[4] See *Cooley v. Board of Wardens of Philadelphia*, 12 Howard 299. Quoted in Anderson, *op. cit.*, p. 20.

dustrial disputes, social and economic planning? To answer this we may assemble such data as the prevalent "consciousness in the community" of "national" and "local" needs, the "areas" of each activity, the alternative public service organisations required to administer particular needs, the financing of each activity, and so on.[5] And on this basis it may be possible to formulate an inventory of indispensable "national" and "local" matters for each particular society, at each stage of its development. But this done, one could never be certain that this "distribution" would in fact correspond with a purely subjective preference for one level of government instead of another in the performance of any of these functions. That is, one might expect the Curtis tests to yield not merely a different group of "national" and "local" activities for different social systems but a different selection of activities for different people in the same political system.[6]

A second view of the division of functions interposes a qualitative factor into the national/local formula. It postulates the condition that if the federal principle is to be satisfied the division of functions should invest both the general and regional governments with "important," "significant," or "high" functions. Thus Sidgwick, for example: "In laying down that the autonomy of the parts of the federal state must be considerable in extent, I mean that we should hardly call a state federal merely because the independence of local governments in certain *minor* matters was guaranteed by the constitution."[7] The precise character of this idea is no less difficult to define than the content of national/local functions. If we presume, for example, that the regulation of any part of social activity is "important" or "significant" for some

[5] See Anderson, *op. cit.,* pp. 18-24.

[6] Compare, for example, the distribution of functions in the U.S. and Indian constitutions. Note also the incessant debate in Australia at each referendum on the "matters" appropriate for "national" and "local" action.

[7] Sidgwick, *loc. cit.* Also Lord Carnarvon, "The real object which we have in view is to give the central government those high functions and almost sovereign powers by which general principles and uniformity of legislation may be secured in those questions which are of common import to all the provinces; and at the same time, to retain for each province so ample a measure of municipal liberty and self-government as will allow and indeed compel them to exercise the local powers which they exercise with great advantage to the community." Quoted, S. Mogi, *The Problem of Federalism,* London, 1931, p. 233. See also Waitz, and Von Mohl, *ibid.,* p. 402, quoted Mogi, *op. cit.,* p. 383.

political purpose or other then this prescription is valueless. What might be implied here, therefore, is either (a) that it is possible to draw a distinction between types of social activity which are "important" and those which are "unimportant" as subjects of governmental control; or (b) that we can arrange the possible subjects of governmental regulation in some scale of importance. If we intend the first we must then ensure that some portion of the "important" functions are vested in both governments; or if we intend the second, we must ensure that neither the general or regional governments are invested only with "minor" matters. These assumptions do not call for comment here. What deserves comment, however, are two things: First, the notion of "important" or "unimportant" tells us little or nothing about the governmental activities which are or are not "important." And for their part the sources do no more than indicate in the vaguest fashion what is of importance both for federal and state activity.[8] Secondly, to designate what is important or "unimportant," or what is of major importance or minor importance as a governmental function raises a set of issues which are not susceptible to the formulation of objective criteria. Obviously the questions *for whom, for what purpose,* and *in what circumstances* a function is or is not important for governmental action will determine the content of any division of functions which applies this condition. Mogi points out, for example, that for Waitz and his contemporaries a distribution effected in this way simply meant that "the collectivity of foreign relations" was committed to the central government and "as much as possible all internal relations" to the regions.[9] But this distribution presupposes a particular historical and political moment in which the conduct of "foreign relations" is deemed important. And we may conceive a different situation, for example a World Federation of all States, in which the activity of "foreign relations" is meaningless.

A third view of the division of functions characterises the main body of nineteenth century juristic writing, and is probably the simplest to state. Briefly, it asserts that the federal principle does not prescribe any physical, moral, or qualitative conditions for

[8] See Waitz, quoted Mogi, *op. cit.*, p. 383.
[9] *Ibid.*

the distribution of functions. It is indifferent to the precise content of the division, and it argues that there is no *a priori* principle by which a distribution of functions could be effected. The definitive element of the federal state is simply in the *form* of the division, not its substance; in the creation of a specific kind of jural relationship between law-making authorities, not in the material quality of the functions vested in the general and regional governments.[10]

If we pause for one moment at this stage to apply any of these three views of the division of functions to our problematic "postman's helmet" federation, it is not difficult to justify its "federal" category. As a matter of historical fact, of course, there has been no such federation. The nucleus of the functions commonly vested in the general governments has, with all the variations of time and place, corresponded fairly closely to a constant pattern in which matters of war, of foreign relations, of overseas trade, etc., have formed the core of federal activity. To acknowledge this, however, is not to invalidate the fantasy of a "postman's helmet" federation, on any other ground than an *ex post facto* historical generalisation. Logically none of these views exclude a federal category. It is conceivable, for instance, that the regulation of "postman's helmets" (or for that matter, white mice) could become a matter of either national or local importance. True, in respect to the "ambit" and the "importance" of the matters vested in the general government, this Gilbertian federation could be easily distinguished from an association of states in which more extensive, or more important, matters were given to the general government. But the mere difference in the content and significance of the powers divided would not—on the present criteria—invalidate their common classification as "federal" states any more than the disparity in the functions of the United States Congress, and an English School-board excludes their common (Diceyan) classification as "non-sovereign law-making bodies." What Sidgwick's view simply enjoins is that matters of "importance" should be vested in the general and regional governments. He does not argue, nor does the legal fiction of co-equal status require, that the distribution of func-

[10] See, for example, Zachariah, Meyer, and von Trietchke, quoted in Mogi, *op. cit.*, at pp. 393, 587, and 790. This is certainly the view we may reasonably associate with Dicey also.

tions should attempt the absurdity of *equating* the scope and the importance of functions vested in the two levels of government.[11]

The greatest obstacle which this hypothetical federal state may have to face is in the test implicitly invoked by Professor Wheare in *Federal Government*.[12] Wheare's view is directly reflected in his analysis of the Weimar Republic and the Soviet Constitution. Of the reasons which persuade him to assign a quasi-federal status to the Weimar Constitution, for example, he refers to the division of functions in this way—"the scope of the powers conferred upon the general legislature is so wide that it is difficult to see what topics of any importance are left to the regional government *if the general legislature chose to exercise its powers to the full*."[13] Or similarly, he writes of the 1936 Soviet Constitution—"Article 14 gives the All-Union legislature such comprehensive powers over almost all spheres of life that it leaves little to the constituent republic, *if the All-Union chooses to exercise them to the full*."[14]

The precise meaning of this criterion and the mode by which we can apply it to any arrangement is again somewhat elusive. How should we read Wheare? To mean, simply that "too much" power should not be vested in the general government and "too little" in the regions; or conversely "too little" in the general government and "too much" in the regions in case either level of government can endanger the other if it should exercise its powers to the full. What then is "too much" and what is "too little"? How can functions be divided so that if exercised to the "full" neither the general government nor the regions will be endangered or deprived of "significant" powers? To answer these questions it is necessary to examine the anatomy of a division of functions.

THE ANATOMY OF DIVISION

The nature of a physical division—for example, of land, money, flour, clothing, marbles—is a relatively clear process. The object to be divided is known, we can stipulate a ratio, effect the division, and measure, weigh or compute the result to test the

---

[11] See von Trietchke, quoted Mogi, *op. cit.*, p. 790.
[12] See K. C. Wheare, *Federal Government*, London, 1946, p. 26.
[13] *Ibid.*
[14] *Ibid.*, p. 27.

fidelity of the division. What do we divide, however, when we divide not an area of land or a number of commodities but the field of those human activities which are or may become the subject of governmental control. First, it is clear that neither the language nor the ideas of a physical division are profitably applicable to this process. Thus, even though Madison can speak of "sums" or "quantities" of power, we cannot quantify all those activities which are or may become the subject of governmental control, we cannot presume that these activities are finite or infinite, and we cannot employ the idea of a ratio except metaphorically. Implicit in all divisions of functions, there is to be sure a legal imagery of an infinite body of present and future political activity – the legal imagery of sovereignty – for which the technique of the "residuary" grant is employed to escape the necessity of denoting its entire content. But whereas the limits of the "residuary" bequest in the division of an estate can be determined because it is material, we can never presume that the "residuary" grant of power in the division of functions is finite or infinite. What is involved here, therefore, despite the legal tidiness of the residuary grant, is not an attempt to map all the world of possible activity prior to division, but simply to identify and group those parts of political activity known to us or conceivable by us within such conventional and variable abstractions as "defence," "agriculture," "trade and commerce," etc.

If we cannot employ the ideas of physical division what then does the "division of functions" involve? To answer this, it is first important to realise that the federal constitution is essentially a political bargain, struck by political bargainers – the "Founding Fathers" – who assemble from a variety of motives to create some degree of permanent union between communities where previously there was none, or to create some degree of diversity where previously there was complete union. It is founded on a particular set of assumptions and expectations as to who should make the law, over what territorial area, over what activities, in what relation the laws of the general and regional governments should stand to each other, what sort of government should prevail, and what benefits will flow from the bargain. The settlement is then enshrined in the form of fundamental law to bear testimony to its terms, and a mode of arbitration is erected to resolve disputes about their meaning. Secondly, the process which goes by the name of the "division of functions" is a unique form of division, containing its own procedure, its own techniques, and its own fictions. What is divided in this process is the world of known or conceivable political activities and the principle of division is fundamentally the principle of the market place, the principle of mutual satisfaction. What functions are vested in the general government, and what left to the regions, what activities are expressed and what implied, what activities are protected, and what activities denied only emerge from an elaborate system of political "horse-trading" in which the variety of interests seeking expression must be compromised. The technique of the "division" varies: specific functions may be vested in the general government, and the "residue" left to the regions, or specific functions may be vested in both, and the "residue" left to the general government or the regions. A general field of activities may be vested "exclusively" in one authority, e.g., health, or it may be divided by geographic analogy, e.g., "intra-state" and "overseas" quarantine; or particular kinds of health activities may be designated, e.g., quarantine, and vested in one authority; or a general field of activity may be shared by two authorities with the proviso that in the event of conflict the laws of one or the other should prevail. There is neither science nor theory in this process. It is not a mathematical division where high exactitude is possible. There is only the skill of translating precedent to local circumstance, and the draftsmanship to express the compromised purposes of the key bargainers in language to satisfy them. McGregor Dawson's comment on the allocation of power in Canada aptly explains the nature of every division of functions in every federal system since 1787:

The original allocation of power was not made . . . on any *a priori* basis; it represented the greatest common measure of agreement that could be formulated among conflicting interests at the time, and the primary test it had to meet was the approval it could command from the federating colonies.

In this view of the division of functions, the question of what is "too much" or "too little" can only be answered in terms of the assumptions and expectations enshrined in the bargain. If, for example, the distribution of functions in the "postman's helmet" federation precisely expresses the desires of those who entered the bargain, then neither "too much" has been given, or "too little" taken, for there is no standard outside the purposes of the "Founding Fathers" by which a grant of power may be deemed "too much" or "too little." To say in answer that a grant of power to one party of the bargain is "too much" because it could, if it chose to exercise its powers to the "full," deprive the other of significant powers, is to presume that by scrutinising the language of the bargain it is possible to know what the complete "ambit" of any power is. Can we have such knowledge?

In a paper read to the International Political Science Association in Zurich in 1950, for example, Professor Wheare considered what were the "minimal" powers necessary to invest in the general government of a Western European Federation, and concluded that the powers of "defence," "foreign affairs," and "taxation" were sufficient. Assuredly he was anticipating the "minimum" powers which the federating states might be prepared to concede, and also the "minimum" powers required to render federal government meaningful. But if we disregard the circumstantial factors, and take these subjects of power to be the "minimum" group of powers vested in all federal governments since 1787, then the vast range of activities in which the governments of U.S.A., Australia and Canada now engage have been validated almost entirely by their power over taxation, defence and foreign affairs.

Clearly, in the experience of federal states, it is impossible to determine the "ambit" of any power, simply because the activities which do or do not come within the ambit of power are ultimately a matter of judicial stipulation. We can know approximately, of course, or be informed at any moment about those activities which have come within the compass of such terms as "defence," or "health" through local usage or local judicial precedent. But obviously we cannot know with any certainty either the total range of activities which these conventional symbols can subsume now or in the future, the manner in which governments will legislate for these activities; or to what purposes these activities will be directed. For example, the activity of regulating entry into a university may serve either the purpose of "education" or "defence"; or the federal power to tax may involve either the right to deprive the states of tax revenues, or only the right to share with the states in the distribution of the

taxpayers' income. What will decide the class of the activity in
the first case and the nature of the right in the second is not
simple definition, political dispute or logic, but only a judicial
contest.

"INDEPENDENCE" AND THE "AMBIT" OF POWER

If this view of the "division" may be assumed, what then
is the nature of the "independence" which members of the
federal state can enjoy within their "ambit" of power? What are
they free to do, and what restraints are they free from within such
imperfect frontiers of action? The conventional answer is this:
that within their "ambit" of power, and the terms of the bargain,
the members of the federal state are free to pursue what ends
they choose, and in what manner they choose *providing they do
not "destroy, limit, or encroach" upon the sphere of each other*. It
is scarcely surprising that a "freedom" so expressed should be
subject to the endless dispute of all the parties to the bargain. But
does the situation allow for a more precise statement than this?

As a first approach we can try to formulate some idea of
the frustrations and restraints from which neither the general nor
the regional governments can be possibly free. It seems obvious,
for instance, that neither the federal nor the state governments
can escape the socio-economic and political conditions which
follow from each other's activities, or through the interaction of
their activities unless we completely arrest political activity.
Wheare, for example, notes that the "financial autonomy" of the
regional governments "is always conditional upon their working
within the framework of currency and credit determined in the
last resort by the general government—so far as such matters are
determined by governments at all."[15] Equally, of course, the
freedom of regional governments to pursue agricultural policies
is conditional upon their working within the framework of federal tariff policy; and conversely, the ability of the federal government to carry out its responsibilities for migration is subject to
those industrial and agricultural conditions created by the regions. To claim an immunity from these conditions is to claim
what is patently absurd, for not even a sovereign state—or for that

[15] Wheare, *op. cit.*, p. 99.

matter an individual in society—functions within a socio-economic vacuum.

The defining quality of these situations, however, is not, as it may appear, the creation of conditions which are by their nature inescapable. For the imperative requirement of all conditions created by federal and state governments—no less than individuals—is that they must flow from a *valid* exercise of power. Thus, for example, a state can free itself from the conditions of a federal tariff, federal currency, or federal banking policy if it can establish that there is no federal right to impose tariffs, control currency, or direct banking; or if it can prove that there is no right to exercise those powers in a particular way. The central question then becomes what constitutes a valid exercise of power? Is it the mark of a "valid" activity that it does not create *any* conditions which "limit," "encroach," or "frustrate" the activity of others; or is it the mark of a valid activity that though it creates such conditions they are only "incidental" to a purpose which is not to "frustrate," "limit," or "encroach" upon the activities of others? Necessarily one enters the realm of "law-talk," because the answer can only emerge for each single activity as it passes through the ritual of the judicial process. In this rite the formal referent is the written "bargain"—the constitution—and the nominal categories of power are simply points of departure for a process which seeks no more than to resolve the clash of interests, and the ceaseless dispute between political ends and legal means within some semblance of legal order. In each system the judicial ideas of the "federal principle," their beliefs about the permissible activity of government, the appropriate canons of interpretation and the manner in which the conflicting interests seek to formalise the principle of action sealed in the "bargain," have each undergone a rich variety of change with changes in judicial personnel, the times and the issues.[16] At any moment in each system, of course, it is possible to give instances as to what constitutes a "limitation" or "encroachment," and what sort of "limitation" is permissible or not. In Australia, for example, the federal government, by its prior right of access to the taxpayer's

---

[16] Switzerland, of course, is a partial exception to this view. See Part I of my article, p. 79.

pocket, can so exercise its power that little or nothing is left to the states; or it can abort state industrial programmes by a change in its tariff or credit policy; or it can materially influence the quality and volume of their public investment, and so on. But there is no logical compulsion in this "wilderness of single instances" to yield one principle of "frustration," "limitation," or "encroachment."[17] It is now axiomatic that what is or is not a "limitation," what is a "valid" or "invalid" limitation *must* (by the very nature of the process chosen to resolve the clash of interests) be what the judges say it is. And the history of judge-made law invites no other view than this: that the parties to the original federal "bargain" can never be certain that the words in which they have clothed their intentions can ever be more than a rough guide to political activity, or that the range of permissible activity at any time after will bear any exact relation to their intentions.

The question then, what is the constitutional "independence," "freedom," or "mastery" which the units of the federal state may enjoy, is not capable of an easy answer. Clearly neither the federal nor state governments can claim to be free from the socio-economic consequences of powers "validly" exercised by one or the other. This is simply one of the facts of federal life so often thrust aside by the high sentiments attending the birth of a federal union. The mode by which federal and state governments exercise their powers may advantage, deflect, predetermine, or abort the policies which each member seeks to pursue. What they are free to do, however, is to employ what powers they have to arrest, diminish, neutralise, or turn to their advantage those conditions they believe inimical to their interest. Their capacity to do so, of course, may vary profoundly with the range of their formal powers, their wealth, and their political influence. We can scarcely equate the manoeuvrability of the federal governments to the states in any federal system, or even among the states, the manoeuvrability of New South Wales with Tasmania, Ontario with Nova ʻScotia, or New York State with Alabama. But to equalise the "independence" of federal and state governments in any one of these three respects, in the number and importance of their powers, the scope and size of their revenue, and in the

[17] See the illuminating article by Dr. Samuel Stoljar, "The Logical Status of a Legal Principle," in *Chicago Law Review*, Vol. 20, No. 2, Winter 1953, pp. 181 *et seq.*

influence they can marshal, is quite impossible, and there is no such pretension in the conventional body of federal theory. *In one sense, and one sense only is the "independence" of all units within all federal systems indistinguishable in degree or kind — the mutually irrevocable freedom of each unit to initiate those measures and pursue those ends it believes to be within its ambit of power.* In this activity — the power to initiate measures — their mastery is complete, and it is never so inviolate again, not even when those activities over which they claim mastery have become accepted as part of the established order and expectations of the community. For once the formal act of initiation, whether through parliamentary or executive action, is at an end, the endurance of their enterprise is conditional (apart from all other qualifying factors) upon their skill in anticipating judicial reaction, upon the absence of constitutional challenge, or in the event of challenge, upon the constant approval of their activity by the courts.

To define the "independence" of federal and state governments in this way is, of course, to define only one and perhaps the most — if not the only — coherent aspect of the "independence" connoted by the "federal principle." It is necessary now to enquire into two further elements of the idea of "independence," the financial means to be master, and the political ability to be master.

"INDEPENDENT AND CO-ORDINATE" FISCAL STATUS

As a beginning let us first note the precise injunction of the "Federalists." "Money," wrote Hamilton, "is with propriety considered as the vital principle of the body politic; as that which sustains its life and motion, and enables it to perform its most essential function. A complete power, therefore, to procure a regular and adequate supply of revenue, as far as the resources of the community will permit, may be regarded as an indispensable ingredient in every constitution." From this premise he urged that the "federal government must of necessity be vested with an unqualified power of taxation," and — with much less of the same grand conviction — that the "individual states should possess an independent and uncontrollable authority to raise their own revenue for the supply of their wants."[18]

[18] See *The Federalist*, The Modern Library edition, New York. Letters 30-36.

Hamilton's precepts find little place in subsequent discussions of federal theory until well nigh the present century. There is an occasional side-long glance at "finance" in several sources[19] but no elaborate concern with fiscal schemes or with the implications of Hamilton's ideas. The travails of the federal system in the last half century, however, have led to this typical reassertion of the "Federalist" concepts. It is not enough, Wheare writes for example, to found a federal system by a division of "sovereign or political power which simply ensures the constitutional equality of the central and regional governments . . ." Clearly "independence" or "equality" in the eyes of the law alone is little or nothing if divorced from means; hence if the federal principle "is to operate not merely as a matter of strict law but also in practice, it follows that *both general and regional governments must each have under its own independent control financial resources sufficient to perform its exclusive functions. Each must be financially co-ordinate with the other.*"[20] This is the characteristic language of mid-twentieth century "realist" federalism, and the question it poses is whether a fiscal scheme can be devised to satisfy the constitutional assumptions of the "federal principle."

The matter can be approached in this way: Let us suppose we are commissioned to prepare a financial settlement which must fulfil these twin specifications; (a) that both federal and state governments should have independent control of financial resources, and (b) that the resources should be sufficient to perform their exclusive functions.[21] It is emphasised, moreover, that no arrangement which safeguards the "independence" of each unit without ensuring it a "sufficiency" of resources, or conversely, "sufficient" resources without the guarantee of "independent" control is acceptable. As a prelude to this task it would be first

[19] See Waitz, and Bentham, in Mogi, *op. cit.*, pp. 384, 277.

[20] Wheare, *op. cit.*, p. 97. *Cf.* Moore and Perry, *Financing Canadian Federation*, Canadian Tax Foundation, Tax Paper No. 6, 1953, p. 55.

[21] A third condition which one school — generally the school of anti-equalisation economists — have projected recently is that a fiscal settlement should not merely satisfy the twin criteria of "independence" and "sufficiency" but also the demands of economic "efficiency." See for example, A. D. Scott, "A Note on Grants in Federal Countries," in *Economica*, Vol. XVII, No. 68, Nov., 1950, pp. 416-22. The issues raised by Scott and others are mainly concerned with the injury to an economy if the constitutional implications of the federal principle are rigidly pursued. This is a "specialist" argument, and my only concern here is to examine the traditional criteria of a federal fiscal settlement.

necessary to consider the nature of its three basic ingredients, (i) the idea of fiscal *"independence,"* (ii) the idea of fiscal *"sufficiency,"* and (iii) the "ambit" of exclusive functions vested in the general and regional governments. Here, however, it will be sufficient to concentrate mainly on the first two concepts.[22]

The body of ideas implicit in the term "fiscal independence" is substantially similar to those invoked by the constitutional notion of "independence" in the exercise of all powers in general. That is, once fiscal sources are divided—in any of the possible combinations—then each unit is free to enjoy its revenue without restriction, infringement, or invasion by any other unit. Each may exploit its resources completely or partially, and apply its revenue to such ends as it chooses, when it chooses. From this situation it is possible to select four integral elements of fiscal "independence": (a) the right to decide when to raise revenue; (b) the right to elect the purposes for which revenue is to be raised; (c) the right to determine the amount to be raised; and (d) the machinery to administer these decisions. A model of perfect fiscal independence would then combine at least these four elements, and conversely the model of complete dependence would be defined as the total absence of these four ingredients. This given, however, one would need to take further into account that between these two points of perfect fiscal independence and perfect fiscal dependence a variety of situations may be found. For example, we might find a situation in which there is a constitutional right to decide the amount to be raised within any one year without the capacity to determine the time when it is to be raised; or the right to elect when loan money should be raised and the purposes to which the money is to be applied but not the amount to be raised; or the right to elect the purposes to which loan moneys are to be applied but not the amount nor the time when such moneys are to be raised, and so on in any possible combination. If we wished then to construct a scale between these two points it would be necessary to determine not merely the degree to which these ingredients were present in any arrangement but also their relative importance to the idea of fiscal independence. For example, it may be argued that it is

---

[22] I have already touched on the problem of defining the "ambit" of exclusive power, and will assume throughout this section that the difficulties are known.

more important to be able to nominate the revenue one wants, and the purposes to which this money is to be appropriated, than to depend on the administrative facilities of another government to satisfy these decisions. Alternatively, it may be more important to elect the precise purposes on which money is to be spent, than the precise amount of money to be raised, or when it is to be raised, and so on again with all the possible variations in value given to particular situations. But clearly, if the relative importance of these situations is determined subjectively then what must emerge is not one scale of fiscal independence but as many scales as there are decision-makers, unless that is, one can assume that the comparative values of these alternative situations must be the same for all.[23]

The second prerequisite—that the resources of each unit should be "sufficient" or "adequate" to perform its exclusive functions—is more difficult. Two preliminary observations can be made. In one sense we may say that the notion of fiscal independence implies a "sufficiency" of revenues. That is, a state is only "independent" if it has "sufficient" resources for its activities, and therefore has no need of assistance. But a state may assert its "independence" in circumstances where, lacking the resources to carry out its functions "adequately," it prefers to abandon or reduce its projects rather than seek help from other governments.[24] These two situations, however, must be distinguished because what the "Federalists" enjoin is a scheme in which the two elements of "independence" and "sufficiency" are so combined that there is no need either for mendicancy or for a pauper state to display its pride. The second observation is this: In the terms of our reference the idea of "sufficiency" is related to a particular body of exclusive functions; it follows, therefore, that since the functions of the general and regional governments vary in number and scope the idea of co-ordinate fiscal status cannot require an equality of resources between these two levels of government. Necessarily there must be a

[23] See Moore and Perry, op. cit., p. 55. "Critical examination of the Tax Agreements is complicated by the multiplicity of the objectives of any division of revenues between the two levels of government. The difficulty is increased by the diversity of views concerning which of these deserves priority." et seq.

[24] See e.g. L. F. Giblin's essay in Federalism in Australia, Melbourne, 1949, p. 89.

difference in the relative magnitude of their means. And this difference can only be offensive to the terms of reference when and if it is possible to demonstrate that relative to their needs one enjoys a superiority of resources over the other.

Given this it becomes important to discover by what standard we should judge whether the allocation of fiscal resources is such that each unit has "sufficient" to perform its exclusive functions. There are two positions to be considered, (a) the relationship between the states, *i.e.*, between units exercising the same functions; and (b) the relationship between the federal government and the states, *i.e.*, between two levels of government exercising different functions.

In the first case if we take the exclusive standard of each unit as the criterion of "sufficiency," then this clearly fulfils the absolute ideal of fiscal independence. To satisfy such a criterion, however, would require a scheme which assured each unit a sufficiency of resources whatever the level of expenditure it believed necessary to satisfy this standard. But this is plainly impossible because we do not inhabit Paradise but a world of limited resources. To be meaningful, therefore, the standard of sufficiency for each unit must be related, at least, to the average or uniform standard of service of all units within the federation. The business of any fiscal scheme then is to ensure that each unit will be able to reach this standard, preferably by its own efforts, and if it fails, to guarantee it the means of doing so — if it chooses. By what means, however, should this guarantee be given? Ideally by enclosing in the constitution an express right which can be asserted by each unit against some determinate federal agency, and by equipping the federal government — for it can be no other organ — with the means of performing an equalising role. Such a right, however, cannot be unconditional, otherwise the claimant could escape with inordinate demands. But if the right is to be conditional, the only mode by which it can be satisfied with due regard to the interests of the two parties — federal and state — is through a body independent of both and whose decisions are binding on the equalising authority, the federal government.

A procedure such as this, of course, can only ensure a meaningful and viable standard of expenditure *as between the states*. But what is a "sufficient" standard of expenditure for a federal government in relation to its functions *vis-à-vis* the states as a whole? In a sense it is true to say that the level of federal expenditure will be determined by its functions, and the very nature of such functions, for example, as "defence," "equalisation," and "stabilisation" requires unqualified fiscal powers. But if it is to be the absolute arbiter of its own standards, then whatever its functions, logically it *must* be vested with such limitless powers. Again, however, our concern is with a world of scarce resources, and unless a federal government is to be left in the exclusive position of deciding what its just share of the taxable income should be—a position most consistent with its own fiscal independence but potentially destructive of others—this dilemma can only be resolved by imposing some kind of external control or external standards on the level of federal expenditure through a device which ensures a "just" distribution of revenue between both levels of government. By what means can this be done? Effectively it can only be through one or a combination of three different devices; first, through an institution which reproduces the procedure of the original constitutional bargain—"horse-trading"—but with this difference that in place of the consultative process which bound no party to its decisions, the decisions of this institution must be equally binding on all parties; secondly, through an institution which rejects the principle of "horse-trading" and compels all parties to submit their needs to arbitration; and thirdly, by incorporating some agreed formula in the constitution. The mode, of course, by which these institutions are composed and the mode in which they function, no less than the way in which the formula is adjusted, will necessarily affect the degree to which one or other level of government can command the settlement. For example, the delegation of all financial policy and management to an independent council or tribunal—the method which seems to excite so many theorists who despair of the ceaseless federal-state conflict over revenue—is possibly the ideal way of ensuring an equitable procedure.[25] But even here its composition and its procedure may vitally affect the interests of the various parties. One would need to distinguish, for instance, between such

---

[25] See the recommendations of tax co-ordination enquiries in Australia in the 'twenties and 'thirties. *Cf.* also the Groves Commission Report on Federal, State and Local Government Fiscal Relations, U.S. Senate Doc. 69, 1943, pp. 5-8.

different forms as a body composed of nominees of each government, or of nominees of the general government only; of an equal number of nominees of each government, or of a greater representation for the general government; of nominees appointed permanently, or nominees appointed for a short term of years, and so on. The probability of variations in the type of institutions and their varying significance, however, is obvious from the pattern of such bodies as the Premiers' Conference or the Australian Loan Council.

In this view of the two terms, "fiscal independence" and "fiscal sufficiency," the central question is — can a financial scheme be devised to satisfy the ideal ingredients of these twin criteria? At the outset, the task of defining the precise responsibilities of each government presents formidable difficulties.[26] If we put this precondition aside, however, it is first clear that a standard financial arrangement cannot be devised for all federal systems. As Dehem and Wolfe have rightly noted,[27] the "data of the problem differ from one federal state to another. The solutions appropriate to each individual case will depend upon the geographic, economic, and cultural characteristics of the country, and also upon the constitutional division of sovereign powers." But given this, is it possible to frame a financial scheme for each system, whatever the political, economic, and constitutional variations, which will fully satisfy our basic terms? The answer shortly is that it has been found impossible to devise such a scheme except for a few rare or ideal situations; for example, where the level of governmental activity creates such a negligible demand upon the national income that it can be satisfied from the most insignificant tax base;[28] or in the ideal case which Dehem and Wolfe formulate — "the country with rather uniform interregional distribution of per capita income, where revenue adequate to finance strictly provincial activities could be derived from provincial public assets and from taxes with negligible interprovincial incidence"; or, of course, in the federal paradise

[26] See *supra*, pp. 232-233.

[27] R. Dehem and J. N. Wolfe, "The Principles of Federal Finance and the Canadian Case," in *The Canadian Journal of Ec. and Pol. Sci.*, Vol. 21, No. 1, Feb., 1955, p. 67.

[28] *Cf.* Hayek's argument that federal government is only viable in conditions of minimal government activity. *Individualism and the Economic Order*, London, 1949.

— if paradise is federal — where the national income is infinite.

The situations for which solutions have been called in the last fifty years do not even closely resemble these conditions. The attempts to frame "just" fiscal schemes have invariably taken place in circumstances of differing regional wealth, differing economic interests, and dynamic levels of governmental activity. It is these conditions, as much as the political antipathy to discriminatory fiscal settlements, which have resisted every attempt to satisfy both ideals of fiscal independence and sufficiency. The experience of federal states is now ample and may be summarised in these four propositions.[29]

First: It has been found impossible to frame permanent fiscal settlements, for these two reasons: (a) it is impossible to predict the cost of government for any long-term period unless we can predict the level of political demand and price movements, and (b) it is equally impossible to predict for any long-term period the revenue yields from any tax fields. *Second:* The increased demand for governmental spending — on welfare policies and war — has multiplied the scale of all governmental transactions, but federal governments, through their superior fiscal and monetary powers, have been better able to meet the increased demands than the states. *Third:* The greater scope and hence manoeuvrability of federal financial powers — and in some cases the constitutional priority of federal tax claims — has placed federal governments in a favoured bargaining position in the choice of remedial measures. *Fourth:* The remedial policies applied by each federal state have varied with the local circumstances — the degree of imbalance between federal and state revenues on the one hand, and among the states on the other; the degree of political forbearance by the federal government in the competition for revenues; and the priority given to "federal" solutions over "logical" tax schemes, "rational" economic policies, and administrative convenience.

If it is impossible then to frame a fiscal settlement which fully satisfies the criteria of "independence" and "sufficiency" in all but ideal — or near ideal — conditions, how can we apply Wheare's categories — "federal," "quasi-federal," and "non-federal" — to the immense variety of fiscal relations which do exist? A conspectus of three or four systems alone — U.S.A., Canada, Australia, Switzerland — reveals variations in the degree to which

[29] See Groves Commission Report, *op. cit.,* esp. pp. 94-117.

states as a whole and individual states rely on federal grants – the
variation may be in the order of ten per cent. to 65 per cent. of
state revenues; in the kind, and the degree of the various kinds of
grants made to the states – for example, obligatory grants (in
pursuance of a formal agreement with the states or constitutional
provision), or discretionary grants (at the discretion of the general government to particular states or states as a whole in the
form of conditional (general or specific) or unconditional grants);
in the kind and the scope of the institutional arrangements
created to deal with the adjustment of fiscal resources – for example, formal or informal, representative or non-representative,
voluntary or mandatory, specific or general; and so on. To arrange these variations along a scale between perfect fiscal independence and perfect dependence it would be necessary to
measure the magnitude of each deviation (given agreement on
what was a deviation) and decide their relative importance. It has
been argued already, however, that since the relative importance
of the various possible deviations is subjectively based it would
be difficult to agree on the point in this scale at which any
particular political unit should be placed. But even if a system of
weights were agreed on so that one could say that Region "x" is
fiscally more independent than Region "y" it would still remain a
purely arbitrary decision to say at which point of this scale the
degree of independence required to satisfy the test of a "federal"
or "quasi-federal" system had been violated. To use the United
States as a model – assuming it were held out as a model of "just"
financial relations – would be scarcely valid given the particu-
larity of its own experience, its economic resources, and the level
of political demand in the American society.

"Independent" Status and the Party System

One final issue now remains – to what extent can the structure
and behaviour of modern political parties be accommodated
within the constitutional assumptions of the "federal principle"?

The integral role of the political party in the machinery and
practice of constitutional government is a fact no longer in
dispute. But while we have noted the conventional requirements
of a dual governmental apparatus for the federal state – legislature, administration, and judiciary[30] – the existing literature is
virtually silent on the type of party system which would fulfil the

[30] *Supra*, section 3, B.

conditions of an "independent and co-ordinate" governmental structure. To employ the traditional principle now, however, without taking this institution into account, is plainly impossible. The exclusion of the Soviet Union from the "federal" category for example, may be argued partly in terms of the excessive body of powers vested in the All-Union government or the centralisation of budgetary policy. But even if the Soviet Constitution gave no offence to the "principle" here, the view which commonly denies its "federal" category is that the monolithic structure of the Communist Party, and the known tendency of the party oligarchy to intrude, direct, and supplant the decision of the Autonomous Republics governments is fatal to the idea of an independent governmental structure. What kind of party system then does the "federal principle" predicate?

In theory one may propose such a model as this: a dual party system – analogous to the dual legislative/administrative machinery – in which the parties are exclusively identified with, and operate at, either the federal or state level; in which the parties are structurally separate from each other in their composition; and in which the parties perform their main business – the nomination and endorsement of parliamentary candidates, formulation of policy, electoral management, and proselytising – completely independent of each other. We need but project such a model, however, to recognise that in no constitutional structure – conventionally termed "federal" – is there any correspondence between this model and the operative party systems. What confronts us instead are multivariant patterns and degrees of decentralisation in the organisation and behaviour of large-scale national parties, a varying set of relations between the party machines and their parlimentary representatives, and varying modes by which federal and state party politicians may influence or coerce each other by manipulation within their common party machinery. In a valuable exploratory essay "Federalism and the Party System"[31] David Truman has inferred that if one were to compare the degree to which the party systems were decentral-

---

[31] See *Federalism Mature and Emergent*, Ed. Arthur W. MacMahon, Columbia University Bicentennial Conference Series, 1955, pp. 115-136. See also, "The Coercion of States in a Federal System," by Arthur Holcombe, in the same volume, p. 137, esp. pp. 143, 150-151. I am also indebted to a very interesting and suggestive research paper written by Dr. D. W. Rawson for the 1954 meeting of the A.N.Z.A.A.S. on "Federalism and the Party System."

ised in the United States, Canada, and Australia, we should find that the national parties were most completely decentralised in the United States, a little less decentralised in Canada, and less decentralised still in Australia. Such a relationship, of course, is not exhaustive, and other systems may be found—for example, the Indian party system and the predominant role of the Indian Congressional Party during the first years of Indian Federation—which might exhibit a higher or lower degree of decentralisation than the United States, Canada and Australia. In any event the implications of such variations in the degree and kind of decentralisation for the federal principle, and the challenge to Wheare's simple categories are again plain enough; but the full scope of the problem is only illustrated if we briefly examine the complexity of the national party system of one country—Australia.

The Australian party system has been often described as "federal" or "confederal" in form. Both terms, however, leave much to be desired. The idea of a "confederality" probably corresponds more closely to their precise organisation, though this term too conceals the marked differences in the degree and quality of a confederal form which may vary from the "tightest of tight" to the "loosest of loose" confederal systems. The Australian Labor Party may more nearly satisfy its popular "federal" description, though here also there are elements—for example, the power of the Federal Conference of the party to intervene in State party affairs on any issue touching the interests of the party as a whole, together with the delegate status of a State-appointed Federal Conference—which suggest that it is much more the "tightest of tight" confederal structures than the "loosest of loose" federal forms. But however we characterise the system, what is the outstanding feature of the three national parties—Labor, Liberal and Country Party—is that the state is the common unity of party organisation for federal and state activity. Here is the professional nerve centre for the main electoral activities—endorsement of candidates, disbursement of funds, and electoral management—for both federal and state politics alike; from here in varying degrees of "tightness" or "looseness" emerges the national superstructure of the three parties; and from here, in varying strength, flows the main directional guide to the conduct of federal-state party relations.

To what extent does this system lend itself to intra-party

manipulation for either federal or state advantage? It is very difficult to give a general answer. In a loose way the intra-party balance between federal and state party interest will depend on the structure and constitutional assumptions of each party machine, its views on party orthodoxy and the status of its parliamentary representatives, the composition of the machine and the nature of its claims on its federal and state representatives, and, of central importance, the disposition of power at any given moment within the party. In all these respects the situation varies between the three main parties.

Of the three national parties, the Australian Labor Party probably offers the most favourable venue for intra-party manipulation, pressure and coercion between the different elements of the machine.[32] As a movement it attaches high importance to two constitutional principles, the necessity for machine control of parliamentary representatives, and absolute conformity to the decisions of the machine. In practice there is an almost incessant tug-of-war between Labor parliamentary representatives and the party bureaucracy in which discipline is the last resort for persistent non-conformity. The official stereotype of its structure is that of a pyramidic and tightly organised democratic movement in which the concern for federal and state matters is divided between two distinct parts of the machine; in federal business, the Federal Conference and Federal Executive; in state affairs, the State Conference and State Executive. In practice, factional quarrels within either segment of the movement often spill over into the other, and the admixture of state and federal parliamentary representatives on both state and federal organs of the machine leaves the way open to a considerable movement of influence into either federal or state arenas. The result is that the real form of the A.L.P. is less a simple pyramid in which policy-making moves along vertical lines, and more the figure of a square in which the four key points are the state machine, the federal machine, the State Parliamentary Labor representatives (S.P.L.P.), and the Federal Parliamentary Labor representatives

[32] See generally, Louise Overacker, *The Australian Party System*, London, 1952, pp. 84-170. See also for a semi-official account of the party as a federal organisation, L. F. Crisp, *The Australian Federal Labour Party*, London, 1955, pp. 1901-1951.

(F.P.L.P.). A conflict for power within the party may be initiated at any one or all of these points, and the consequent pressure may move in varying strength in any direction vertically, horizontally or diagonally from any point of this structure.

Within this machine, for example, it has been possible for a State Labor Premier to engineer the downfall of a Federal Labor Prime Minister by using a State member on the Federal Executive to lead the revolt; conversely it has been possible for the Leader of the F.P.L.P. to join in the removal of a State Labor Premier by marshalling opposition to him on the State Executive of the party. It has been possible for a state machine in conflict with the federal machine to interpret the wishes of the movement on a federal question, and expel or threaten to expel federal members who adhered to the ruling of the Federal Executive.[33] Through this machinery it has been possible for a Federal Labor Prime Minister to persuade a State Labor Premier to accept the decision of the Federal Executive on uniform taxation instead of allying himself with Liberal State Premiers in a challenge to its validity. It has been possible for a State Labor machine to discipline a State Labor Premier for refusing to collaborate in policy approved by a rival political faction in the Federal Executive. It is through this machinery again that a Federal Labor Leader of the Opposition could with the support of the Federal Executive of the party issue instructions to State Labor Governments on policy towards the Communist Dissolution Bill, or that a State Labor Executive favourably disposed to the bill could bring pressure to bear on the Labor majority in the Federal Senate to withdraw its opposition to the bill. And through this machine it has been possible to coerce and threaten State Labor members of Parliament who resisted the extension of federal powers in referenda sponsored by the Federal Labor Governments,[34] and for the Leader of the F.P.L.P. to protest to State Labor Premiers for collaborating with non-Labor Federal Governments on policies attacked by the Labor Opposition in the Federal Parliament.

Nominally, few of these Labor stratagems are available to the

[33] Overacker, *op. cit.*, pp. 127, 150, 158, 163.
[34] *Ibid.*, p. 116. And see Crisp, *op. cit.*, pp. 111-141, esp. p. 132 *et seq.*

Liberal Party, given the relatively modest pretensions of the party machine, the pre-eminence of its parliamentary leaders, the rigid insistence on state party autonomy, the identity of federal and state policies, the diversity of state organisation, the diffusion of policy-making at the federal and state levels, and the disavowal of the more dramatic forms of Labor party discipline.[35] Yet if there is no large scale evidence of any intrusion of federal into state, or state into federal affairs through intra-party pressure one would still need to note that "in some states leading federal members of the Liberal Party have an important influence on state parliamentary affairs";[36] that the party, despite its formal dissociation, still operates within the shadow of large extra-party economic interests which at one time did, and still could, determine the balance between federal and state interests on specific issues; and that an influential Liberal Federal Prime Minister may bring pressure to bear on the policy and strategy pursued by State Liberal Premiers or Liberal Opposition by the offer of advantage or consideration.

With the Country Party, on the other hand, a sectional movement described by Overacker as "hardly more than a loose alliance of independent state chieftains, each jealous of his own autonomy," supporting little more than a token federal organisation, troubled by dissension between federal and state leaders on important points of policy, and with a discipline over its members in two of its three state machines comparable to Labor regimentation, one would need take much less account of the rare possibility of federal manipulation of the state machine than the periodic attempts of the state machines (notably the Victorian Country Party) to "extend their authority to federal members in the Commonwealth Parliament"[37] by threatening their party endorsement if they refuse to follow state directions on specific items of federal policy, or consort too closely with its political enemies in federal politics.

If we go no further with this short view of the three Australian parties, the difficulties of accommodating this system to the model of a "co-ordinate and independent" party structure, or of applying Wheare's criteria to a single national system which

---

[35] See Overacker, op. cit., pp. 240-270.
[36] Rawson, op. cit.
[37] Overacker, op. cit., pp. 234-237.

exhibits such diversity of form and behaviour among its parties, are unmistakable. To ask, for example, how does the party system affect the "independence" of federal and state legislators we need to ask which party is in command of each of the seven centres of government, and equally which party is in Opposition at each of these points. That is, one would need to ask whether the relationship of a Liberal Federal Government to a Liberal State Government is more or less "federal" than the relationship of a Labor Federal Government to a Labor State Government, or Labor Opposition, and so on. If we consider the complex relations which such combinations imply and if we take into account the greater complexity of comparing the relations of a single, non-homogeneous system such as this with other national party systems of even greater diversity, then the serious misgivings about the adequacy of the traditional "federal principle" when confronted with political data of this kind, are not without cause.

CONCLUSIONS

The tendency of the foregoing analysis and argument has already foreshadowed the nature of these conclusions. As a preliminary, however, let me state what seem to be the issues involved here. For my purpose, the conventional terms by which Professor Wheare defines the "federal principle" need not excite any dispute. What is at issue, however, are two things: (a) whether the "federal principle" is a distinct and exclusive principle of organisation if it connotes only jural and formal properties, or whether it can be equally distinct if we introduce the extra-legal ingredients implied by Professor Wheare; and (b) whether the "federal" and "quasi-federal" categories – on either view of the "federal principle" – are sufficiently useful to describe the realities within the federal form.

In the first instance it is clear that if we seek some principle of classification to justify the "federal" category of the United States, Australia, Switzerland and Canada, it cannot be anything so vague as – "the principle which makes the United States the society that it is" – for no other society can be precisely what the United States is. And obviously Professor Wheare has no principle as imperfect as this in mind. The distinctive principle of these four societies is more precisely this: that in each case

power is so divided between the general and regional governments that each, within a sphere, is co-ordinate and independent. And for him the defining properties of this relationship
appear to be the four elements I have named, (a), (b), (c) and (d) —
shortly, co-equal jural status, self-sufficient governmental machinery; fiscal autonomy, and some viable balance in the distribution of functions. However, it has been argued that the only
stable, clear and communicable properties which give an exclusive identity to these four countries by contrast with South
Africa, for example, are the first two factors, one defining the
purely formal jural relations, and the other, their governmental
apparatus. For the rest there are multiple variations in their fiscal
relations, in the political influence or pressure, which may be
exercised through different party systems, and in the scope and
importance of their activities. Insofar as Professor Wheare groups
these four countries within a common category and excludes all
others, we can presume that these variations are negligible or
unimportant. But outside his personal intimations, it is difficult
either to divine the degree of independence which must exist
between the general and regional governments over the whole
field of their power relations, or to discover a sufficiently general
guide to what is a "negligible" or "important" deviation to allow
his classificatory technique to be applied. It may, of course, be
possible to resolve these difficulties by employing some doctrine
of the "reasonable man" — and no doubt this is what Professor
Wheare invokes by the use of the term, "predominantly" federal.
His own difficulties with this test, however, suggest its latent
dangers. It is hard to resist the view, indeed, that if the "federal
principle" is to convey a distinct and univocal idea of organisation, it should only connote the two formal properties we have
already described.

A conclusion such as this does not render the idea of a "federal" union either meaningless or vague. On the contrary, the
desire to create such a state is simply a desire to engage in a
particular form of union, structurally and legally distinct from all
other modes of union. Yet while this activity is related to a
conventional form and a stereotype set of purposes, it is no more
possible to predicate the precise motives, postulates, and understandings, or predict the life which will ensue from the choice of
this form of union than one can predicate the motives which lead

to marriage or to predict the relationship which will ensue from the form in which the union is legally consummated. It is scarcely conceivable that all parties to the federal bargain at all times and in all places seek the same things, in the same proportions, for the same reasons; or that the intensity of the preferences among those who seek just that much more strength for the national government, or for the regions, should be the same. The various lengths of the documents, the various clauses, the use of different safeguards, the institutional innovations, suggest only faintly the complex of interests at work. At best the federal compact can only be a formalised transaction of a moment in the history of a particular community.

If a single form of union can clothe such a multiplicity of life — India, Central African Federation, America, Canada, Australia, and potentially the Caribbean Federation — by what means can one best characterise the life inside the form? The distinction between form and practice to which Professor Wheare draws attention is, if course, vital. Obviously the form of union may be modified, perverted, or entirely ignored. And it would be absurd to say, for example, that one cannot distinguish between the formal pretensions of the Russian constitution and life inside Russia, or that we cannot distinguish between the kind of "independence" which the Canadian or Australian regions enjoy compared to the Autonomous Republics of the U.S.S.R., any more than it would be difficult to describe the kind of "independence" which English County Councils or the South African provinces or the French prefectures enjoy by comparison with the Autonomous Republics. In each case one can describe the relations of any two levels of government within a single political system in terms of their constitutional relations (formal and customary), the scope and importance of the activities they perform at any time, the extent to which, and the methods by which they may influence, or coerce each other, the kind and degree of administrative separation or interdependence, the precise nature of their fiscal relations, and so on until all the possible formal and informal media of their interaction have been exhausted. But given this, could we profitably employ either the single category of "federal," or the dual category of "federal" and "quasi-federal" to comprehend the immense variations in the kind and degree of power relations which express themselves both within and between units clothed in "federal" or "quasi-federal" form? On a purely formal view of the "federal principle" it would be impossible to apply a category founded exclusively on jural assumptions to extra-legal data. There are no degrees in the dichotomy of legal independence and dependence to take sufficient account of political and social nuances. Wheare's position, however, is different. In his case if agreement can be secured on the meaning of "independence" in all its extra-legal forms of power, then it is logically possible to apply a "federal," "quasi-federal," or "quasi-quasi-federal" category if at each point of the multiple and dynamic set of relations one could erect a stable differentia capable of distinguishing the degree and kind of independence appropriate to each of these categories. But even if this were practical, one might seriously doubt the adequacy of these categories. To compress these multiple variations within these concepts is not merely to lose in descriptive reality, but to disfigure reality to serve categories of limited service.

What conceptual value then does the "federal principle" have if it is circumscribed in this way? For the student of politics the maximum utility of this concept is not in doubt. Its main value is to inform him of a particular kind of jural relationship in which general and regional governments may be joined, and the formal institutional arrangements in which this relationship should be expressed. Other than this it can tell him little of the precise distribution of functions between two levels of government, the range and influence of their functions, the precise set of fiscal relations created, the party system and the power structure within each party, the degree of cohesion and diversity in the community, their political skills and dispositions, their attitudes to the formal garment, or their wealth, traditions and usages. And for this reason he can predicate neither weakness nor strength, radicalism nor conservatism, flexibility nor rigidity in its institutions. These attributes, if they are meaningful, are functions of the society, not its legal form alone. To the question then what value can such a formal principle have which can say so little, it would not be ungallant to use the answer Dicey gave to his critics when they accused him of distorting the relations of the Belgian Parliament and an English School-board by classifying them both as "non-sovereign law-making bodies":

There is, it is said, a certain absurdity in bringing into one class things so different in importance and in dignity as, for example, the Belgian Parliament and an English School-board . . . No doubt when features of likeness between things which differ from one another both in appearance and in dignity are pointed out, the immediate result is to produce a sense of amusement, but the apparent absurdity is no proof that the likeness is unreal or undeserving of notice. A man differs from a rat. But this does not make it the less true or the less worth noting that they are both vertebrate animals.[38]

[38] A. V. Dicey, *Law of the Constitution*, London, 1926, 8th edition, p. 88, footnote 1.

2   *A Note on the Nature of Federalism*

William S. Livingston

Federalism as a Juridical Concept

Almost every treatment of federal government and its problems has begun with the assumption that the problem here concerned is one of legal formalism and formal jurisprudence. Nearly all theorists have been at pains to point out that a federal constitution is a device for associating a number of distinct political and constitutional entities in such a manner that a new body is produced which is above and different from those that have come together. But the component states still retain their identity, sacrificing to the collectivity only such powers and functions as are necessary for the implementation of the purposes for which the association is formed. Or, as it is described in some instances, the powers of the central government are devolved upon the subordinate bodies in such a way that both central and regional units are thenceforth endowed with certain powers and functions of which neither can be deprived by the other. This is

From *Political Science Quarterly*, LXVII, 1 (March 1952), pp. 81-95. Reprinted by permission of The Academy of Political Science and the author.

to say that the central government's functions cannot be assumed by the local governments, or the local governments' by the central. Each is placed in relation to the other in a position of autonomy; neither is subordinate and each may exercise within its sphere the full extent of its powers. There is also substantial agreement among writers on federalism that the extent of these powers is strictly limited by the simultaneous existence of comparable, though never identical, powers in the other unit. The problem thus becomes that of the proper delineation of these spheres. Where is the boundary between the central and the component governments to be drawn? How much power does the central government have and how much power do the local units have? This attempt to quantify power seems to be characteristic of the juridical approach to the problems of federal government.

In order that this line of demarcation between the two governments may be precise and understood by all it is ordinarily considered necessary that the constitution of a federal state be written. Most writers have held it impossible for a distribution of this nature to be produced by the slow evolution of institutions such as is found in Great Britain. The experience of federal governments in the modern world is cited to show that in fact they all do have written constitutions. Only a written constitution, it is held, could precisely assign powers and functions in the necessary manner.

Once the distribution of powers is made, the accounts continue, it must be protected; and this requires that some kind of obstacle be put in the way of constitutional change. If the component units have entered the federation on the understanding that they are to possess certain rights and functions, then these must not be taken from them except in circumstances where some agreed-upon criterion demands such reassignment. Conversely the powers of the general government must not be alienated unless this is clearly necessary. In order to protect the allotment of powers to local and central units, the constitution must be *rigid*. By this is meant simply that to amend the constitution a procedure different from (that is, more difficult than) that of ordinary legislation is to be used. Indeed, since Lord Bryce published his *Studies in History and Jurisprudence* the definition of a rigid constitution has turned on this very point. A rigid constitution, as contrasted with a flexible one, has come to mean one that can be amended only by a procedure more difficult than that by which ordinary laws are made.

This procedure for constitutional amendment in a federal state, it is ordinarily said, must be designed to protect the federal allocation of governmental powers and functions. Since one of the purposes of employing a federal rather than a unitary constitution is to assure the different units of their proper and agreed-upon share in governmental activity, the power to amend the constitution cannot be lodged in either the general government exclusively or in the local governments exclusively, for this would permit the one to take from the other without its consent those functions that it desires to retain. Hence the federal system necessitates an amending procedure in which the consent of both the general and the local governments must be secured before any change can be made. But, the accounts continue, this does not mean that the consent of all the local governments is necessary, for this would effectively cripple the federation and prevent all important change; it would also, according to some, transform the federation into a confederation. But the procedure must consist of some form of consent on the local level as well as some form of consent on the national level. Usually the need for local concurrence takes the form of a requirement that a majority or more of the component units must consent to the amendment, though the means by which this consent is secured and measured vary greatly.

It requires little demonstration to show that the constant emphasis throughout this chain of thought is on the legal aspects of federal organization. The questions are always of a legal nature. How much power? What vote is required? Upon what right may this or that action be based? Does it violate the constitutional distribution of powers? Does it violate the principles of federalism? The ordinary treatment of federalism is based upon a legalistic foundation and its problems are treated as problems of constitutional law.

THE OPERATION OF FEDERAL INSTITUTIONS

This is assuredly a convenient method of approaching the problem and in many instances it is the only possible one. But it is not the only one. If a question arises that requires a legal answer, it can be answered only in legal terms. But the validity of such an answer is limited to the frame of reference within which the question is posed. Legal answers are of value only in the solution of legal problems. And federalism is concerned with many other problems than those of a legal nature.

Above and beyond this legalism there is an aspect of federalism that has been largely ignored. The essential nature of federalism is to be sought for, not in the shadings of legal and constitutional terminology, but in the forces — economic, social, political, cultural — that have made the outward forms of federalism necessary. Federalism, like most institutional forms, is a solution of, or an attempt to solve, a certain kind of problem of political organization. It is true, on the whole, that federal governments and federal constitutions never grow simply and purely by accident. They arise in response to a definite set of stimuli; a federal system is consciously adopted as a means of solving the problems represented by these stimuli.

Whether a constitutional structure may properly be called federal, however, depends not so much on the arrangement of the institutions within it as it does on the manner in which those institutions are employed. Institutions have a habit of serving purposes other than those for which they are designed. The passage of time produces changes in the purposes of any society and these new purposes are reflected in new modes of operating old institutions which frequently retain their original forms. Thus a society may possess institutions that are federal in appearance but it may operate them as though they were something else; and, what is more likely, it may possess a unitary set of institutions and employ them as though they were federal in nature. The institutions themselves do not provide an accurate index of the federal nature of the society that subtends them.

FEDERALISM AS A SOCIOLOGICAL PHENOMENON

This leads us another step forward in the analysis. We have said that institutions may not be suited to the actual needs of the society and this point will be explored in greater detail later. If one could know exactly how the institutions are operated, one would have a much more accurate picture of the nature of the society itself. But the picture would still be incomplete and unclear; for institutional devices, both in form and in function, are only the surface manifestations of the deeper federal quality of the society that lies beneath the surface. The essence of federalism lies not in the institutional or constitutional structure but in the society itself. Federal government is a device by which the federal qualities of the society are articulated and protected.

Every society, every nation if you will, is more or less closely integrated in accordance with its own peculiar historical, cultural, economic, political and other determinants. Each is composed of elements that feel themselves to be different from the other elements in varying degrees and that demand in varying degrees a means of self-expression. These diversities may turn on all sorts of questions – economic, religious, racial, historical; any of these can produce in a certain group within the population a demand for such self-expression. Furthermore, these diversities may be distributed among the members of a society in such a fashion that certain attitudes are found in particular territorial areas, or they may be scattered widely throughout the whole of the society. If they are grouped territorially, that is geographically, then the result may be a society that is federal. If they are not grouped territorially, then the society cannot be said to be federal. In either case coherence in the society may depend on the devolution upon these groups of the exercise of functions appropriate to the diversities that they represent. But in the first case only can this take the form of federalism or federal government. In the latter case it becomes functionalism, pluralism or some form of corporativism.

I realize that in using the term federal only in this restricted territorial sense I am taking from it some of the meaning attributed to it by writers who profess to see federal elements in the various forms of pluralism, such as feudalism or corporativism. But I suggest that these writers have added a meaning that was not there before and one that introduces an element of confusion into the term. No government has ever been called federal that has been organized on any but the territorial basis; when organized on any other it has gone by another name.

It is true that the geographical diversities may not always follow the boundary lines of the component units. In many countries, and particularly in the United States, the operation of the federal system has displayed patterns of diversity that are more nearly associated with regions or groups of states than with the individual states themselves. This is easily understood. Federalism embraces not merely a diversity of opinion on one issue but a whole pattern of diversities on a number of issues. It can scarcely be expected that state boundary lines will be adequate to mark off areas in which opinions differ on all possible questions. Indeed on many, or even most, questions the state boundaries will be of little significance in thus delimiting the areas of diversity. Federal organization is not perfect in every case.

No one supposes that it is, however. Component states exist because of some great significant diversity of such importance that it is felt that only a federal organization can offer it sufficient protection. Day-to-day issues may easily and reasonably produce alignments that follow regional lines. Regionalism in this sense is a valid manifestation of the federal principle. It conforms to the criterion suggested above, namely, that the diversities in the society be grouped territorially. It should be noted, moreover, that regionalism in the politics of a federal country is made possible only by the federal allocation of functions to the states themselves. The fact that several states within a larger region are dominated by similar opinions and hence unite in an effort to transform these views into policy does not detract from the importance of the states as the basic units of the federal system.

On the other hand, federalism becomes nothing if it is held to embrace diversities that are not territorially grouped, for there are then no territorial units that can serve as components of the federal system. I readily agree that this is a question of the definition of federalism and that society can be organized in accordance with any principle upon which there is substantial agreement among the members of the society. But if the distribution of powers, which is the essential feature of the federal structure, is made between the nation as a whole and component units that are functional in character, such as industries, trade unions, churches, and so on, then the traditional and, I think, necessary quality of federalism is lost. We confuse two distinct principles when we apply the terminology of federalism to a society organized on a functional basis.

It may be objected that the federal division of powers among territorial areas is in reality functional, since these areas differ from one another on questions of a functional character. I agree. But the important point is that they are territorially organized.

Such areas naturally differ in opinions, in composition, in interests, in function. This, however, only brings us back to the point that they differ. If there were no functional differences, there might be no need for federalism. But the point that must be emphasized is that these functional differences are territorially grouped; and thus they provide a reason for and a demand for a federal system of government.

FEDERAL INSTITUTIONS AS A REFLECTION OF SOCIETAL DIVERSITIES

The nature of a society is roughly reflected in the external forms of its political and constitutional arrangements; and it is true that the extent to which the society is federal can be more or less accurately measured by the extent to which these external forms are federal. The institutional patterns reflect the federal quality of the societies in varying degrees; they may be more or less "federal" in the way in which they manifest the degree to which the political society behind the institutional façade is integrated or diversified. But the institutional patterns and the constitutional structure are far from an adequate test of the federal qualities of the society; dependence upon them alone can lead to serious error in assessing the nature of the society itself.

If these did serve as an accurate measurement of the society, the problems of the constitution maker and of the political analyst would be much simpler and this essay would not have been written. But the weighing of the various forces that go into the making and maintaining of a political community is an extremely difficult task. Those who devise institutions can never be sure that the institutions they devise will accurately represent the nature of the society or will be adequate to the needs they are designed to fulfill. Moreover, social patterns are constantly changing. What may be good for today will very likely be outmoded and less adequate by tomorrow. Finally, institutions mean different things to different people; the same set of institutions may produce widely different results when adopted and operated in different communities. Hence there can be no assurance at any time that the institutional patterns fit the needs of the society below.

From this it follows that the real nature of the society cannot be divined merely by an analysis, however brilliant and profound, of the institutions only. No amount of reading of constitutions can properly inform the analyst about the societies served by those constitutions. The nature of the political society can be examined only by observing how the institutions work in the context of that society. It is the operation, not the form, that is important; and it is the forces that determine the manner of operation that are more important still.

THE SPECTRUM OF FEDERAL SOCIETIES

This is no less true of federalism than it is of any other form of political organization. Federalism is a function not of constitutions but of societies. Viewed in this way, it will be seen that federalism is not an absolute but a relative term; there is no specific point at which a society ceases to be unified and becomes diversified. The differences are of degree rather than of kind. All countries fall somewhere in a spectrum which runs from what we may call a theoretically wholly integrated society at one extreme to a theoretically wholly diversified society at the other. Some are more unified than others; some are more diversified than others; and the differences between adjacent societies in this spectrum may be so slight or so incommensurable as to be incapable of assessment. But that there is a gradation is clear from observing societies that are widely separated in the spectrum.

As one moves from one end of this hypothetical spectrum to the other the societies encountered are more and more diversified. And the more diversified the society, the greater is the necessity of providing some means for articulating the diversities; for these diversities are nothing less than tensions and as tensions they demand and require means of self-expression. But there is no point at which it can be said that all societies on one side are unitary and all those on the other are federal or diversified. If a society contains territorial groups that are so different from the rest of the society that they require some instrumentality to protect and articulate their peculiar qualities, then the society is likely to provide some means for the creation of such an instrumentality. One such circumstance doubtless does not make a society or a constitution federal. But two or six or twenty may produce a result that may be properly so called.

It cannot be said that when a society is just so diversified, it requires a federal constitution. In the first place we are unable to quantify social and political forces to the degree necessary to warrant such a demarcation; and secondly the forces themselves are incommensurable. (Which is more diversified, a society rent by religious schisms or one in which the members are divided by differences of language?) Societies employ instrumentalities for the expression of diversities in accordance with what men in particular societies think is necessary; and this view of what is necessary and what is not will vary considerably from society to society. Thus some societies which would seem to be highly diversified are able to get along with a set of institutions that seems to be nearly unitary; and, conversely, some that seem quite unified adopt institutions that we call federal. It may be that one especially strong unifying tendency in a society, such as a long historical tradition of unity, will overcome diversities of economic interest, language and the like which, in another society, with a weaker historical tradition, would necessiate federal institutions.

TYPES OF DIVERSITIES

The social diversities that produce federalism may be of many kinds. Differences of economic interest, religion, race, nationality, language, variations in size, separation by great distances, differences in historical background, previous existence as separate colonies or states, dissimilarity of social and political institutions—all these may produce a situation in which the particular interests and qualities of the segments of the larger community must be given recognition. At the same time these differences must not be too great, else the community must break up into independent groups. Federalism cannot make coherent a society in which the diversities are so great that there can be no basis for integration.

There is no way to estimate the relative weights of these factors except in results; we have observed already that they are largely incommensurable. But it seems clear that some are more significant than others, at least within a single society. For example, a society that enjoys a uniformity of social and political background can still hold together despite deep cleavages in other matters. The point is that the diversities and similarities are of many different kinds and when taken together they produce a total picture of the extent to which the society is integrated or diversified.

The total pattern of these diversities produces a demand for some kind of federal recognition of the diversities. This demand must in most cases meet a counterdemand (or inertia, which equally a force) for increased unity or integration. These two demands or forces—the one impelling toward autonomy and independence for the component units, the other impelling toward centralization and the suppression of diversity—meet each other head on; the result of their conflict is the federal system. The federal system is thus an institutionalization of the compromise between these two demands, and the federal constitution draws the lines of this compromise. The constitution will be more or less federal in accordance with the relative strength of the two demands. Thus societies in which the demand for integration is stronger than the demand for decentralization will produce a set of institutions that is more nearly unitary; and a contrary situation will produce a contrary result. It is in this sense that federalism is a matter of degree and not of kind. The varying degrees of federalism are produced by societies in which the patterns of diversity vary and in which the demands for the protection and articulation of diversities have been urged with more or less strength. But what determines the federal quality of the government is not only the constitution that draws the lines of the compromise but the whole pattern of instrumentalities that are employed as a result of these demands.

TYPES OF INSTRUMENTALITIES

The diversities within a society require certain instrumentalities for their expression and protection. Just as the diversities take many forms, so do the instrumentalities; the latter are designed to fit the needs of the former. But the relation and correspondence between the diversities and the instrumentalities that express them will vary from society to society. A diversity that requires one kind of instrumentality for its expression in one social complex will require another kind in another social complex. So also similar instrumentalities in different social complexes will serve different kinds of diversities. It is this fact that has been largely ignored by most analysts of federal institutions.

We are too prone to say that federal constitutions must contain a certain five or eight or ten characteristics and that all constitutions lacking any of these are not federal. Such a set of criteria ignores the fundamental fact that institutions are not the same things in different social and cultural contexts. Two societies equally diversified with respect to a particular matter may require very different instrumentalities for the implementation of that diversity. By the same token, similar institutions or instrumentalities in different social contexts may serve to implement dissimilar diversities.

The word "instrumentality" is a broad one and necessarily so; but we must be clear about what is meant. First of all, it does not mean merely a clause in the constitution, though such clauses may be examples of such instrumentalities and it may be said that the provisions of the constitution are a good rough guide to the pattern of instrumentalities, though they become less adequate with the passage of time. But the word includes not only the constitutional forms but also the manner in which the forms are employed; it includes the way in which the constitution and its institutions are operated. Beyond this, moreover, it includes many things that are far from constitutional in importance in the ordinary sense of the word. It includes such things as habits, attitudes, acceptances, concepts and even theories. It includes perhaps the rules of the American Senate, the make-up of the Canadian cabinet, the zeal of the Baptist Karens in Burma. All these may serve as instrumentalities for the expression of the diversities within a society, and whether a country is federal or not may best be determined by examining the pattern of these instrumentalities and not by checking its constitution against an *a priori* list of the characteristics of a federal constitution.

Federal Constitutions and Federal Instrumentalities

Indeed the documentary constitution may be a poor guide in attempting to discover whether or not the society itself is federal. Several South American countries have adopted federal constitutions and yet an examination of those countries reveals a rather high degree of integration. Are we to infer that Soviet Russia is more federal than, say, the United States because it provides in its constitution for a right of secession?

Other examples may better illustrate the point. It is meaningless to insist that the Union of South Africa is unitary and not federal because of certain characteristics of its constitution. I should be quite willing to agree that the component units may be overwhelmed by the central government, if the testimony of the constitution is to constitute the only evidence. But I should at the same time insist that what is significant is, not what the constitution says, but how the people of South Africa employ it. The fact is that in many instances South Africa operates its institutions as though its constitution were federal; it works federally despite the unitary character of its legal forms. If one examines the South African polity from a strictly legal or constitutional point of view, it is clearly unitary. But if one probes deeper into the processes of politics one quickly perceives that federalism is still an operative principle in that society.

A similar argument may be advanced in regard to Great Britain, a country whose constitution is most often cited as being typically unitary. Many elements of British public life are witness to the vitality of the federal principle in British society. Indeed there would seem to be an operative right to secede from that community, exemplified by the withdrawals from it in recent years of such elements as Burma and Ireland. If Northern Ireland or Scotland, or perhaps even other elements, were to seek actively for secession, it seems most unlikely that the right would be challenged. A right of secession as an operative idea in a society suggests diversities of a rather acute nature and places that society, as far as the particular point is concerned, well over toward the diversity side of the spectrum of federalism. Federal elements in Great Britain take other forms as well. Northern Ireland has its own parliament; Scotland has its own courts and legal systems as well as its own church. Scotland, furthermore, is especially protected in the House of Commons by a Scottish Committee which deals with questions pertaining to that area. If the central government were to attempt to abolish any of these institutions, the outraged complaints of injustice would bear adequate witness to the extent to which this society is diversified and to the necessity of providing these instrumentalities for the articulation and protection of the federal qualities.

Even France under the *ancien régime*, which is ordinarily considered to have been a very highly centralized executive state, manifested certain federal qualities. The laws and customs of the provinces were far from standardized. Each had its own legal code, its own body of customary law, its own historical tradition and a very considerable degree of local patriotism.

THE CAUSAL RELATION BETWEEN FEDERALISM AND ITS INSTRUMENTALITIES

The point has been made that the pattern of forces within the society changes with the passage of time. Society is never static but changes constantly in accordance with the interplay of the various dynamic forces within it. As a result, the diversities within the society wax and wane in intensity so that the need for their articulation increases or decreases. A complex of psychological and sociological factors may require one type of instrumentality at one time and another type at some other time. As the nature of society changes, demands for new kinds of instrumentalities are created and these demands are met by changing or abolishing old instrumentalities and substituting new ones in their place. But it can scarcely be hoped that the instrumentalities will keep pace with the changing pattern of social relationships, and as a result the pattern of instrumentalities tends to lag behind the changes in society itself (though it may be observed that the functioning of the instrumentalities will not be so rigid in this respect as the constitutional forms).

This is complicated further by the fact that the instrumentalities, once put into operation, become rigidified and acquire a status of their own. They become substantive instead of merely adjectival; they become ends in themselves instead of merely means toward other ends. Their procedures become standardized; they may take on an honorific quality; they become matters of pride to the diverse elements that they serve; and ultimately the instrumentalities enter into and become part of the psycho-sociological complex itself.

This is by no means an unusual occurrence; almost every society manifests this tendency in one form or another. The Scottish Committee of the British House of Commons, mentioned above, is an example. This Committee was at the outset a device, an instrumentality, to permit the organized expression of Scottish opinion on affairs that directly concerned Scotland; it is still that. But it is also much more, for it has become a thing of value in itself, a thing to be preserved because it is an essential part of the federal relation between England and Scotland.

Another example is the Supreme Court of the United States which began as a mere court of law. But as judicial supremacy developed in the United States the Supreme Court became more and more an institution that connoted the maintenance of justice in federal relations in this country. (It came to mean many other things as well, but it is the federal arrangement that concerns us here.) Few men now claim that the Court is a mere court of law; and few men would dare to disturb its position without serious consideration of the effects of such a change on the shifting balance of national power and state power. The Court has ceased to be a mere instrumentality and has entered into the psycho-sociological complex that determines the nature of the instrumentalities.

Another example is to be found in the United States themselves. America adopted a federal constitution at the outset because the elements that were to make up the new country were so diversified that they could be brought together in no other form. But since that time the Federal Constitution has continued in force and has collected around it all the aura of a highly revered institution. As other states have entered the union they have taken their places in the federal arrangement and have found that all the perquisites and particularities of the established states have accrued to them. Although at the time of their entry these later states may not have been sufficiently diversified to justify such special treatment, they rapidly acquired such consciousness of individuality that they would now be unwilling to part with the instrumentalities that permit the expression of that individuality. It is doubtful that the two Dakotas warranted the dignity of separate statehood at the time of their entry into the union; but who can deny now that, having lived as states for a number of years, they would look with disfavor upon any proposal to deprive them of their individuality by merging them into one? The Constitution, which endows the states with the characteristics of diversity, treats them indiscriminately and thus tends to create diversity where none previously existed. The Constitution with its federal plan, though designed as an instrumentality, has become a part of the complex of sociological and psychological values that constitutes the pattern of diversities. It is no longer merely an instrumentality serving to protect and articulate the diversities; it has itself become a part of that complex of values which *is* the pattern of diversities and which determines the pattern of the instrumentalities.

Thus the problem of the student of federalism is made much more difficult, for he cannot clearly distinguish between society and the instrumentalities it employs. Similarly with the problems of the statesman; he cannot devise means to accomplish new ends without disturbing the old relationship, for the old means have themselves become ends and the old techniques have become values.

The effort to draw the distinction must be made, however; for otherwise we end by confusing cause with effect and by attributing to the instrumentalities values that belong properly to the anterior diversities. The student of federalism must probe deeper than the institutional patterns, for these are but the products of the diversities in the society; it is to the pattern of these diversities that we must go if we would assess the federal qualities of the society.

II

THEORIES

3 *Federalism: Origin, Operation, Significance*

WILLIAM H. RIKER

THE POPULARITY OF FEDERAL CONSTITUTIONS

The recent popularity of federal constitutions is not surprising because federalism is one way to solve the problem of enlarging governments — a problem that is one of the most pressing political concerns in the modern world. Like so many other modern problems, this one is a consequence of rapid technological change. Each advance in the technology of transportation makes it possible to rule a larger geographic area from one center, to fill a treasury more abundantly, to maintain a larger bureaucracy and police, and, most important of all, to assemble a larger army. There seem to be enough ambitious politicians in the world at any one time to guarantee that at least one government will use the new technology of transport to enlarge its area of control. And, once one government enlarges itself, then its neighbors and competitors feel compelled to do likewise in order, supposedly, to forestall anticipated aggression. Hence it is that technological change and a sense of competition together guarantee that governments will expand to the full extent that technology permits.

At the dawn of written history, most governmental units were tiny, consisting typically of an urban place and a few square miles of farms and villages. But with technological advance, imperial dominions became possible. Some of these in the ancient Near East and central and south Asia were based on the domestication of the horse; others like the Egyptian and Chinese were based on the exploitation of a river system as a channel of transport. The Roman empire is especially interesting for it was first created by control of the Mediterranean (*mare nostrum*) as a channel of transportation and was expanded by the invention of the Roman roads to control western Europe. Even so, the ancient empires were small by modern standards and at its height Rome probably ruled less land and fewer people than are now ruled from any one of these cities: Washington, Ottawa, Brazilia, Moscow, New Delhi, Peking, and Canberra. A necessary condition for these numerous large governments of today is of course innovation in transportation. First came the navigational discoveries (compass, triangular sail, sextant, trigonometry, etc.) that permitted the so-called expansion of Europe and, second, the innovations in land transportation (the steam railroad, the automotive engine, road building and earth moving, the airplane, etc.)

The initial form of most of the great modern governments was empire. That is, large territories were accumulated by conquest when the technologically sophisticated Europeans subdued the relatively primitive inhabitants of America, Asia, and Africa. Thus were created the Spanish, Portuguese, Dutch, British, French, German, Russian, and Belgian empires. Of modern empires, only the Austrian, Turkish, and Chinese involved the conquest of territory inhabited by people as technologically sophisticated as the conqueror and even in these cases the conqueror had some kind of technological superiority in transportation and military equipment.

The collapse of imperialism forces a constitutional alternative on all successful rebels: Since they necessarily rebel within the subdivisions established by the imperial power for its own convenience in governing, one alternative is to establish the freed subdivisions as independent political units. But the subdivisions, coordinated as they have been by the colonial office in the center, are not usually large enough to take advantage of the technological conditions that made the empire possible in the first place. Hence, if the newly independent subdivisions stand alone as political entities, they are highly vulnerable to yet a new imperialism. This is what happened, for example, to the Balkan rebels against the Austrian and Turkish empires. Freed from one imperial master as a result of 19th-century revolutions and World War I, and yet too small to support large armies, they fell victim in World War II to Hitler's abortive Third Reich and then to Stalin's Communist hegemony. The whole of Africa and the Near

East is now Balkanized in a similar way and it is not fanciful to suggest that something of a similar future awaits these new nations. The other alternative for successful rebels is to join several former imperial subdivisions together. But if they join the subdivisions in one centralized political unit, then the rebels have merely exchanged one imperial master for a lesser one. Thereby much of the justification for rebellion is lost. The subdivisions can, however, be joined in some kind of federation, which preserves at least the semblance of political self-control for the former subdivisions and at the same time allows them (by means of the government of the federation) to make use of the technological advantages in the size of treasuries and armies and thus to compete successfully with their neighbors.

In this sense federalism is the main alternative to empire as a technique of aggregating large areas under one government. Although it probably does not so clearly assure large treasuries and armies, it does assure them to some degree—and it avoids the offensiveness of imperial control. It is this combination of attributes, I believe, that accounts for the 20th-century popularity of the federal kind of constitutional bargain and explains why today all the governments of large territories (except China) have federal constitutions at least in name.

CONDITIONS OF THE FEDERAL BARGAIN

As bargains, the acts of making federal constitutions should display the main feature of bargains generally, which is that all parties are willing to make them. Assuming that they do display this feature, one may ask what it is that predisposes the parties to favor this kind of bargain. From the theory set forth in the previous chapter, I infer the existence of at least two circumstances encouraging a willingness to strike the bargain of federalism:

1. The politicians who offer the bargain desire to expand their territorial control, usually either to meet an external military or diplomatic threat or to prepare for military or diplomatic aggression and aggrandizement. But, though they desire to expand, they are not able to do so by conquest, because of either military incapacity or ideological distaste. Hence, if they are to satisfy the desire to expand, they must offer concessions to the rulers of constituent units, which is the essence of the federal bargain.

The predisposition for those who offer the bargain is, then, that federalism is the only feasible means to accomplish a desired expansion without the use of force.

2. The politicians who accept the bargain, giving up some independence for the sake of union, are willing to do so because of some external military — diplomatic threat or opportunity. Either they desire protection from an external threat or they desire to participate in the potential aggression of the federation. And furthermore the desire for either protection or participation outweighs any desire they may have for indepedence. The predisposition is the cognizance of the pressing need for the military strength or diplomatic maneuverability that comes with a larger and presumably stronger government. (It is not, of course, necessary that their assessment of the military-diplomatic circumstances be objectively correct.)

I shall briefly examine two widely asserted fallacies about the origin of federalism.

One is the ideological fallacy, which is the assertion that federal forms are adopted as a device to guarantee freedom. Numerous writers on federalism, so many that it would be invidious to pick out an example, have committed this ideological fallacy. It is true, of course, that federalism does involve a guarantee of provincial autonomy and it is easy to see how some writers have confused this guarantee with the notion of a free society. Indeed, in certain circumstances, for example by encouraging provinces to have different policies or even simply to be inefficient, federalism may provide interstices in the social order in which personal liberties can thrive. And I suppose it is the observation of this fact that leads one to the ideological fallacy.

The worst error involved in this fallacy is the simple association of (1) federalism and (2) freedom or a non-dictatorial regime. Only the most casual observation of, for example, the Soviet Union or Mexico demonstrates, however, that even though all the forms of federalism are fairly scrupulously maintained, it is possible to convert the government into a dictatorship. In the two examples mentioned, the conversion has been accomplished by a strict one-party system, which suggests that the crucial feature of freedom is not a particular constitutional form, but rather a system of more than one party. But in other countries, e.g., Brazil, Argentine, imperial Germany, even federalism and a multi-party system have been unable to prevent dictatorships, so probably some even more subtle condition is necessary to maintain free government. What it is I cannot say, but I am certain that there is no simple causal relationship between federalism and freedom.

Alongside the rather crude ideological fallacy is the subtler and initially more impressive reductionist fallacy, which is the assertion that federalism is a response to certain social conditions that create some sense of a common interest. On the basis of a theory of this sort, British colonial administrators have encouraged a number of federalisms, some successful, some not. It is the fact of some failures that is interesting—for they indicate the inadequacy of the theory. Perhaps the most exhaustive statement of this kind of theory is contained in the work of Deutsch and his collaborators,[1] who produced a list of nine "essential conditions for an amalgamated security-community" of which class the class of federalisms is a sub-class:

(1) mutual compatibility of main values; (2) a distinctive way of life; (3) expectations of stronger economic ties or gains; (4) marked increase in political and administrative capabilities of at least some participating units; (5) superior economic growth on the part of at least some participating units; (6) unbroken links of social communication, both geographically between territories and sociologically between different social strata; (7) a broadening of the political elite; (8) mobility of persons at least among the politically relevant strata; and (9) a multiplicity of ranges of communications and transactions.

There are many defects in such a list. It is apparent that these conditions are not sufficient to bring about amalgamation for, if they were, federalisms like the Central American Federation would never have broken up or a pan-Arabic movement would reunite the Arabic parts of the former Turkish empire. Nor are all these conditions necessary, for a great many successful amalgamations have violated some or even all of them, *e.g.*, the Swiss confederation seems to have violated conditions (1) and (2) during most of its history and 19th-century colonial empires violated almost all conditions. If these conditions are neither jointly necessary nor sufficient, it is hard to imagine in what sense they are "essential."

The trouble with the Deutsch list is that it attempts to reduce

[1] Karl Deutsch, *et al., Political Community in the North Atlantic Area* (Princeton: Princeton University Press, 1957) p. 58.

the explanation of the political phenomenon of joining together to an explanation of the social and economic condition of the population. In bypassing the political, in bypassing the act of bargaining itself, it leaves out the crucial condition of the predisposition to make the bargain. What this list amounts to is a set of frequently observed conditions in which politicians can develop a predisposition to unite in some way or another. But it omits any mention of the political conditions in which, given some of these and other social and economic conditions, the actual predisposition to bargain occurs. The theory I have set forth, on the other hand, is confined to the political level entirely. It assumes some sense of common interest, of course, and then asserts the invariant conditions of forming one kind of larger political association, namely, federalism. (Incidentally, by confining the theory to a specific kind of amalgamation, the theory has a political focus that Deutsch and his collaborators failed to achieve.)

THE INVENTION OF CENTRALIZED FEDERALISM

The federal relationship is centralized according to the degree to which the parties organized to operate the central government control the parties organized to operate the constituent governments. This amounts to the assertion that the proximate cause of variations in the degree of centralization (or peripheralization) in the constitutional structure of a federalism is the variation in degree of party centralization.

There are strong *a priori* arguments for the validity of this assertion of a causal connection. Suppose the officials of the central government wish to centralize to a degree greater than the formal constitution of the federalism contemplates (*i.e.*, suppose these officials wish to break the federal bargain in their favor). Suppose further that these officials are the leaders of a party that also operates constituent government through subordinate leaders. That is, suppose the parties are highly centralized. Then, it would seem that all the constitutional and institutional prohibitions guaranteeing constituent governments against revision of the federal bargain would be ineffectual. If, on the other hand, the officials of the central government do not have partisan supporters operating the constituent governments, they may expect some opposition to their breaking of the guarantees.

Whether or not the opposition is strong enough to maintain the bargain depends of course on a variety of institutional circumstances. But whether or not the opposition occurs at all seems to depend initially on a partisan difference between the central and constituent leadership. There is even some empirical evidence supporting the notion that the degree of partisan unity between the constituent and central governments is closely related to changes in the federal relationship. In another place,[2] Schaps and I devised a measure of the degree of partisan disharmony between the two levels of government and, when we correlated the index of disharmony by eight recent bienniums in the United States with the absolute amount of litigation between the two levels of governments in the Supreme Court, we obtained a coefficient of correlation of about +0.8, which is within the 2 per cent level of confidence. This finding suggests that to a very high degree variations in the federal relationship, especially variations in the ability of constituent governments to conflict with the central government, depend on variations in partisan relationships between the two levels.

What is suggested by this finding about a barely visible feature of federalism in the United States is also suggested by a much grosser observation of other systems. Thus, consider the federalisms in which the central government is invariably able to overawe the constituent governments, *viz.* Mexico, the Soviet Union, and Yugoslavia. One other characteristic these three political systems share is the fact that one and only one political party rules all levels of government. If the theory just set forth is correct, it is the feature of one-partyism that causes the rupture of the federal bargain. At the other extreme, consider the federalisms in which constituent governments can overawe the center, whereas central officials cannot overawe them. There are relatively few governments in this category (since it verges on the complete collapse of the federal bargain), but Nigeria offers at least one contemporary example. If the theory here set forth is correct, there should be many parties in Nigeria and the national levels of these parties should have little or no influence over the constituent levels. Such in fact is the case, for the main party

[2] William H. Riker and Ronald Schaps, "Disharmony in Federal Government," *Behavioral Science*, Vol. 2 (1957) pp. 276-90.

leaders prefer to hold office in the constituent governments rather than in the central government. Thus at both extremes of variation in the federal relationship, it appears that the variations in partisanship are causally related to variations in federalism. Since in the instance of the United States, the same causal relationship appears, one easily infers that the same causal connection is valid for all systems in all categories.

The exact nature of this causal connection can best be examined by asking how to measure the federal relationship according to the partisan variation. Once one asks this question, it is immediately apparent that there are involved two kinds of relationships between parties at the two levels: (1) the degree to which one party controls both levels of government; and (2) the degree to which each potential governing party at the national level controls its partisan associates at the level of constituent governments.

WHAT MAINTAINS FEDERALISM?

1. The division and sharing of administrative responsibilities, which is often said to be at the heart of federal arrangements, has little or nothing to do with maintaining the bargain. In the United States such centralization as has occurred seems to have been occasioned by technological considerations and to have had little effect, one way or another, on the bargain. Certainly in the period most crucial for its maintenance, some functions were centralized and others peripheralized, which suggests the genuine irrelevance of this consideration. In seven other federalisms there seems to be no rhyme or reason for the degree of administrative centralization except administrative traditions and convenience. Again there seems to be no connection between centralization or peripheralization in decision making and centralization or peripheralization of administrative functions.

2. It is true that federalism is maintained by the existence of dual citizen loyalties to the two levels of government. But this assertion is almost a tautology. Federalism means the existence of two levels each to some degree able to decide questions independently. Without loyalty to each of the two levels, both could not continue to exist. Besides being tautological, this statement tells us little about the degree of centralization in a federalism.

Many writers wish to utter a much stronger companion statement: Federalism is maintained by the existence of dissident provincial patriotisms. Although this sentence appears to be true in many instances (*e.g.*, the United States, where a gradual decline in provincialism seems to accompany some centralization, Canada, Brazil, etc.), it does not appear to be true of Australia or Argentina, where provincial patriotisms seem to be relatively weak.

Hence, in a larger sense one can say the federal bargain is maintained by loyalties to both levels, but one cannot always say that it is maintained because of the need to satisfy a dissident provincialism such as that of the South in the United States or of French Canadians in Canada.

3. Whatever the general social conditions, if any, that sustain the federal bargain, there is one institutional condition that controls the nature of the bargain in all the instances here examined and in all others with which I am familiar. This is the structure of the party system, which may be regarded as the main variable intervening between the background social conditions and the specific nature of the federal bargain.

4. It is theoretically possible but practically difficult to measure the structure of the party system.

4   *Approaches to the Study of Federalism*

ANTHONY H. BIRCH

FEDERALISM AS A PROCESS

An attempt to develop a flexible model of federalism has been made by a number of writers who refer to federalism as a process rather than as a static pattern of government. C. J. Friedrich attempted to summarize this approach in a paper presented to the Sixth World Congress of the International Political Science Association and it will be convenient to quote

From *Political Studies*, Vol. XIV, No. 1 (1966), pp. 18-33 (Sections III-VIII). Reprinted by permission of The Clarendon Press (Oxford, England) and the author.

from his summary.[1] Friedrich describes a federation as "a union of groups, united by one or more common objectives, but retaining their distinctive group character for other purposes."[2] This description can be applied not only to a federal state but also to an alliance, a functional association of states, or a union of groups within a state (such as the Trades Union Congress). Federalism is said to be the process of federalizing; that is, the process of achieving a union of groups which retain their identity. It follows that "federalism may be operating in both the direction of integration and differentiation. For both the transformation of the British Empire into the Commonwealth of Nations and that of European states into a United States of Europe (as envisaged and initiated) are federalizing processes."[3]

This approach thus directs our attention to one of the features of postwar politics: the development of a wide variety of political systems and organizations in which decision-making is divided between a central authority and a number of regional authorities. This, broadly speaking, is what federations which conform to Wheare's model have in common with those that do not conform to that model, and what both have in common with several other forms of political association. Scholars who follow this approach seek to identify the factors making for integration and those impeding integration in a variety of situations, and have shown that the social and economic forces at work are often the same, even though in one context they contribute to nation-building while in another they contribute to international integration. To view federalism in this way is to view it in a broad perspective which helps us to understand some of its features and draws our attention to what may appropriately (if inelegantly) be called its dynamics.

There is, of course, a certain price to pay. If federalism is defined in such general terms there may be difficulty in deciding

---

[1] The quotations which immediately follow are from C. J. Friedrich, "New Tendencies in Federal Theory and Practice" (mimeographed, 1964). See also Friedrich's chapter in Elmer Plischke (ed.), *Systems of Integrating the International Community* (Princeton, 1964); and the work of K. W. Deutsch and his associates.

[2] p. 2.

[3] p. 2. See also Ernst B. Haas, *The Uniting of Europe* (London, 1958) and "International Integration: European and Universal Processes," in *International Organisation*, vol. 15 (1961).

whether certain political systems are to be regarded as federal at
any particular time. For Friedrich the difficult case is the Soviet
Union. On page 5 we are told that "the hitherto common invasion
of the sphere of power of the republics of the Soviet Union
argues against the presumption that the Soviet Union constitutes
a genuine federalism"; on page 10 we learn that "the evolution of
Soviet federalism suggests that within limits the absence of
constitutional democracy is no bar to the federalizing process";
and on page 16 it appears that "in the Soviet Union the formal
federalism of the government structure is rendered largely nuga-
tory by the integrating force of the C.P.S.U." But every classification has its borderline cases and this particular difficulty may not
be very important, since the test of this approach to the study of
federalism must be the success of those who follow it in identifying the factors which influence the speed and direction of
progress in the federalizing process.

It is hazardous to generalize about such a considerable body of
literature but it seems safe to say that the factors generally
suggested as important are economic, social and cultural. The
factors most commonly identified as creating the conditions for
federal integration are the expectation of economic advantage
and the existence of social and cultural bonds which generate a
feeling of community. K. W. Deutsch and his collaborators have
listed nine conditions as "essential conditions" for what they call
an "amalgamated security-community" (which would include all
the forms of union with any reasonable claim to be regarded as
federations).

These conditions include "a distinctive way of life," expectation of economic gains, and "unbroken links of social communication."[4] But what is conspicuously absent from the list is any
mention of the political circumstances in which the politicians
who alone can create an amalgamated security-community are
likely to do so. Without this the list is potentially misleading, to
put it no higher. W. H. Riker has pointed out that the evidence of
history shows that these nine conditions are neither necessary
nor sufficient for the amalgamation of political units, which
prompts him to ask the pertinent question of how they can be

[4] K. W. Deutsch *et al.*, *Political Community and the North Atlantic Area*
(Princeton, 1957), p. 58.

considered "essential."[5] Riker's own approach focusses directly on the political aspects of federalism.

FEDERALISM AS A BARGAIN

Riker defines federalism in a very simple and formal way, saying that a constitution is federal if it provides for two levels of government, each of which has at least one area of action in which it is autonomous, and each of which has "some guarantee (even though merely a statement in the constitution)" of its contained autonomy within its sphere.[6] He notes that this kind of constitution is always the result of a political bargain which takes place in a historically unique situation, but he proceeds to an examination of these situations which yields the discovery that two conditions have always been present. He concludes that these conditions should be regarded as necessary conditions for the striking of a federal bargain. The first condition is the existence of politicians who wish to expand the area of territorial control, either "to meet an external military or diplomatic threat or to prepare for military or diplomatic aggression,"[7] but prefer to expand without the use of force. The second condition is the willingness of the assenting politicians to surrender part of their independence, either because "they desire protection from an external threat" or because "they desire to participate in the potential aggression of the federation."[8]

The other question with which Riker deals is that of the conditions for the maintenance of a federal system. Here again his examination of historical evidence leads him to a single, but more tentative, conclusion: that whether or not a federal system survives depends on the nature of the party system that develops. It does not, that is, depend on the division of governmental powers, on the extent of governmental activities, or on the

[5] W. H. Riker, *Federalism: Origin, Operation, Significance* (Boston and Toronto, 1964), pp. 15-16.

[6] Ibid., p. 11. He does not worry about the hypothetical problem posed by Mackenzie and Chapman of a system in which the regional governments enjoy only the power to determine the shape of postmen's helmets, though he comes near it when he suggests at one point that the question of whether the Soviet Union is a federation depends upon whether the republics have genuine autonomy in the sphere of cultural affairs. See W. J. M. Mackenzie and B. Chapman, "Federalism and Regionalism," in *Modern Law Review*, vol. 14 (1951).

[7] Riker, op. cit., p. 12.

[8] Ibid.

survival of provincial loyalities and a belief in states' rights:
these factors influence the nature and working of the federal
system, but it is the structure of the parties which determines
how long the system itself is maintained.

Though these conclusions can be outlined in a few lines, they
are not insubstantial. Given that the model of federalism is
sketchy enough to permit the inclusion of twenty or more somewhat diverse systems, it would be absurd to expect a comparative analysis to produce many generalizations. Riker's conclusions are a significant achievement, provided the evidence supports them. It is also interesting to see that Riker's approach to
the subject enables him to deal in a specific and useful way with
some of the social factors with which Livingston was concerned
but which he did not make explicit, such as the nature and effects
of regional cultural differences and the changing pattern of
citizens' loyalties to different levels of government.[9]

The Value of These Approaches

It is a little difficult to compare the value of these approaches to
the study of federalism because although the aims of the authors
overlap they are nevertheless not the same. Wheare's aim is to
make possible a detailed comparative study of the small number
of federal systems which conform to his model. The aim of
writers like Friedrich and Deutsch is to elaborate the forces and
conditions, thought to be mainly social and economic, which
facilitate and stimulate the federalizing process.[10] Riker's aim is
to establish the conditions, claimed to be entirely political,
which are necessary for the making and maintenance of the
federal bargain as he has defined it. These approaches can be
compared only in respect of the fact that each points to a set of
conditions in which a new federation is likely to be created.
They cannot usefully be compared in respect of their other
virtues, such as Wheare's discussion of constitutional and administrative problems in federation, Deutsch's discussion of other

[9] Ibid., pp. 103-16. The analysis is brief and the evidence is somewhat uneven
as between one country and another, but this does not affect the value of the
conceptual framework.

[10] I do not intend to suggest that Friedrich and Deutsch agree on everything,
only that their approaches to the study of federalism are similar enough for it to
be appropriate to include them in the same category in this paper.

forms of economic and political integration, and Riker's discussion of the conditions for the maintenance of federal systems.

The conditions which are proposed by these authors as necessary for the creation of a federation can be summarized as follows. K. C. Wheare considers that most, if not all, of six conditions must be satisfied:

1. a sense of military insecurity and of the consequent need for common defence;
2. a desire to be independent of foreign powers, for which union is a necessity;
3. a hope of economic advantage from union;
4. some previous political association;
5. geographical neighbourhood;
6. similarity of political institutions.[11]

K. W. Deutsch and his collaborators postulate nine conditions:

1. Mutual compatibility of main values;
2. a distinctive way of life;
3. expectations of stronger economic ties or gains;
4. a marked increase in political and administrative capabilities of at least some participating units;
5. superior economic growth on the part of at least some participating units;
6. unbroken links of social communications, both geographically between territories and sociologically between different social strata;
7. a broadening of the political elite;
8. mobility of persons at least among the politically relevant strata;
9. a multiplicity of ranges of communications and transactions.[12]

W. H. Riker regards two conditions as pre-eminent:

1. A desire on the part of the politicians who offer the bargain to expand their area of influence by peaceful means, usually either to meet an external military or diplomatic threat or to prepare for military or diplomatic aggression and aggrandizement;
2. a willingness in the part of the politicians who accept the bargain to give up some independence for the sake of union, either because they desire protection from a military or diplomatic threat or because they desire to participate in the potential aggression of the federation.[13]

The following sections of the paper will be devoted to a brief discussion of developments in Nigeria, in East Africa, and in Malaysia, with the hope that these examples will cast some light

[11] See Wheare, op. cit., pp. 37-38.
[12] See Deutsch *et al.*, op. cit., p. 58.
[13] See Riker, op. cit., p. 12.

on the value of the three approaches to the student who wishes to analyse the factors involved in the establishment of a new federation.

THE NIGERIAN FEDERATION

The main outlines of this story are well known and need not be repeated.[14] It is clear that in Nigeria the last four of Wheare's conditions were present and it is arguable that the second condition was also present: certainly the British Government wanted Nigeria to remain united and would have delayed independence if one or more regions had insisted on separation, though it is not likely that independence would have been long delayed. Wheare's first condition was not present, as the former French colonies which surround Nigeria did not present any kind of military threat. But as Wheare stipulates only that most of the six conditions must be present the case of Nigeria supports his generalization.

Of Deutsch's conditions, numbers 3, 4, 5, 9, and (with some reservations) 6 were present. But the Muslim and aristocratic north had a different way of life and was dominated by a different set of values from those which obtained in the two southern regions; it is doubtful whether federation was accompanied by a broadening of the political elite; and there was little mobility of top persons between regions.[15] The Nigerian example therefore confirms Riker's view that Deutsch's nine conditions cannot be regarded as essential.

Riker's own account of the Nigerian situation is somewhat misleading. He cites the expansionist ambitions of Ghana as the external threat, saying that "during the time just before and during the Nigerian achievement of independence, Nkrumah's emphasis on Pan-Africanism was at its height and no Nigerian leader could fail to be aware of the proximity of the western (and depressed and minority) region of Nigeria to Ghana."[16] In fact the western region was the most prosperous of the three and at the

[14] See James S. Coleman, *Nigeria: Background to Nationalism* (Los Angeles, 1958); Kalu Ezera, *Constitutional Developments in Nigeria* (Cambridge, 1960); and Richard L. Sklar, *Nigerian Political Parties* (Princeton, 1963).

[15] There had been some mobility of junior government officials from the East to the North, but the programme of "Northernization" was launched to counteract this.

[16] Op. cit., p. 31.

time of the bargain its leaders showed no disposition whatever to sympathize with Nkrumah's ambitions.[17] However, it is certainly true that diplomatic considerations were a factor in the establishment of this federation. The two groups whom it is reasonable to regard as the proponents of continued political union were the British and the leaders of the N.C.N.C. The British were clearly motivated by diplomatic considerations and the N.C.N.C. leaders, having played a dominant role in the nationalist movement, hoped to have a large influence on the politics of an independent Nigeria and saw great diplomatic advantages in the fact that, if it remained united, it would be the most populous country in Africa.[18]

The western and northern leaders can appropriately be regarded, in Riker's terms, as the acceptors of federation. Both wished to preserve their own leadership in their own area and had some fears of the ambitions of the N.C.N.C., a party which was to some extent the vehicle of an ideology, as opposed to the western and northern parties which were based on tribal and cultural organizations. But the western leaders knew that an independent state of western Nigeria would be in a very precarious position because of the tribes minority in the west and the strength of the N.C.N.C. in organizing both these tribes and certain dissident elements among the Yoruba peoples (for in-

[17] The writer acted as consultant to the western region government from 1956 to 1958 and feels able to report this with some certainty. It is also the case that the western leaders' attitude to Ghana was well known in West Africa: it was expressed in speeches and in frequent editorials in the Action Group newspaper, the *Daily Service*. Further, in the federal elections of December 1959 the Action Group announced its "opposition to any form of political union among the West African States." (See R. O. Tilman and Taylor Cole (eds.), *The Nigerian Political Scene*, London, 1962, p. 128). It was not until June 1961 that Chief Awolowo, by then disappointed in his personal political ambitions, changed his mind on this score: an extraordinary reversal of view which was one of a succession of steps which led eventually to his imprisonment for treason. His policies up to 1960 are explained and illustrated in *Awo: the Autobiography of Chief Obafemi Awolowo* (Cambridge, 1960).

[18] Of course economic and social considerations also motivated the N.C.N.C. leaders: Riker's point is not that diplomatic considerations must be dominant, only that they must always be present. It is also true that the N.C.N.C. leaders were over-optimistic about the political influence they could exert in a federation, believing as they did that they would be able to offset the numerical preponderance of northerners by winning a fair number of seats in the northern region in association with their allies in the Northern Elements Progressive Union.

stance, in Ibadan). Moreover, they knew that a claim for independence would immediately precipitate a conflict over the
status of Lagos. Feeling that a two-state federation of southern
Nigeria would also be dominated by the politically ambitious
easterners, the western leaders therefore accepted the idea of a
federation of three states, hoping to ensure that the powers of the
central government would be fairly restricted.

The northern leaders accepted federation with more reluctance, partly because they were fairly content with the status quo
and thought that it would be a poor exchange if British rulers
were replaced by southern Nigerians. However, once it became
clear that the colonial régime was reaching its last days the
northern leaders had to face the prospect that regional independence would leave the north extremely poor (the poorest of the
three regions), with a grave shortage of middle-grade officials
(the north being far more dependent on British officials than the
other two regions), and in a precarious position because their
traditional enemies in the south could cut off their communications with the coast at a moment's notice. They therefore agreed
to accept the proposal for a federation, strengthened by the
knowledge that the population of the north would entitle it to at
least half the seats in the federal legislature.[19]

The situation in Nigeria was therefore more complex than
Riker suggests, and is unusual in the sense that the potential
threats which acted as inducements to those who accepted the
proposal came from other parts of the federation, not from other
countries. But it is of course true that considerations of political
power and diplomacy were a factor in the establishment of this
federation. It follows that the Nigerian case can probably be
regarded as an example of Riker's rule, provided that the rule is
so interpreted or amended as to allow the threat to come from
prospective partners in the federation as well as from outside. An
amendment to cover this will be suggested below.

[19] The differences of attitude between the regions were reflected in many of
the negotiations. Thus one of the main subjects of controversy at the 1957
Constitutional Conference was the control of the police, the British and the
eastern leaders wanting federal control while the western and northern leaders
wanted regional control. Again, in their submissions to the Fiscal Commission
of 1957-8 the government of the eastern region proposed a more centralized
tax system than that advocated by the governments of the western and northern
regions.

68   ANTHONY H. BIRCH

THE PROPOSED FEDERATION OF EAST AFRICA

The idea of a federation of the East African territories that were
until recently administered by Britain has been intermittently
under discussion for over forty years. It was advocated by Winston Churchill when he was Colonial Secretary in 1922 and by L.
S. Amery when he was appointed to that office in 1924. It was
investigated by a series of commissions and committees during
the following years, all of which reported with varying degrees of
emphasis that the idea had economic advantages but political
and administrative drawbacks. After 1931, when a Joint Select
Committee of Parliament canvassed opinion in Kenya, Tanganyika, and Uganda, one of the main obstacles was the feeling
among Africans that such a development would extend the area
of influence of the European settlers who already had a good deal
of influence in the government of Kenya.[20] From then until the
independence of these countries became imminent constructive
discussion focussed on the development of common services and
economic integration, not on federation as such.

At the end of the World War II the three territories had a
common market (instituted in 1927), a common currency, a single
court of appeal, and a single system of posts and telegraphs.
There was an annual governors' conference which was replaced
in 1948 by the East Africa High Commission, with a Central
Legislative Assembly and power to administer a number of
common services. These included rail transport (as from 1949),
civil aviation, docks and harbours, the collection of income tax,
locust control, and research organizations in medicine, agriculture, and veterinary science. In December 1961, when Tanganyika became independent, the High Commission was replaced
by the East African Common Services Organization. The functions of EACSO were substantially the same as those of the High
Commission, but its executive was responsible to the three
territorial governments instead of to the British Government and
its constitution provided for amendment by agreement of the
three governments.[21] There was, therefore, a considerable mea-

[20] See *Reports of the Joint Select Committee in Closer Union in East Africa*,
Cmd. 3254 and 3378 of 1931.

[21] For an analysis of the structure and role of EACSO, see J. S. Nye, Jr., "East
African Economic Integration," in *Journal of Modern African Studies*, vol. 1
(1963).

sure of functional integration in East Africa when the idea of
federation was given new life by Julius Nyerere in June 1960.

Speaking at Addis Ababa, Nyerere proposed that the four East
African territories (including Zanzibar) should federate as soon
as they achieved independence, and he went so far as to suggest
that Tanganyika would be willing to see its own independence
day postponed by a few months if the four territories could then
be given independence simultaneously. He repeated this suggestion at the P.A.F.M.E.C.A. meeting at Nairobi in January 1961,
saying: "The feeling of unity which now exists would be whittled
away if each country gets its independence separately and becomes open to the temptations of nationhood and the intrigues of
those who find their strength in the weakness of small nations."[22]
In Kenya this proposal got a mixed reception. The Legislative
Council passed a resolution declaring that federation was both
economically and politically desirable, but the government rejected as impracticable the suggestion that independence should
be synchronized. In Uganda the leaders of all three parties took
the view that it would be premature to discuss federation before
the country's own constitutional problems were resolved.[23]

However, the leaders of Kenya and Uganda became more
ready to talk about federation after they had achieved what
seemed to be solutions to their internal constitutional problems,
and in June 1963 a joint statement pledging their governments to
the goal of federation was issued by the President of Tanganyika
and the Prime Ministers of Kenya and Uganda. In this statement
federation was commended both as a step towards Pan-African
unity and as a move which would bring economic benefits to the
area. It was announced that to achieve these aims: "a working
party is being established which will prepare a framework of a
draft constitution for the Federation of East Africa. It will report
back to a full conference of East African governments," to meet in
"the third week of August."[24]

In the event this confident prediction was not fulfilled. The

[22] Quoted in A. J. Hughes, *East Africa: the Search for Unity* (London, 1963),
p. 233. In saying this Nyerere may also, of course, have been motivated by the
desire to press the British Government to bring forward the dates of independence for the other territories.
[23] Ibid., pp. 231-4.
[24] The full statement is printed in an appendix to Hughes, op. cit.

working party failed to reach agreement and the conference was not held. During 1964 the army revolt in Tanganyika, the revolution in Zanzibar, and the subsequent "amalgamation" of Tanganyika and Zanzibar effectively occupied President Nyerere's attention, and there are signs that his future international involvements may be to the west and the south rather than to the north. Meanwhile economic co-operation between the East African countries has been under strain and some restrictions have been imposed on the free trade of commodities between them. In June 1965 the government of Tanzania announced its intention to withdraw from the common market and to establish its own currency.

These are the bare bones of the story of the proposed East African Federation. The question with which we are concerned is how this story should be interpreted. Should the student adopt Wheare's approach, looking for a mixture of geographical, economic, and political factors; or Deutsch's, with its heavy emphasis on economic and social factors; or Riker's, with its exclusive concern with the political, diplomatic and strategic aspects of the situation?

There can be little doubt that the first inclination of nearly all commentators is to concentrate on the economic and social factors. Four main arguments have led people both to commend federation in East Africa as desirable and to predict it as a probable development. First, the common market has stimulated economic development and a federal union with complete internal free trade would be even more beneficial.[25] Second, it should not be assumed that the common market and EACSO will survive for long after self-government unless a further step towards unity is taken: functional integration of this kind is to be regarded not as a point of equilibrium but as a stage in the federalizing process, with political union as the next stage. Third, overseas investors tend to be more willing to invest in a large country (provided it appears to have a fair chance of political stability) than in a number of small countries.[26] Fourth,

[25] In the common market there are a number of artificial impediments to trade between territories. See *Report of the East African Economic and Fiscal Commission*, Cmnd. 1279 of 1961, pp. 15 and 63.

[26] See, for instance, the report by the Federation of British Industries on the prospects of investment in Nigeria.

territorial boundaries in East Africa are entirely arbitrary, often cutting tribal communities in two; while tribal rivalries might be more easily contained in a federal union in which no tribe would comprise more than four or five per cent. of the population.[27]

All these arguments and others were canvassed at a conference on the problems of East African federation which was sponsored by the University of East Africa and held at Nairobi in November 1963. The general tendency of participants in the conference (most of whom were politicians from the three mainland territories) was to discuss federation in terms of economic and social advantages on the one hand, political and administrative difficulties on the other.[28] The advantages were agreed to be very considerable; the difficulties (e.g. the fact that the states had slightly different institutions and the problem of giving the states some influence over federal planning decisions) did not seem insurmountable. Yet at the time of writing the proposal for a federation is in eclipse. This is the problem of this approach, spotlighted by the fact that in East Africa all of Deutsch's nine conditions appear to be satisfied. So, for that matter, are all but the first two of Wheare's conditions.

It is evident that although economic arguments loomed large in the discussions over federation, the situation cannot be understood simply in these terms. One indication of this is that the negotiations do not appear to have taken the shape they would have done if economic considerations had been primary. There is substantial agreement among economists that Kenya has derived most of the benefit from the common market, that Uganda's benefits have been very small, and that Tanganyika may not have benefited at all.[29] If there were more complete economic integration the territorial disparities in terms of benefit would necessarily be greater, except in so far as Tanganyika and Uganda were either compensated by fiscal means or given special advantages

[27] On this last point see Burudi Nabwera, *Federation* (mimeographed, Nairobi, 1963), p. 3.
[28] It will be appreciated that this is a personal impression. The main papers of the conference have been published in Colin Leys and Peter Robson (eds.), *Federation in East Africa* (Nairobi and London, 1965).
[29] See, for instance, Dharam Ghai, "Territorial Distribution of the Benefits and Costs of the East African Common Market," in Leys and Robson, op. cit., where it is argued that Tanganyika has suffered a slight net loss from the operation of the customs union.

in the planning of industrial location.[30] Since all the straws in the wind pointed to increasing strains within the customs union after the participating governments gained full independence, with the possibility of Uganda and/or Tanganyika taking protective measures, the economic logic of the situation required that Kenya should propose federation as a way of safeguarding the customs union and that the other countries (particularly Tanganyika) should demand guarantees of fiscal compensation and a sizeable influence in planning decisions as a price of their agreement. Instead, Julius Nyerere proposed federation and has consistently taken the view that the three governments should commit themselves to political union before bothering about details of that kind. From the economic point of view, this makes no sense at all: it makes sense only if Nyerere's primary motives were political and diplomatic.

If the latter assumption is made, Nyerere's role as the proposer of federation can be interpreted as a move to expand the area of influence of himself and his party, and to create a large East African state which would be in a good position to assume the leadership of the Pan-African movement. The reluctance of the governments of the other countries, particularly Uganda, to accept the proposal can be interpreted as the natural reluctance of political leaders to surrender autonomy when they were under no external threat and either did not desire to participate in the diplomatic aggression that union would make possible or did not feel confident they would have anything but a subordinate role in the proposed federal government.

Nobody would suggest that this is the whole truth of the matter. The suggestion is the more limited one that this approach enables the student of politics to pick out the factor—namely a prospect of political, diplomatic or strategic gain for all parties— which must be present if the negotiations for federal union are to succeed. The so-far abortive attempts to form a federation of East Africa would seem to afford striking confirmation of the value of Riker's contribution to the theory of federalism.

THE ESTABLISHMENT OF THE FEDERATION OF MALAYSIA

This example is clearer than that of East Africa because diplomatic and strategic considerations were openly paramount in

[30] See Benton F. Massell, *East African Economic Union* (Santa Monica, 1963), *passim.*

Malaysia. The story in a nutshell is that federation was proposed first by the government of Singapore, anxious to transfer control of internal security and allied matters to Kuala Lumpur; was proposed secondly by the British Government, worried about Singapore and anxious to give the Borneo territories independence without leaving them in a hopelessly vulnerable position in relation to Indonesia; and was accepted by the government of Malaya, mainly because of its concern about the possibility that Singapore might might otherwise become a threat to the security of the area.

The proposal for some form of merger between Singapore and Malaya was made by successive chief ministers in Singapore between 1955 and 1960—first by David Marshall, then by Lim Kew Hock, and then by Lee Kuan Yew. The proposals were unacceptable to the Malayan Government mainly because the inclusion of the predominantly Chinese electorate of Singapore would upset the delicate balance of multi-racial politics by means of which the Malays, with fifty per cent. of the population of Malaya, have contrived to control the political situation.

However, in the first five months of 1961 the Tunku Abdul Rahman (Prime Minister of Malaya) changed his mind on this issue. One factor in this was the imminence of the end of the five-year agreement made in 1958 whereby internal security in Singapore was controlled jointly by the governments of Singapore, Malaya, and the United Kingdom. Another was that Lee Kuan Yew succeeded in persuading the Tunku that the People's Action Party (the ruling party in Singapore), though left-wing, was firmly anti-communist and more reliable than any likely alternative. Allied to this was the growth of opposition from the extreme left in Singapore and the loss of a by-election which shook public confidence in the ability of the People's Action Party to win the next general election.[31] These developments increased the disposition of the Malayan leaders to see the advantage and indeed the necessity of a merger which would put defence and internal security in Singapore under the control of a federal government at Kuala Lumpur.

In this same period the British Secretary for Commonwealth Relations proposed to the Tunku that it would be advantageous to include the three British Borneo territories with Singapore

---

[31] See Michael Leifer, "Politics in Singapore," in *Journal of Commonwealth Political Studies*, vol. II (1964).

and Malaya in a federation. The convenience of this to the British Government was clear; its great attraction to the Malayan Government was that it would enable the Chinese and left-wing electorate of Singapore to be offset by the inclusion of a considerable non-Chinese and not-left-wing electorate in the Borneo territories. In May 1961 the Tunku announced that he saw advantages in the creation of a federation which would include both Singapore and the Borneo territories, and the matter was henceforth the subject of public discussion and private negotiation.

The public discussion emphasized the concern of government leaders with the possibility that Singapore might become the Cuba of Asia. Lee Kuan Yew delivered twelve broadcast talks in the autumn of 1961 which were intended to expose communist attitudes in Singapore and to justify his government's decision to join the proposed federation.[32] He insisted that the main fear of the communists and their allies was that internal security in Singapore would pass into the control of Kuala Lumpur; that the communist object was either to secure the abolition of the Internal Security Council and the subsequent independence of Singapore by itself or else to keep Singapore under British rule, so that their opposition to the government could "be camouflaged as an anti-colonial struggle";[33] and that it was his government's intention that security in Singapore would in fact be transferred to an elected federal government which could not be accused of colonialism. The Tunku took a similar line, saying in a speech to publicity officers of his party that:

The most important point is that the constitution of Singapore will come to an end and with it two issues will be faced: firstly, whether Singapore becomes independent; and, secondly, whether Singapore should merge with the Federation of Malaya.

It is impossible to grant independence to Singapore because of the danger of its going communist, and if it goes communist it would with the help of the communist powers try to overrun the whole of Malaya. . . . Therefore to prevent this most unhappy and disastrous state of affairs occurring, the only course open to us would be to accept Singapore as a member of the Federation of Malaysia.[34]

[32] See Lee Kuan Yew, *The Battle for Merger* (Singapore, 1962), which comprises the text of these talks together with twelve documentary appendixes.

[33] Ibid., p. 45.

[34] Speech printed in *Malayan Times*, 25 September 1962, quoted in Gordon P. Means, "Malaysia: a new Federation in Southeast Asia," in *Pacific Affairs*, vol. 36 (1963).

The private negotiations took place at first between Lee Kuan Yew and the Tunku, and subsequently involved the spokesmen for the Borneo territories. They first established the main terms for the merger between Singapore and the mainland, which related to citizenship, to representation in the federal legislature, and to Singapore's wish (which was granted) to retain control over education and labour. Bargaining continued from July 1961 until the very eve of the inauguration of the federation,[35] and resulted in an extremely complicated set of constitutional arrangements in which the different states of the federation enjoy differing degrees of autonomy.[36] Despite this flexibility the terms offered proved unacceptable to the rulers of Brunei, which has remained outside the federation. The details of the constitution are not relevant to this article, but it is worth noting that Singapore, with a population of 1.6 millions, was given only 15 seats in the federal legislature, whereas Sabah and Sarawak, with a combined population of 1.2 millions, have 40 seats between them.[37] The governing Alliance Party of Malaya moved quickly into the Borneo territories and in the first elections for the federal legislature (the Dewan Ra'ayat) it won all 16 seats in Sabah and 20 of the 24 seats in Sarawak. Since it won 89 of the 104 seats in Malaya in 1964 it had 125 members in a house of 159 seats, in which all the Singapore representatives (12 People's Action Party and 3 Barisan Sosialis) were in opposition. The Borneo territories thus filled the role for which they were cast, but whether the Alliance Party will continue to be so successful there must be a matter for speculation. If racial tensions were to increase this would probably weaken its position, since it would be seen as a Malay-dominated party in states in which only a minority of the population are Malays.[38]

[35] Nine points were not agreed until 8 and 9 July 1963, when Lee Kuan Yew and the Tunku settled them in meetings in the Ritz Hotel, London, one or two of the agreements being jotted down on the back of an envelope, photographs of which were subsequently published by the Singapore Government. See *Malaysia Agreement: Exchange of Letters*, Misc. 5 of 1963, Singapore.

[36] For details, see *Malaysia Agreement*, Cmnd. 2094 of 1963; H. E. Groves, *The Constitution of Malaysia* (Singapore, 1964); Milton E. Osborne, *Singapore and Malaysia* (Data Paper 53 of Cornell University Southeast Asia Programme, Ithaca, N.Y., 1964); and Wang Gungwu (ed.), *Malaysia: a Survey* (London, 1964).

[37] The official justification of this was that Singapore retained control of education and labour, which are federally controlled in the Borneo territories.

[38] See Robert O. Tilman, "Elections in Sarawak" and Frances L. Starner, "Malaysia and the North Borneo Territories," both in *Asian Survey*, vol. III (1963).

This outline of the formation of the Federation of Malaysia is substantially different from that given by Riker, who cites the possibility of Indonesian aggression as the only threat and regards the British and the Malayan Governments as the proposers of federation and the other territories as the acceptors.[39] I do not think that his account can be accepted in its present form. Malaysia is a federation which would almost certainly not have been created in the absence of threats to the security of one or more of the participating territories, but the threats were as much internal as external, and it was a desire for protection that motivated the proposers (Singapore and Britain, on behalf of the Borneo territories) as well as the acceptor. It follows that this example is not quite covered by Riker's generalizations as they are now formulated. Since the Nigerian example was also one in which the threats were internal, I suggest that the generalizations stand in need of amendment to cover situations of this kind. The following proposition is offered as a substitute for the two conditions proposed by Riker:

A necessary condition for the establishment of a federation is that the political leaders of all the territories involved should believe that union would either (a) help to protect one or more of the territories from an external or internal threat, whether actual or potential, to the security of the established regime or (b) enable them to benefit from the improved diplomatic or military position that the larger unit could be expected to enjoy; though it is not necessary that the considerations influencing the leaders of the various territories should be identical.

It should also be noted that all of Wheare's six conditions were present in Malaysia (provided 800 miles of ocean are not regarded as a bar to "geographical neighbourhood"). Of Deutsch's nine conditions only numbers 3, 4, 5, and 9 were satisfied.[40]

[39] See Riker, op. cit., p. 31.

[40] This analysis is not invalidated by the fact that Singapore has left the Federation since this article was written. The reason for the rift is that the dominant Malay elements in the Alliance Party are not willing to tolerate electoral competition from a non-Malay party led by Lee Kuan Yew. In the objective situation little has changed, but there has been a shift in the assessment by Malay leaders of the relative importance of the threats to their position from (a) the possible election of a pro-communist government in an independent Singapore and (b) the development of a challenge to their political power from a Chinese-led Malaysian party deriving leadership and finance from Singapore. However, this development may indicate the importance for the maintenance, as distinct from the establishment, of a federation of some of the social factors discussed by Deutsch et al.

CONCLUSION

It may be appropriate to conclude with a very brief comment about method. My own belief is that the kind of comparative study most likely to be fruitful is that which takes as its starting point the existence of somewhat similar arrangements which have evolved or have been devised in a limited number of countries, themselves not entirely dissimilar, to meet similar needs. The object of this kind of study is to show how these arrangements have been modified in the course of time by the pressure of circumstance and by differences in the political traditions of the countries involved, and how far interesting points of similarity remain.

The approach followed by Riker and by Deutsch is unlike this in that, instead of beginning with similarities and showing differences, they begin with a large variety of different situations and try to establish uniformities. This method is inherently more difficult, not only because no scholar can be expected to have a detailed knowledge of more than a few countries but also because the method involves such a radical process of abstraction and generalization that the sense of concrete reality is apt to disappear. But in spite of these difficulties, Riker has succeeded in establishing the importance of certain kinds of political consideration in the formation of federations, and this may be counted a real, if limited, gain in a period in which it seems fashionable to assume that economic and social factors are preeminent.

5   *Federalism and the Party System*

DAVID B. TRUMAN

In the representative governments characteristic of the
Western World the interdependence of constitutional forms and
types of political party is a fact, obvious enough in its simple
statement, but complex and baffling when the observer under-
takes to explain these interrelations as they bear upon past
changes in the political life of a people or to anticipate the form
and direction of developments in the future. The need to organize and to lead a mass electorate has given rise, even in political
systems paying the merest lip-service to the values of democracy,
to party forms basically different from the cliques and cabals
which bore the name in an age when the political drama was
played before a smaller and more select audience. Constitutional
practices, whether formal and written or informal and customary,
have presented the engineers of power with both advantages and
handicaps in terrain and material to which their structures have
been adapted, especially in systems where an attachment to
constitutionalism has imposed limitations upon the techniques
and tactics of the politician.

Yet even the most superficial glance at these interdependent
elements will indicate that the cast has altered the mold, whether
subtly and implicitly, as in the case of the American Electoral
College, or directly and openly through formal amendments and
legislative enactments. A search for origins and for trends is thus
bedeviled by the tendency to treat in linear, cause-and-effect
terms a relationship which is circular and elusive. At whatever
point the circle is entered appear the dangers of assumptions too
hastily made and generalizations too easily arrived at. These

From Chapter 8 in *Federalism: Mature and Emergent*, Arthur W. MacMahon,
editor, Russell and Russell Publishers. Reprinted by permission of the Trustees
of Columbia University.

dangers are augmented when the constitutional structure to be examined is federal, where diversity of practice and complexity of organization are endemic.

The questions that make this interdependence significant lie close to the core of the underlying paradox of federalism.[1] In the formative phase of a federal system the question of survival—of maintaining a minimal degree of union and of giving some measure of reality to formal powers of central direction—challenges the adaptive and adjusting potentialities of party, even in the context of a restricted electorate. Maturity, on the other hand, focuses upon the party system, as the representative device most responsive to the underlying values of personality, such questions as whether the perpetuation of decentralizing forms must eventuate in restricting a centralized power to govern which a developing popular consensus would otherwise support; whether federalism, as structural fact rather than as doctrine, must spawn an extra-constitutional system of party power which places limits upon the adaptability of the scheme as a whole and forces a choice between an inhibiting political veto and a drastic alteration of the whole pattern, perhaps through violent means.

I

To speak loosely of "the party system," especially when dealing with federalism in the United States, is to run the risk of begging the central question in this inquiry, for the nature of the party enterprise rests on the extent to which the elements collectively designated by the term actually constitute a system. Differentiating factors of structure and function bisect the "system" from various directions and in bewildering fashion, creating patterns of autonomy and subordination, some stable and some fluid, which seriously embarrass generalization.

The structural elements of party can be classified in the conventional fashion—following the formal, frequently statutory provisions for the diversity of committees, conventions, and individual functionaries—by national, state, and local levels. Such classification, while formally appropriate, is likely to take insufficient account of the extent to which the persistent and

[1] See the opening chapter in this symposium by Arthur W. Macmahon.

effective relationships among men and groups of men active in party affairs are clustered around one or a number of individual offices located on one or two or all three levels of the formal hierarchy.

It is a commonplace to point out that the party on the national level in the United States is, and throughout the country's history has been, focused on the presidency. Such national or interstate machinery as exists is primarily, though not exclusively, concerned with the nomination and election, perhaps especially the renomination and re-election, of a President. So much is this the case that, despite the practice by both parties since 1928 of maintaining at least a nuclear national headquarters in continuous operation and despite the normal efforts of the defeated presidential candidate to give substance to his titular leadership, the party which has failed to win the White House presents a somewhat truncated, if not fractionated, appearance, which it is likely to retain until after the next nominating convention. Moreover, when the presidency is not at stake both parties show strong symptoms of "mid-term atomization."[2]

The essential supportive structures for members of the Congress typically are not national or interstate. The chairmen and staffs of the national committees provide some services and assistance for duly nominated candidates for the Congress. The organizationally separate and often jealously independent campaign committees maintained by the "parliamentary" parties in the Senate and the House of Representatives seem to perform much the same sort of function, although their activities have never been closely studied.

The party in the Senate and the House of Representatives is not without significance as a means of allocating positions of power and influence in the legislative branch or even as a vehicle for the formulation of public policy,[3] and the "record" of the congressional parties is not irrelevant to the fortunes of aspirants for election or re-election to the Congress. But the risks and sanctions to which most members of Congress are particu-

[2] The phrase is V. O. Key's. See *Politics, Parties, and Pressure Groups*, 3d edition, New York, Thomas Y. Crowell Company, 1952, p. 515.

[3] Julius Turner, *Party and Constituency: Pressures on Congress*, Baltimore, The Johns Hopkins Press, 1951.

84   DAVID B. TRUMAN

larly sensitive have their focus within the states and localities. The relationships which the legislator has established and maintained within the constituency are primary and crucial; others are secondary and incidental. This seems to be the case despite the evidence that, especially in the case of the House of Representatives, the bulk of the voters in general elections cast their ballots on the basis of party preference rather than attachment to the personal qualities of individual candidates for the national legislature; that is, party percentages in most districts tend to shift in the same direction. This is the case in presidential years, when the party is in a sense symbolized in the person of the chief candidate, but is equally apparent in the midterm elections.[4] This paradox seems to point to the underlying significance of the nominating as against the electoral function of party structure, of which more will be said below.

At the state and local levels the structural patterns are varied and complicated, but not essentially different in kind. The significiant organizations in the states may be centered upon the governorship, with control reaching down effectively into the counties and municipalities, or upon the United States Senators or upon both in some form of combination. Specialization in the localities may be built individually or in combination around the positions of mayors, sheriffs, or other prime sources of patronage and power such as the office of surrogate in the counties of New York State. Such specialized structures may include a variety of other elective offices, such as seats in the state legislature, in the United States House of Representatives, and even in the Senate. As often as not, however, congressional candidates will operate through more or less independent organizations of their own creation, even in the general election campaign. In the case of Representatives, this is often a reflection of the relative indifference of the more inclusive state and local organizations toward the congressional ticket, as compared with more lucrative sources of patronage. Senators may function independently for quite different reasons. Not only are they more conspicuous in

---

[4] See the data presented in Key, *op. cit.*, chap. 17, and his paper, "The Veterans and the House of Representatives: A Study of a Pressure Group and Electoral Mortality," *Journal of Politics*, Vol. 5 (1943), pp. 27-40. This pattern is not to the same degree discernible in the case of Senators, since they are likely to enjoy a greater degree of personal prominence.

the political affairs of their constituencies and secure in their positions for a longer period of time, but also they are likely to command other means of political power in greater abundance, including federal patronage.

The structural scheme of parties in the American federalism thus displays a confusing complexity, both in its formal aspects and in its informal operation. The system, to the extent that it can be given the name, is composed of a tremendous variety of elements imperfectly and rather unpredictably articulated, capable of showing a remarkable degree of separatism and autonomy. Moreover, the degree of articulation which exists to make the system is of a peculiar sort. The relationships between the more obscure and the more prominent elements in the system show a defensive, unilateral quality. In areas where general elections mean anything, it is a rare local or state party unit which, personal and factional feuds aside, is indifferent to the vote-pulling power those occupying the principal positions on the ticket. But the concern is in a sense parasitic, to derive support from the leading figure on the ticket rather than to supply it. Given the tendency of voters, even when the form of the ballot does not help, to simplify their tasks by voting a "straight ticket," state and local elements are understandably interested in a nominee at the top of the list who may carry the whole slate into office with him. But these segments of the system are able, in marked degree, to cut themselves off from the head of the ticket when the latter is regarded as a handicap and succeed with remarkable frequency in checking the effects upon them of a swing of voting sentiment adverse to the occupant of the top place.[5] Similarly, there are significant relationships between the presidential party and the "constituency parties," illustrated by the common appeal by a member of the Congress for executive adoption of a particular policy or for a favorable presidential announcement in order to improve the prospects of hard-pressed candidates in special areas, but these carry no guarantee of reciprocal support either on the floor of the Congress or in subsequent election campaigns.

[5] This point is tentatively demonstrated in V. O. Key, Jr., "Partisanship and County Office: The Case of Ohio," *American Political Science Review*, Vol. 47 (1953), pp. 525-32. Cf. Harold F. Gosnell, *Machine Politics: Chicago Model*, Chicago, University of Chicago Press, 1937.

II

Although the system—made up of the presidential parties, the "parliamentary" parties, the constituency parties, and the various other state and local aggregations—is structurally unstable and disjointed, the distribution of power within it is not even or merely haphazard. Here again, however, the danger of hasty generalization is great. It is customary to refer to the distribution of power within the American party system as decentralized. This is the generally accepted view, yet its implications in the context of federalism and for possible future trends are not clear unless some account is taken of the relative significance of the various functions of the party and of the degree of decentralization of power in connection with the most important of them. Parties, in any representative system, perform a composite of functions, including nominating candidates for public office, mobilizing an electorate for their support, distributing patronage and other perquisites of public position, developing and protecting those formulas for social adjustment and accommodation which we collectively refer to as public policies, and a host of less obvious and self-conscious services. In different places and at different times one or another of these may be more conspicuous than the rest, which vastly complicates the tasks of historians and comparative analysts of the political process. Except perhaps in those political situations where a basic consensus is lacking or is being challenged, however, the nominating function seems to be the most fundamental or at least the most persistently focal. This has been strikingly the case in the United States since at least as far back as the caucuses and juntos of the later colonial years and, especially on the national level, conspicuously so since the great changes in the period associated with the name of Andrew Jackson, when the presidential party assumed most of the characteristics it displays today. It is around the nominating function that the states in recent decades have constructed the most elaborate and complicated systems of statutory regulation, and the intensity of feeling associated with the spread of the direct primary in the first decade of the present century reflected in part a recognition of the fundamental importance of the nomination process. James Bryce made no more acute observation concerning the American scene than he did when he noted that the nomination of candidates for public office was not only the most important but the most distinctively American function of party organization.[6]

It is in connection with the nominating of candidates that the decentralization of power in the American party system is most apparent. Looking at the presidency it is clear that the changes in practice which developed in the eighteen-twenties — changes largely of degree, perhaps, but of such measure that their significance can scarcely be exaggerated — involved an increase in the importance of localism in the selecting process. The congressional caucus had been the instrument of a limited and comparatively homogeneous national elite, disposing of an office which had little of the quality of popular symbolism that it possesses today. Its members were not, of course, lacking in attachment to states and sections, but theirs was a national and central power reflecting the effects of close association in the institutional frame of the national legislature. The shift of initiative to the state legislatures and later to the national delegate conventions was a response to demands from more heterogeneous elements in the population and eventuated in a shifting of the power of decision, if not of initiative, from the national to the state or local level.

In Jackson's day, and for decades thereafter, the utility of the national convention lay not only in the announcement of a defensible nomination, but also in the sharpening of an effective electoral mechanism. In fact, the first national convention of the Democratic party was apparently more a rally to spur Jackson's state and local cohorts into vigorous activity than a device for selecting the candidate, as, in fact, conventions in which incumbent Presidents have sought renomination have usually been ever since. In later years the leaders of state and factional delegations had not only convention votes to market among the managers of aspiring candidates but also a canvassing and electoral organization as well. Both were needed, even though the former were of more immediate importance.

Perhaps the most significant, if largely undocumented, change in recent years, a change which may account for some of the recent criticism of the national convention, is that the election-

[6] James Bryce, *The American Commonwealth*, 2d edition, New York, Macmillan and Company, 1891, Vol. II, p. 73.

88   DAVID B. TRUMAN

eering functions of the presidential party have become increasingly centralized while the power over nominations remains decentralized. Although those voters who alter their choices late in the campaign may be strongly influenced, as the survey studies indicate, by personal solicitation,[7] the presence of the presidential candidates in every living room, by way of radio and television, reduces the need for an army of canvassers in presidential campaigns as the development of the metropolitan press alone never did. In recent presidential elections both the behavior and the informal testimony of many urban functionaries support this interpretation; the circulars and posters are still distributed to the local clubs and headquarters, but the effort necessary to put them in the hands of individual voters is recognized as being of little or no value. State and local leaders are not powerless or completely unnecessary in the electioneering efforts of the presidential party, but both central direction and central execution of a presidential campaign have become in recent years not only a possibility but in large measure an actuality.

Yet the nomination function, excepting the renomination of an incumbent President, remains essentially decentralized. Despite such devices as the presidential primary and the centrally directed pre-convention efforts of the leading aspirants, local and frequently extraneous considerations not only enter into but even dominate the selection of delegates and the horse-trading decisions behind the scenes at the convention. In fact, the evidence clearly suggests that in areas where one-party dominance, as in the South, operates to avoid disturbance to distinctive local practices, the only significant function of a state party may be to select reliable delegates to interstate party councils. The leaders of the presidential party may no longer need to rely heavily upon a decentralized machinery for conducting an election campaign, but they are still dependent on forging a cohesive coalition of state and local leaders for the opportunity to conduct one.

Decentralization of the nominating function is more striking and more significant as it affects Senators and Representatives.

[7] Paul F. Lazarsfeld, Bernard Berelson, Hazel Gaudet, *The People's Choice*, 2d edition, New York, Columbia University Press, 1948, pp. 150-158.

Regardless of the method of selection, by one or another form of the predominant direct primary or by convention, the influences which are chiefly responsible for the selection of candidates are local rather than national. The importance of this fact is merely underscored by the evidence that, under normal conditions, in about half the congressional constituencies, success in the primary is tantamount to election.[8] This is typically due to the "one-party" complexion of many such areas, but it may result as well from the individual candidate's effectiveness in creating or associating himself with an organization within the constituency which can assure his selection or redesignation. The implications for the party system are much the same in either case.

Even a casual glance at the career lines of Senators and Representatives, as well as of state and local officials from whose ranks they are normally recruited, will indicate that most of them have had long and intimate association with the areas which they represent, more than is required by the symptomatically significant custom demanding residence in the district from which the legislator is chosen. No precise data on this point exist in the literature, but the impression is that a member of Congress is more likely than the average of the population to have been born, raised, educated, and trained in the area from which he is chosen. A constituency, perhaps especially an urban one, may take up a comparative newcomer who has achieved sudden prominence, but his survival is likely to depend ultimately upon his knowing his constituency, not in abstract, intellectual terms, but through supportive associations with individuals and groups. He must have satisfactory "connections," either with the leadership of a dominant party organization or with influential individuals primarily concerned with assuring his continuance in office or a combination of the two.

These connections may not be able to assure his election; the fortunes of the national party may be ebbing so rapidly that nothing can assure his individual survival or the nominee of the opposing party may more successfully exploit local dissatisfactions. But the aspirant will have no chance even to face these risks, except as he chooses to attempt a normally unsuccessful

[8] Cortez A. M. Ewing, "Primaries as Elections," *Southwestern Social Science Quarterly*, Vol. 29 (1948-49), pp. 293-98; Malcolm Moos, *Politics, Presidents, and Coattails*, Baltimore, The Johns Hopkins Press, 1952.

"independent"· candidacy, unless he has the support necessary for nomination.

The structure responsible for nominating the legislative candidate need not be parochial or anti-national in its attitudes. This is not its principal significance but rather the fact that it is the locus of discretion in the nominating process. In its operations it need display no dependence upon, no functional association or identification with, the leadership of the presidential or the "parliamentary" party. Bryce made the point effectively in a brief comparison of local party organizations in Britain and the United States:[9]

An organization which exists, like the political associations of England, solely or mainly for the sake of canvassing, conducting registration, diffusing literature, getting up courses of lectures, holding meetings and passing resolutions, has little or no power. . . . But when an organization which the party is in the habit of obeying, chooses a party candidate, it exerts power, power often of the highest import. . . .

Decentralization of the functions of nominating and promoting the election of members of the Congress is reflected in a lack of cohesion on important policy matters within the "parliamentary" parties — within the party in either House and between the party in one chamber and "the same" party in the other — and in fairly frequent rejection of the legislative leadership of "the party's" President when it "controls" the White House. It is too easy to underestimate the influence of party affiliation upon legislative voting and to ignore the evidence that it is more reliably predictive of such behavior than any other factor so far identified.[10] But on controverted issues of prime significance the leaders of the "parliamentary" parties not infrequently find themselves in the minority among their nominal following or split into two opposing wings, and the Administration may have to count on appreciable support from a segment of the "opposition" in Congress for the enactment of a basic portion of its legislative program, often despite extraordinary efforts by a popular President through public appeals and pronouncements, efforts which depend for effectiveness upon their infrequent use.

This state of affairs leads to criticism of the party system and

[9] Bryce, op. cit., Vol. II, p. 76.
[10] Consult the evidence in Turner, Party and Constituency. Turner's data are confined to the House of Representatives.

demands for party "responsibility" by those who desire a central place among the functions of party for the formation of a more coherent and enforceable program. Of such criticisms the recent report of the American Political Science Association's Committee on Political Parties may be taken as representative.[11] A common shortcoming of such appeals, illustrated in the committee's proposals, is that in their enthusiasm for programmatic elegance they tend to underestimate the significance of the decentralized nominating function. It seems unlikely that any amount of policy talk in local meetings or of platform writing by interstate bodies will increase discipline within the congressional parties or cohesion within the Administration as a whole, unless they are preceded by a centralization of the risks and sanctions associated with the selection of candidates for seats in the legislature. It may be doubted, in fact, whether in any party system dominated by two major aggregations, even in a country less extensive and socially less complex than the United States, cohesion is provided primarily by the programmatic element rather than by a central leadership whose policy tendencies are but vaguely known and whose displeasure with a parliamentary follower is enforceable at the nominating stage. If the legislator's risks are localized, he will look in that direction when making difficult choices on matters of public policy.

III

The American party system thus tends to be characterized by decentralization of power with respect to its most crucial function, by structural confederation, and by a lack of coherence in matters of major policy. What have the facts of federalism to do with this? To what extent is this an inescapable consequence of the federal system itself? Federalism, by the constitutional protection of constituent governments, creates at least the possibility, as Herbert Wechsler has argued,[12] that the states will control the composition and influence materially the legislative processes of the national entity. If, as Arthur Holcombe suggests,

---

[11] *Toward a More Responsible Two-Party System,* A Report of the Committee on Political Parties, American Political Science Association, Supplement, *American Political Science Review,* Vol. 44, No. 3, Part 2 (September, 1950). Also published as a separate volume (New York, Rinehart and Company, 1950).

[12] Herbert Wechsler's chapter in this symposium.

the national political party is the principal agent for restricting these tendencies,[13] its effectiveness in the United States has been something less than complete. Is the molding force of the federal system itself such that a party system operating within it must inevitably show the characteristics of political organizations in the United States?

This is a question of considerable importance for an understanding of the American experience and for an estimate of its potentialities in the future. It is a question which the Committee on Political Parties tends to avoid by treating party organization as a matter dissociated from that of governmental structure. Thus it asserts that: "In the case of the American party system, the real issue is not over the federal form of organization but over the right balance of forces within this type of organization."[14]

The basic political fact of federalism is that it creates separate, self-sustaining centers of power, privilege, and profit which may be sought and defended as desirable in themselves, as means of leverage upon elements in the political structure above and below, and as bases from which individuals may move to places of greater influence and prestige in and out of government. This does not mean simply that a socio-economic interest group, dominant within a state or, more typically perhaps, a group of contiguous states, will utilize state powers to protect itself from assault both from within the area and from the national center. This is true enough; it merely restates the facts underlying the original choice of a federal rather than a unitary structure for the second American constitution, and it points to the familiar fact of sectional politics present through most of our history and recurrent with each wave of state creation.

The separate political existence of the states in the days of the nation's industrial and political maturity, on the other hand, provides effective access to the whole governmental structure for interest groups whose tactics may be local or sectional but whose scope is national. Separatism, whether within the federal system or in the form of a specious demand for making a governmental activity "independent of politics" at whatever level of the structure, has frequently been a refuge for interests bent on defen-

[13] See the chapter by Arthur N. Holcombe.
[14] *Toward a More Responsible Two-Party System*, p. 26.

sive or evasive action, and the "states' rights" argument has often had about it an air more of expediency than of principle. This is not new. But it is the fact of federalism which permits an interest group or other enterprise of national scope, in alliance with lesser interests which may be primarily local or sectional, to prevent or negate action on the national level and to insure inaction or indulgence in the states. It was not merely Yankee stubbornness and dedication to local self-government which in the thirties prevented federal action to foster integrated development of the Connecticut River Valley. Such sentiments may have been more than mere expedient romanticism, and they might alone have affected the outcome of the proposal and the fortunes of elected state officials and members of Congress, but they received significant support and direction from private utility interests whose reach was nationwide.[15] Nor were the interests exclusively local or sectional, though such were allied at least peripherally, which induced the Congress to alter in favor of state action a Supreme Court decision asserting or permitting national control of insurance. These illustrations are not cited by way of indictment but merely of illustration. In the maturity of the federal system the existence of the states as self-contained centers of power permits the use of them and associated party units by interests which are state or local only in a tactical sense. This is not equivalent to the separatism of a geographically defined interest, though it appears in the same garb and owes its significance as a technique to the continued existence of the states as power centers. Its effects on the party system are conducive to neither centralization nor cohesion at the national level.

In viewing the states as channels of access for interest groups, however, it is easy to forget that elective positions within the states, especially the governorships, are prizes in themselves and that the political "game" may be merely a means from the viewpoint of the interest group leader but is likely to be an end in itself for many of the more active partisans. It is perhaps a commentary on the instrumental, almost a-political attitudes of many academic observers of politics that they lay such stress upon the American parties as alliances of socio-economic interest

[15] William E. Leuchtenberg, *Flood Control Politics: The Connecticut River Valley Problem, 1927-1950*, Cambridge, Harvard University Press, 1953.

groups. They are, of course, alliances of groups, but parties are not distinguishable exclusively or even primarily in terms of their socio-economic policy content. In varying but important measure they are purely political, focused upon securing and holding power for their leading elements as an end in itself. The grand patterns of sectional and perhaps class alliances which have successively dominated our presidential politics for periods lasting up to several decades can in the large view perhaps be explained most meaningfully in terms of socio-economic interest. But at shorter range the detailed patterns take on a more exclusively political appearance.[16] There is here no intended implication of petty place-seeking but rather a suggestion that to aspire to be among those who govern and to associate for that objective as an end in itself is both normal and honorable. The evidence which indicates that enduring attachment to a party is for many voters a loyalty independent of, though not dissociated from, socio-economic interest[17] supports the assumption that similar attachments to party, clique, and faction exist among the more active elements in political organizations.

The significance of this point in the present context is that, given the multitude of elective positions in the system (only partially a consequence of federalism) and given the absence of a clearly defined and recognized path from one position to another in the loose hierarchy of political careers (a consequence more of a decentralized party system than directly of federalism itself), conflicting but interdependent clusters of loyalty and aspiration build up around various positions in the governmental structure. Thus, within a given "party," the career aspirations and prospects of a state governor, a United States Senator, and a member of the House of Representatives are likely to be ambiguous to one another or to others in the political structure with whom they must deal. Each may want one of the other offices; the governor and Senator may both have presidential ambitions which are mutually exclusive; the Senator or the Representative, though occupying a "national" office, may hope to move to the governor-

[16] I am here dissenting in part from the view expressed by John Fischer in his contribution to the symposium. Cf. my comments in *The Governmental Process*, New York, Knopf, 1951, pp. 279-81, 509-10, and *passim*.

[17] There are interesting data on this point in the recent study of the 1952 presidential election by Angus Campbell, Gerald Gurin, and Warren E. Miller: *The Voter Decides*, Evanston, Illinois, Row, Peterson and Company, 1954.

ship and is likely to be far more closely dependent upon the state governor, from considerations either of preference or of expediency, than upon the leaders of the "parliamentary" party or upon a President bearing the same party designation. This is a simplified and hypothetical example,[18] but it illustrates the role played by the offices established in the federal structure, and especially the state governor, in fractionating and decentralizing the party system, in encouraging the development of largely independent, hostile, and internally cohesive factional groupings.

The connection between these tendencies and the existence of federalism should not, of course, be overstated. The basic phenomenon of clique and personal rivalry is familiar enough in all organizations, including political parties. The point of significance here is the extent to which the federal structure tends to give these free rein. It is symptomatic of the function in the party system of state political positions, especially the governorship, that of the forty-three major candidates in the twenty presidential elections from 1876 through 1952 (counting three candidates in the elections of 1912, 1924, and 1948), only seven, excluding the thirteen incumbent Presidents, came to the nomination directly from a national political position, such as a seat in the Congress or a cabinet post; five were nominated from non-political positions of national or regional importance, and the remaining eighteen were drawn from state political roles, mostly governorships. Such nominations are, of course, available under normal conditions only to governors of the large doubtful states, but the disruptive potentialities of the governorships are not confined to presidential races. The governor who merely seeks to retain his office through an effective organization covering major sections of the state is in a position to influence the fortunes and the choices of members of Congress, and a Senator or Representative who is aiming at the governorship is likely to be peculiarly solicitous of interests located in his home state.[19]

---

[18] In some states, of course, party organizations have been disciplined enough to establish a relatively clear and enforceable *cursus honorum*, as recently in Virginia. See V. O. Key, Jr., *Southern Politics in State and Nation*, New York, Knopf, 1949, chap. 2.

[19] The basic incompatibility of elements in the party structure is underestimated in the report of the Committee on Political Parties when it looks to local party meetings to give local party organizations "a stronger sense of loyalty to the

These three factors derived from the existence of the states as separate and largely self-sustaining power centers — channeling the claims of local socio-economic interest groups, inviting their use as leverage against federal action by interests which are only tactically local, and providing for competing and frequently incompatible nuclei of decentralized intra-party conflict — are, of course, interrelated. In various combinations they go a long way toward indicating that there is something inherent in federalism which induces decentralization and lack of coherence in a party system.

But it is not sufficient merely to show that federalism has had some effect upon the nature of the party system. The important question of how much effect it has remains unanswered and to a precise degree unanswerable. It can easily be pointed out that decentralization and lack of cohesion frequently are apparent within the state parties, where factors other than federalism are influential. Could the like of these account in considerable measure for the peculiarities of the system as a whole? Would the American party system have developed essentially its present characteristics if the Founding Fathers had established a unitary constitution? The question is hypothetical but not irrelevant.

IV

Before turning to an examination of some of the influences other than federalism that have molded the American parties, it may be instructive, or at least suggestive, to examine briefly two other federal systems, Canada and Australia, for evidence of similar effects of federal organization. The comparison cannot be conclusive, since, as in all such efforts, it is impossible to differentiate the effect of other influences and state in precise terms the consequences of basic constitutional structure. But contrasts may be revealing even when comparisons cannot be made with exactness.

In both Canada and Australia the major parties are obliged, especially in the former, to take account of the geographically

---

entire party" and when it proposes a Party Council "representative" of various elements, including the party's state governors. See *Toward a More Responsible Two-Party System*, pp. 39 ff., 47.

defined differences which underlie the federal structure. Viable national political structures, as would be expected, must reckon with sectional issues, attitudes, and interests. Yet despite this obvious fact both have seen the development of national parties more centralized and considerably more cohesive than those in the United States.[20]

In Canada there is considerable variation in the formal structures of the major parties, and within the parties the patterns differ from one province to another and between rural and urban constituencies, as in the United States. In Quebec, whose politics are not unlike those of the American South, parties are more loosely organized, and purely personal and factional influences have considerable significance. At the national level the only party organization of importance is the parliamentary party. Below that is the somewhat more complex provincial party organization and the constituency (riding) organization.

The fact of federalism introduces potential cleavages into the party system, yet normally the leader of the parliamentary party, especially if he is also Prime Minister, can count on the disciplined support of those elected with him, and a majority Government usually can survive throughout its permissible statutory life of five years. In Dominion elections, to be sure, it is not unusual for the outcome nationally to be affected by the existence of local or provincial hostilities clustered around other points in the federal structure and largely irrelevant to national questions.

Such centrifugal influences as exist within the Canadian parties seem to be associated, as in the United States, with decentralization of the nominating function and with the use of provincial governmental positions as points of resistance. Nominations for the Dominion parliament are made by the constituency organizations through various procedures generally lacking the complexity of their American equivalents, a point perhaps not without significance. These constituency organizations, perhaps espe-

[20] In this section I have relied heavily upon Alexander Brady, *Democracy in the Dominions*, 2d edition, Toronto, University of Toronto Press, 1952; Robert M. Dawson, *The Government of Canada*, Toronto, University of Toronto Press, 1947; H. McD. Clokie, *Canadian Government and Politics*, 2d edition, London, Longmans, Green and Company, 1945; and Louise Overacker, *The Australian Party System*, New Haven, Yale University Press, 1952.

cially in Quebec, are a good deal more independent in their decisions than are those in Britain, and the provincial and national parties have no formal or acknowledged power to withhold designations or to control the local decisions. A member of parliament who is not in the best of standing with the Government may be renominated if he nevertheless retains the confidence of the constituency committee, but this is less likely to occur if he is known to be in disfavor, and the national party leader may, especially if he is Prime Minister, be able to punish, by indirect means, the recalcitrant by seeing that he is deprived of his nomination.

The national party's organized contact with the individual voter is through the mechanism of the provincial party association, which directs the electioneering efforts in the constituency. The provincial organization has dual loyalties, to the national party and to the provincial leader. These may become divided, as happened in the not entirely unprecedented break in 1940 between Prime Minister Mackenzie King and Mr. Mitchell Hepburn, the leader of the Liberal Party in Ontario and the provincial prime minister. In a fashion not unrecognizable to Americans, the latter made use of his position in the provincial government to embarrass the national leadership. Clokie's comment on the incident was that it illustrated "one of the penalties paid for federalized politics when there is no appropriate political organization to coordinate the entire national party."[21] This was an extreme case; the more common threat is merely that the provincial party will be more interested in winning power in the province than in promoting the interests of the national party leadership.

The Canadian party system thus shows the influences of the federal structure, but it is in rather sharp contrast to the United States in degree. This is not the place to attempt an exhaustive analysis of the reasons for the contrast, but one or two prominent factors should be cautiously mentioned. These seem to be associated with the parliament-cabinet system, operating under conditions at least analogous to those in Britain. In this connection it is tempting to seize upon the absence of a separation of powers as

[21] Clokie, *op. cit.*, p. 95.

the crucial element, but as a simple constitutional fact it is not convincing. However, the consequence that it involves no separate popular election of the head of the government is significant, in that it implies narrowing and rather sharply defining the alternative lines of succession to the positions of principal influence. The subtle differences in the role of prime ministers, at the national level and in the provinces, flowing from retention of representatives of the Crown in the chief ceremonial positions, are not unimportant. But the chief fact seems to be that the positions of provincial prime ministers, to say nothing of a variety of other governmental and nongovernmental positions, are not points from which direct succession to the most important political post can take place. As a point of leverage the provincial prime ministership, or leadership of the minority party in a province, may be useful, but it is not readily convertible into peak national leadership. In fact, it appears that sectional hostilities are more likely to focus upon a provincial leader than upon a Dominion statesman. The advantages of political ambiguity, which adhere to the governor of an important state or to a presidential aspirant whose prominence rests on a nonpolitical career in the United States, lie with the experienced politician at the national level. This seems to produce a somewhat cooptative pattern of succession which, buttressed by a skillful and thoroughly un-British use of patronage when the party is in power, increases dependence upon the party leader. In the hands of a gifted politician such as a Laurier or a Mackenzie King — historically not unimportant political facts in themselves — the system can produce long and durable national leadership and reduce the disruptive influences of federalism to a minimum.

Associated with and in some instances flowing from these basic factors are a number of supportive influences of apparently less fundamental importance, such as the power of dissolution, simpler and less frequent elections, resulting in a more informal and less sustained party activity at the local level, and the striking dominance of the national party leader. The last of these involves an assumption within the constituency that a member of parliament will support his party in the legislature or resign, which considerably reduces the significance of decentralized nominations.

The main features of the Australian situation are succinctly expressed by Louise Overacker in the closing sentences of her informative study:[22]

In spite of its federal structure and a strong sense of particularism among the member states, unified, disciplined parties with Commonwealth-wide organizations developed. Even the Senate, created to safeguard state interests, has become a body in which divisions are along strict party lines.

This state of affairs is traceable to the existence of the remarkable Australian Labor Party, not only in the sense that it applies most completely to that party but also because the A.L.P., far more than the Liberal Party in Canada, has developed a structural pattern to be imitated by other political groupings as well as a substantive position for them to react to.

Superficially the structure of the A.L.P. resembles the general pattern in Canada. However, the primary emphasis given to the movement has not only attached extraordinary importance at both the state and Commonwealth levels to the parliamentary caucus, which the elected member is pledged to support, but has also produced a federal structure of state and interstate conventions whose relations with the parliamentary parties in the matter of policy-making are not always clear or harmonious.

While discipline within parliamentary parties is high, it is not always so striking in the structure as a whole, and decentralization is even more conspicuous. State party leaders have successfully repudiated the positions taken by federal leaders in referendum campaigns, and the leader of the party in New South Wales was able for five years, from 1932 to 1937, to dominate the party within the state even though his group had been formally expelled by the federal party. These occurrences are not necessarily typical or increasing in frequency, but they point to the fact of federal structure as a source of decentralizing leverage. Ambiguity in lines of succession is not as marked as in the United States, but its equivalent seems to be supplied by control by the state leadership over nominations, both state and federal, and over the financing of campaigns. The influence which they can thus exercise over the composition and conduct of the parliamentary parties appears to warrant Overacker's characterization of

[22] Overacker, *op. cit.*, pp 327-8.

them as "masters in their respective bailiwicks" and "lords of their own domain."[23]

Parliamentary discipline is less marked and decentralization is considerably more evident in the new Liberal Party, as in its predecessors, but its tendencies seem to be in the direction of a development similar to that of the A.L.P. The Country Party, clearly more a product of underlying social differences than of the structure of federalism itself, has never achieved a strong central organization.

At least in the case of the A.L.P. the contrasts with the American situation seem, as in Canada, to be more marked than the similarities. For this the parliament-cabinet system, with its partial reflection of British practices, is undoubtedly in part responsible. The importance of the individual national party leader is not as great as it has been in Canada, but, in the hands of a John Curtin, it is apparently possible so to use the machinery of party conference, caucus discipline, and the solidarity pledge as to offset state control of nominations.

But the chief significance of the Australian system for Americans is that matters of constitutional form are far less important than in Canada. The degree of discipline and of centralization which marks the A.L.P., and its rivals by partial adaptation, is fundamentally a reflection of underlying social conditions. Early land policies and patterns of settlement, imposed upon the peculiarities of Australian geography, and a course of economic development which restricted the emergence of a significant middle class and the dominance of middle-class values, resulted in the early appearance of a highly class-conscious labor movement unlike anything in the United States or Canada. Australian politics have been proportionally bitter and marked by lines of conflict drawn in class terms. Their significance is that these lines cut across geographic jurisdictions and minimize, even if they do not eliminate, the centrifugal effects of constitutional structure. These lines, moreover, are old, older than Australian federalism itself. As Overacker puts it, "Not only does the Australian Labor Party antedate federalism but in a sense it became a national party even before Australia was a nation."[24]

[23] *Ibid.*, pp. 100, 319.

[24] *Ibid.*, p. 30. For a comment on similar phenomena in interest-group organization, cf. Truman, *op. cit.*, p. 121.

The Canadian and Australian experiences thus seem to indicate that, although the structural fact of federalism produces tendencies toward decentralization and lack of cohesion in the party system, a variety of other political or social influences may minimize the effect of such tendences sufficiently to permit the development of a centralized power to govern consistent with the degree of underlying popular consensus. In the American case, apparently, these additional political and social facts have accentuated or at least perpetuated the centrifugal tendencies.

V

It seems clear that the structural fact of federalism is not alone sufficient to account for the peculiar characteristics of the American party system, though it may be fundamental. Additional influences must be identified and accounted for. Yet any effort to identify the additional forces in the American experience and to assess their relative importance is in a sense, likely to be artificial. It sets the analyst to the unenviable task of cutting apart what is a seamless web of multivariant and interdependent factors with the prospect that he will end up with a set of separate elements whose chief significance lies in their interaction.

The foregoing discussion of Canada and Australia suggests the relevance of the separation of powers, the constitutional arrangement which seems to attract the attention of critics most easily. If the present analysis is sound, however, it is not the partial constitutional isolation of executive from legislative functions or the accompanying system of checks and balances that is of chief interest. Attempts to encourage or to develop means for improving communication and collaboration between the White House and the Congress are, in this context, essentially palliatives, though commendably constructive ones of considerable potential significance. It is the separate election of chief executives at both levels, and perhaps all three, which seems relevant here. Governors have often succeeded in imposing their leadership upon state legislators and presidents have with varying degrees of success bridged the long mile from Capitol Hill to 1600 Pennsylvania Avenue. Nevertheless the separate election of chief executives has multiplied and thereby rendered ambiguous the lines of succession within the governmental structure, and ambiguity of this sort seems almost certain to encourage independence and parallelism in party structures rather than coherence and centralization. As long as Presidents may be recruited from Congress, from the governorships, or from the cabinet (as well as from outside of political life), and as long as men in any of these positions may reasonably aspire to any of the others, decentralization and lack of coherence are likely to appear in many subtle but significant ways. The hypothesis is rhetorical, but if gubernatorial aspirants could be recruited only from within the state legislature or only from among the principal executive positions and if presidents were drawn exclusively from the Senate, or, in Jeffersonian fashion, from the hierarchy of the cabinet, the reasons for independent and poorly articulated party structures would be reduced.

But if the separation of powers is relevant, it is not sufficient. Such elements of structure would not alone be controlling, particularly in face of the kinds of factors which orginally produced a federal scheme and which give it vitality today. Looking broadly at such factors over the sweep of the years, one gets the impression that, with one great exception, our politics has been carried on at relatively low temperatures. Except for the conflicts leading up to the Civil War, the issues generally have been of moderate intensity or, when heated or persistent, have been considerably tempered by a timely improvement in prices or in the level of industrial and commercial activity. Operating in the context of a large domestic market and a rapidly expanding economy, unrestricted by the kinds of factors which stoked the fires of conflict in Australia, our politics has been occupied with parceling slices of a pie that has had a way of expanding when awkward choices were imminent, not only over the relative sizes of the portions, but over who might partake and who must go without. Until very recently, moreover, our controversies have been for the most part domestic.

Our domestic, low-temperature quarrels have taken full cognizance of the geographically defined diversities which are still a reality within the country. In fact, the system has frequently exaggerated them; in a viable polity, and the survival value of the American scheme need not be argued, cleavages along local or sectional lines are not likely to dominate the scene in the presence of intersecting issues of great significance, especially if the latter have their origin on the international plane. In the absence of such issues, and occasionally in default of a recognition of their import, Americans have been able to engage in locally or regionally based disputes which have not infrequently had the appearance of political luxury. The argument is not that all these geographically defined issues have been without substance, although some of them clearly have, but rather that their prominence is in part owing to the absence of more intense, intersecting issues and that collectively their impact on the party system has been decentralizing and disintegrative. These conditions, if this estimate is valid, may help account for tendencies toward a decentralized politics within many of the states as well as in the nation as a whole.

In no respect is the quality of American politics, in contrast with Australian, more clearly indicated than in the labor movement. No substantial proportion of American wage earners has ever developed strong class attitudes. Given our characteristically uninhibited methods of settling and exploiting a rich and virgin continent, the steadily expanding economy, and the resulting high social mobility, the dominant values of the society have been "middle-class" and individualistic. So thoroughly have these values been accepted by the wage-earning population that the labor movement throughout its history has been haunted by the problem of cohesion. For decades this problem was dealt with in the organized sector of labor more by a reliance on differences within the working-class population than on cleavages between class groupings. From the "plain people" movements of the eighteen-sixties to the industrial unionism of the nineteen-thirties and nineteen-forties, American workers have been more likely to divide along sectional, commodity, even ethnic and religious lines — all essentially decentralized — than to consolidate along the shadowy boundary of social class. For good or ill, the American political system has not been faced with the intersecting issues churned up by a class-conscious labor movement.

A further consequence of the low-temperature, domestic quality of American politics is the high visibility of the organized interest groups which have developed around the lines of cleavage and specialization in a complex, industrialized society. Many of these are local or sectional only in a tactical sense, as noted earlier, but all of them are on occasion highly significant, in the absence of other sorts of controversies, as elements in the calculations surrounding the nomination function, even though they may not be overtly active in this respect. Moreover, even when, in partial consequence of their own characteristically federal structures, they have been rent by divisive controversy, their local or state components are no less likely to be influential in the facilitation or disruption of political careers and in the determination of legislative action at state and national levels.[25]

In this connection it is worth while to point out that a considerable element of localism has inevitably been injected into American politics, regardless of constitutional structure, by such factors as the patterns of immigration from Europe. Immigration itself has rarely provided a controversy of national scope, and nativist movements have been conspicuous on occasion but of no lasting significance. Ethnic issues as such, perhaps excluding the Negro question, have not had the impact on national politics that they have had, for example, in Canada. But with the tendency for individual nationality groupings to concentrate in particular areas, especially in the cities, and to find in their common rootlessness and frequently in the experience of discrimination and exploitation a basis in addition to national origin for cohesion and interdependence, they have constituted a means to power and influence for locally oriented political organizations outside and inside their own ranks.

It is these geographically defined factors, accentuated by a low-temperature, domestic politics, which give major force and relevance to the possibility of state control over the composition of the national governing bodies, through the electoral college and related means, which Herbert Wechsler points out in his chapter. Structural elements in the system — some, it is argued here, inherent in federalism — alone encourage an irreducible minimum of decentralization and disruption in the party system. But it is as these reflect the underlying pace of the political process and as they are harnessed to regionally differentiated issues and clusters of organization that they find their most impelling dynamic.

As in other national systems, moreover, there are additional governmental arrangements which support and in some in-

---

[25] See Truman, *op. cit.*, chaps. 2, 6, 10, and *passim.*

stances reflect the decentralizing tendencies apparent in the process as a whole. Not the least important of these is the practice of frequent elections specified by the calendar and the related constitutional provision for unequal terms of office. Decentralizing in intent, they have operated to accentuate localized concerns, especially in the midterm primaries and elections at the national level. But in a system in which any election may be relevant to all others in an area, whether they are held simultaneously or not, the very frequency of elections and campaigns can accentuate and exploit local and transitory animosities and consolidate localized patterns of control. This point had never been more dramatically illustrated than it was in the tragic years leading up to the Civil War. During the decade of the eighteen-fifties "the baneful influence of elections almost continuously in progress, of campaigns never over,"[26] accentuated local and sectional hostilities. Aided by the fact that at that time elections to the Congress were not held at a uniform date throughout the nation, the upthrust of localism further crippled already imperfect efforts to forestall a fatal break. In Nichols' words, "The incessant procession of artificially ordered election conflicts frequently meant nothing more than the routine return of pleasurable electioneering excitement; but in the 1850's it had become dangerous." "It was," he points out, "harder for the statesman at the capital city to calm the emotions stirred in these countless local contests when their representatives brought them to Washington."[27]

The difference between this fateful decade and the more normal course of our politics is one of degree, the more so as a multiplicity of local elections may support a professionalized corps of politicians whose organized relationships within the area can be utilized to resist an effort at centralization.

A representative and significant response to such an effort is provided by the Hatch Act of 1939. Stimulated by Franklin Roosevelt's awkward and ill-fated attempt at a "purge" of rebellious Representatives and Senators in the Democratic primaries of 1938, a bipartisan combination in the Congress took steps to forestall the possibility that a centralized party leadership could

[26] Roy F. Nichols, *The Disruption of American Democracy,* New York, Macmillan, 1948, p. 515.
[27] *Ibid.,* pp. 5, 7.

be built upon presidential patronage, through the device of a statutory prohibition against political campaign activity by federal employees below the policy-forming level, whether they are in the classified civil service or not. This was an effort at insurance against an extremely remote contingency, since the requirement of senatorial confirmation and the practice of senatorial courtesy have made patronage a comparatively feeble instrument of centralized leadership except in the opening months of an Administration or for purposes of securing renomination for an incumbent President. It is impossible to estimate precisely the effects of this restriction or of the comparable provision in the 1940 legislation restricting the annual expenditures of national committees, but at minimum their enactment testifies to the strength of the decentralizing tendencies.

VI

In a federal system decentralization and lack of cohesion in the party system are based on the structural fact of federalism, but, it has been argued here, the degree to which these become the dominant characteristics of the distribution of power within the political parties is a function of a variety of other governmental and social factors which are independent of the federal structure or are merely supportive of its tendencies. Within the American structure there clearly are limits beyond which centralization and coherence in the parties may not go. Nevertheless, accepting the argument that the national political party is the most responsive instrument of restraint upon federalism's centrifugal tendencies, it may be appropriate briefly to inquire into the circumstances which might produce a gradual shift in the locus of power within the American parties.

It seems clear that the prospects for such a shift must rest fundamentally upon the emergence or intensification of a dominant and persistent set of interests and issues which will tend to cut through rather than to unify constituencies, especially the states, and which demand standardized national solutions. These would imply a more intense and urgent, perhaps a more explosive, politics; that would seem to be the price of change. Here is not the place to attempt a detailed examination of any such issues, but it seems entirely possible that their most likely source would lie in the problems of an increasingly urbanized and industrialized society, as Arthur Holcombe suggested more than twenty years ago in his anticipation of the replacement of sectional by class politics.[28] Another complex of such issues may emerge or may be in process of emerging out of the problems besetting the new American leadership on the international scene.

Neither of these complexes of issues appears to hold much promise of startling immediate developments within the party realm. In the unlikely event of an increasingly even industrialization of all the states, it is by no means certain that an expanding economy will not so check the importance of intersecting issues of full employment, social security, and the like, that the demands of commodity and of section will still be dominant. Nor in such circumstances is it at all sure that leadership forces will not prefer the occasional inconveniences of a decentralized politics to the less manageable potentialities of an opposite trend. And in the realm of foreign policy it is by no means clear that an emerging consensus on direction and general posture will not leave the center of the stage free for geographically defined issues of pace and of precise application.

These obstacles aside, the dominance of issues capable of dividing major constituencies internally presupposes their emergence or evocation in sections now monopolized by a single party and the development of a vigorous and genuine bipartisan pattern. This result is not likely to be the work of a single day and not only because of the stubborn disinclination of voters to alter partisan attachments once they have been formed, though this is a factor of no inconsiderable importance. Rather, as V. O. Key has amply demonstrated in his study of the South, a single-party monopoly based on the assertion or defense of a dominant sectional interest tends to inhibit the identification and expression of intersecting national issues. It induces a fluid factionalism along personal and clique lines incapable of the organization necessary to sustained expression of such issues from within and to effective response to their assertion from without.[29] Moreover, the purely political advantages of a one-party monopoly are considerable and not to be surrendered without resistance. Only

[28] Arthur N. Holcombe, *The New Party Politics*, New York, W. W. Norton, 1933.
[29] Key, *Southern Politics*, chap. 14 and *passim*.

the most intense conflict over persistent issues is likely to prevail over efforts by an invigorated majority party to capture the leadership of an emerging opposition and to hamstring its efforts with all the statutory and polemic resources at the command of an entrenched group.

The federal structure itself imposes no insuperable obstacles to a shift in the locus of power within the party system, but it seems improbable that the country will soon dispense with the talents of the politician skilled in the manipulation and reconciliation of decentralized and recalcitrant power blocs.

6 *American Political Parties and the American System*

MORTON GRODZINS*

A distinguished Indian scholar recently said that he thought it was a fraud and a mockery to call American parties by that name. They had no program, they had no internal solidarity. The reasoning is familiar and easy to follow. A foreign student finds it hard to designate as a "party" a political group that controls a majority of the Congress but cannot formulate and by its own votes pass a program; that stands together only, and not always then, for national elections, for matters of patronage, and for the organization of the legislative business; that in convention chooses a leader and presidential candidate by unanimous vote and then, in Congress, forces that leader as President to depend upon defections from the other side.

From *Western Political Quarterly,* Vol. XIII, No. 4 (December 1960), pp. 974-998. Reprinted by permission of the University of Utah, copyright owners.

* This paper is a product of the federalism workshop of the University of Chicago, a research and training program carried out with support from the Ford Foundation. For helpful criticism of an earlier draft, I am indebted to Kaspar D. Naegele, Harry H. Eckstein, and Lee Benson, all colleagues during 1958-59 at the Center for Advanced Study in the Behavioral Sciences.

The purpose of the following pages is to comment on the functional consequences of this unique party arrangement for the larger governmental system in which it operates. How does the operation of American parties affect the operation of the American government? The argument, in a single sentence, is that the parties function to preserve both the existence and form of the considerable measure of governmental decentralization that today exists in the Unites States. The focus of attention is, therefore, upon the classic problem of a federal government: the distribution of power between the central and peripheral units. Yet there is little in what follows concerning formal, or constitutional, power relationships. The word "sovereignty" does not appear. Decisions of the Supreme Court are not emphasized. The concern of the paper is not juridical concepts or the sporadic umpiring of the courts, but the day-to-day pattern of who does what under whose influence; not the theoretical locus of supreme powers, but the actual extent of the sharing of decision-making in legislation and administration among the central, state, and local governments.

THE PARTIES AS DECENTRALIZERS

To say that parties function as decentralizers is not to say that parties cause decentralization. The two statements are of a different character. Saving a discussion of the difference between *function* and *cause* until later, we ask: how, specifically, do the American parties contribute to decentralization in the American system of government?

The Basic Sharing in Legislation. They do so, first of all, by determining in legislation the basic sharing of functions between the federal government on the one hand, and state and local governments on the other. Lord Bryce described the "working relations" of the national and state governments in the following words:

The characteristic feature and special interest of the American Union is that it shows us two governments covering the same ground, yet distinct and separate in their action. It is like a great factory wherein two sets of machinery are at work, their revolving wheels apparently intermixed, their bands crossing one another, yet each set doing its own work without touching or hampering the other.[1]

[1] James Bryce, *The American Commonwealth* (London: Macmillan, 1890), I, 318.

Classic works are sometimes responsible for classic errors. Bryce was wrong, even for the period of his own observations, in describing the federal government and the states as "each . . . doing its own work without touching or hampering the other." The American system is pre-eminently a system in which functions and responsibilities are shared among the federal, state, and local governments.

The federal government's participation in what are usually conceived to be state and local functions is widespread indeed.[2] But it is not our concern here. That concern is with the sharing of federal programs by the states and localities. And the first point is the basic one that "federal law is generally interstitial in its nature,"[3] limited in objective and in any given area of service or regulation building upon the main body of legal relationships defined by state law. It is difficult to find any area of federal law that is not affected in important ways by state law. Federal criminal statutes utilize state standards in defining federal crimes. Federal licenses are not granted unless applicants meet licensing requirements established by state laws. Federal tax laws are largely concerned with property relationships created and defined by the states. Substantive rights established in federal statutes have their enforcement left largely or wholly to the states (though in exceptional cases Congress gives exclusive jurisdiction to the federal courts). Even in fields that on their face concern exclusive federal spheres of action – that of patents, for example – the mixture of law occurs. Patent laws do not displace either the police or tax functions of the states, and patent rights are subordinate to a given state's authority over property within its limits.

Examples of this sort could be multiplied endlessly. The important task is to understand how the American parties operate to produce this characteristic mixture of American law.[4] Now, as

[2] A simple listing of *Federal Services to Cities and Towns* by Robert H. Blundred and Donoh W. Hanks, Jr., covers more than seventy pages and ranges from "abbatoirs" and "accounting" to "zoning" and "zoo administration" (Chicago: American Municipal Association, 1950). A full documentation of the sharing hypothesis will be contained in future publications of the federalism workshop of the University of Chicago.

[3] Henry M. Hart, Jr., and Herbert Wechsler, *The Federal Courts and the Federal System* (Brooklyn: Foundation Press, 1953), p. 435.

[4] It bears repeating that I am here discussing functions, not causes. An explication of the causes for the mixture of laws would take into account historical and

in the first days of the republic, the local as opposed to the national orientation of most members of the national Congress leads to legislation that gives important responsibilities to states and localities.

The entire development of grant-in-aid programs generally supports the sharing hypothesis. The grant device from this perspective allows the federal government to utilize its purse powers while sharing with the states important responsibilities in program definition and administration. Two specific examples will demonstrate the process. These are "hard cases." The hard case as a method of analysis means choosing those data—or those events or problems—which seem most likely *not* to support the hypothesis being considered. The National Airport Act of 1946 and the unemployment insurance provisions of the Social Security Act of 1935 are hard cases with respect to the sharing hypothesis because there existed compelling reasons for establishing both programs without state participation.

The issue that vexed Congress with respect to the postwar airport bill was a direct sharing question: should local governments, particularly large cities, deal directly with the Civil Aeronautics Administration or should the flow of applications and funds between large cities and the CAA be "channeled" through state agencies? The cities, as represented by Mayor Fiorello LaGuardia of New York and the United States Conference of Mayors, supported direct city-federal negotiations; the states through the Governors' Conference demanded channeling. An impartial observer, if one could be found, would almost certainly have concluded that the cities had the better case. The states had few and rudimentary airport authorities and contributed from 1933 through 1945 less than one per cent of total national airport expenditures. Federal funds were preponderant (75 per cent), the federal-local pattern then existing had proved successful, and federal administrative officers testified that, for larger airports, they preferred to deal directly with local authorities.

---

constitutional factors. The states existed before the union, and the Constitution, providing reserved powers to the states, established in the first place no impetus for the national definition of exclusive areas of national action. The common law background of American institutions also impedes the massive summary and codification of law that would have to precede an exclusive occupation of given fields by the federal government.

The Governors' Conference took a strong stand in favor of channeling,[5] and the Senate version of the bill was amended so as to channel all federal aid to airports through state agencies. The amendment was proposed by Republican Senator Owen Brewster of Maine, a former governor and former chairman of the executive committee of the Governors' Conference. The roll-call vote on the Brewster mandatory channeling amendment was as follows:

	Republicans	Democrats	Progressives	Total
Yea	24	15	1	40
Nay	7	26		33

Party influence is apparent, but party control plainly not: the Republicans, a clear minority in the Senate of the 79th Congress, could not have won without the fifteen Democratic defectors and thirteen Democratic non-voters. The crucial factor bringing victory to the states was not party affiliation. It was the conduct of senators who had once served as state governors. Sixteen former governors voted. Twelve were in favor of the amendment. Party identification made little difference: five of six Republican former governors and seven of ten Democratic ones supported the channeling amendment. Whereas 52 per cent of the senators who were not former governors opposed the amendment, 75 per cent of the former governors approved it. If the latter had divided their votes in the same way as their fellow senators did, the amendment would have been defeated by one vote rather than winning by seven.

The Brewster amendment represented an extreme victory for the states and the principle of shared functions. Later in the debate it was pointed out that some states had no airport programs or indeed no legislative authorization at all to concern themselves with airport development. A further amendment, passed without discussion and by voice vote, authorized the CAA to carry out airport projects directly with localities in those states which could not themselves participate for lack of the necessary legislation. The states could share in airport development, said the Senate, if they were in the least way prepared to do so. The choice was the states'. Only if they failed to provide enabling

---

[5] In addition to the several resolutions of the Conference, telegrams from 46 governors endorsing channeling were read into the record.

legislation for their own administrative agencies would the federal agency deal directly with local governments.

The House version of the bill was originally reported out by the Committee on Interstate and Foreign Commerce with no channeling provision whatsoever. It was amended on the floor with virtually no discussion and by voice vote to provide: "Nothing in this act shall authorize the submission of a project application by any municipality or other public agency which is subject to the law of any State if the submission of such project application by such municipality or other public agency is prohibited by the law of such State."[6] The bill was easily passed by the House in this form. The Conference Committee was presented in the two versions of the bill with what would seem to be a distinction without a difference. The Senate version provided for channeling of all funds through state agencies, but if states did not have appropriate agencies, then direct federal-local relationships were authorized. The House version said nothing about channeling, but any state by its own initiative could make channeling mandatory and thus prohibit direct federal-local negotiations. In both cases, the states clearly could control the administrative handling of the federal program. Nevertheless, the state governors and the former governors who were senators tried hard to have the Senate version of the bill adopted. Republican Senate members of the conference committee for a time held fast as a group. The conference committee remained deadlocked for four months. The bill finally reported and passed was substantially the House bill: affirmative state action was required if federal airport funds were to be channeled through state agencies.

The history of the 1946 National Airport bill is notable for the clear view it gives of the cross-cutting of party by other lines of influence. It is equally significant for the opposite views taken by the states, on the one hand, and the larger cities, on the other, in this case competing for participation in the sharing process. The role of the Congress was in many ways that of mediator, seeking in Senator McCarran's words "to effect a compromise" between

---

[6] A subsequent attempt to require channeling was initially defeated, then passed by teller vote, and finally shelved by a roll call. The final defeat was by a vote of 185-170, 164 Democrats and 20 Republicans opposing the mandatory channeling; 133 Republicans and 36 Democrats favoring it.

state and local views.[7] The strength of the idea of shared functions was perhaps most marked in the unstated assumption by all concerned that the federal government would not do the airport construction job alone. Constitutional authority, fiscal predominance, administrative ease, and military necessity might have justified this course of action. There is no evidence to indicate that any responsible group or agency seriously considered it. The states did not get all they wanted in the bill. But their failure to achieve full victory carried no sting. The power to compel channeling — which was the power to insure their full sharing in the airport program — remained exclusively a state power.

The Social Security legislation of early New Deal days is a more important case illustrating the political process by which the states insure their basic sharing in national programs. The legislation may indeed have marked a turning point in the federal system. If the social security program had been established as an all-federal one, as it very nearly was, the American government might look very different today. In a revealing aside in the course of a book review, Rexford Guy Tugwell described how close he and Harry Hopkins came to establishing Social Security as a program administered completely by the national government:

As an historical matter it was not hard to see that the states had declined in importance as responsibilities had gravitated to Washington.... And it was not a mistake to think that the states were obsolete and ought to be superseded by regions; the mistake was in thinking that it would be the policy of President Roosevelt to enhance the federal power (of which he was talking a good deal in those days of crisis) at the expense of that of the states. He seemed to conclude finally that both powers could be enhanced at the same time.... The evidence that he still clung to the Brandeis-Frankfurter view was not supplied until there occurred the intra-administration struggle within the Committee on Social Security. In this struggle Harry Hopkins and the writer [Tugwell] put up what seemed to them to be a sound argument against decentralization to the states. Miss Perkins' advisers were determined to use the social security system to bolster up the states. This appeared to be so costly an undertaking that it might jeopardize the system and, anyway, it would artificially interrupt the natural desuetude of the states. On an

---

[7] U.S. Congress, Senate, Sub-Committee on Aviation of the Committee on Commerce, *Hearings, Federal Aid for Public Airports*, 79th Cong., 1st Sess. (March 13-23, 1945), p. 114.

historic occasion Mr. Hopkins and the writer asked the President if it was wrong to go on objecting. The answer was not clear; but it was plain that the objections were not going to win his support. The objectors then withdrew from the committee and from then on neither had any contact with the formulation of the report, the shaping of the law, or its subsequent administration. Both regarded it as perhaps their worst defeat.[8]

There existed, as a matter of fact, several solid justifications for joint federal-state programs. The sharing-of-functions controversy raged most hotly over the administration of unemployment compensation. For one thing, the 1933 Wagner-Peyser Act had established employment offices on a federal-state basis (replacing an older all-federal program). This clearly "helped to fix the mold into which the unemployment insurance system was to be cast."[9] For another, a number of states already had operating systems of unemployment insurance and argued that a new federal-state program would be less damaging to ongoing activities than an all-federal one, especially since the systems were quite diverse. Wisconsin's system provided for compensation reserves on a plant or industrial basis, which probably would have been impossible to maintain under an all-national program, and a former Wisconsin official, Edwin E. Witte, was executive director of the Cabinet Committee on Economic Security which was drafting the new federal legislation. Third, it was believed that a federal-state system would have greater constitutional security than an all-federal one. Miss Perkins put great weight on this point.[10] Finally there were many arguments put forward with respect to the desirability of state experimentation, decentralization, and local participation.

None of these considerations or any combination of them was controlling. Mr. Tugwell is completely accurate in his recollection that the unemployment compensation program came very close to being established as an all-federal one. In addition to the general argument with respect to the "natural desuetude" of the states, there were good technical reasons for establishing an all-

[8] R. G. Tugwell and E. C. Banfield, "Grass Roots Democracy—Myth or Reality?" *Public Administration Review*, X (Winter, 1950), 48, 50.

[9] Paul Douglas, *Social Security in the United States* (New York: McGraw-Hill, 1936), p. 32.

[10] Frances Perkins, *The Roosevelt I Knew* (New York: Viking, 1946), p. 291.

federal unemployment compensation program. The movement of workers and the consequences of unemployment were clearly national in scope, and a nationally uniform unemployment insurance scheme seemed highly desirable. Many relief and other depression programs had been administered directly from Washington. The states, administratively and financially, were in poor condition.

In the eyes of those directly concerned, the weight of the argument was in favor of the all-federal unemployment compensation program. Miss Perkins has revealed that the Cabinet Committee in fact made, relatively late in its deliberations, a formal decision to recommend such a program. But the decision was reversed in favor of the collaborative federal-state programs. The final decision was not made for technical reasons, but for political ones. Miss Perkins has written:

> After long discussion we [the Cabinet Committee] agreed to recommend a federal system [without state participation]. We went back and informed colleagues in our own Departments. Within the day I had telephone calls from members of the Committee saying that perhaps we had better meet again.
>
> There was grave doubt, our latest interviews with members of Congress had shown, that Congress would pass a law for a purely federal system. State jealousies and aspirations were involved. So we met again, and after three or four hours of debate we switched back to a federal-state system.[11]

The depression crisis, weighty technical considerations (although some technical advice was on the other side), the powerful influence of Tugwell, Hopkins, Wallace, and Morgenthau, the existence of overwhelming Democratic majorities in both houses — all of these favorable factors were not sufficient to produce an all-federal unemployment compensation system. They were not sufficient because of decisive political considerations. The distribution of power within the majority party made an all-federal system impossible. Virtually the whole debate on the unemployment compensation bill, as introduced in its federal-state collaborative form, revolved around criticism of the power given to federal administrators. Amendments to the bill, proposed by

[11] *Ibid.*, pp. 291-92. Miss Perkins does not mention Tugwell's or Hopkins' views, but notes that Henry Wallace and Secretary of the Treasury Morgenthau argued for the all-federal system.

Democrats and passed with Democratic votes, drastically curtailed even the limited power initially provided federal agencies.
When the Cabinet Committee was making a following for its
proposal and when the proposal itself was altered by the Congress, the localism of the legislator was the controlling factor.
The lack of party solidarity produces through national legislation
the marble cake of shared functions that characterizes the American federal system.

Legislative Involvement in the Administrative Process.[12] The
second manner in which undisciplined political parties establish
the character of the American system is through the impact of
congressmen and senators on national administrative agencies.
The congressional interference is constant, effective, and institutionalized. It may be pegged on the broadest issues of national
policy or on purely personal considerations, but it is most
frequently exercised on behalf of local interests—individual,
group, and governmental.

Some aspects of the process of legislative involvement in
administrative affairs are formalized and well known. Administrative justifications before subcommittees on appropriations; the
routine hearings before permanent legislative committees and
subcommittees; and the work of special investigating or "watchdog" committees provide natural access points for members of
the Congress to press constituency interests upon administrative
officials. The Legislative Reorganization Act of 1946 made explicit the responsibility of the standing committees: each "shall
exercise continuous watchfulness of the execution by the administrative agencies concerned of any laws, the subject matter of
which is within the jurisdiction of such committee...."[13] Both
houses also have committees on Government Operations, each
spawning a number of subcommittees. The House of Representatives has found the (Moss) Subcommittee on Government
Information a tool for looking into all sorts of administrative
processes on behalf of local constituents. The Congressional
Committee on Printing has assumed a number of direct administrative responsibilities. Joint Committees of the Congress and
the executive have for many years made decisions concerning

---

[12] I am greatly indebted to Kenneth E. Gray, a member of the federalism
workshop, for aid on this section of the paper.
[13] 79th Cong., 2d Sess., 60 *U.S. Stats.* I, 832.

the purchase of land for wild life refuges and national forests.[14]
The General Accounting Office is a creature of Congress with
important and pervasive executive functions.

The legislative involvement with executive business has been
aided by a number of statutes in recent years that require administrators to report either past actions or future plans to Committees of Congress or to Congress as a whole. The 1955 Defense
Appropriations bill, for example, required the Secretary of Defense to secure prior consent of the House and Senate Appropriations Committees before turning over departmental functions to
private industry.[15] The Secretary of the Air Force, by a 1949
statute, was required to "come into agreement with" the House
and Senate Armed Forces Committee before acquiring land for
guided missile proving grounds.[16] Sometimes the statutes
provide merely for "consultation" between congressional committees and administrative agencies; sometimes for reports;
sometimes for a suspensive veto that Congress or one of its
committees can exercise over administrative action.[17] An example of the last sort of control is provided by the Internal Revenue
code which stipulates that the Commissioner of Internal Revenue may not make a tax refund or credit in excess of $200,000
until thirty days after he submits a report to the Joint Committee

[14] See Paul H. Appleby, *Policy and Administration* (University of Alabama
Press, 1949), pp. 8-10.
[15] Department of Defense Appropriations Act of July, 1955, Sec. 638. 69 *U.S.
Stats.*, p. 321. The President strenuously opposed this provision, and it was
eliminated in 1956.
[16] 63 *U.S. Stats.*, I, 66.
[17] Lease purchase agreements are subject to direct committee supervision.
Public Law 519, 83d Cong., 2d Sess. (1954), amending the Public Buildings Act
of 1949, reads (Title I, Sec. 411(e) and Title II, Sec. 202(g)): "No appropriation
shall be made for purchase contract projects which have not been approved by
resolutions adopted by the Committee on Public Works of the Senate and House
of Representatives respectively...." Identical statements are included in legislation relating to the Post Office and General Service Administration. See the
review of such statutes in J. Malcolm Smith and Cornelius P. Cotter, "Administrative Accountability: Reporting to Congress," *Western Political Quarterly*, X
(June, 1957), 405-15. Concurrent resolutions by Congress, as well as statutes, are
used to terminate administrative powers, require administrative action, and veto
administrative acts. See Cornelius P. Cotter and J. Malcolm Smith, "Administrative Accountability to Congress: the Concurrent Resolution," *Western Political
Quarterly*, IX (December, 1956), 955-66. See also Kenneth T. Kofmehl, "Congressional Staffing: With Emphasis on the Professional Staff" (Ph.D. dissertation, Columbia University, 1956).

on Internal Revenue Taxation. The Joint Tax Committee maintains a "branch office" in the Bureau of Internal Revenue where members of the Committee's legal staff review administrative recommendations for tax refunds and credits and do not cavil at recommending that the legislative committee reverse administrative determinations.[18]

A general scrutiny of administrative stewardship is made possible by this elaborate formal network of legislative-administrative relationships. But the very nature of the reporting and consultation statutes, as well as the local propensities of the members of Congress, substantially turns the system into one in which, for better or worse, the legislator serves as the watchdog of national administrative actions on behalf of local constituents. The system formally provides for extensive joint responsibilities by congressional committees and administrative officers in the making of administrative decisions. Administrators in effect must "pre-clear" their actions with the appropriate subcommittee, in some cases with individual members. At the very least, an opportunity is provided congressmen and senators to register protests — in many cases having the effect of a veto — with respect to problems affecting their constituencies. At its worst, the system makes it possible for an individual member to bludgeon an entire department on behalf of local causes.

The formal and legally specified overviews of administrative action by legislative committees frequently encounter strenuous opposition by executive officers and are in some cases subject to constitutional objection. In any case, informal understandings are far more important than the provisions of law for producing continuous legislative involvement in administrative affairs. Rivers and Harbors legislation caricatures the process. Members of Congress nominally serve as officers of the leading interest group (the Rivers and Harbors Congress), and the Corps of Engineers has established procedures for entertaining local viewpoints in the field and for implementing them in Congress, subject only to whatever measures of control can be mustered by the Bureau of the Budget and the President. Institutional caricatures, like others, make overt what elsewhere may be hidden. Thus the

[18] See Sec. 3777 of the Internal Revenue code. In 1949-50, almost 1,000 cases involving $766 million were reviewed in this fashion.

Committee on Interstate and Foreign Commerce instructs the Department of Commerce and the regulatory agencies with respect to the imposition of licensing fees.[19] A House subcommittee prevents the Department of Defense from closing military hospitals that, according to defense officials, are no longer necessary.[20] The House Armed Services Committee, in an effort to keep military post exchanges from competing with local retailers, works out detailed, informal agreements with each of the services concerning what may and may not be sold at post exchanges. Regulations of the services implement these legislative-administrative settlements.[21] Appropriations hearings provide the stage for securing many commitments of this sort.

The most important and pervasive method of legislative participation in the administrative process is through activities of individual legislators on behalf of local constituents. Workers on the Hill call this their "case work." Alben Barkley had a story illustrating both the range of services rendered and the sometime ingratitude of the recipients:

I called on a certain rural constituent and was shocked to hear him say he was thinking of voting for my opponent. I reminded him of the many things I had done for him as prosecuting attorney, as county judge, as congressman, and senator. I recalled how I had helped get an access road built to his farm, how I had visited him in a military hospital in France when he was wounded in World War I, how I had assisted him in securing his veteran's benefits, how I had arranged his loan from the Farm Credit Administration, how I had got him a disaster loan when the flood destroyed his home, etc., etc.

"How can you think of voting for my opponent?" I exhorted at the end of this long recital. "Surely you remember all these things I have done for you?"

"Yeah," he said, "I remember. But what in hell have you done for me lately?"[22]

Barkley's joke is a form of caricature, and again it reveals what is widespread but frequently unrecognized. The joke in fact may be documented. Its exact counterpart is found in a letter to a constituent written by Texas Congressman Wright Patman. Mr.

[19] *Cong. Rec., Daily Digest*, 83rd Cong., 2d Sess. (March 30, 1954), pp. 239-40.
[20] *Chicago Daily News*, May 3, 1957.
[21] Field notes, Washington, D.C., February 11, 1958. Consultation on what may be sold in commissary stores has a statutory base. See H.R. 12738, Sec. 613, Department of Defense Appropriations Bill, 85th Cong., 2d Sess.
[22] Alben W. Barkley, *That Reminds Me* (New York: Doubleday, 1954), p. 165.

Patman was angry when he wrote his letter because he had heard that the constituent was supporting another candidate for the Congressman's seat. The Congressman reviewed his relationships with his constituent over a period of twenty years. On no fewer than twenty occasions Mr. Patman had interposed himself in administrative matters on behalf of this single voter and his family. Ten of Mr. Patman's acts concerned the Post Office Department (the Congressman not only secured jobs for his constituent and members of his family, but saved them from being dismissed when they misappropriated funds); two concerned part-time jobs with the Bureau of the Census; one involved an authorization of veterans' payments to students in a school founded by his constituent; three concerned loans from the Reconstruction Finance Corporation, the Small Defense Plants Administration, and the Public Housing Administration; and three concerned War Department matters involving the names of ROTC officers who might make good candidates for insurance sold by the Congressman's constituent.[23]

The very tone of Mr. Patman's letter indicated his belief that all of this activity was perfectly normal and proper. He was doing what congressmen do naturally. Senator Lehman of New York spent considerable personal sums to augment his staff, the largest fraction of which devoted itself to constituent problems. Not that senatorial staffs are picayune. Senator Douglas revealed in 1957 that his offices in Washington and Chicago had twenty-one employees whose total salaries amounted to $119,222.[24] A good fraction of these people were involved in the simple process of opening the Senator's mail and finding an easy way of handling it — a form response, a stereotyped referral slip, or a request for a pamphlet from one of the departments. These processes involve little direct contact with the administration, though in more than a few instances the proper response, even if a canned one, is dependent upon a phone call to a bureau or a corridor conversation with a bureau representative.

Aside from clerical workers, Senator Douglas' personal staff in

[23] The letter was placed on March 23, 1956, into the record of the Subcommittee for Special Investigations of the House Committee on Armed Services investigating the sale of life insurance to prospective members of the military service. It was reprinted in the *Reporter*, July 12, 1956, pp. 19-22.

[24] *Chicago Sun Times*, March 27, 1957, p. 10.

1958 included three full-time persons in a Chicago office and five in Washington. Some of their work was concerned with publicity, party and campaign relations, and the Senator's obligations in legislation. But their principal task was to place problems of the Senator's constituents before the appropriate administrative offices in the way best calculated to achieve the constituents' satisfaction—and, it goes without saying, the constituents' votes for the Senator.[25]

The examples of Senators Lehman and Douglas are good ones because they should remove any doubts concerning the propriety of such acts of involvement by the legislator in administrative matters. In these matters, as in others, Messrs. Lehman and Douglas provide models of the ideal senator. There is no hint of venality or impropriety in these activities. They are a normal part of a senator's business. Senator Douglas' complaint is only that the government does not provide him with enough money to maintain an office staff large enough to do all the things he thinks ought to be done in response to the needs of his large constituency.

The looseness of the party system makes all of this activity possible. It also minimizes partisanship, producing an individualistic competition with bipartisan overtones. Congressional and senatorial staff members form a pool of expertise, not least of all

[25] The essential difference in the roles of American and English legislators is made clear when one compares their respective office staffs. Unless the M.P. holds a ministerial post, the government does not even provide him with an office. Since M.P.'s usually can't afford to pay for their own office accommodations in the neighborhood of the Parliament, most of them have no office at all. And the idea that twenty-one people at an expenditure of more than $100,000 a year would not be sufficient for an M.P. to do his job properly would only arouse the utmost mirth. Again, unless he holds an official post, the M.P. is not even supplied with a personal secretary from government funds. This does not mean that a British M.P. neglects to nurse his constituency. "Holding surgery" to listen to constituent complaints and proposals is a well-established part of a member's routine. But his course of action is not a demanding one with respect to the departments. Except for matters of information, the M.P. must take up his constituent problems with the ministers concerned, themselves controlled by party decisions, and on no issue may he transgress party policy or embarrass party stewardship or, as American legislators do as a matter of course, join with opposing members *contra* party *pro* locality. An opposition member has greater latitude, but still not that of successfully badgering bureaucrats up and down the line in behalf of local interests. If he tries this course of action, he is politely referred to the appropriate ministerial officer who, as a member of the majority party, has a powerful platform from which to respond.

in casework problems, and a member of one party may have staff members of another. Congressional delegations often join forces without regard to party for city, state, or regional matters. For example, the California congressional group for a number of years has been formally organized for such purposes, and the entire West Coast delegation also works as a single unit in pursuit of regional interests. A senior congressman from a given state will often speak and act on behalf of the entire delegation. When it becomes known that a state's Republican senator is less efficient than his Democratic colleague in case-work matters, Republican voters (including mayors and state legislators) find their way to the Democratic senator's office. They receive service all the more prompt and energetic because of the delight that the Democratic member and his staff have in building fences where none existed before. Even this minor partisan pin-pricking may be absent. For example, Colorado Senators Millikin (Rep.) and Johnson (Dem.) maintained a common office, jointly staffed, to give service to those with general state problems. Correspondence from the office carried the signatures of both senators. This co-operation continued for twelve years without a major disagreement.[26]

Although no exact calculation of the magnitude of the case work is possible, one can be sure it is very large indeed. The Office of Price Administration during the calendar year 1944 averaged 1,397 congressional "contacts" a week (phone calls, letters, and visits), an average of more than two for each five working days from each member of Congress. Peak periods were higher. In one twenty-week period of 1943, for example, congressional letters alone averaged 842 weekly.[27] Data for less

[26] Field notes, February, 1958. The relationship was apparently a unique one. See *Roll Call* ("The Newspaper of Capitol Hill" published weekly by Capitol employees), February 12, 1958.

[27] Tabulated from "OPA and Congress," and "Report of Congressional Mail," Office of Price Administration, National Archives, Record Group 188. For technical reasons, all of these tabulations are underestimates. A report by an OPA official, Frank Ketcham, estimated (and probably overestimated) that from 1943 through 1946, the agency received 150,000 letters and telegrams and 300,000 telephone calls from members of Congress. See "Legislative Supervision of the Office of Price Administration" (typescript, 1947), National Archives, Office of Price Administration, Record Group 188.

OPA kept a separate record of *public* criticisms made of its operations by

vulnerable agencies during less intense periods are also available. In the ten working days between May 21 and June 4, 1958, the Department of the Interior received by actual count 553 pieces of congressional mail, plus an estimated 200 phone calls, an average of 75 congressional contacts per day.[28] The Office of Legislative Liaison of the Air Force averaged 3,000 "monitored" congressional contacts a month (as of the winter of 1958), and this did not count the personal contacts of the three Senate and four House liaison officers who were on full-time duty in the Capitol and House and Senate office buildings. (The Army, Navy, and Department of Defense each have separate liaison staffs.) The congressional liaison office of the Department of Health, Education, and Welfare, according to an official estimate, responds to 500 congressional phone calls a month, and this, one can be sure, is only a fraction of the total number of calls to the many bureaus and field offices of the Department. An official tally by the Department of Agriculture recorded 5,564 letters from Congress during 35 working days, a daily average of 159.[29]

The administrative agencies seek to service congressional requests more effectively by establishing special liaison staffs and by institutionalizing procedures for congressional contacts. The Air Force in 1958 had, under the command of a major general, 137 people (55 officers and 82 civilians) working in its

---

members of Congress. This recounts a lengthy list of bitter attacks in committee hearings, in public speeches, and on the floor of both houses. The March 1, 1944, entry is more meaningful than most others. It says simply: "No Congressional criticism this day." *OPA and Congress* (a duplicated intra-office information sheet), March 6, 1944.

[28] The count was of mail processed by the Correspondence Control Office in the Secretary's office. Many bureaus in the department, for example the highly decentralized Bureau of Land Management, undoubtedly handle congressional mail directly. The number given, therefore, is an underestimate. The phone calls are similarly underestimated.

[29] U.S. Congress, House, Subcommittee of the Committee on Appropriations, *Hearings, Department of Agriculture Appropriations for 1959*, 85th Cong., 2d Sess. (1958), p. 865. Magnitudes of interference are also impressive when measured from the side of the individual congressman or senator. In a single week, for example, one mid-western senator received 122 constituent letters which required 100 separate contacts with administrative agencies, involving 30 different bureaus or offices in twelve departments as well as twelve additional federal agencies. Kenneth E. Gray will further analyze these data in later reports.

Office of Legislative Liaison.[30] Every congressional contact, except those made directly by Air Force officers, who worked in the
House and Senate office buildings, was "controlled" (the word
was used to indicate the desire to render more rapid service),
nine copies of a route slip being distributed strategically to the
personnel concerned. Many agencies have rules that require
congressional requests to be answered within a limited time (24
or 36 hours), and many others require all but routine responses to
carry the Secretary's signature.

A similar institutionalization occurs within the congressional
offices. We have already noted the specialization of function
within the staffs. In addition, a given staff develops systems of
priorities in handling cases; there are so many that all cannot be
given an equal amount of time. Priority ratings are influenced by
the source of the request (an old friend, a heavy campaign
contributor, or a city mayor get special attention), but they are
sufficiently flexible to bring out full effort when a "good case" —
in terms of injustices done, or publicity potential, or constituency
reaction — comes from an unknown and uninfluential constituent.
Priority values determine whether a request is handled with a
perfunctory phone call or routine reference — "just to get it from
our desk to theirs"[31] — or with a full-scale assault upon administrative offices. The latter may start with a staff assistant making a
casual inquiry and end with the congressman or senator meeting

[30] Field notes, January, 1958. For analysis of Liaison Offices, their numbers,
functions and costs, see U.S. Congress, House, Committee on Government
Operations, H.R. No. 2947, *Availability of Information from Federal Departments and Agencies,* 84th Cong., 2d Sess. (1956). For questionnaire and responses, see U.S. Congress, House, Committee on Government Operations,
*Replies from Federal Agencies to Questionnaire Submitted by the Special Sub-
committee on Government Information of the Committee on Government Operations,* 84th Cong., 1st Sess. (1955).

[31] Even with respect to the most perfunctory inquiries, a member of Congress
usually wants it to appear to the constituent that a special and "justifiably
privileged" service has been rendered, whether that is the case or not. Staff
members and administrators play this game knowingly with each other. When a
service is rendered to a constituent that an administrative agency was going to do
in any case and it only appears that congressional interference had something to
do with it, full credit is likely to be publicly accorded the congressman by all
hands. Staff members call this a "fall in" case. A special kind of "fall in" case is
the practice of administrative agencies to inform congressmen and senators in
advance of the decisions to spend money or build public works in their areas,
thus allowing the members of Congress to make the announcements in the local
newspapers.

personally with a cabinet secretary, or attacking an agency on the floor, or introducing a bill, or asking for a special investigation. The institutionalization of interference also includes establishment of standards for ignoring or rejecting constituent requests, based upon considerations of decency and propriety, as well as for defining acceptable and unacceptable modes of dealing with administrative officers. Both sets of standards vary from member to member and from staff to staff. It is not difficult to find examples of the abusive congressman demanding, as the price of his support, that an inordinate fraction of funds for a particular agency be spent in his district, or that normal procedures for rotation of military assignments be abrogated for a son of his important constituent. (By the same token, there exist administrators who promote their bureau, their project, or themselves by encouraging congressmen to expect such special considerations.) More generally, congressional involvement is amiable. It is directed at producing rapid and full consideration for constituent and district interests. It expects impartial treatment without favoritism,[32] but it also demands special consideration for hardship cases and other special circumstances. It assumes an adversary quality only when the normal give and take between legislative requests and administrative adjustment breaks down.

The legislator's ability to command information from the administrative agency, on the one hand, and his access to press, television and radio, on the other, produce a double sanction. Administrators know that any failure to satisfy congressional requests may result not only in congressional penalties, ranging from criticism to new legislation, but also in adverse publicity. Both sorts of penalties are avoided whenever possible, although where congressional requests are immoderate, administrative officers have recourse to both legislative and public means of defense. The typical means of avoiding clashes and of promoting the continuous executive-legislative collaboration necessary for administrative action is through the mechanism of "pre-clearance." Pre-clearance works in both directions. Legislators informally work out in advance with administrators what they later formally request. More relevantly here, administrative officers

---

[32] All congressional inquiries lead to two forms of favoritism. They hasten the consideration of the particular problem raised; and they move the decision from lower to higher levels of the administrative hierarchy.

clear contemplated actions in advance with strategic subcommittees and members of Congress. The clearance is sought not only for new legislative and budget requests but also for contemplated administrative actions. Important clearance activities of this sort are those that seek advance approval of the congressmen and senators who represent localities to be affected by what a national agency is planning to do. Mechanisms of clearance range from a phone call to a Congressman to full-scale conferences between bureau chiefs and committee chairmen with staff members from both sides in attendance. The informal periodic reporting of agencies to subcommittees is a particularly effective means of pre-clearing administrative acts.

The widespread and in many ways unpredictable character of legislative interference in administrative affairs has many consequences for the tone and character of American administrative behavior. From the perspective of this paper, the important consequence is the comprehensive, day-to-day—even hour-by-hour—impact of local and state views on national programs. No point of substance or procedure is immune from congressional scrutiny. No point of access is neglected: from phone calls to regional offices to conferences with agency heads and the chief officers of the Bureau of the Budget; from cocktail conversations to full committee investigations. A very large portion of the entire weight of this impact is on behalf of individual constituents, group interests, and state and local governments. It is a weight that can alter procedures for screening immigration applications, divert the course of a national highway, change the tone of an international negotiation, and amend a social security or flood control law to accommodate local practices or fulfill local desires.

Virtually the whole process of legislative participation in administrative affairs would be impossible if the American party system were more tightly controlled from the top. With disciplined parties the free-wheeling interference of individual members on behalf of local constituents could not take place. It would not be tolerated. If members of the parties were responsive to their leadership, if they were committed to a program, if they were subject to discipline in the event of defection from that program, the administration of policy would be unified and controlled. The individual legislator would have less access to the administrator and less influence in altering administrative direction in terms of non-party interests. To a corresponding degree there would be diminished the leavening of national administrative programs by state, local, and other group interests, interests that are so energetically represented by members of the Congress.[33]

The Administrator as Politician. Bluntly put, it can be said that the inability of national political leaders to control the legislative members of the party accounts, *ipso facto*, for their inability to control the national administration. Stated positively, the undisciplined party system impels administrators to seek political support for their programs. The parties do not supply this support, and administrators and their programs cannot survive without it. This leads to the third important manner in which the parties affect the operation of the American system: they make the administrator play a political role.

The previous discussion makes clear why some administrative officers walk in fear of the telephone. A bureau chief in the Department of Interior once told an interviewer that half of his fellow chiefs prayed each morning: "Oh Lord, let not the chairman of my appropriations subcommittee call me this day." But if a bureau chief is craven before a congressman, how then can he follow the directives of his own administrative superior? If a

---

[33] The discovery that pressure groups in Great Britain are vastly influential does not in any way alter this point. Indeed, it strengthens it. As Samuel H. Beer has pointed out, the relationships between interest groups and government in Britain are "quasi-corporative." The "individual legislator, and the legislature generally, under cabinet government occupy a less important position." The American legislative committees have no British counterparts. Interest groups in Britain are agglomerated in large associations, and they must focus on winning the support of the Minister and Chancellor of the Exchequer. In the United States there are more points at which pressure can and must be applied. Party control means precisely that pressure upon government can be effective only if approved by the party. Pressure groups therefore work in areas where party discipline is not exercised and, more importantly, in areas where their scope of effectiveness is defined by party and party-leader decisions. The American contrast—where, in Beer's words, "pressure politics is so much noisier and less tidy"—rests upon the lack of party control. See Beer's two excellent articles, "Pressure Groups and Parties in Britain" and "The Representation of Interests in British Government," *American Political Science Review*, L (March, 1956), 1-23; LI (September, 1957), 613-650. Also W. J. M. MacKenzie, "Pressure Groups in British Government: Historical Background," *British Journal of Sociology*, VI (June, 1955), 133-48; S. E. Finer, *Anonymous Empire* (London: Pall Mall Press, 1958); J. D. Stewart, *British Pressure Groups* (Oxford: Clarendon Press, 1958).

legislator can substantially interfere with the operation of an administrative office, how can a group of administrative offices concert their efforts into a unified program?

Administrators need not be craven. Some welcome conflict with congressmen; some are polite but unresponsive, and some just plain hide; some can find protection by appealing to other legislators; some serve other masters who themselves may be influential with significant congressional blocs; some are successful in protecting their own view and their agency program by deftly juggling the opposing views of congressmen, constituent groups, administrative superiors, and others concerned. The very multiplicity of pressures upon administrators provides opportunities for discretion, independence, and invention.

These activities of the administrator do not sound significantly different from the activities of many congressmen. And they are not. The higher administrator, as Paul Appleby and others have made clear, performs an intrinsically political role.[34] The reason such a role is possible for the administrator is the same reason that accounts for the interference in administration on the part of the legislator. The administrator can play politician, just as the politician can play administrator, because the parties are without program and without discipline.

The administrator's response to the unprotected position in which the party situation places him is a natural one: he seeks support where he can find it. One ever-present task is that of nursing the Congress of the United States, that crucial constituency which ultimately controls his agency's budget and program. For this task he may partially depend on the clients his agency serves. To take an easy example, the Veterans' Administration can rely to some degree upon veterans' organizations to reward congressional supporters and punish congressional opponents of V.A. programs. But this is neither a quick nor a certain process. And it is necessary for the administrator to lubricate the continuous interaction his agency has with the Congress and individual congressman by a sympathetic consideration of, if not downright

[34] Paul Appleby, op. cit., and Big Democracy (New York: Knopf, 1945); Norton E. Long, "Power and Administration," Public Administration Review, IX (Autumn, 1949), 257-64; Herbert A. Simon, Donald W. Smithburg, and Victor A. Thompson, Public Administration (New York: Knopf, 1950), pp. 381-401; Harlan Cleveland, "The Executive and the Public Interest," Annals, CCCVII (September, 1956), 37-54.

accommodation to, congressional requests. This is the administrative basis of the successful congressional case work we have
already considered. An additional point can now be made clear.
The case-work relationship works both ways. Not only is the
congressman dependent upon administrative accommodation; a
more fundamental truth is the administrator's dependence upon
the congressman.

From the administrator's side, the servicing of congressional
requests is to build the political support without which the
administrative job could not continue. The servicing role sometimes takes an extreme form. "We try to consider ourselves part
of the senators' staffs," an agency liaison officer recently told an
interviewer. This posture is sometimes assumed to offset the less
accommodating attitudes of bureau workers who view congressional interference with something less than receptivity. But
even the completely task-oriented administrator must be sensitive to the relationship between case work requests, on the one
side, and budgetary and legislative support, on the other. "You
do a good job handling the personal problems and requests of a
Congressman," a White House officer said, "and you have an
easier time convincing him to back your program."[35] Thus there
is an important linkage between the nursing of congressional
requests on local matters and the most comprehensive national
programs. The administrator must accommodate to the former as
a means of gaining support for the latter. Other considerations of
course affect congressional support of administrative programs.
But the importance of administrative service to members of
Congress is evident at every hand, particularly in the size and
cost of the liaison staffs themselves. At least five staffs – Army,
Navy, Air Force, Veterans' Administration, and Civil Service
Commission – maintain quick-service offices on Capitol Hill.
Other liaison officers headquarter themselves in the offices of
friendly congressmen or senators. Liaison with the highest executive officers is close and continuous. "Pre-clearance" of administrative acts works at every level, a cabinet officer consulting
a subcommittee chairman on important points, a liaison clerk
calling a freshman congressman on others.

The need for executive offices to build their own political
support is the principal cause of that conflict which characterizes

[35] Quoted in *Wall Street Journal*, June 16, 1959.

American administrative life — among departments and among bureaus within departments. It accounts for the relative immunity of some agencies from presidential control; and the stronger the source of independent support, the more immune the agency is. It explains why an act of legislation may not at all define the real power of an administrative office.[36] The necessity put upon administrators to build political support also provides the sociological base for Charles G. Dawes' otherwise enigmatic statement that "every member of the Cabinet is the natural enemy of the President."[37]

One result of administrative politics is that the administrative agency may become the captive of the nationwide interest groups it serves or presumably regulates. In such cases no government may come out with effective authority: the winners are the interest groups themselves. But in a very large number of cases, states and localities are also influence winners. The position of states and localities may be directly tied to nationwide interest groups: the United States Conference of Mayors has been at one with the Congress of Industrial Organizations, for example, in urging federal urban renewal programs. In other cases, the state or local views (frequently opposed to each other) may be represented on their own: as when a congressman hastens the transfer of a defense airport to a municipality, or a group of congressmen aids state welfare officers in bringing about changes in federal public assistance rules, or a bureau chief, under pressure from city lobbyists and the state delegation (one of whom is a key figure in the bureau's appropriations subcommittee), orders the establishment of a field office where it otherwise would not have been.[38] The complete

[36] A price control law wrung from a reluctant Congress by an amorphous and unstable combination of consumer and labor groups is formally the same as a law enacting a support price program for agriculture backed by the disciplined organizations of farmers and their congressmen. [But] the differences for the scope and effectiveness of administration are obvious." Long, *loc. cit.*, p. 257.

[37] I am indebted to Louis Brownlow for the Dawes quotation. Richard F. Fenno, Jr., supplies an overview of the literature on presidential-cabinet relationships and an illuminating case study of the divisive effects of independent sources of support in "President-Cabinet Relations: A Pattern and a Case Study," *American Political Science Review*, LII (June, 1958), 388-405.

[38] Local officers even attempt to use this route of influence to alter *state* policies. See the testimony of Mayor Richardson Dilworth of Philadelphia before the (Fountain) Subcommittee of the Committee on Government Operations, House of Representatives, 85th Cong., 1st Sess., *Hearings*, Part I, pp. 357-58.

mobilization of a state or locality produces maximum potency. A group of state legislators and administrators will travel to Washington with the governor's blessing, accompanied by leading businessmen and several administrative specialists from state offices. They will convene a meeting which is attended by both of the state's senators and a majority of the state's congressmen. The federal administrators summoned to such a meeting perforce pay careful heed to the requests of the group.

Bureaucrats and the bureaucratic system in the United States do not at all follow the model classically set forth by Max Weber. The system is not described by his term "monocratic control," control by one from the top. Such control must be predicated upon the existence of a program—defined, administered, and policed by an organized majority. The United States congressional majority is relatively unorganized. It has no single program, no single leader, no effective means for political punishment, and therefore no easy mechanism for controlling the political activity of the bureaucrat. Lack of political program and control compels political activity on the part of the administrator. Without this activity he runs the risk of having no program to administer. The total impact of the political role of the bureaucrat is not unmixed. He may use his political power to aggrandize his own position and his own agency, thus shifting the power focus to the center. He may produce, or be forced into, a situation in which no government is in effective control. But always he must find support from legislators tied closely to state and local constituencies and state and local governments. The political activity of the administrator, like the administrative activity of the legislator, must often be turned to representing state and local interests in national programs.

The Multiple Crack. Those who have discovered the politics of the administrator have not made sufficiently clear that his political attributes are not unique. His role in politics is matched by that of other individual citizens and other professional and vocational groups. The political system gives all groups the privilege of playing politics. The administrator is in a somewhat privileged position, but it differs in degree, not in kind.

This suggests a fourth manner in which parties crucially affect the operation of the American system. Weber predicted that "the living machine which is bureaucracy, in co-operation with the inorganic-physical-machine, is bringing about the structure of super- and sub-ordination which will characterize the future. In that structure human beings will be forced into impotent obedience—like fellaheen in the ancient Egyptian state." What a misreading of the current American situation this is. The picture is not one of obedience. It is one in which individuals and groups attempt to influence governmental policy at every step of the legislative-administrative process.

We call this the "multiple crack" attribute of American government. "Crack" has two meanings. It means fissure, a place for individuals and groups to make their views known; in this meaning crack is almost synonymous with what the literature discusses as "access."[39] But access alone is too static a concept. Crack also means a wallop, a smack at government in an attempt to influence policy.

If the parties were more disciplined, the result would of course not be a cessation of the process by which individuals and groups impinge themselves upon the central government. But the present state of the American parties clearly allows for a far greater operation of the multiple crack than would be possible under the conditions of centralized party control. Local and other interests make themselves felt in the British system. But it would be difficult to adduce any case in which British interests act as American ones characteristically do: finding and attempting to exploit cracks at literally uncountable points in the legislative-administrative process. If legislative lobbying (from the committee stages to the conference committee) does not produce results, those seeking action meet with the cabinet secretary. His immediate associates are petitioned. Bureau chiefs and their aides are hit. Field officers are put under pressure. Campaigns are instituted by which friends of the agency apply a secondary influence on behalf of the interested party. A conference with the President may be urged. Attempts may be made to activate the wife of the President or other members of his immediate family.

To these multiple points for bringing influence must be added the multiple voices of the influencers. Consider, for example, those in a small town who wish to have a federal action taken, whether it be to amend a flood control law, or to secure a sewage

[39] Pendleton Herring, *The Politics of Democracy* (New York: Norton, 1940), p. 431; David B. Truman, *The Governmental Process* (New York: Knopf), pp. 507-8.

disposal grant, or to have a surplus plant sold to a local business-man. The easy merging of public and private interests[40] at the local level means that at selected points in the decision-making chain the local Chamber of Commerce speaks; at other points it is the Rotary Club; at others the mayor or city manager, and at still others an engineering consultant or fiscal specialist. In many matters the state or national professional organizations of local officials can be enlisted. In almost every case individual con-gressmen and senators, and not infrequently whole state delega-tions, will make the local cause their own. Federal field officers who service localities not infrequently assume local views. So may elected and appointed state officers. Friendships are ex-ploited, and political mortgages called due. The voices are many, but the cause is one. Many people and groups may accumulate pressures at a single point, and, according to rough criteria of efficiency, forces are allocated where they will do the most good. If a phone call to a congressman is deemed helpful, it will be made by a person or group close to the congressman. If a confer-ence in a senator's office will expedite matters, someone on the local scene can be found to make such a conference possible and effective. If technical information is needed, technicians will supply it.

All local causes, of course, need not be so energetically or efficiently pursued, and even if the need exists the skill and energy may not. The competition of interests — within single localities, between them, between localities and other interests, and between localities and states — complicates the process. Ac-ceptance of a given locality's view may be dependent upon the defeat, but more typically it rests upon the ignorance or acquies-cence of other interested groups. Despite all qualifications, two facts are indisputable. The lack of central discipline within the party system makes the multiple crack possible and profitable for those who exploit it. The effect of the multiple crack is further to disperse decision-making power within the institutions of the central government and between the central and peripheral governments.

[40] The mixture of the public and private in American governmental affairs will be the subject of later publications by the University of Chicago federalism workshop.

A NOTE ON DIVERSE FUNCTIONS; AND ON THE DISTINCTION BETWEEN
FUNCTION AND CAUSE

The discussion thus far has attempted to demonstrate how the
party system is reflected in the governmental system and particularly how the undisciplined parties function to produce governmental decentralization. It should be made clear that this view
(a) does not preclude the parties from functioning in other
fashions, and (b) does not involve any simple causal relationship
between party and governmental processes.

The first point can be briefly disposed of. The literature
abounds with analyses that see the party system as having quite
different consequences for government. One such consequence,
for example, is alleged to be the difficulty of setting a general
course of policy for the government as a whole. A related result is
said to be that special interests gain undeserved governmental
privileges. A third is that disunited parties deprive voters of clear
choices and make it impossible to tell who is responsible for
particular acts of government. Still a fourth alleged consequence
is that the parochialism of party members makes parties "meaningless and even dishonest in the mind of the public."[41] And so
the list could be continued. No attempt can be made here to
assess the validity of such analyses. It can only be said that the
functional consequences of party arrangements are undoubtedly
numerous and include many consequences not related to the
issue of decentralization. The decentralizing functions of parties
and their consequences for political life may be highly valued;
and other functional consequences may be considered disadvantageous to particular purposes at particular times and at some
times threatening to the nation as a whole. One task of political
analysis is to delineate such contrary consequences (and contrary
evaluations) of political institutions and processes.

The principal theme of this paper is that the party system acts

[41] See A Report of the Committee on Political Parties of the American Political
Science Association, "Toward a More Responsible Two-Party System," pub-
lished as a supplement to The American Political Science Review, XLIV (Sep-
tember, 1950). The quotation is from James MacGregor Burns, Congress on Trial
(New York: Harper, 1949), p. 46. See also E. E. Schattschneider, Party Govern-
ment (New York: Rinehart, 1942). This literature is critically reviewed in Austin
Ranney, The Doctrine of Responsible Party Government (Urbana: University of
Illinois Press, 1954).

primarily to foster decentralization in government. Yet it is easy
to show that on occasion it has done the opposite, as when, for
example, demands for action by the central government follow
the failure of parties to organize effective programs under the
auspices of state governments. Thus, even with respect to decentralization, the consequences of parties for government are not
simple and do not always move in one direction. Again, political
analysis must separate the functional strands and decide in
which direction the more important truths lie.

The distinction between function and cause is a more complicated matter. In tracing party functions in terms of governmental
decentralization, there is no implication that the parties alone
cause decentralization. In fact, parties in the United States do
stand in an immediate causal relationship to governmental
processes and specifically to governmental decentralization. But
it would be a great error to ignore other, more general, causal
factors.

In the first place, it can easily be shown that the causal
relationship between party and government is a reciprocal one.
For example, many of the formal constitutional provisions that
were established to prevent even a majority faction from achieving complete control of the national government also militate
against the organization of the majority faction itself. The substantial control over elections given to the states; the electoral
college system (combined with the extra-constitutional nominating convention); the fixed terms for President, senators, and
congressmen; the composition of the Senate; the amendment
process; the appointment procedure and tenure for Supreme
Court justices—these as well as other constitutional provisions
can be said to "cause" party disunity. Directly and through the
function of parties they also "cause" decentralized government.[42]

No formal amendment procedure is needed to alter many
constitutional practices. But it is clearly not true that the Constitution is no longer important in establishing the distribution of

[42] For relevant discussions see Herbert Wechsler, "The Political Safeguards of
Federalism: The Role of the States in the Composition and Selection of the
National Government," in Arthur W. Macmahon (ed.), *Federalsim, Mature and
Emergent* (New York: Doubleday, 1955), pp. 97-114; Austin Ranney and Will-
moore Kendall, *Democracy and the American Party System* (New York: Har-
court, Brace, 1956), especially chap. 21.

power between the federal government and the states. The latitude of interpretation that is possible with respect to the interstate commerce clause cannot equally be applied elsewhere. The simple, clearly stated, unambiguous phrases – for example, the President "shall hold his office during the term of four years" – are subject to change only through the formal amendment processes. And it is this sort of constitutional statement that is at once an impediment to the tight organization of both government and parties. If the terms of the President and members of Congress were not so firmly defined in the Constitution, the power of party leaders to enforce discipline would be immeasurably increased. Similarly, state constitutional provisions, such as those providing for the independent election of state administrators and for the direct primaries in the nomination of candidates for the governor's office, have the effect of splintering state parties and, by extension, of impeding the development of structured national parties and national party government.[43] The parties become a chief avenue for the achievement of decentralized government. But governmental (here formal constitutional) factors are partially responsible for the manner in which parties are structured. So government "causes" the form of party; party "causes" the form of government.

Second, a wide range of factors not directly related to the party-government interrelationship contributes to governmental decentralization. One certainly is in the form of creed; the opinion of Americans, as molded by tradition and history, that places a high value on the grass roots, local initiative, and vigorous local institutions. Another is pride in locality and state, and allegiance to them, fostered by the nation's size, the different speeds of cultural and industrial development, and the varieties of regional, if not state, histories. The sheer wealth of the nation can also be shown as a cause of governmental decentralization. It renders possible the sharing of governmental largesse by many groups, including the state and local governments, provides leeway for experimentation and even waste, and renders unnecessary the tight organization of political power that is found

---

[43] V. O. Key, *American State Politics: An Introduction* (New York: Knopf, 1956), especially chaps. 3, 4, and 7.

when the support of one cause necessarily means the deprivation of another.

Other social and economic forces are important for the decentralized structure of American government. All of them may variously make themselves felt (1) directly on government; (2) directly on parties; (3) through parties on government; and (4) through government on parties. To take only the most obvious sort of example, the lack of deep, divisive schisms with respect to basic economic issues in the American society makes possible a viable government in which the executive is controlled by one party, the legislature by another. So social structure directly affects government. The same basic unity on economic matters allows parties to be only marginally unlike and permits members of one party to support the other party on many issues. So social structure affects parties and through parties affects government. Even more elaborate causal chains could be constructed if they served any useful purpose. In fact, they rarely do. The only point here is to make clear that many cultural factors are causal for both undisciplined parties and decentralized government. Reciprocally, it can also be shown that party and government processes reflect back on the culture. The open government and the open society may be conceived as separate entities; but they markedly affect each other.

Third, a cause of party disunity and governmental decentralization also exists in the mediating role that parties play between society, on the one hand, and government, on the other. This is a special case of the reciprocal influence of social factors and party organization. Norton Long has outlined, without providing the empirical evidence, the manner in which the present disunity of the parties serves significant social groups: businessmen and professional workers, farmers, ethnic groups, and state and local office-holders.[44] The argument, in brief, is that sizable population groups believe that they profit from the present organization of parties and that they might be deprived (or at least not equally indulged) if parties became more programmatic and unified. On the other hand, no easily organized, powerful groups are presently deprived, or believe they would be appreciably in-

[44] Norton E. Long, "Party Government and the United States," *Journal of Politics*, XIII (May, 1951), 187-214. For historical evidence see Herbert Agar, *The Price of Union* (Boston: Houghton Mifflin, 1930).

dulged, by greater unity. Proof of the argument involves one in difficult methodological problems. Yet it contains a fundamentally sound perception. If majority social groups in the country were convinced of the advantages of party unity, constitutional barriers might make the task of creating unified parties more difficult, but those barriers would hardly be controlling. Party disunity and governmental decentralization are partially the direct consequences of the rewards that they give to significant social groups.

Finally, it must be clear that the party function, if it is not the sole cause for governmental decentralization, must be considered one cause. The parties themselves are institutions of power and importance. They are not mere weather vanes moved by the shifting winds of law, ideology, wealth, and social structure. They supply breezes of their own. Members of Congress express their own will, as well as that of constituency groups, in their devotion to the seniority principle for committee assignments and the right of unlimited debate in the Senate. The state governors and other local party chiefs play roles that they would not play in a system of centralized parties, and it is to their personal and professional advantage to maintain those roles. Cash for careerists is one consequence of disunited parties.[45] Status and power are others. Issues of sociability, of personal ambition, of honest (and dishonest) graft, of the patronage of prestige, of intraparty institutional stability are all involved. In the view of those most concerned, these factors are inseparable from their view of the welfare of the nation, however narrow or exalted that view may be. The party-government relationship, in other words, can be understood as a closed system, with the parties standing as a relatively independent social force. Their undisciplined character is the product of their internal dynamics, as well as of other factors. When the parties function to encourage governmental decentralization, they also, therefore, are one cause of that decentralization.

This discussion barely touches the complexities involved in separating functional from causal strands.[46] The causes of party

[45] My colleague, Lewis A. Dexter, has emphasized this point.
[46] See Herbert A. Simon, *Models of Man* (New York: Wiley, 1957), Part I, "Causation and Influence Relations"; Carl G. Hempel, "The Function of General Laws in History," in Herbert Feigl and Wilfrid Sellars (eds.), *Readings in Philosophical Analysis* (New York: Appleton-Century-Crofts, 1949), pp. 459-71;

disunity and governmental decentralization are numerous, over-lapping, and reciprocal. Lack of unity in parties and the institutions of decentralized government (including constitutional factors) mutually support each other. A series of extra-governmental factors, ranging from social structure through ideology to national wealth, are in part responsible for the character of parties and government. Direct benefits accruing to defined social groupings act to support the disunity of party structure and decentralization in governmental operations. And the internal dynamics of parties — the diverse rewards they produce for those who operate them — can be considered as a cause of their own character as well as of their decentralizing impact on government. The larger point here is only to emphasize the difference between causes and functions. But once one sees the anthropological unity of society, government, and party—which is only another way of recognizing the seamless web of cause and effect—the problems involved in altering any single aspect of the design become more apparent. At the very least it is clear that changes at one point necessarily involve some changes at other points.

Conclusion

In summary then, the parties function to maintain a division of strength between the central government and the geographical (and other) peripheries. Anything that tightened party control at the top would decrease strength at the bottom. This would have the effect of decreasing the importance of the four characteristics of the system discussed above. If control from the top were *strictly* applied, the characteristics might entirely disappear. To be specific, if disciplined and programmatic parties were achieved:

(1) It would make far less likely legislation that takes heavily into account the desires and prejudices of the highly decentralized power groups and institutions of the country, including the state and local governments.

Ernest Nagel, "The Logic of Historical Analysis," in Herbert Feigl and May Brodbeck, *Readings in the Philosophy of Science* (New York: Appleton-Century-Crofts, 1953), pp. 688-700; Paul F. Lazarsfeld and Morris Rosenberg (eds.), *The Language of Social Research* (Glencoe: Free Press, 1955), especially section II, on "multivariate analysis." A basic paper on functional analysis is Robert K. Merton, "Manifest and Latent Functions," in his *Social Theory and Social Structure* (Glencoe: Free Press, 1949), pp. 21-81.

(2) It would to a large extent prevent national legislators, individually and collectively, from intruding themselves on behalf of non-national interests in national administrative programs.

(3) It would deprive administrative officers of a large part of their political weight, a weight often used to foster state, local, and other powers.

(4) It would dampen the process by which individuals and groups, including state and local political leaders, take multiple cracks at the national government in order to steer legislation and administration in ways congenial to them and the institutions they represent.

Alterations of this sort could only accompany basic changes in the organization and style of politics which, in turn, presuppose fundamental changes in the parties' social base. The sharing of functions is, in fact, the sharing of power. This sharing is the hallmark of modern American federalism. To it can be traced in large part the continued important participation of state and localities in virtually all programs of government: the marble cake of administration. It accounts, with historical consideration added, for the fact that federal and state laws share, rather than exclusively occupy, areas of service and regulation. It provides the basis for states and localities to exercise an extraordinarily wide range of informal influence over federal legislation and administrative programs, an influence that is sometimes channeled through members of Congress but which is also manifest through the activities of professional organizations and direct "cracks" at federal agencies by state and local officers. It indicates, in sum, the existence of a substantial devolution of power in the American political system.

Physicists have postulated the existence of sub-atomic antiparticles that exhibit characteristics opposite to those of particles. One is tempted to say that it would be appropriate to consider American political parties as antiparties. The classical party functions are functions of gathering together segments of power and welding them as one. The American parties, as we have seen, do the opposite: they characteristically serve to disperse power. In this sense they are antiparties, not parties. The future may see national and world developments leading to a transformation of the antiparties to parties. Many voices are raised to urge that such developments would be in the national interest.

And it is remarkable how many of those who believe in the desirability of disciplined parties which will focus power, see trends and social forces moving in that direction; while those who believe not, see not.[47]

Whether such a development is occurring, or whether it would be desirable if it did occur, is not the subject of this essay. But clearly the disciplining of parties, whatever its advantages, would exact a price. The undisciplined parties function to produce the measure of decentralization of government that exists in the United States today. In the sweep of history, this conclusion emerges from a series of ironies. The constitutional fathers rigged a government to dissuade the formation of political parties and to prevent concentrations of power under the aegis of parties in the national government. They did this by establishing a system of separations, within the federal government and between the federal government and the states.

The first irony is that the formal separations have become relatively unimportant. The second irony is that, instead of preventing the formation of parties, the fathers' scheme has aided in producing a pattern of weak nationwide parties. The final irony is that the devolution of power that remains in our governmental system follows from the dynamics of parties. What the fathers abhorred—the parties—serves to produce what the fathers sought—devolved power. The path may be perverse, but the constitutional intent has been substantially fulfilled.

[47] See the several works by E. E. Schattschneider, and notably with respect to the emergence of national, disciplined parties, his "United States: The Functional Approach to Party Government," in Sigmund Neumann (ed.), *Modern Political Parties* (Chicago: University of Chicago Press, 1956), pp. 194-215; also Part III of the report of the Committee on Political Parties of the American Political Science Association, cited above; Paul T. David, "The Changing Party Pattern," *Antioch Review*, XVI (Fall, 1956), pp. 333-50.

7   *Federalism and the Party System in Canada**

STEVEN MULLER

The purpose of this article is to suggest that there is a causal and necessary link between Canada's achievement of a relatively stable and coherent two-party system in the Dominion parliament and the considerable variety of parties established in the Canadian provinces. Normally such parties as the Co-operative Commonwealth Federation (C.C.F.) and Social Credit are characterized as splinter parties in a national two-party system. This is in part quite justified. These parties do compete for seats in the Dominion parliament and have never attained a very large representation there. But classification of these parties, and of the Union Nationale in Quebec, merely as national splinter parties obscures the true nature of Canada's party system. It may be useful to conceive that within the context of Canadian federalism, the national party system has two distinct layers, and that these are mutually inter-dependent but can be separated for purposes of analysis. One layer of the national party system services the parliamentary institutions at Ottawa. The other layer applies to the tension between the Dominion government and the governments of the provinces.

It is suggested here that as ruling parties in one or more provinces, the so-called splinter parties of the first layer constitute an essential part of the second layer of the Canadian party system. As elements of this second layer, parties such as the C.C.F. or Social Credit are not merely also-rans for power in the Dominion parliament. Far greater is their importance as factors in the federal balance of powers between Ottawa and the provinces. The maintenance of this federal balance is perhaps the

Reprinted by permission of the author.
*Prepared for delivery at the 1961 Annual Meeting of The American Political Science Association, St. Louis, Missouri, Sheraton-Jefferson Hotel, September 6-9, 1961.

most acute problem of Canadian politics. It is, in fact, so acute that a special dimension of the national party system appears to have emerged to oblige it.

The argument that follows therefore assumes that a party that wins power in a Canadian province plays three major roles. Obviously, it functions within the party system of its particular province; it is a factor in the top layer of the national party system, which involves control of the Dominion parliament; it also functions in the second layer of the national party system, which balances central and sectional interests within the federal structure. The roles of provincial ruling parties within provincial party systems and as contributors to the party politics of the Dominion parliament have been variously studied, but too little recognition is evident of their special function as a safety valve for sectional interests. The hypothesis is advanced that this special function is performed within the second layer of the national party system, and that the effectiveness of the stable two-party process in the Dominion parliament depends upon its fulfillment. It also seems that the character and operation of the second layer of the Canadian party system is unique, and that it owes its existence to the complex, inexorable logic of Canadian federalism.

The Canadian Confederation is not inherently stable. It is a truism that divisive forces threaten Canada's national unity. Everyone is aware of the problem of the French Canadians, self-consciously nationalistic, rooted in their language, their church, their customs, and therefore different from other Canadians. In fact, the situation of the French Canadians is so dramatic, their destiny so colorful, that over-concentration on the social problem for national unity they represent may blur recognition of other centrifugal forces no less powerful. These are primarily economic in origin. It must never be forgotten that the natural economic drift of North America runs, like the course of its rivers and mountain ranges, on a north-south axis. Canada has created her national economy on an east-west axis in defiance of nature. Penned between the frontier of the United States and a vast arctic hinterland, the Canadian economy has no vertical, only horizontal mobility.

The problem thus posed for Canadian national economic development has never been solved, although its difficulties have failed to defeat Canadians, who have manfully fought and to an extent subdued them. There are in Canada at least four major and quite distinct economic regions: the Atlantic Maritimes, the industrial and commercial heartland of Quebec and Ontario, the Western prairies, and the Pacific Coast. The logic of economic geography would link each to a southward partner region in the United States; the logic of national politics yokes them together. The compulsion of political nationalism is characteristically negative. To be Canadian is above all to be North American without being American (i.e., pertaining to the United States — and the usage galls north of the border), or British, or French. A common defiance of external pressures remains the most important factor that unites Canadians with conflicting interest — the bluenose from the Atlantic Coast, the French Canadian, Irish Canadian, British Canadian, the farmer of East European descent in the prairies. There is a sharp difference here between Canada and the United States. In the States, clashing interests of sections and diverse peoples were and still are being overcome by an unrivalled homogenizing national prosperity, created essentially within the national frontiers and financed by domestic capital. Canada is poorer and lacks economic self-sufficiency. She has depended on London and New York for capital investment. At the sacrifice of a shared, homogeneous North American prosperity, she has austerely defied absorption into the economy of the United States. Her various regional interests — economic and social — retain their separate vigor virtually undiminished. The national politics of Canada involves a tense and struggling adjustment between national and sectional power quite different from the United States.

II

Canadian political institutions reinforce and cater to this tension. Confederating in 1867, in pursuit of greater autonomy from Britain and in fear of the ambitions of a United States still in arms after the Civil War, the statesmen of the first four Provinces adopted federalism. They sought to make a nation; some hoped that their projected system would one day evolve into a unitary regime; but at the time French and British Canada could live as one only within a federal pattern that guaranteed their differences. The national purpose of the Fathers of Confederations is clearly evident in the British North America Act. In contrast to the Constitution of the United States, which had just endured the war between the States, the B.N.A. Act assigns both the general and residual powers of government to the Dominion, not the Provinces. By means of lieutenant-governors appointed by the Dominion government, the latter could disallow provincial legislation.[1] The design was created for the conquest of sectionalism from the Center.

But it was not to be so. It is commonly known that the decisions of the Judicial Committee of the Privy Council abridged the general powers of the Dominion governments and enhanced the legislative powers of the Provinces.[2] After 1887, it is equally clear, the power of disallowance of provincial acts came to be less and less frequently used. What is often not emphasized sufficiently is that this frustration of the hopes of national supremacy over sectionalism was not merely the result of caprice on the part of alien judges. Professor Brady is right in maintaining that these decisions "gave judicial expression to the upsurge of provincialism, evident from the early eighties to the decade after the First World War."[3]

In 1867 Canada consisted of Ontario, Quebec, Nova Scotia and New Brunswick. By 1905 Ontario and Quebec had been vastly enlarged, and the Dominion had nine Provinces: Manitoba was created in 1870, British Columbia joined in 1871, Prince Edward Island in 1873, and Alberta and Saskatchewan were established in 1905. Sectional development, fed by immigration, was proceeding rapidly. Macdonald's national policy, inherited and adapted by Laurier, had linked the nation east to west by rail, maintained a tariff barrier against economic aggression from the United States, and had hugely lessened dependence on Britain. The nation existed, but sectional differences had grown apace with its progress. At the very heart of Canadian federal politics a classic pattern of tension between Dominion and Provincial governments was fully developed, around the focal point of financial relations. Dominion-Provincial financial arrangements symbolize Canadian diversity more validly than the problem of

[1] B.N.A. Act, 91; 58, 56, 90.
[2] See especially *Tennant vs. Union Bank* (1894) and *Snider vs. Hydro-Electric Commission of Toronto* (1925).
[3] Alexander Brady, *Democracy in the Dominions*, 3rd ed., Toronto, 1958, p. 46.

STEVEN MULLER

the French Canadians; and as a symbol and a fact they offer a rather neglected clue to the nature of the national party system.

I will not include here a detailed review of the manifold intricacies of Dominion-Provincial financial relations in Canada.[4] Suffice it to explain that, from Confederation onward, the Dominion government has necessarily subsidized the Provincial governments. Deprived by the federal constitution of revenues from external trade, but not released under that constitution from their diverse functions, the four original Provinces received subsidies in the form of per capita grants and debt allowances from the Dominion. The terms fixed for these subsidies were meant to be final, and they were embodied in detail within the constitution itself.[5] In fact, they have been subject to constant bargaining and revision ever since Nova Scotia obtained "better terms" almost at once, in 1869. The number of Provinces and the divergent pressures grew; the alteration of subsidies has been virtually continuous.[6]

The problem has had an extra dimension ever since British Columbia and Prince Edward Island were first given additional subsidies in the early 1870's in lieu of land turned over to federal public domain. Time and again the Provinces have besieged Ottawa for better terms; final settlement has succeeded final settlement. After the impact of the depression and the Second World War the present basis for an approach to the problem was developed. This involves the exchange of increased and adjustable subsidies to the Provinces for exclusive "rental" by the Dominion government of the personal income tax, corporation taxes, and succession duties.[7]

[4] The best account of the matter up to the Second World War can be found in J. A. Maxwell, *Federal Subsidies to the Provincial Governments in Canada*, Cambridge (Mass.), 1937.

[5] B.N.A. Act of 1867, 118.

[6] Professor Dawson counts "over twenty special revisions and three general revisions since Confederation." Robert MacGregor Dawson, *The Government of Canada*, 2nd ed., Toronto, 1954, p. 120.

[7] The rental of the taxing power had to be devised because of the ambiguity of the British North America Act, which in section 91 (3) gives to the Dominion parliament the right of "The raising of Money by any Mode or System of Taxation," but in section 92 (2) gives to Provincial legislatures the power of "Direct Taxation within the Province in order to the Raising of a Revenue for Provincial Purposes"; thus exposing Canadians potentially to confiscatory levels of double direct taxation. Dawson hypothesizes the resident of Alberta who had an income of $1,000,000. In 1938, before the post-war rental schemes went into

III

For our present purposes the significance does not lie in the constitutional and technical labyrinth enclosing the problem, but in the basic fact that the governments of the Provinces, meaning, of course, the parties that control them, inevitably must struggle and bargain for higher subsidies with the government at Ottawa, meaning, of course, the majority party in parliament. This is true even when the party in power in a Province is nominally the same as the party in power in Ottawa. And here we approach the nature of the second layer of the Canadian national party system.

In the first layer, two groups of adversaries are pitted against each other in the Dominion parliament in what is essentially a two-party system. These are parliamentary parties in nature, with relatively weak national organization. They operate in the British parliamentary context, which decrees that elections come irregularly and with little advance warning. (The sharp contrast with the regularity of Congressional elections in the United States and with the galvanizing national impact of the Presidential election must be noted.) For effective organization these national parliamentary parties depend upon the services of provincial organizations. The textbooks advise that "the provincial association is the effective head of the party organizations in Canada."[8]

These provincial associations may bear the same name as the national parliamentary party, but they are in fact nearly autonomous. A national parliamentary party may in a Dominion election usefully be served by a provincial organization wholly autonomous and bearing a distinct and different name. The classic illustration of this is the role of the Union Nationale in Quebec. In its post-war heyday it helped the Liberals nationally to capture the bulk of Quebec's seats in the Dominion parliament in four elections, and aided the Progressive-Conservatives in a fifth. Also, dominance of a province by a provincial party organization does not guarantee that the organization will deliver federal representation to its nominal partner in the Dominion parliament. Social Credit governed in Alberta and British Columbia in 1958, but all of Alberta's and most of British Colum-

---

effect, he would have been liable for 105% of this amount in Dominion and provincial income taxes. Dawson, *op. cit.*, p. 123.

[8] Thus Dawson, *ibid.*, p. 529.

bia's seats in the last federal election went to the Progressive-Conservatives, and none to Social Credit.

This is no doubt confusing, but it is nevertheless logical, and the logic is that of the second layer of the national party system. Centrifugal sectional forces are very strong in Canada. These forces are to a large extent institutionalized in the politics of the Canadian provinces. These politics, and the parties that control them, are inevitably pointed toward conflict with Ottawa. And it is therefore true, as Professor Dawson suggests, that "while it may be advantageous for a Dominion Government to have its own party in power in the provinces, it may well be that a Provincial Government is more secure if it is politically opposed to the party in power in Ottawa."[9]

The logic of the second layer lays down its own classic cyclical pattern. A Dominion government will be established with a majority in the federal parliament that rests on the support of a majority of the provincial party organizations. As that government stays in power in Ottawa, the governments of the provinces will gradually turn against it. Where the parties in power in the provinces bear the same name as the party in power in Ottawa, these parties in the provinces will tend to face defeat. To complete the cycle, a majority of party organizations in the provinces hostile to the government in power at Ottawa will in the end elect the opposition party to office in the Dominion parliament. Thus, for example, when the Liberal party under Mackenzie King returned to power in Ottawa in 1935, Liberal parties were in power, alone or in coalition, in all of the then nine provinces except Alberta, where Social Credit had just come into office. When the Liberal party was defeated in the Dominion election of 1957, Liberal parties remained in power, alone or in coalition, in only three of the provinces; and in two of these, Manitoba in 1958 and Prince Edward Island in 1959, Progressive-Conservative governments came into office at the next provincial election.

In this fashion, the two layers of the national Canadian party system interact, and their inter-relationship is perhaps the most complex and unique phenomenon in Canadian politics. To win a Dominion election, a party must appeal for a national consensus, in face of all the divisive forces rampant on the political stage.

[9] *Ibid.*, p. 574.

From the birth of the Dominion it was apparent that a party appealing exclusively to either French Canadians or British Canadians could not hope to encompass a national consensus. In fact, such a party would, in its very nature, embody a threat to Canada's survival as a single nation. Total hostility from either of the two main racial groups also dooms a party's national chances. Flaws of leadership and historical circumstances deprived the Conservative party of the capacity to appeal to French Canadians for decades after the First World War. Until recently, therefore, it seemed that the Conservatives were doomed to be in opposition at Ottawa as a normal matter of course. To achieve national consensus and a national majority, parties must surmount not only social but economic divisions as well. This they can do mainly by advocating strong government to promote national economic development, which holds the promise of increased prosperity for a country still underpopulated, and still far from able to make full use of enormous natural resources. Strong national leadership, to keep the country together, to combat external pressures, and to develop the economy despite adverse geographical factors—this Canada needs and has usually received. It is what the parties successful in Dominion elections promise.

The themes are perennial: a national policy of energetic promotion, be it of a national railway or of natural gas; the vigorous assertion of separateness from the United States, running the gamut from protective tariffs to the attempt to force a distinctly Canadian culture into being. Only the theme of the British connection has altered, with the reality of completely achieved autonomy. The old negative separatist tone appears to be giving way to a more positive search for a forceful Canadian contribution to the Commonwealth. As all observers since Lord Bryce have noted, ideological questions play little role in Dominion politics. National circumstances do not encourage them.

Strong leadership at Ottawa appealing to Canadian nationalism, however, is never so strong as to be able to destroy the centrifugal forces at work. Sectional interests remain and must be somehow accommodated. In the absence of effective institutions to accommodate them within the Dominion government itself, they express themselves in the second layer of the party system. For practical purposes, sectional interests translate themselves into issues of provincial rights. What Canada requires is balance. Strong national leadership is required if the country as one is to survive at all. Yet national leadership which attempts to eliminate, or even override, sectional claims would be destructive. Therefore, provincial centers of power must exist to counter the power at Ottawa and keep it within bounds. However, a rigid, permanent conflict between Dominion and provinces would be intolerable. So the power in the provinces, as in Ottawa, must be flexible. At times the provinces must sustain leadership at Ottawa, at other times frustrate it.

IV

This is the essence of living Canadian federalism, and it is largely accomplished in the interplay between the parties in the provinces and the parties in the Dominion parliament. What is distinctively Canadian in the process is the vigor of provincial rights and what they represent, as well as the fact that the struggle for balance between them and the wider national interest is institutionalized in the party system. It is more usual in federal systems to find this struggle, often less severe than it is in Canada, institutionalized within the federal apparatus itself. So it is in the United States, chiefly within the Congress. But not in Canada, where the federal parliamentary institutions are unsuited to this purpose.

The Canadian House of Commons does not represent the provinces. Seats are allocated among and within the provinces roughly on the basis of population. The two forces in conflict in the House are normally the party of government and the opposition, which in the British tradition acts as a potential alternative government. Never far from the prospect of the next election, both government and opposition party must, as we have seen, bear in mind the need to appeal to a national consensus. To protect their political future, both attempt to mute and smother manifestations of divisive sectional forces. More than the government party is able to, the opposition party may choose to pose as the champion of provincial rights, and thus of sectional interests. But its freedom of action is also restricted. It dare not press issues to the point where its own opportunity to rally a national majority is endangered. Nor dare it make such commitments to provincial rights as will prevent its capacity for strong national leadership should it come to power at Ottawa. Operating under the authority of the Cabinet much as in Britain, the Canadian House of Commons tends very much to be the place where the policies of the government are put forth and enacted and where the two major parties in contention strive respectively to maintain or to achieve their appeal to a national majority.

It is well known that the Canadian Senate is not an effective institution, either for the accommodation of thrusting provincial interests or for most other purposes. This body of aged appointees, the great majority of whom owe their tenure to political services rendered in their more active days to the government that named them, does not even represent the provinces equally.[10] Even at the outset of Canadian Confederation the Senate was designed less as an organ of federal representation than as a bulwark of social conservatism. And, as Professor Brady points out, whatever federal role was intended for the nominees for life has now been largely diluted, since they are not compelled to possess a practical accountability to their provinces or their regions.[11] A weak second chamber, the Canadian Senate plays only a minor role in the parliamentary process, and virtually no significant role at all in Canadian federalism.

Within the Dominion Cabinet, to be sure, all or at least most of the provinces are represented. The process of Cabinet-making in Canada is made exceptionally difficult by the need of the ruling party to maintain its national strength by squeezing into the government as extensive a representation as possible from the ten provinces. However, such representation flows primarily only in one direction. It lacks a genuinely reciprocal character, and thus it does not serve to institutionalize the struggle for the federal balance completely in the Cabinet. The governing party does not pick a Cabinet in order to resolve federal conflicts. It

[10] The normal membership of the Canadian Senate is 102. In essence the body is designed to give representation to four major geographic areas. Thus Ontario and Quebec each have 24 Senators; the Western provinces have 24 Senators in all, six each for British Columbia, Manitoba, Saskatchewan and Alberta; and the Maritimes originally had 24 Senators, ten each for Nova Scotia and New Brunswick and four for Prince Edward Island. With the entrance of Newfoundland the balance was altered by the addition of six Senators for the island.

[11] Brady, *op. cit.*, p. 522.

seeks to have ministers from every province to demonstrate its truly national character and to sustain as widespread an allegiance as possible. There is a crucial overlap of purposes which falls short of identity.

In one sense a minister (or ministers) from a province does, of course, represent it. He can express a provincial or regional point of view, dispense some patronage and otherwise play an effective partisan role on behalf of his provincial party. But as a member of the Cabinet oriented toward the British model he is not consistently an effective bargainer for provincial interests. Only at the very formation of a government does he have an opportunity to make a really strong case for his province. An effective leader of the party in control of a province who is asked to join a Dominion Cabinet being formed can make his acceptance conditional upon *quid pro quos* that will benefit his province. Once in office, however, his ability to work for the provincial interest is limited by the practice of Cabinet solidarity. The collective decisions of the Cabinet are of necessity oriented toward preservation and promotion of the national consensus. And most men will temper their advocacy of a provincial case once it is clear that they will pay with a loss of office if they persist too far.

It is hard to be absolutely clear on this point. Obviously a Prime Minister and a Cabinet majority will go to great lengths to avoid a rupture that would see one of their number resign on the sensitive issue of provincial rights. Any Cabinet formed by the ruling party at Ottawa will seek to retain the strongest fealty possible from among affiliated or allied provincial parties, and to accede to the needs of the latter whenever practicable. But the momentum of divergent forces is never arrested; no balance of forces is permanent. Provincial demands, especially financial demands, are by their very nature insatiable. Better terms here, a boon there are inevitably followed by demands for still better terms, bigger boons. As a Dominion government stays in power it becomes impossible to gratify continually all that is sought by the provinces, even those governed by allied parties. In fact there is a danger that provincial demands feed on satisfaction. If too much is given by Ottawa too soon, the point may very early be reached within the Cabinet where the line is drawn against provincial pressures.

V

It is here, then, that the logic of the second layer asserts itself most forcibly. Within a province the feeling is apt to grow that the provincial cause—most often symbolized by financial terms though it may in actuality have a far more complex composition—is no longer best served by having the ruling party in the province represented in the Cabinet of the ruling party at Ottawa. Such representation may have resulted in recognized initial benefits to the province. But soon there may be talk that the province's representative (or representatives) has been in Ottawa too long, that he no longer stands for the provincial interest. It may not be immediately practicable, or indeed desirable, to change parties both in the province and in Ottawa, and thus to await the next great stride in the provincial cause at the moment of formation of the new Dominion Cabinet. But it may very well seem of advantage to overturn the ruling party in the province. This puts at the head of the provincial government men who no longer belong to the ruling party at Ottawa, but who at least will therefore be free to put the provincial case forward without reservation.

There are conflicting considerations involved, of course. Is it indeed wiser to trade muted advocacy of the provincial cause within the Dominion Cabinet for strident efforts made outside the pale? Where the ruling party in the province and the ruling party in the Dominion are affiliated under the same name, prudent concessions from Ottawa may long persuade provincial voters to continue support of the affiliation and not to rupture it. Of greater interest to the argument at the moment is the alternative of keeping in power in a province a government not affiliated to either of the two major parties in contention at Ottawa. Is this perhaps the strategy that gives the most effective flexibility to the provincial case?

Such an autonomous party, in essential control over the province, is free to bargain with both of the contending parties at Ottawa each time there is a Dominion election. It will be rewarded each time that it supports a winner at Ottawa. True, it is not likely to be rewarded with direct partisan representation within the Dominion Cabinet. On the other hand, however, its leaders remain free to criticize and differ with the Dominion government as they choose. The leaders of the ruling party in the Dominion can never ignore the autonomous party in the province as long as it rules there and has the effectively dominant provincial electoral organization. A Dominion election is always in the offing, and for the Ottawa leaders each Dominion election means that the process of bargaining for support from provincial organizations must be resumed.

No doubt the leaders of the two major parties in contention at Ottawa find such thinking vexatious and deplorable. But its potential appeal for the voters of a province seems real and apparent. The most virulently divergent pressures away from national consensus exist among French Canadians and in the West. It is then perhaps no accident, that until 1960 Quebec voters for years chose to support the Union Nationale in the province while usually voting Liberal in Dominion elections. Also, the Western provinces, with the very recent exception of Manitoba, are each in the control of a party not affiliated with either of the main contenders for Dominion power. Social Credit appears to be thoroughly dominant within Alberta and British Columbia, and not since the war has the C.C.F. lost control of Saskatchewan.

These circumstances are scarcely understandable except in terms of Canadian federalism and a second layer of the national party system. The so-called ideology of Social Credit seems scarcely relevant to the conduct of provincial government by the party, and of almost equal irrelevance to its voters. The Union Nationale, given the leadership of the late M. Duplessis and French Canadian nationalism, was and is not encumbered with an ideology that could be so labelled. There is, of course, a socialist-progressive point of view that distinguishes the C.C.F. ideologically, but there is little evidence of its relevance to provincial voting in Saskatchewan. It seems most likely that voters in general support these provincial parties with a pragmatic perception of the federal circumstances under discussion, i.e., with recognition of the two layers comprising the national party system.[12]

[12] My thesis is supported by brief suggestive statements made by F. H. Underhill, "Canadian Liberal Democracy in 1955," in G. V. Ferguson and F. H. Underhill, *Press and Party in Canada*, Toronto, 1955, pp. 27-46, and by Dennis Wrong, "The Pattern of Party Voting in Canada," *Public Opinion Quarterly*,

VI

Two obvious dangers attend this conception of an autonomous or nearly autonomous ruling party within a province as the most effective bargaining agent with Ottawa. Both have been evident in Canadian politics. The first is that dominance of provincial politics by one party will breed corruption and neglect or abuse of power. It is at this point that the third dimension of the party system relates to the two national layers. Sometimes the political situation within a province will prevent voters from continued support of the traditionally dominant party, even if the effectiveness of the latter in bargaining with the Dominion government is undiminished. This may be the result of evident flagrant abuses of office held too long and too securely. Or it may follow, as in the recent case of the Union Nationale in Quebec, the loss by the traditional ruling party of its dominant personality.

In the event, the replacing of a ruling provincial party which was not affiliated with either of the two major parties in the Dominion Parliament is hard to assess in terms of its impact on both layers of the national party system. Usually, such a provincial party could be replaced only by a provincial party affiliated with one or the other of the two Ottawa contenders. The first question must be whether the shift in the province is temporary and is soon to be undone again, after the repudiated party has undergone internal reform. The second question, if the shift seems semi-permanent, is whether the victory of a provincial party affiliated with one of the two parties in the Dominion Parliament signals an alteration in Ottawa. For example, with regard to Quebec today, it is not yet clear whether the Union Nationale will make a comeback soon within the province, or whether its fortunes have suffered a lasting reversal. And it is even less clear whether the success of the provincial Liberal party in Quebec signals the return of the Liberals to power in Ottawa or not. What is rather more clear is that lengthy dominance by one party is,

Summer 1957, pp. 252-264. It runs directly counter to the views of Howard A. Scarrow as expressed in his "Federal-Provincial Voting Patterns in Canada," *Canadian Journal of Economics and Political Science,* May 1960, pp. 289-298. Mr. Scarrow attempts a comparative manipulation of Canadian provincial and United States state election statistics and concludes from this effort, which proves sterile, "that no simple formula is likely to provide an adequate understanding of the motivation underlying split or alternating elections within a federation."

despite disadvantages, habitual in Canadian politics, both at the Dominion level and in many of the provinces.

The second danger consists of the possibility of sterile deadlock or destructive hostility between the Dominion government and the governments of one or more of the provinces. This is in fact a constant potential threat within the structure of Canadian federalism. It is a threat not often realized because it is suicidal. The basic fact of the matter is that most Canadians are fully aware both of the need for strong national leadership that will hold the country together, and of the pressures of centrifugal forces pulling away from national unity. Awareness means more than recognition in this case. It means acceptance. The existence of centrifugal and centripetal forces is taken for granted, as is the tension between them. They serve as a basis for all Canadian political calculations.

Quite naturally both forces are embodied in the constitution, which demands their interaction. The Dominion must finance the provinces because it depends on governmental services only the provinces can render. The latter cannot function without the financial support of Ottawa, nor without the context of a national consensus which the Dominion government represents. Both forces are also institutionalized in the national party system, requiring the parties at Ottawa to bargain with provincial parties, either as such, or more frequently as the governments of provinces. To bargain is the antithesis of deadlock or naked hostility. Prolonged bitterness between Dominion and provincial governments can work to the advantage of neither.

Nevertheless, there have been occasional lapses into excess. Two illustrations of unusual interest come to mind. One is the famous quarrel in 1940 between the Ontario Liberal administration led by Mitchell Hepburn and the Dominion Liberal government headed by Mackenzie King. This reached its peak when the Ontario legislature, dominated by the provincial Liberal party, passed a motion of censure on the conduct of the war effort by the Dominion government. Thus challenged, Mackenzie King went to the country and was returned to power with an increased majority. The number of Liberals returned to the Dominion Parliament from Ontario declined by only one, from fifty-six in 1935 to fifty-five. At the next provincial election in Ontario, in August 1943, the provincial Liberal party was crushingly defeated. (Mitchell Hepburn had earlier resigned as provincial Premier, on 21 October 1942.)

Of particular significance is the fact that this open breach occurred between a provincial and the Dominion party nominally affiliated under the Liberal name, which suggests that such nominal affiliation does not destroy the near-autonomy of a provincial party organization. Also of interest is the result of the conflict for the provincial party. Undoubtedly there was some feeling in Canada in the early years of World War II that the King government was not sufficiently vigorous in its war effort at Britain's side, and the voters of Ontario were as a group perhaps more loyal to the British connection than those of other provinces. However, the head-on challenge to the Dominion government flung down by the Ontario Liberal administration went too far in its expression of a divergent interest. Implicitly rebuked by King's success in the Dominion elections of 1940, and bitterly divided within itself, the provincial Liberal party lost its hold on Ontario.[13]

The other illustration is the notorious "five-cent speech" delivered by Mr. King in 1930. Speaking during the depression, Mr. King said:

"So far as giving money from this federal treasury to provincial governments is concerned.... I might be prepared to go a certain length possibly in meeting one or two of the western provinces that have Progressive premiers at the head of their governments, but I would not give a single cent to any Tory government.... May I repeat what I have said? With respect to giving moneys out of the federal treasury to any Tory government in this country for these alleged unemployment purposes, with these governments situated as they are to-day, with policies diametrically opposed to those of this government, I would not give them a five-cent piece."[14]

Shortly after this speech the Liberal Administration of Mackenzie King fought a general election. The speech was extensively used against the government. In the election the Liberals were defeated. No one could claim that they were defeated solely or even primarily because of Mr. King's utterance. Still, there can be little doubt that his statement was excessive and

[13] For Mackenzie King's reaction to Hepburn's challenge and his judgment on the Liberal defeat in Ontario in 1943, see J. W. Pickersgill, *The Mackenzie King Record, Volume I,* Toronto, 1960, pp. 62-65, 568-571.

[14] Canadian House of Commons, *Debates,* 3 April 1930, pp. 1227-8.

disastrous. Were such a view to become policy for a Dominion government vis-à-vis provincial governments affiliated with the opposition party at Ottawa, the basis of Canadian federalism would be destroyed. In Canada the center can no more wipe out sectional divergence than the latter can hope to override the center.

Of the greatest interest, however, is Mr. King's allusion to his willingness to deal with Progressive premiers, or in other words with leaders of provincial parties not affiliated with either of the two main parties at Ottawa. His statement invites the suggestion that there may well be a positive benefit at the first layer of the Canadian party system that derives from the existence at the second level of provincial parties both nominally and actually autonomous. It was remarked above that the leadership of both of the major parties in contention at Ottawa probably deplores the existence of autonomous parties in the provinces. No doubt a Liberal Prime Minister of the Dominion would, for partisan reasons, much prefer to have provincial Liberal parties in power in every province, just as a Conservative Prime Minister at Ottawa would welcome the unanimous support of provincial Conservatives prevailing everywhere. But how would politics in the Canadian national parliament be served if only the same two parties in contention at Ottawa were available to provincial voters?

The pressures of Canadian federalism, as we have seen, dictate that in time the conflict between provincial forces and a government confirmed in power at Ottawa is bound to intensify. The classic cycle of the two layers would therefore indicate that, for example, a Liberal government that had come into power with the support of provincial Liberal parties dominant in most or all of the provinces would soon find itself confronted with hostile Conservative provincial parties coming to power in most or all of the provinces. It would then be rather rapidly succeeded by a Conservative government at Ottawa, which would in turn then undergo the equivalent experience.

At least two very grave disadvantages would inevitably seem to follow. First, the precarious national consensus of Canada would suffer. Governments at Ottawa would alternate more rapidly than is now the case, which is not necessarily desirable in itself.[15] It would also seem certain that they would succeed or fall increasingly on the divisive issue of provincial rights. Secondly, each alternation at the Dominion level would presumably be accompanied by the characteristic rewards granted to provincial supporters. The process of pressure for better terms would be opportunistically accelerated, and the present basis of Canadian federalism would be rapidly eroded.

Such dire results might be avoided only if the two Dominion parliamentary parties could discipline and manage their provincial affiliates. This, however, is unlikely to happen so long as provincial governments and political processes serve divergent social and economic forces which are indelibly part of the very essence of Canadian nationhood. With these considerations in mind, the prevalence of parties in office in several provinces that are not affiliated with either of the two contenders for Dominion power may be seen as a vital safety valve in the Canadian political process.

By voting Social Credit into provincial power, for example, the voters of British Columbia can effectively express sectional interest, albeit in the guise of provincial identity, without necessarily damaging thereby the delicate balance of national unity. The autonomous provincial parties in power appear uniquely free to negotiate with both parties at Ottawa. It may well be that this fact offers a vital flexibility, not only to the voters of the provinces, but to the entire national party system. In this sense, then, these autonomous parties in power in the provinces are not merely splinter groups also represented in the Dominion parliament. They constitute part of a second layer of the national Canadian party system, and it is in large measure to their existence that the stable parliamentary life of Ottawa owes its viability.

Professor Brady has written that "Federalism is the most distinctive achievement of Canadian democracy."[16] It is also true that the success of a national system of democratic politics in Canada is *per se* a magnificent achievement in the face of great odds. A century ago John Stuart Mill asserted: Free institutions

[15] For the argument that Canadian circumstances make the relatively extended rule of one party in the Dominion parliament advantageous, see my "Massive Alternation in Canadian Politics," *Foreign Affairs,* July 1958, pp. 633-44.

[16] Brady, *op. cit.,* p. 65.

are next to impossible in a country made up of different national-
ities. Among a people without fellow feeling, especially if they
read and speak different languages, the united public opinion
necessary to the working of representative government cannot
exist."[17] For Canada at least, Mill's dictum does not hold, though
the experience of other nations well justifies his warning. Essentially it is Canadian federalism that has made the difference.
More attention is justified to the ingenious and complex political
process which animates the successful federal democracy of the
Canadian nations. Within this process a two-layer national party
system appears to have developed.

[17] John Stuart Mill, *Representative Government*, Oxford, 1948, p. 292.

8   *Party Discipline Under Federalism:*
     *Implications of Australian Experience**

AARON WILDAVSKY

Australia has a federal system and a parliamentary form
of government. This mixture of institutions found separately in
the United States and Great Britain provides the student of
politics with an opportunity to test generalizations usually made
only on the basis of data in one or the other of these two
countries. Does federalism prevent control of national legislative
parties by national party bodies outside the legislature? Is federalism incompatible with a high degree of party cohesion and
discipline in the national legislature? What are the possibilities
of national control of state party organizations? Even partial

From *Social Research*, 28 (Winter 1961), pp. 437-458. Reprinted by permission of
Social Research, an international quarterly edited by the Graduate Faculty
(New School for Social Research).
    * AUTHOR'S NOTE—I am indebted to Henry Mayer and Robert Parker for
helpful critical comments on this paper. Some of its material is based on personal
interviews and conversations with Australian officials.

answers to such questions require comparative analysis in which the consequences of federalism for different political systems are appraised. In this paper I shall examine the answers suggested by case material on the most disciplined political party in Australia, the Australian Labour Party (ALP), focusing on the interrelationships among the ALP's Federal Executive, its members in the federal legislature, organized in the Federal Parliamentary Labour Party (FPLP), and its state party organizations. This analysis will then be used to comment more generally on the effect of federal structure on political parties, with special reference to American problems.

I

The harsh conditions under which Australia's settlers labored, confronted with a vast, dry, sparsely populated continent, have impressed their logic and their lessons on even the most obtuse. And perhaps the greatest of these lessons was the need for group solidarity to insure survival by doing for the individual what he could not do alone:[1] solidarity to keep from perishing from heat, thirst, or hunger; solidarity to improve working conditions, to protect employers against unionism, to insure the doctor and the journalist a proper station in life; solidarity, above all, to force the government to do all the things that private citizens and their associations found it impossible to do for themselves. In the political arena solidarity has come to represent a value in itself as well as a means to securing certain practical ends. Few words sound so derogatory on the Australian tongue as those that are applied to the despicable creature who deserts his friends and "scabs" or "rats" for the enemy. In a society that values solidarity, the union and branch members of the ALP take pride in assuring the devotion of the legislator to the movement he represents by their sufferance.

The visible manifestation of the ALP's emphasis on solidarity is found in two firmly established practices — the pledge and the caucus. All candidates for public office on the ALP ticket must sign a pledge committing them to carry out the party's platform,

---

[1] The importance of solidarity is stressed by J. D. B. Miller, *Australian Government and Politics* (London 1954), and by W. K. Hancock, *Australia* (London 1930). The related concept of "mateship" has been used by many authors.

withdraw from the election if they lose their bid for pre-selection endorsement, to support the party in all cases where the fate of a government is at stake, and, in most states, to support the decisions of a majority of the ALP (the "caucus") in Parliament, except on certain matters of conscience. The result is a degree of party discipline equaled by few of the world's parliamentary democracies.[2] Enforcement of these disciplinary practices is almost entirely in the hands of the state organizations, which are the centers of party activity.

Although the organization of the ALP differs somewhat from state to state, certain general comments can be made.[3] The State Conference writes the state policy platform, chooses representatives to federal party bodies, and selects the State Executive. Representation on the conference is therefore all-important. The majority of delegates come from affiliated unions, while a much lesser number represent local party branches. Since the conference meets for only a few days (it has been said that its normal state is dissolution) the prize for which the party factions compete is control of the State Executive.

Between conferences the State Executive is supreme. It controls most party funds, grants and refuses charters to local branches, interprets the rules determining eligibility for party membership and for voting at conferences, and may refuse party endorsement to any candidate for government office even if he has the support of his local branch. We are here particularly interested in the fact that the State Executive is empowered to issue binding instructions to the State Parliamentary Labour Party (the party's representatives in the state legislature), and frequently exercises this right. An adroit Labour premier may get his way by stressing electoral necessity or playing rival union factions off against each other, but where the unions (and hence the State Executive) are united, the premier is likely to be in a subservient position. "A labour leader may stoop to conquer," J.

[2] The best account of this subject is that by J. D. B. Miller, "Party Discipline in Australia," in *Political Science* (Wellington) (March and September 1953). Details of the pledge vary from state to state.

[3] A detailed account of ALP organization at the state level may be found in Louise Overacker, *The Australian Party System* (New Haven 1952) Chapters 4 and 5. The federal bodies are covered by L. F. Crisp, *The Australian Federal Labour Party, 1901-1951* (London 1955).

A. McCallum declares, "but, none the less, stooping, not conquering, appears to be his characteristic position."[4]

If there is anything that may be considered the cardinal rule of labor politics in Australia it is this: if a substantial majority of the interested unions within a state are agreed on a particular policy, there is nothing that can stand in their way except their own self-restraint. By choosing to exercise their controlling voice on the State Executive, the unions may compel the members of the State Parliamentary Labour Party to bow to their wishes or risk expulsion from the party. The State Executive's relationship to the State Parliamentary Party depends to a considerable extent, therefore, on the degree of unity among the trade unions that control the bulk of votes on party affairs.

The fact is, however, that often the unions are not united. The view that labor is a purely homogeneous interest is untenable in Australia. Sources of conflict are many and varied, and not sufficiently well understood. All that can be done here is to list some of the more persistent quarrels: the Australian Workers Union (AWU), a catch-all union with a rural base and significant industrial representation, versus other unions, which regard it as a "body snatcher" constantly trying to increase its membership at their expense; strong industrial unions that prefer direct strike action versus weak unions that feel they are better served by sticking to the legal arbitration courts; communists in some unions versus the so-called Industrial Groups, supported by Catholic Action; the Australian Council of Trade Unions (ACTU), a loose grouping of Trades and Labour Councils in large cities, versus the AWU, the Industrial Groups, and unions led by communists; some union leaders versus others in struggles for personal advancement among men of working-class background who lack other avenues of mobility.[5]

The existence of a federal structure is also a fruitful source of conflict. Federal structure plays a generally important part in

[4] J. A. McCallum, "The Economic Basis of Australian Politics," in W. G. K. Duncan, ed., *Trends in Australian Politics* (Sydney 1935) p. 110.

[5] See Miller (cited above, note 1), Appendix C, pp. 215-19; Kenneth Walker, "Australia," in W. Galenson, ed., *Comparative Labor Movements* (New York 1955); D. W. Rawson, "The A.L.P. Industrial Groups," in *Australian Quarterly*, vol. 26 (December 1954) pp. 30-46; Herbert Weiner, "Reduction of Communist Power in the Australian Trade Unions," in *Political Science Quarterly*, vol. 69 (September 1954) pp. 390-412.

Australian political life. There were states before there was a
nation. Most of the major interest groups and all of the political
parties were organized on a state basis before they formed
national organizations. Enjoying a separate existence, state organizations have developed an interest in perpetuating that
existence, which is defended by a large corps of personnel who
benefit from this arrangement. It is this structural fact, rather than
underlying differences between the states, which characterizes
Australian federalism.[6] The national parties are less a reflection
of the economic and social diversity of the states than an arena for
clashes of national interests. This helps to explain why the
attempt to transplant American political institutions to Australia,
at least by making the Senate based on equal state representation, has failed abysmally. The Australian Senate, dominated by
party discipline and interest-group solidarity, has never acted as
a representative body for the states. But the fact remains that
federalism is woven into the fabric of party and associational life.

Since the establishment of the federal government in 1900, the
ALP has been plagued by the difficulty of reconciling its emphasis on unity with the divisive pressures fostered by the federal
system. That system creates rival union and party hierarchies
whose interests, both personal and group-centered, may conflict.[7]
A proposed national law may work unequally in different states,
with the result that the legislation is favored by the unions in one
state and opposed by those in another.[8] The unions in one state
may have a considerable stake in keeping the Labour Party in
power in their area, and may therefore urge the ALP federal
legislators to forgo unpopular acts that might react unfavorably
on the state party's chances at the polls. With elections held at
irregular intervals all over the country, an unpopular act may be
punished in a constituency other than that in which it originated.

Above all, the ALP, whose State Executives have always been
supreme, has had to work out the problem of relationships with

[6] P. H. Partridge makes this point in his excellent paper, "The Politics of
Federalism," in Geoffrey Sawer, ed., *Federalism* (Melbourne 1952).

[7] H. V. Evatt's book on former New South Wales Labour Premier W. A.
Holman, *Australian Labour Leader* (Sydney and London 1945), contains numerous examples of how federal structure confuses the lines of political conflict and
cooperation.

[8] For an illustration see A. B. Wildavsky, "The 1926 Referendum," in A. B.
Wildavsky and D. Carboch, *Studies in Australian Politics* (Melbourne 1958).

the FPLP, the party's representatives in the federal Parliament. One possible solution to this dilemma would have been no national party apparatus outside the FPLP; this would have permitted the state parties, possessing powerful disciplinary weapons, to go their own ways and dictate the actions of their members in the FPLP. Another solution would have been a national party body, independent of all state ties, which would exercise complete control over the state organizations and the FPLP; this would have eliminated political forces based on state boundaries as important elements in the ALP's power structure, and would have converted the FPLP into a cipher. Neither of these extreme alternatives has been adopted.

The Federal Conference, composed of six delegates from each state party, is the supreme body in the ALP. It is empowered to issue binding policy for the entire party, and to determine the legitimacy of state parties. In the intervals between conferences (as with the State Conferences, this means most of the time, since the Federal Conference normally occurs once in two years) these potentially vast powers are exercised by the Federal Executive, which was established in 1915 after thirteen years of states-rights opposition, centered in the populous state of New South Wales. The interests of the states of small population were safeguarded by four provisions: equal representation from each state; selection of two delegates each by the existing state political organizations; transaction of business only by a quorum of seven members, drawn from at least four states; and convocation of special Federal Conferences by the Executive only on demand of four states.[9] The word "delegate" has been used advisedly, since the members of the Federal Executive speak for their respective State Conferences and Executives, who may remove them at any time and substitute more pliant souls.

The confederate structure of the Federal Executive results in a situation wherein four states — Queensland, South Australia, West Australia, and Tasmania — with considerably less than half the total population and party membership, control eight of the twelve votes in that body. These states may not have geographic interests separate from those of Victoria and New South Wales, but their most influential unions, particularly the AWU, exercise

[9] See Crisp (cited above, note 3) pp. 52-53.

far more than a proportionate voice in the decisions of the
Federal Executive. Together, or with votes from either of the
more populous states, the small states are in a position to control,
or at least veto, the Federal Executive's decisions.

Serving as the ALP's mechanism of national unity, the Federal
Executive possesses the formal right to dictate binding instructions to the FPLP, and is also empowered to determine the
legitimacy and composition of the party's state organizations.
Opponents of the Labour Party in Australia are fond of charging
domination of national parliamentary life by "outside interests"
under the cloak of the Federal Executive; the ALP's supporters
counter that the Executive is ultimately responsible to the party's
rank-and-file and hence is more democratic than the "capitalist
conspiracies" that secretly govern the Liberal and Country parties.[10] I consider both these views essentially incorrect; by
neglecting the influence of federalism, both sides overrate the
importance of the Executive as a vehicle for compelling the
FPLP to do things it does not wish to do. The standard charge of
ALP dictation by "outside" bodies has more validity in at least
some of the states (in Queensland, for example, the State Executive recently broke the state labor government without reference
to the voters). But what may be, in the states, an active, "tough,"
or compelling party machine is not basically that on the federal
level. As a basis for examining this question in more detail, let us
look now at several specific instances of Federal Executive
relations with the FPLP and also with party officials in the states.

II

Apparently the first attempt by the Federal Executive to exercise its rights over the FPLP occurred at its second meeting, in
January 1916. At that time, according to Crisp's account (p. 56),
"it passed, by eight votes to three and in the face of a passionate
defence by Hughes [then leader of the FPLP], what amounted to
a censure on the Labour Government for abandoning the 1915
Referendum for wider Commonwealth powers. . . . Hughes was

---

[10] For more sophisticated criticisms of the Federal Executive see Leicester
Webb, *Communism and Democracy in Australia* (New York 1955) pp. 35-37; and
"Australia: Labour and Communism," in *Round Table* (London), vol. 41, no. 162
(March 1951) pp. 182-86. For a rebuttal by a learned Labour Party member see
Crisp (cited above, note 3) pp. 6-12.

reported to have stamped out of the Executive meeting and to have threatened to leave the Movement unless the Executive swallowed its words (which it did next day by an eight to three vote)." The weakness of the Executive at this early stage was also apparent when it failed to take any action whatever on the conscription issue, which split the FPLP during World War I.[11]

In 1926 a nationwide referendum was held to decide whether power to determine wages through arbitration courts was to continue to be shared between the states and the federal government, or was to be exercised solely by the latter.[12] Although the ALP had previously advocated federal control, it became bitterly divided on the issue. The FPLP, led by its members from Victoria (the only state then without a labor government), favored the referendum proposal to shift powers over arbitration to the federal sphere, but some unions in the five states where Labour Party governments were in power felt that state courts would be friendlier than federal courts operating under a management-dominated Nationalist Party. The State Executive of the New South Wales party, whose union supporters were benefiting from particularly advantageous actions under the incumbent Lang labor government, threatened the federal legislators from that state with loss of endorsement in future elections if they dared to support the position taken by the FPLP. The Federal Executive then stepped into the picture and decided that in the presence of so much dispute it would be wise to leave the matter an open question. Although the New South Wales Executive protested vigorously, the Federal Executive succeeded in protecting the FPLP against state disciplinary measures.

In succeeding years it became apparent that only disaster could result from a situation in which six different State Executives might pledge their FPLP members to support six different courses of action. After an unhappy experience in the marketing referendum of 1937, in which the Queensland Labour Party succeeded in controlling the votes of its FPLP members, the Federal Executive voted eight to four that "no State Executive may direct members of the Federal Parliamentary Labour Party in regard to matters affecting the Federal Platform and/or

[11] See Overacker (cited above, note 3) pp. 121-22.
[12] See Wildavsky and Carboch (cited above, note 8) pp. 7-71.

proposed legislation which the ... Party has to deal with in the [Federal] legislature." But this could not prevent quiet sabotage on the part of any State Executive disposed to use for that purpose its power of denying endorsement for federal office.

Meanwhile another significant incident had occurred—in 1931, in the midst of the depression. Since 1929 the FPLP had had a large majority in the House of Representatives but only a minority in the Senate, and because legislation must receive Senate approval, the FPLP's pet measures were either defeated or postponed. The only way to end the divided government would have been to call for a Double Dissolution, whereby all Senators and members of the House would have faced the voters at an election. But in 1931 many in the ALP feared that a defeat at the polls would leave them at the mercy of the opposition in the midst of the great depression. After other remedies failed to secure Senate approval, the leaders of the FPLP came to believe that only a deflationary policy could meet the economic emergency and receive the support of the opposition parties. In concert with the opposition, the FPLP adopted a plan of financial retrenchment, which included a 20 percent slash in wages and pensions and drastic cuts in social services. Many in the ALP felt betrayed, and looked to the Federal Executive to order the FPLP to reverse its policy. The Executive duly met and issued a statement that mirrored its predicament: "The Executive of the Australian Labour Party is opposed to ... reductions of wages, pensions, and social services.... The Executive is convinced that a Nationalist Ministry ... would be abhorrent to the workers.... It is of the greatest importance that the Labour Ministry should remain in office ... to prevent the enemies of Labour from enforcing a ruthless policy of aggression against the hard-won rights of the workers."[13] In other words, maintaining the FPLP in power was considered more important than rejection of a plan humiliating to labor.

Another major event began in 1950, when Liberal Party Prime Minister R. G. Menzies introduced a bill providing for the dissolution of the Communist Party.[14] From the start the labor

[13] *Round Table*, vol. 21, no. 84 (September 1931) p. 903. Other material on this case is from Warren Denning, *Caucus Crisis: The Rise and Fall of the Scullin Government* (Paramatta, New South Wales, 1937).

[14] The factual material in this discussion is from L. Webb. *Communism and Democracy in Australia: A Survey of the 1951 Referendum* (Melbourne 1954).

movement was intensely divided on this issue. The prime consideration was the fact that the ALP, a minority in the House of Representatives, held a commanding majority in the Senate. If the party voted down the bill, as it wished to, Menzies would be able to appeal to the country under a Double Dissolution of Parliament. Fearful of going into an election on the communist issue and of losing its Senate majority, the Labour Party was in a quandary, and the Federal Executive was called into session. In consultation with the leaders of the parliamentary party, the Executive recommended that the principle of the bill be accepted, but that amendments be sought to safeguard the law from certain abuses. The FPLP caucus voted to accept the recommendation. Several months elapsed as the bill went through various stages. Some amendments were made, but not enough to satisfy the FPLP. Within the party and the unions the argument raged at fever pitch. The split in the party was clearly indicated when the Federal Executive met again and there was a six-to-six tie on the question. At the last minute, however, the party in West Australia had a change of heart, and called another session of the Federal Executive. By an eight-to-four vote the Executive then ordered the FPLP to cease its opposition to the Communist Dissolution Bill. The order was carried out. It may be that the Executive was telling the majority of Labour parliamentarians what they wanted to hear, and rescuing them from the prospect of a difficult election campaign.

A more recent episode may be cited as a final example of relations between the Federal Executive and the FPLP. In March 1959 a proposal was made to increase the salaries and allowances of members of Parliament. The Liberal Party government supported the proposal and, with a few amendments, succeeded in having it approved by both houses. There was a great deal of criticism in the press, however, and several Labour Party State Executives and affiliated trade unions came out against the legislation. The FPLP decided that basic salary allowances should be approved, but that other increases should be rejected. In the party outside of Parliament, opposition to the FPLP decision was apparent, and some looked to the Federal Executive to reverse it. The head of the Executive, F. W. Chamberlain, first stated that the matter was one to be decided by the FPLP, and then resigned in protest against its decision. Later, Chamberlain declared that he would have called a meet-

172   AARON WILDAVSKY

ing of the Federal Executive to reverse the FPLP decision if time had permitted. At a meeting of the Federal Conference of the ALP in May, Chamberlain was persuaded to accept reelection, and a motion was passed deeply regretting the FPLP's action. Nevertheless the FPLP decision prevailed.[15]

As has been indicated, the Federal Executive was given the right to suspend or remove an existing State Executive from office and replace it with another. The pattern of Federal Executive intervention in state affairs was set during the 1920s, in reaction to the disputes that continually rent the New South Wales Labour Party.[16] When things threatened to get completely out of hand, or when there was a danger of the conflict spreading to other states or affecting the party's electoral chances, the Federal Executive intervened. With considerable regularity it deposed one state faction and put another in its place. Analyzing the local reaction, D. W. Rawson has written that "The attitude of the New South Wales party to Federal intervention was simple. Those who controlled the party condemned it, those who were seeking to control the party welcomed it."[17]

The general pattern in New South Wales was for the Federal Executive to call a "unity" conference. Frequently the rules were changed in such a way as to assure victory for a particular faction. At times the disadvantaged faction refused to take part in this type of prearranged unity, and formed its own party (laying claim to the legitimate title of "Labour"). The crucial battle was then fought out in the ensuing elections, perhaps over a period of years, with final victory going to the faction that obtained the best results at the polls. Regardless of what its original decision may have been, or whether it had a contrary instruction from the Federal Conference, the Federal Executive, like Thrasymachus, decided that justice was the interest of the stronger. It ended up by throwing its support to the faction most popular with the electorate, formally designating it as entitled to bear the proud name of the official New South Wales ALP.

[15] D. W. Rawson, "Australian Political Chronicle, The Commonwealth," in *Australian Journal of Politics and History*, vol. 5, no. 2 (November 1959) pp. 226-27.
[16] See V. G. Childe, *How Labour Governs* (London 1923).
[17] D. W. Rawson, *The Organization of the ALP, 1916-1941* (unpublished Ph.D. dissertation, Australian National University) p. 53.

In 1955 the Federal Executive intervened in Victoria. During the years after World War II a faction had gathered around the Industrial Groups and, backed by Catholic Action,[18] had achieved predominance in the Victoria Executive by winning over a large percentage of the branches and a considerable amount of union support. Serious conflicts arose when a substantial section of the unions, with a majority in the Melbourne Trades Hall, felt endangered by Industrial Group influence and sought to put its own representatives in to control the Executive. At that time H. V. Evatt, leader of the FPLP, came out with charges of a Catholic Action plot to subvert and dominate the ALP. With the Federal Conference in the offing, the Federal Executive, controlled by opponents of the Industrial Groups, decided to suspend the Victorian State Executive, which had been specially indicted by Dr. Evatt, and to hold a "unity" conference in that state under direct Federal Executive supervision. The Federal Executive took care to alter rules of representation that had been in force since 1939, to make sure that the unions not controlled by the Groupers would dominate the conference. The State Conference duly elected a new Executive, and sent new delegates to defeat the Industrial Groups at the Federal Conference in Hobart. Thus outmanoeuvred, the Grouper forces in Victoria proceeded in time to form their own anti-communist labor party, and similar breakaway labor parties were subsequently formed in other states.

III

The cases presented above provide the basis for a few generalizations concerning the Federal Executive's relationship to the FPLP and the state machines. As regards the FPLP, its intervention occurs only when there is a deep split within the movement as a whole, not only between leading personalities but between unions. Thus the Federal Executive's intervention reflects not so much its special relationship to the FPLP as the presence of a

[18] See Henry Mayer, "Catholic Action in Australia," in *Voice* (December 1954) pp. 22-23, 33; the exchange of letters between H. W. Arndt and B. A. Santamaria, published as an article, "The Catholic Social Movement," in *Australian Journal of Politics and History*, vol. 2, no. 2 (May 1957); Tom Truman, *Catholic Action and Politics* (Melbourne 1959), and "Catholics and Politics in Australia," in *Western Political Quarterly*, vol. 12, no. 2 (June 1959) pp. 527-34; Henry Mayer, ed., *Catholics and the Free Society* (Melbourne 1961).

problem that has divided the entire labor movement. Moreover, the Executive does not preempt or cut short the discussion phase of policymaking, but acts only after the issue has been extensively debated in party circles. In the arbitration-referendum and the depression-policy cases the Executive did not meet until long after the FPLP had arrived at its decision. Even in the case of the bill calling for Communist Party dissolution, the Executive's final binding action took place after the issue had been agitated in and had split the unions, branches, state organizations, and FPLP.

Yet the Federal Executive did call for a direct reversal of FPLP policy in regard to the latter bill. Although some labor parliamentarians may have wanted to hear this instruction, it is likely that the FPLP would have continued to resist the bill if the Executive had not intervened. The crucial question arises, therefore, whether this single instance signifies an important change in the relationship between the Federal Executive and the FPLP, or whether it will remain an isolated incident. The preponderance of evidence and a consideration of the functions that the Executive performs leads, I believe, to the conclusion that so long as the Executive remains a federal organization it will dictate to the FPLP only at rare intervals.

When an issue arises that splits the party, the State Executives, who control their delegates to the Federal Executive, are likely to be guided by their least common denominator—maintaining the FPLP in power where it can aid them and their union supporters. This means preventing the FPLP from doing anything that would lead to the loss of federal and state elections. In the hurried circumstances surrounding the convocation of the Federal Executive, what is sought is not some new program, which would probably cause greater dissension, but a means of avoiding the immediate difficulty and retaining at least the outward unity of the movement. Thus the Executive acts to protect the FPLP from divisive pressures originating in less than a majority of the six states, as in the arbitration-referendum case; or to help maintain the FPLP in power by protecting its ability to advocate a policy unpalatable to some sections of the party, as in the depression-policy case; or to protect a majority of states (and possibly the FPLP itself) from unpopular action, as in the dissolution case. The stereotyped picture of the Federal Executive as a mechanism for constantly browbeating reluctant parliamentarians hardly fits the facts.

To be sure, any student of Australian politics must face the vexing problem of how to make generalizations about institutions in a federal system without unduly complicating his analysis by including the multiple consequences of interaction between the state and federal levels. In focusing in one set of relationships — Federal Executive intervention with the FPLP in regard to specific policies — I do not in any way wish to imply that other relationships do not exist. For example, it is true that the Federal Executive may help determine the outcome of struggles in the state labor parties. It is also true that federal parliamentarians are to a considerable extent controlled by these parties. Hence the Federal Executive, through its powers over state machines, may indirectly compel some federal parliamentarians — those who belonged to the state faction against which the Executive has intervened — to do things they do not wish to do. Such relationships, however, are of only tangential interest to the fact, stressed here, that the Federal Executive rarely dictates to the FPLP.

There are, to begin with, many matters with which the Executive is not concerned, and others on which it has no desire to take a stand. At the federal level, legislation in regard to wages and hours, potentially the most fruitful source of conflict, has been removed from parliamentary consideration and turned over to arbitration courts by the Constitution, a circumstance that many Labour Party politicians do not find at all distressing. The leader of the FPLP may have his own connections with the state machines and large unions, and thus be able to exert pressure against the Executive. Or he may enjoy a close and friendly relationship with the Executive, and use this special access to ward off undesired pressures from other party and union bodies, as J. B. Chifley is said to have done.

The very nature of the Federal Executive militates against an overly active role. It is not a body in continuous session, but meets regularly only twice a year. A special session must be called before other meetings may be held. Its membership drawn from widespread geographic areas and is constantly changing. In these circumstances it is difficult to create and maintain an organizational spirit that might develop demands of its own and take an interest in keeping the FPLP under a collective thumb. Matters are eased along by the fact that several FPLP members are generally chosen as members of the Executive, and hardly have an interest in making things difficult for themselves.

But in the end, the Federal Executive, despite its powers over the state machines, is composed of state delegates who must follow the orders of their respective State Executives. If the Federal Executive does not exercise close and continuing supervision over the FPLP it must be because the several State Executives are divided on the question, are uninterested, or are unwilling to permit such a relationship.

The difficulties of the power relationships that result in a maintenance of the status quo become apparent once we consider the existing alternatives to the Federal Executive. One would be a total lack of extraparliamentary machinery capable of giving orders to the parliamentary body. But this would be entirely alien to the doctrine and traditions of the ALP; it would permit a return to the situation in which the federal parliamentarians were subject to divergent voices within each state; it would enable New South Wales and Victoria, as the states with the largest representation in the federal House of Representatives, to exercise a controlling voice if they wished to do so and could agree among themselves. Another alternative would be a permanent body, continuously in session, composed of delegates elected by the State Executives or by the party members of each state. But this is precisely what the state party officials do not want. Such a Federal Executive would only institutionalize the conflicts between the state parties; it would be called on not to frame a minimum agreement for the moment but to agree on a general program for every issue that came up; it would either become a poorer and more quarrelsome substitute for the FPLP or lead to disillusionment by gravitating back to a function no more vigorous than that existing today. And in the unlikely event that the small-state party machines would permit a popularly elected Federal Executive, rather than one chosen, as now, on the basis of equality of state representation, the sources of discord would be multiplied tenfold.

In short, an independent Executive would not only compete with the FPLP but also be in continual strife with the state organizations, which would have to control it or accept an inferior status in the party. There appears to be no way for the Federal Executive to be made much more influential and active in relation to the FPLP without at the same time making it a rival center of power to all the state parties.

The present Federal Executive represents an institutional compromise between state control of the FPLP and a national political machine independent of the state organizations. In return for accepting Executive control, slight and sporadic as it is, the FPLP receives some protection against unwanted orders from state machines, added support when faced with unpopular political decisions, and relative insulation from a number of conflicts dividing the extraparliamentary body. The question has never been whether the FPLP should remain without any direction from its parent body, but rather for whose benefit this limited direction should be carried on. What the ALP faces is not a choice between the Federal Executive and no extraparliamentary control of the FPLP, but one between the Executive and far more onerous forms of central direction. The Federal Executive represents the minimum form of extraparliamentary control of the FPLP possible under Australian conditions.

But although the Federal Executive's direction of national affairs has been overestimated, its influence on the party's internal affairs can no longer be minimized. Its increasing power has altered the tactics of intra-party warfare. Normally an "out" faction in a state is faced with the long, difficult, and frequently unsuccessful task of obtaining enough union and branch votes to take control of a State Conference. This is no longer indispensable. The dissident groups now have the far easier and quicker alternative of trying to gain support from the Federal Executive and using it as a lever with which to lift the "in" group out of office. This conclusion is subject, however, to a major long-run qualification. The opposition faction seeking Federal Executive intervention must be supported by the voters. Otherwise its so-called victory will eventually evaporate at the polls. When the faction in whose favor the Executive has intervened has lost support among the voters, the Executive has invariably changed course and formally ratified the existing preponderance of power in the state. So long as the results of intervention must be ratified by voters circumscribed within limited geographic boundaries, the Federal Executive will have to pay careful attention to state sentiments.

IV

The foregoing discussion of the ALP Federal Executive suggests at least the possibility of comparison with problems relevant to American federalism, such as party discipline and the
relationship of the National Committees to the Congressional
parties (and may be relevant also to British concern over extraparliamentary control of parliamentary parties). A key distinction
between federalism in the United States and in Australia must,
however, be borne in mind. While both countries have federal
structures — separate state and national governments — only in the
United States are underlying economic, ethnic, religious, and
other diversitites centered in distinct geographic areas corresponding roughly to state and sectional boundaries. Let us call
this "social federalism," to distinguish it from the "structural
federalism" that characterizes both countries. In analyzing the
effect of federalism on American political parties it is difficult to
separate out the consequences of structural federalism from
those of social federalism, because the two factors are found
together and react on each other. Since social federalism is
largely absent in Australia, the consequences of structural federalism may be viewed more clearly there — consequences that
might occur in the United States even if its pervasive social
federalism were to disappear.

Perhaps the most obvious proposition to be derived from
Australian experience is that structural federalism does not
necessarily prohibit the existence of highly disciplined political
parties in the national legislature. So long as the most significant
cleavages of interest in the political community do not regularly
take place along state and sectional boundaries, as they tend to in
the United States, but occur along class, occupational, or other
non-geographic lines, as in Australia, the clash of interests may
lead to disciplined parties. This consideration supports David
Truman's conclusion that prospects for change in the locus of
power within American parties "must rest fundamentally upon
the emergence or intensification of a dominant and persistent set
of interests and issues which will tend to cut through rather than
to unify constituencies, especially the states, and which demand
standardized national solutions."[19]

[19] David Truman, "Federalism and the Party System," in Arthur Macmahon,
ed., *Federalism Mature and Emergent* (New York 1955) p. 133.

What federal structure does do, as study of the ALP Federal Executive indicates, is to make extraparliamentary control of parliamentary parties exceedingly difficult — or, in terms of American equivalents, it hampers National Committee control of the Congressional party. When all states are given the same representation on the controlling body, the states of small population have a vastly disproportionate voice in the determination of national policy, and the large states seek ways of evading this. And the alternative of making representation proportionate to population not only would be bitterly resisted by states of small population, but also would alter or abolish the party's federal structure; the extraparliamentary body would then become a rival center of power against all state parties, which would have to resist, to accept a completely subordinate status, or to pass out of existence altogether.

Failure to consider the consequences of federal structure has led many writers on British politics to conclude that an institution like the ALP Federal Executive must prove destructive of traditional parliamentary democracy. Samuel Beer asserts that "rule by an extra-parliamentary body ... is incompatible with Cabinet Government," and R. T. McKenzie, too, has no doubt that such rule "is in fact incompatible with parliamentary government."[20] "Parliamentary government" is largely a system of conventions, which may differ from country to country. The convention referred to here holds that members of a parliament must not be placed in the position of taking orders from an outside body. Presumably, the adherents of this convention recognize that many of a parliament's decisions may be strongly influenced by elements of society not directly represented in it. What they object to, it appears, is the giving of direct orders to a party in parliament with the expectation that they will and must be carried out. Consideration of the adequacy and viability of this convention would be outside the scope of this paper, but it must be emphasized that in Australia parliamentary government and the Federal Executive exist side by side. Under the limiting conditions fostered, if not imposed, by federal structure the practice of extraparliamentary dictation to the parliamentary

[20] Samuel Beer, "Great Britian: From Governing Elite to Organized Mass Parties," in Sigmund Neumann, ed., *Modern Political Parties* (Chicago 1956) p. 51; R. T. McKenzie, "Policy Decision in Opposition: A Rejoinder," in *Political Studies*, vol. 5, no. 2 (June 1957) p. 180.

party is quite different from what it would be in a country like Great Britain, where the party structure has long since been nationalized.

Writers on American politics can hardly be accused of failing to consider the importance of federalism. Yet the resistance of structural federalism to greatly increased National Committee influence on American legislative policies has not been sufficiently appreciated. If it were, prognostications of increased power by the National Committees would not be so frequently or so confidently made.[21] For the purposes of argument, let us assume ideal conditions for such an increase in power. We may imagine that various secular trends have led to the weakening of social federalism as an important factor in American politics. If we let our imaginations go, we may also suppose that the separation of powers has been abolished, that something like a parliamentary system has taken its place, and that all national parties are as cohesive and disciplined as the fondest of the party-government reformers might hope. In Australia every one of these "ideal" conditions exists, and yet structural federalism has prevented effective, continuous extraparliamentary control of the parliamentary party. If Australian experience has any relevance for the United States, those who pin hopes for party reform on the National Committees are bound to be disappointed, no matter what happens to the legislative parties.

Nothing that has been said here should be interpreted as denying that an organization like the National Committee may occasionally manage to take temporary control of some state machines. Even apart from the importance of social federalism, those who benefit by a federal structure may intervene in a single state's affairs now and then, in order to safeguard common interests—as is evident from the record of the ALP Federal Executive. But this is a far cry from the creation of a national party body, independent of the state organizations, which would constitute a threat to all of them. It would be no easy task to persuade the state organizations and officials who would lose by the nationalization of the party to cut their own throats.

---

[21] See, for example, Hugh A. Bone, *Party Committees and National Politics* (Seattle 1958); Sydney Hyman, "The Collective Leadership of Paul Butler," in *Reporter*, vol. 21 (December 24, 1959) pp. 8-12; Stephen K. Bailey, *The Condition of Our National Parties*, Fund for the Republic, Occasional Paper (1959).

The crux of the problem is that states within a federal system are, in fact, unequal in population, national resources, and other bases of influence, even though they are likely to be given equal votes in determining the policy of an extraparliamentary body. This granting of equal representation to unequal states may be tolerable so long as the extraparliamentary body performs the minimal functions necessary to keep the party going as a national entity, but becomes intolerable if that body seeks to be the center of national policymaking. The more influential it becomes, the more serious the struggle over who shall control it. Equal representation disadvantages the large states, representation proportionate to population disadvantages the small ones, and direct national representation without reference to states disadvantages existing state organizations. So long as parties have a federal structure the extraparliamentary body of the party cannot aspire to more than occasional intervention in the legislature without seriously antagonizing some large section of the party. In a word, federal structure represents a more intransigent obstacle to the nationalization of political parties than is generally recognized.

9 American and German Federalism: Political Differences

Arnold Brecht

American federalism, from its inception, was an integral part of the country's democratic institutions. It originated in the same ideas that underlay bills of rights, town meetings, and the Declaration of Independence. Men who in all matters wanted to be independent of British power overseas wished in their local affairs to be free from interference by some far-away central government, just as in their personal matters they desired to be left alone by any kind of government. But they were ready to handle their common affairs in common. Thus, after a short transitional period, foreign affairs, defense, interstate commerce, currency, and similar matters of national concern were considered appropriate subjects be to handled by the federal government, while others were retained for the states, and some were withdrawn from the reach of any government.

American federalism, therefore, was no mere makeshift designed as a substitute for something else that had been lost. It was a *creed* — part and parcel of the democratic creed. In giving federal power and state power each its due, "Dual Federalism" was indeed regarded as a great democratic innovation, fitted to solve many troubles in the world. It entitled Americans to the honor of "having solved for the destinies of man the problem of his capacity for self-government," said Madison. Federalism was "the best guardian . . . of the liberty, safety, and the happiness of man." It was "the last hope of true liberty on the face of the earth."[1]

From Chapter 1 in *Federalism and Regionalism in Germany: The Division of Prussia* by Arnold Brecht (Oxford University Press, 1945), pp. 3-7. Reprinted by permission of the New School for Social Research and the author.

[1] *The Writings of James Madison* (New York, 1910), vol. 9, pp. 68, 136, 430 (note), 521, 605; E. S. Corwin, *The Twilight of the Supreme Court* (New York, 1934), p. 8.

185

German federalism had a different political origin. Little in it stemmed from democratic ideas. The German Confederation *(Der Deutsche Bund)* of 1815-66 was a makeshift, a stopgap, designed to replace the weak bonds constituted by the emperor and the few existing imperial institutions which until the end of the Holy Roman Empire had interlocked the multitude of Germanic states. With the emperor gone, no ties, either actual or symbolic, were left. The Confederation was considered the most suitable substitute. An alliance of the former tenants-in-chief was the logical consequence of the elimination of the overlord, against whose powers they had conducted a merciless war of attrition for hundreds of years.

True, American federalism too replaced ties that had been indirectly provided by Great Britian. But here the federal structure was given a popular basis, and the new bonds rapidly grew much stronger than the old ones had been. In contrast the German Confederation was one of princes and not of peoples. And it was weak. Princes joined forces mainly for the mutual defense of their independence and sovereignty. Each was anxious to retain for his state its separate foreign policy, army, police, currency, and customs barriers. While America discarded a similarly imperfect union within six years after the War of Independence, Germany continued hers for more than fifty years. Only a few minor concessions to the popular trends toward liberty and unity were included in the German Covenant, and the weak central powers of the Confederation were often used to help trample down these movements. Feudalistic features prevailed in the states. German liberalism, therefore, as well as democratic anti-monarchism and national patriotism aligned themselves against this brand of federalism, with its emphasis on princely independence. While the term *federalist* in the United States came to be applied to advocates of a strong federal government, the German term *Föderalist* was used for one who opposed all but the weakest federal government in favor of state independence.

Bismarck's federal constitution of 1871 greatly strengthened federal power, bringing foreign affairs, interstate commerce, currency, and other matters under exclusively federal control. But it preserved the technical character of an alliance of princes. It began with the words:

His Majesty, the King of Prussia on behalf of the North-German Federation; His Majesty, the King of Bavaria; His Majesty, the King of Württemberg; His Royal Highness, the Grand-Duke of Baden; and His Royal Highness, the Grand-Duke of Hessen and of the Rhine—the latter for the section of the Grand-Duchy situated south of the river Main[2]—conclude an eternal federation to protect the federal territory and the law of the land as well as to promote the welfare of the German people. This federation shall be known by the name of German Reich and shall have the following Constitution.

This undemocratic preamble was not changed until the empire collapsed in 1918. Actually, however, it had long been out-moded. Universal interest in the national Reichstag, which was divided not by states but by national parties; national legislation, rapidly growing in all spheres of life; nationwide business not hampered by internal customs barriers; popular feeling and common experience—these and other factors made the national union a matter of the people and the pride of the common man long before the revolution finally did away with the princes whose alliance had created the empire.

There was a change in regime in 1918 not in the Reich alone, but separately in each of the twenty-five constituent states. Twenty-two princes were expelled, or withdrew, by separate action, and three aristocratic city senates had to submit to popular control. If we may use the word revolution for any enforced change in regime, there was not one revolution but twenty-six, although it has sometimes been doubted whether, in the sociological sense of the term, there was any revolution at all. William II himself made a desperate attempt to hold his position as king of Prussia by abdicating only the throne of German emperor, but he had to quit the Prussian as well.

In the beginning, the problem of federalism did not bother the masses very much. Their gravest domestic problem in the first two months, apart from bread and demobilization, was the choice between communism on the model that had been established in Russia a year before—that is, dictatorship by the proletariat or its "vanguard"—and democracy on western models, based on free elections. Friedrich Ebert never wavered in his choice. Whatever weakness he may have shown in other respects, he

---

[2] The section of Hessen north of the river Main was part of the North-German Federation of 1866, and was therefore represented by the Prussian king, as presiding officer of that federation.

steered the boat with a firm and resolute hand through the revolutionary storms that threatened to push it toward some kind of socialistic dictatorship, and he brought it early into the democratic port of general elections for a constituent assembly.

This was a vital decision. Demands for a dictatorship of the proletariat constituted not only a powerful storm but also, to socialists, a luring siren; it was likely from the outset that the socialists would fail to obtain a majority and that thus fidelity to democratic principles might deprive the workers of the greatest opportunity they had ever had to introduce the socialist system to which they adhered. It was, therefore, a decisive factor in German history that Friedrich Ebert meant to be a Social *Democrat,* who refused to give the lie to his democratic convictions simply because the hour was favorable to establish a dictatorship.[3]

The result of the elections held on 19 January 1919 was an assembly in which the socialists, although by far the strongest group, failed indeed to obtain the coveted majority, while three parties together, all bent on establishing a genuinely democratic constitution—the Social Democrats, the Liberals (called Democrats), and the Catholic Center—commanded more than two-thirds of the votes. They framed the Constitution of Weimar.

The preamble of the new Constitution dropped any reference not only to the princes but also to the states. It read:

The German People, in their united branches [*Stämmen*] animated by the will to renew and stabilize their commonwealth [*Reich*] with liberty and justice, to preserve peace at home and abroad, and to promote social progress, have given themselves this Constitution.

While in the imperial Reichstag the people had shared legislative powers only within the framework of a constitution not designed by them, they now drafted their own constitution through their freely elected representatives. They drew up similar constitutions in each separate state, bringing every government, federal and state, under their control.

The difference in origin of German and American federalism could then have seemed a matter of the past. But the historical differences continued to affect the present. There remained most

[3] See Appendix A on the dual source of Ebert's authority. This is not the proper place to describe the historical consequence which Ebert's policy and the communists' opposition to it had with regard to the renascence of the army.

conspicuously the disproportionate size of Prussia and the scattered remainders of small principalities, for neither of which there is any analogy in the United States. Furthermore, relics of other times exercised a remarkable influence on popular feelings and especially on the traditions of state bureaucracies, which often continued to think of their authority as issuing from the Past rather than from the People. In addition, German and American federalism remained distinct in their approaches to the problems of distribution of powers between the national government and the state governments.

There also prevailed a remarkable difference in the share the states had in the federal government. This share was in some respects more strictly secured in Germany, where the delegates to the Federal Council (*Bundesrat,* called *Reichsrat* after 1919) were appointed by the state governments and acted under the direction of the latter, than it is in the United States, where popularly elected senators express their personal views. The states themselves, or their governments, and not the delegates, were members of the German Federal Council.[4] But this strong feature of state power was offset by another—a weakening— factor in the democratic period, for the Weimar Constitution authorized the Reichstag to pass, with a two-thirds majority, any act or even amendment to the Constitution, over the veto of the Federal Council. The one recourse left the Federal Council in such a case was a popular referendum. Yet only when an amendment to the Constitution was at issue could the Council itself ask for the plebiscite; in matters of ordinary legislation this was left to the Reich President, who could not be compelled to act by the Federal Council.[5]

Actually there was no case in which the Reichstag ever passed an amendment to the Constitution over the veto of the Federal Council. Ordinary legislation, however, was so passed in a number of cases, and in none of them was a popular referendum called on the matter.

In view of the fact that a two-thirds majority of the Reichstag could bypass the declared will of the Federal Council, it is a matter of theoretical controversy whether Germany during the

---

[4] Articles 61 and 63 of the Weimar Constitution. Only the delegates of the Prussian provinces had a personal vote. See below, Chapter II and Appendix D.
[5] Articles 74 and 76.

democratic period was still a "federal" country. But whatever our academic vocabulary, the practical importance of the Federal Council and of state rights remained great enough to justify the traditional classification of democratic Germany as federal. The direct membership of the states in the Federal Council was one of the reasons for this practical weight of both the states and the Council.[6] And only by a *breach* of the Weimar Constitution could Franz von Papen and Adolf Hitler, in July 1932 and February 1933, free themselves of Prussia's democratic cabinet and of its influence on the Federal Council.

[6] See F. F. Blachly and M. E. Oatman, *The Government and Administration of Germany* (Johns Hopkins Press, Baltimore, 1928), pp. 52 ff., for a good appraisal of the importance of the Reichsrat, and especially for a clear exposition of its functions in the administrative field. This book is still invaluable for Anglo-American students of German administration.

10   *Federal-State Collaboration in the Nineteenth-Century United States*[*]

DANIEL J. ELAZAR

FEDERALISM: COOPERATIVE OR DUAL

The operation of the American federal system in the nineteenth century has been the subject of much discussion and some examination since the New Deal and the so-called "rise of cooperative federalism." It has generally been assumed that federalism in practice, like federalism in theory in the nine-

From *Political Science Quarterly*, 79 (June 1964), pp. 248-281. Reprinted by permission of The Academy of Political Science and the author.

[*] This essay is based on a study of intergovernmental collaboration in the nineteenth-century United States, conducted under the auspices of the Workshop in American Federalism, University of Chicago, and financed by the Ford Foundation. The major product of the study is the writer's book, *The American Partnership* (Chicago, 1962) which presents the data summarized below in greater depth and detail. Particular acknowedgment is due the Institute of Government and Public Affairs, University of Illinois, which provided me the time and facilities with which to prepare this essay.

teenth century (which is here taken to include the entire period between 1790 and 1913) has been dual federalism, in which the federal and state governments pursued virtually independent courses of action during a period when government activity was, in any case, minimal.[1]

Dual federalism has been defined by Clark, among many others, as "two separate federal and state streams flowing in distinct but closely parallel channels." Perhaps the best definition of the term was that given by Chief Justice Roger B. Taney in the name of the United States Supreme Court, in *Ableman v. Booth* (21 Howard 506), at the height of the era of dual federalism, in 1858: "The powers of the general government, and of the state, although both exist and are exercised within the same territorial limits, are yet separate and distinct sovereignties, acting separately and independently of each other, within their respective spheres." Dual federalism as a doctrine has been expounded at various times by presidents of the United States (particularly while vetoing federal aid measures);[2] by the United States Supreme Court (particularly in opinions restricting the powers of government—federal or state—to act);[3] by spokesmen for the South (particularly when justifying slavery, segregation, or secession);[4] and by conservative business interests (particularly

[1] This thesis has been most persuasively stated by George C. S. Benson in *The New Centralization* (New York, 1941) and Jane Perry Clark in *The Rise of a New Federalism* (New York, 1938), and has been repeated by such eminent authorities as Arthur N. Holcombe in *Our More Perfect Union* (Cambridge, Mass., 1950). A variant thesis, which argues that federal-state administrative cooperation existed in the early days of the Republic and was then replaced by strict dual federalism, has been advanced by Edward S. Corwin (inventor of the term "dual federalism") in *The Twilight of the Supreme Court* (New Haven, 1934) and in other books and by Leonard D. White in his great four-volume study of American administrative history, *The Federalists* (New York, 1948), *The Jeffersonians* (New York, 1951), *The Jacksonians* (New York, 1954) and *The Republican Era* (New York, 1958).

[2] See James D. Richardson (ed.), *Messages and Papers of the Presidents* (Washington, D. C., 1908), for exemplary statements by Thomas Jefferson, James Madison, James Monroe, Andrew Jackson, Franklin Pierce, James Buchanan, and Grover Cleveland, among others.

[3] See, for example, *Collecter* v. *Day* (11 Wallace 113), the Slaughterhouse Cases (16 Wallace 36), *Munn* v. *Illinois* (94 U.S. 113), *Hammer* v. *Dagenhart* (247 U.S. 251), and *Ponzi* v. *Fessendan, et al.* (258 U.S. 254).

[4] The classic statement of the Southern viewpoint is that of Alexander H. Stephens, *A Constitutional View of the War Between the States* (Philadelphia, 1868).

when seeking to avoid government regulation). The doctrine has been expounded as representing classic American federalism so long and so forcefully that it has been accepted, by students of American institutions and others, as fact.

The central hypothesis of this study is that the traditional picture of nineteenth-century American federalism is unreal, that federalism in the United States, in practice if not in theory, has traditionally been cooperative, so that virtually all the activities of government in the nineteenth century were shared activities, involving federal, state, and local governments in their planning, financing, and execution. The pattern of sharing in American federalism was established, in its essentials, in the first decades after the adoption of the Constitution. This study seeks to explain how that pattern has continued to evolve since then. Its central conclusions are that the theory of dual federalism was not viable when applied to concrete governmental problems in specific situations even in the early days of the Republic; that dual federalism when interpreted to mean demarcation of responsibilities and functions has never worked in practice; and that, while the amount of governmental activity on all planes in relation to the total activity of American society (the "velocity of government") has increased, the governmental activity that existed in the nineteenth century was shared in much the same manner as governmental activity in the twentieth century. All this is true despite formal pronouncements to the contrary, made by the political leadership of the day who spoke in terms of demarcation but practiced cooperation.

THE ELEMENTS OF COOPERATIVE FEDERALISM

The roots of cooperative federalism are entwined with the roots of federalism itself. It was during the colonial period that the four elements which later coalesced to form the pattern of intergovernmental cooperation first appeared on the American scene. Among these elements were a federalist theory of governments,[5] a dual governmental structure, some specific cooperative

[5] For a discussion of this theory of federalism, see Carl Becker, *The Declaration of Independence* (New York, 1958), Chap. III. Part of the theoretical debate over the nature of the British Empire prior to 1776 centered on specific cases of parliamentary agents engaging in unconstitutional unilateral action within the colonies rather than conforming to the constitutional patterns of crown-colonial cooperation as they were conceived by the colonists, though the discussions were not phrased in those terms.

programs, and some administrative techniques for intergovernmental collaboration.[6]

These four elements of theory, structure, program, and technique can be traced through the subsequent evolution of the
American governmental partnership. They were first combined
under a general American government by the Second Continental Congress after the declaration of American independence in
1776. Consequently, the patterns of intergovernmental cooperation that developed informally during the Revolutionary War
antedate even the Articles of Confederation. That document, the
first written constitution of the United States, implicitly provided
for collaboration in a manner highly reminiscent of the then
recently sundered relationship between colonies and crown, as it
had been viewed in American political theory and as it was
embodied in the structure of colonial government institutions.
Even the programs requiring collaboration (defense, taxation)
were much the same. With the development of a national policy
of grants-in-aid based on the Western land in the Northwest
Ordinances of 1785 and 1787, the creation of the Confederation-
sponsored Bank of North America in 1784, and the general
reliance of the Confederation Congress on state officals to execute its actions, the colonial techniques of collaboration were
also embraced by the Confederation.

It is unquestionably true that collaboration under the Articles
was over-dependent on the actions of the states and often failed
in practice. This was, of course, purposely changed with the
adoption of the Constitutuion in 1789 and in the course of its
translation into action during Washington's first administration.
While the "intentions of the framers" are always subject to
dispute, it seems safe to say that the Constitution is oriented to
neither cooperative nor dual federalism per se. It provides for
dual institutions, some cooperative programs, and a wide range
of concurrent powers which can either be divided between the
federal government and the states or shared by them in various
cooperative programs. By and large, the decision of the American
people has not been to separate functions by government but to
maintain dual institutions which share responsibility for the
implementation of specific functions. This "decision" has not

[6] For a discussion of land grants in the colonial period, see Mathias N. Orfield,
Federal Land Grants to the States, With Special Reference to Minnesota (Min-
neapolis, 1915), Part I, 5-30.

been made through a prior conscious design but through a continuous series of specific decisions involving concrete programs. The continuing evolution of the theories, structures, programs, and techniques of the federalism that emerged from this process is what we today term cooperative federalism.

THE ARCHITECTS OF COOPERATIVE FEDERALISM

Just as the founding fathers did not perceive the future role of political parties in the United States, it seems that they did not plan on the development of cooperative federalism as we know it. The majority of the theoretically-oriented founding fathers either viewed the federal system as dual and separate with the states having the dominant role and the powers of the federal government confined to those objects specifically enumerated in the Constitution or as one in which the national government would have the dominant role while the states were to become relatively weak repositories of residual local powers.

The men who became the architects of American federalism did not view the federal system as one in which there was to be either a perpetual struggle between the federal and state governments for dominance or an irrevocable separation of their respective functions for the sake of amity between them. Avoiding the premises of legalistic thought, they did not view the two planes as rivals, but as partners in government who were to share responsibility for a wide range of activities for the mutual benefit of the nation as a whole and for its constituent states.

These architects did not leave a formally organized and recognized body of theory behind them because they wrote of their theories almost exclusively in response to specific practical problems. Nevertheless, examination of their official reports and other documents which they produced during their public careers does reveal some coherent patterns of thought on the proper nature and goals of American federalism.[7]

---

[7] Some of the most important of these documents setting forth the cooperative approach are: Albert Gallatin, "Report on Roads and Canals," *American State Papers: Miscellaneous*, I, 724-921 (April 4, 1808); John C. Calhoun, "Report on Roads and Canals, communicated to the House of Representatives, January 14, 1819," in Calhoun, *Works* (New York, 1855), V, 40-54; Calhoun, "Report on the Condition of the Military Establishment and Fortifications, Communicated to Congress by the President, December 7, 1824," *ibid.*, 141; Mahlon Dickerson, *Report on the President's Message as Respects the Distribution of the United States Surplus*, 21st Congress, 1st Session, December 1830.

Foremost among the men who led the movement toward intergovernmental cooperation to meet the problems of a dynamic society were Albert Gallatin and John C. Calhoun, who pioneered the formulation and implementation of cooperative programs during the first four decades of the Republic. Aside from these two principal architects of American federalism, many people made major contributions to the development of the federal system as we know it. Other top-ranking officials in the federal executive branch, particularly in the Treasury, War, and Interior Departments, led the federal government into the field of specific cooperative activies when cooperation, as such, was not popular as a doctrine. The professionals in the federal and state goverments, who were interested in promoting specific programs for the benefit of the whole nation and its constituent parts, provided cadres for the initiation and implementation of cooperative programs in undramatic ways while the rest of the country virtually ignored them and the governments they served. The advocates of specific programs, who were not in or of government at any level but who wanted to see the development of certain public activities at all levels (or regardless of level), provided a basis for the mobilization of popular support in those cases where government did take part. Finally, much of the development of the system was stimulated by the members of the Congress of the United States and the several state legislatures who, because of their interest in the general welfare or as an outgrowth of their local concerns, supported intergovernmental cooperation in those fields of endeavor which seemed most necessary to them despite an overall theoretical disposition to limit government in general and to separate by level those few activities that were considered to be of legitimate governmental concern.

Cooperative Federalism Between 1789 and 1848

American federalism has evolved over three historical periods, all bound together by the thread of intergovernmental collaboration. A strong case can be made to demonstrate that the three periods of federalism correspond to the three major periods in post-colonial American history generally. The particular characteristics of federalism in these three periods can be identified by the forms of intergovernmental collaboration that predominated in each, though in every period the other forms of cooperation existed alongside the predominant ones. The difference between the three periods is not a difference in the nature of intergovernmental cooperation but in the predominant forms by which such cooperation was effected.

The first period encompassed the formative years of the American nation and its federal system, including the Revolutionary and Federalist eras, the flourishing and subsequent decline of the Jeffersonians, and the rise of "Jacksonian Democracy." When it came to a close in the mid-eighteen-forties, the United States had fought its second war of independence, turned its back on Europe to concentrate on westward expansion, and was just completing the continental expansion of the nation's boundaries.

This was also the period in which the mercantilist orientation of the American economy which openly allotted to government a major share in the economic development of the nation persisted and finally declined, to be replaced by the laissez-faire persuasion which, at least in theory, denied government any but a minimal role.[8] In fact, the last decade of this period was marked by the fluidity and confusion characteristic of a change in eras, both in the economic and governmental realms, since the changes in the forms of federalism coincided with the changes in economic organization.

This first period contributed refined versions of the vital ideas of natural law and constitutionalism to the American mystique, as expressed in the basic documents that emerged from the Revolutionary era. As part of this set of ideas, the concepts of federalism were defined and refined as well. Dominant in this formative period were the activities of the major architects of pre-twentieth-century cooperative federalism, Gallatin near the beginning and Calhoun near the end.

The major vehicles of intergovernmental cooperation in this period were the joint stock company (in which federal, state, and local governments, as well as private parties, joined to invest in corporations established to undertake specific projects, usually in the realm of internal improvements and banking) for long-term cooperative projects, and the cooperative survey (in which the

[8] For a discussion of the mercantilist approach in American political economy during this period, see Curtis P. Nettels, "British Mercantilism and the Economic Development of the Thirteen Colonies," *The Journal of Economic History*, XII (1952), 105-14.

federal government would send or lend Army Engineers to the states to survey and plan internal improvement projects) coupled with the widespread use of federal technicians by the states as a means of providing federal services-in-aid to the latter. During this period the majority of the states then in the Union did not have extensive federal lands within their boundaries, so the tone of cooperation was set by programs designed for the states without public lands. Cooperation in the field of banking was the most formally structured on a nationwide basis. Internal improvement programs usually involved formal arrangements, but were almost always tailored to specific situations in each state and even for each project. Federal aid to education was vital, but generally consisted of "back-door financing" through federal "reimbursement" of certain state-incurred expenditures with the implicit understanding that the funds would be used for education. The major continuing programmatic concerns of American government had already emerged during the first period. They were the extension of internal improvements, the maintenance of a sound nationwide fiscal system, the establishment of appropriate educational facilities, and, to a more limited extent, the provision of necessary public welfare aids.

In the field of internal improvements, the first period was given over, in the main, to water transportation, primarily through canals, and, to a lesser extent, to overland transportation via wagon roads. One of the best examples of federal-state collaboration in canal construction was the opening of the Dismal Swamp Canal, connecting Norfolk, Virginia, with Albemarle Sound in North Carolina. In 1816, after several abortive local attempts to construct a canal through the Great Dismal Swamp of Virginia, the State of Virginia joined the State of North Carolina, the City of Norfolk, and private investors in the creation of a joint stock company to implement a canal plan prepared by the Army Engineers in 1808 as part of a national blueprint for internal improvement.

Informal cooperation between state and federal officials was developed to advance construction. This included federal assistance in securing a supervising engineer for the state (1816), as well as a second survey by qualified federal engineers (1817). This cooperation involved the highest administrative levels of both the federal government and the state, including the Presi-

dent of the United States; the Secretaries of State, Treasury, and
War; the diplomatic corps; government bureaus such as the Army
Engineers, the governor of Virginia, his agents, and the Virginia
Board of Public Works. Some of this cooperation came about
through direct interlevel contracts made through the normal
administrative channels. Part of it came about through the state
officials' use of the services of their senators and representatives
in Washington.

Ten years later, despite the company's efforts and further
informal federal-state collaboration, the canal had still to be
completed. Despite periodic state subsidies, the company still
lacked the requisite funds. In 1826, the Virginians, with the
active assistance of the War Department, were able to persuade
Congress to invest $150,000 in the project and, in that way, to
acquire 600 (out of a total of 1,240) shares in the company. Once
the federal government became a partner in the enterprise, it
provided the additional professional and administrative services,
as well as the needed funds, for the completion of the project.
Despite the oratorical denunciations of "states'-rights" Virginians, this federal "intervention" succeeded in bringing the canal
to a state of readiness by 1828. For the next three decades the
federal government and the State of Virginia continued their
cooperative efforts to maintain and improve the canal. Though
the formally cooperative aspects of the program came to an end
with the coming of the Civil War, the canal is still in use as an
important part of the intracoastal waterway system.

Closer examination of the details of this program reveals the
three major areas of federal-state cooperation characteristic in
projects of this nature: construction of the canal, maintenance
and improvement of its facilities, and control over the administration of its operations. The first two areas involved both fiscal aid
and the services of governmental personnel. The third involved
cooperation between federal and state officials. While the federal
government did not become a full partner in this enterprise until
it was already under construction, once it did enter the partnership its role became a crucial and even dominant one. Yet this
did not come about through the lessening of the state's power but
through a coincidence of interest (often made explicit in the
correspondence between state and federal officials at the time)

between the state and federal governments. To ensure this coincidence of interest the state as a whole and the locality involved both had means of influencing federal policy and actions through their senators and representatives.

Administration of the canal was a joint federal-state venture. The federal executive delegated the power of proxy (to represent the federal interest in the project's administration) to the Collector of the Port of Norfolk and detailed other federal personnel to aid in the construction of the canal. The state executive, pursuant to earlier acts of the Legislature, provided for the State Board of Public Works to act as proxies and supervisors for the state which, through its greater direct role in the company (which was a quasi-official state agency) became primarily responsible for actual construction. Cooperative procedures were then developed by the two sets of officials involved. Construction and, later, maintenance proceeded under the direction of the company, supervised by the State Board of Public Works and utilizing federal engineers and equipment. The company reported to the state and to the federal government and the State Board also reported to the Treasury and War Departments. Company policy was decided by its board of directors dominated by the United States and the State of Virginia, whose representatives operated in concert within a community of interest. The few attempts to change company policy that were made were in every case directed against both governments by the non-governmental shareholders rather than by one against the other.

The case of the Dismal Swamp Canal is typical. By the third decade of the nineteenth century, the pattern of intergovernmental cooperation was already clear in projects such as this one, of which there were many. Changes were indeed made in subsequent years but they were changes designed to improve the mechanisms rather than to modify the basic relationships. While federal control over standards tended to grow, state control over processes grew as a counterbalance.

Collaboration under the Constitution in the fiscal field may be said to have begun with federal assumption of the states' Revolutionary War debts in 1790. During the seventeen-nineties, federal reimbursement of state debts already paid, coupled with the sale of state lands, furnished sufficient income for most of the states to maintain themselves without resorting to taxation.[9] Though the level of state governmental activities was low prior to 1816, the states began to develop a tradition of spending money with relatively little responsibility for raising revenues. This was coupled with a developing, albeit unrecognized, reliance on the federal government for funds to initiate and support the major programs of each era. While it may be argued that the reimbursement funds "rightfully" belonged to the states in the first place, in the last analysis they came from the federal treasury and were used for projects which the states would not have been able to finance alone because of local opposition to increased taxation.

Two other major cooperative fiscal programs were established by the first Congress. The first involved the levying of a direct tax among the states, which were given quotas based on the constitutional formula and required to raise and deliver the taxes to the federal government. Direct taxes were levied in the above manner intermittently over the next century. The second program involved the inauguration of a central banking system for the United States through the chartering of the first Bank of the United States as a federal-controlled agency.

Federal involvement in the banking system is almost as old as banking as an institution in this country. When the first Bank of the United States was established in 1791, only four other banks existed in the entire United States and one of these four, the Bank of North America, had been chartered by the Confederation Congress as a quasi-national bank.[10]

In the early period, the great majority of banks were either state-owned, joint stock companies in which the state was a major shareholder, or controlled by the state through special charter provisions. The Bank of the United States, a government-controlled bank under federal auspices, served as the fiscal and banking arm of the federal government and manager of the federal deposits. In this capacity it dominated the American financial scene prior to 1800. According to Shultz and Caine, "Through its

[9] William J. Shultz and M. R. Caine, *Financial Development of the United States* (New York, 1937), 117-18.
[10] Bray Hammond, *Banks and Politics in America, from the Revolution to the Civil War* (Princeton, 1957), 144.

branch organization it cooperated with and to some extent controlled the newly-created state banks throughout the country."[11]

Under this first and subsequent national banking programs, a significant amount of intergovernmental cooperation developed. Some of this cooperation was formally written into law by both nation and state, while some of it evolved informally in response to obvious situations and needs. The directors of the Bank, which was located in Philadelphia, did not originally intend to establish branches in other parts of the country, but pressures from stockholders in other cities soon forced them into widespread branch banking, primarily because so few banks existed outside of the Northeast. Four branches were opened in the spring of 1792 after some attempts were made to absorb the four existing state banks. This latter move was resisted by many of the same people who had previously supported creation of the national bank against those who felt it to be a threat to states' rights as well as a corrupting influence in an agrarian society. Just as they recognized the need for some centralized banking institution, they also feared too much centralization and resisted any attempts to eliminate the system of dual institutions which makes cooperative federalism possible.

The United States Bank soon began to function as a clearing house and source of capital for the various state banks, as well as serving as fiscal arm of the federal government. As such it was accepted as an asset by the more conservative banks and as an undesired threat by the more reckless and speculative ones. Hammond describes its operation in these words:

Being the main government depository and having offices in the principal commercial cities, the Bank was the general creditor of the other banks. It had the account of the largest single transactor in the economy — the federal government — and the receipts of the government being mostly in the notes of state banks and these notes being deposited in the Bank, it could not help being their creditor. By pressing them for payment of the notes and checks received against them, the Bank automatically exercised a general restraint on the banking system. . . . This restraint upon bank lending came later to be designated central bank control of credit.[12]

[11] Shultz and Caine, 125.
[12] Hammond, 198-99.

Congress allowed the Bank's charter to expire in 1811, despite administration support for its renewal, as a result of the opposition generated by a coalition of extreme states'-rights conservatives and spokesmen for Eastern businessmen interested in speculation on the frontier, where less control over fiscal matters would aid their highly speculative ventures. As in the debate of 1791 and in many subsequent debates over similar subjects, the arguments this coalition used against the Bank were those of constitutionality, but the motivations were those of business. On the other hand, the new agrarians, primarily Westerners, wanted to maintain the National Bank precisely because the state banks had already proved their inability to meet what were, in essence, national needs, in particular those related to westward expansion.

The nation soon discovered how useful the central bank had been. The War of 1812 brought with it serious fiscal problems for the federal government and the states, many of which could have been avoided had a central bank been in existence. In 1816 Congress reversed itself and voted the establishment of the second Bank of the United States. The reversal was made possible by a parting of the speculator — states'-rights coalition. While the speculators continued to oppose central banking as interfering with their opportunity to manipulate the nation's fiscal affairs, a number of states'-rights advocates supported the new federal bank as an aid to the states in their struggle, often against the speculation interests, for fiscal solvency. They were led to take this position as a result of the contrast between their experiences with the intergovernmental collaboration that had developed between the states and the first Bank and their experiences with "free" banking between 1811 and 1816. Indeed, their major demand in preparing the charter for the second Bank was that its collaborative aspects be strengthened. Cooperative federalism in the banking field was already being used to develop a system in which the duty and ability of the states to take action was both stimulated and guaranteed by the federal government.

The most forceful argument for federal responsibility in monetary matters, from the constitutional point of view, came from John C. Calhoun, who had assumed Gallatin's role as leading architect of cooperative federalism in his generation. His statement, in this case as in so many others, has a most modern ring. It was Calhoun's view that when any private enterprise (in this case the financial interests) grows strong enough to exercise a power granted to the federal government under the Constitution (in this case, control over the soundness of the currency) it must be subject to regulation in the public interest. This regulation is best achieved by reassumption of the power by the federal government, in the interests of the public and of the states.[13]

The charter that was finally enacted made it quite clear that the second Bank was a continuation of the first. Thus it may be said that the same national banking system served the country for forty of the forty-five years between 1791 and 1836. The new charter gave the federal government the power to require the Bank to establish at least one branch in each state, under certain conditions. In addition, the bank was specifically designated as the principal depository of the United States Treasury, though the state banks, which had inherited the federal deposits after the demise of the first Bank, under a different cooperative program were allowed to keep some deposits because they were so dependent on them to stay solvent.

Even without the National Bank, cooperative relationships had developed between the U. S. Treasury and the state banks. The latter served as federal depositories and disbursing agents during periods when the National Bank did not exist and also parallel to it when it did. As long as the mercantilist view of the role of government in the economy prevailed for a majority of the nation, this cooperation continued. It was only when this view was abandoned due to changing times that the forms of cooperation created under it became inadequate.

After 1828 the operations of the U. S. Bank centered around forcing the state banks to adopt more conservative banking practices. This attempt came just as the more radical and speculative business elements were attaining political power under the Jacksonian Democracy. As a result, their cries that the Bank was strangling business expansion in the interests of a few wealthy Eastern capitalists fell on willing ears and doomed the second Bank in much the same manner as the first had been. Even so, the political struggle that led to Jackson's veto of the recharter bill in 1832 sealed the fate of the Bank more because of conflicts

[13] Calhoun, *Works*, II, *passim*.

between persons in the political arena than for reasons of principle, and certainly did not imply a rejection of federal-state collaboration.

Beginning in 1833 the $6,500,000 in federal deposits were gradually withdrawn as the funds were spent (gradually, to prevent a sudden collapse of the nation's finances, a tribute to the role played by the Bank as the central force in the national monetary system). Newly received funds were deposited in the state banks once again, as they had been after the demise of the first Bank, where they remained until the establishment of independent federal depositories in the eighteen-forties.

The first century of the American Republic witnessed a struggle between advocates of a national banking system designed to bring some measure of national order to the fiscal scene and advocates of maximum local control over the money system. For forty years prior to the administration of Andrew Jackson, the nationalists were successful in perpetuating a centralized, cooperative, banking system. In the eighteen-thirties the tide turned and the localists were able to decentralize the system. During the Civil War, the passage of the National Banking Act of 1863 signified another turn in the direction of order through the creation of a uniform national currency and nationally applied bank standards which in themselves gave rise to a new cooperative regulatory program in which the federal and state governments shared in the regulation of the newly created national banks. Finally, the creation of the Federal Reserve System in 1913 brought both the national and local approaches together in a workable compromise.

Collaboration in the field of education in the states without public lands was less direct in the early period. Before 1837, one major means by which federal assistance for the establishment of public schools was made available was through the reimbursement process. It has already been indicated that federal assumption of the states' Revolutionary War debts and the general government's reimbursement of those debts already paid by the states provided the bulk of the states' revenues prior to the War of 1812. During that conflict, and subsequent ones through the Spanish-American War, the federal government again had to rely upon the states for a major share of the immediate financing of the nation's war effort. Whenever necessary, the states raised, equipped, and supplied their troops with the promise of federal reimbursement after the cessation of hostilities. While the War of 1812 marked the high point in the role of the states in financing a war effort, reimbursable state defense expenditures continued to be made for Indian conflicts, international border disputes, and even for major national wars, throughout the nineteenth century.

Federal reimbursement of war expenditures provided the states with larger amounts of revenue for use in providing domestic services than would otherwise have been possible for the states to raise through universally unpopular taxation. Furthermore, in the negotiations for reimbursement, the states' Washington agents and congressional delegations were often able to have expenditures of less than strict legitimacy included in the final accounting. This was possible because it soon became widely understood and accepted that federal reimbursement funds would be used by the states wholly or partly to finance the establishment of free public educational systems. Here, as in the case of internal improvement and fiscal organization, the problem of education was simultaneously of both local and nationwide concern and, consequently, was attacked by all planes of government. In the public land states, the federal-state-local partnership could operate through the medium of the land grant by which the federal government provided potentially handsome endowments for public education from elementary school through the university. Constitutional scruples on the part of a strong and determined minority prevented the direct, overt extension of federal aid to those states without public lands. However, since the felt need for federal assistance and stimulation in the field of education remained, the reimbursement system was seized upon to provide an acceptable alternative to formal grants-in-aid.

Thus it was that the states would file claims for reimbursement with the War Department, with the necessary substantiating documents, and then would secure congressional approval for any out-of-the-ordinary claims by letting it be understood that the funds involved would be used to promote education, often through the creation of a permanent fund that would provide annual benefits. In some states, such as Virginia, the interest on the invested reimbursement funds provided the state's sole contribution to public education for decades. Even in New

England they were influential and important, particularly in stimulating the states to enforce their own compulsory school laws which were often ignored when left entirely to the local communities.

In 1837, the United States Treasury surplus was distributed among the states by a formula based on each state's population. While the strict constructionists prevented formal earmarking, a provision was inserted in the act of Congress making the distribution a loan and providing for recall of the funds should the federal government deem it advisable (that is, if the funds were used by the states for purposes other than the two implicit options of education or internal improvement). Though the Panic of 1837 ended the surplus distribution in less than a year, and the one attempt to revive it in 1841 also failed in a year's time, the amount of funds accruing to the more populous Eastern states did much to offset the national imbalance that resulted from federal grant-in-land assistance to the Western states. Furthermore, by federal and state law as well as through local custom, the surplus distribution monies, like the proceeds of the land grants (and, in most cases, the reimbursements), were placed in earmarked permanent investment funds whose incomes were used for the support of education year after year. In a majority of the states, these permanent funds have remained in existence, albeit with the original federal funds diluted by other increments. During the nineteenth century they became administrative devices which stretched the impact of federal aid to education over the years, renewed its impact annually, and gave the states a lever by which to gain control over school systems and educational endeavors in order to raise educational standards.

While social welfare programs were fewer in the early period, significant advances in that field were also made through federal-state-local collaboration. A few examples will suffice. Government support for education for the handicapped had its origins in the Hartford Asylum for the Deaf and Dumb founded in 1817 under private, church-supported, auspices and transformed into a public institution in 1819 through a federal land grant and cooperative arrangements with the six New England states. The successful federal-state partnership in this pilot project stimulated the creation of schools for the deaf and dumb in other sections of the nation. The drive for better treatment for the insane led to the development of state insane asylums in the mid-nineteenth century, many of which were initially constructed through the use of federal land grants, reimbursement funds, or the surplus distribution. Veterans of the nation's wars were awarded lands, the pre-Civil War equivalent of pensions, through federal-state cooperative projects. Less formally, a network of marine hospitals for the nation's seamen was constructed and maintained along the sea coasts and inland waterways by joint federal-state action. Each of these early welfare programs involved not only a sharing of fiscal responsibility, but the development of routinized administrative collaboration to bring the programs to fruition. It was this routinized administrative collaboration which set the tone and the pace for cooperative federalism in the period.

COOPERATIVE FEDERALISM BETWEEN 1848 AND 1913

The landmark that comes closest to marking the end of the formative period and the beginning of the second era in American federalism was the Mexican War. After the war the questions of manifest destiny, commercial expansion, and political democracy that had provided the impetus for government activities during the first period gave way to concern over slavery, industrialization, and the settlement of the newly acquired Far West, opening up a new set of problems for government.

While the great land grant programs which dominated the second period were created during the formative period, and even antedated the other forms of cooperation, they were almost entirely confined to the public land states, which did not become major factors on the American political scene until the Age of Jackson and did not begin to set the national pace until the middle of the nineteenth century. The second period can be considered to begin from the time when land grant programs became the predominant form of intergovernmental cooperation, that is, when their impact on government became greater than any other form of cooperative federalism and other forms of cooperation began to be measured in relation to the level of collaboration in the public land states. The transition from the formative period began during the Jackson administration, with the demise of the U. S. Bank, the greatest of all the joint stock companies, and the distribution of the surplus revenue in 1837 which was partly designed to balance the land grants to the Western states. By mid-century, the states admitted to the Union after ratification of the Constitution outnumbered the original thirteen. Though not all of the former were public land states, the majority shared in the problems of the West. They provided the support necessary for the establishment of the land grant as a major means of implementing national policy. The Land Grant College Act of 1862 marks the triumph of this policy, in that it was applied without distinction to all the states, east and west.

The second period lasted for the remainder of the nineteenth century. During this period the patterns of American democracy evolved after 1775 were subjected to their greatest domestic tests. In the political realm, there was the challenge of classical states'-rights, secession, disunion, and reconstruction. In the economic realm the complex of radical individualist and anti-government doctrines known as laissez-faire was the order of the day. The slavery issue and its outgrowth, segregation of the Negroes, tore at the fabric of American democratic ideals. Politically, this was the Republican era. The Democratic party, in power as the nation's majority party at mid-century, was already declining. During the first decade of the second period, the Republican party wooed and won more or less of a majority of the voters who turn to it as the best vehicle available to respond to the era's major issues. Though challenged by Populists from its own ranks and by a Democracy led by the resurgent South, the Republican party managed to maintain its position throughout the period.

Between 1848 and 1913 the hope of the American people lay in the West as never before or since. The West, whatever it may have been in reality, became the shining haven of the American dream. It was this period that added the refined idea of the frontier to the American mystique and, in reality, it was in the West that cooperative federalism flourished and matured. The great land grant programs set the tone for intergovernmental cooperation in the older states because of their expansion in the new ones. Uniformly structured land grants for internal improvements and education dominated the stage, supplemented by various types of federal subsidies, new cooperative developments in the regulatory field, and by an increasing amount of informal cooperation among professionals on all levels of government. Through the land grant the impact of the federal government was felt in almost every field of activity throughout the West and in most of the East.

During the second period, as in the first, problems of internal improvement, fiscal organization, education, and public welfare were the dominant continuing concerns of government on all planes. However, during this period, there was a paradoxical intensification of support for the theory of dual federalism simultaneous with a sharpening of the structures and techniques of cooperative federalism and an expansion of collaborative programs into new fields.

The actual transfer of federal lands to the states under the terms of a grant-in-land was begun in 1802, with Ohio's achievement of statehood. Under the terms of the Northwest Ordinance of 1785, Ohio received a grant of one section of land per township, designed to go directly for the establishment and support of public schools. This school grant was subsequently extended, with some modifications, to every new public land state. Experience soon demonstrated that the purposes of the grant would be better achieved if it were administered by the states rather than by local government and if a minimum price for the lands were established in the federal grant. The grant was also expanded to include up to four sections per township by the end of the century. Later conditions imposed by Congress included the requirement that any lands sold be disposed of at advertised public sales only.

This first land grant program contained within it the seeds of many of the principles and procedures that were evolved in later federal grants-in-aid, both land and cash. The grant was a general one, applicable to all states carved out of the public domain as a matter of course, though, because it was applied to new states only as they were organized, specific legislation was necessary to apply the grant in each case. The amount of the grant was set down in the general law and was uniform for all the states organized while the general law was in effect. Finally, the grant was not a gift. It came with specific conditions attached, including an obligation on the part of the state to create township or state-administered permanent trust funds based on the proceeds of the sale or leasing of the granted land to be used exclusively for the promotion of public elementary education and an obligation on the part of the federal government to provide indemnity lands where the designated school sections were otherwise pre-empted. It is true that the conditions attached to this first grant were rudimentary; however, these rudimentary conditions were expanded and tightened as experience proved necessary.

Ohio also received the first land grants for higher education and for internal improvements. As the first state to be carved out of the federal public domain, it was the testing ground for many of the early land grant programs. Yet Ohio was only the first of the thirty public land states to receive grants-in-land for programs falling within the scope of all four continuing concerns of government. Of the other twenty states, all, with the possible exception of Hawaii, have received land grants for programs in two or more categories. It would not be amiss to say that virtually every major governmental function in the public land states benefited from federal land grants directly or indirectly. The grants directly stimulated, financed, or helped to finance vital governmental operations. Indirectly, the pervasiveness of the public domain, and the need for its proper disposition to enable a state to grow, served to involve the state government either formally or informally through the political process in all federal land activities that took place within its boundaries. In this manner the public domain came to serve as the integrating factor in the development of cooperative action between the federal government and the states.

Federal land distribution programs fell into three basic categories. First was the system of land grants made by the federal government to the various states to aid them in developing education, internal improvement, and welfare programs. Over the years grants were made to the states for elementary education, higher education, general internal improvements, land reclamation, river and harbor improvements, public buildings, public institutions, and veterans' benefits. These grants were designed to make basic contributions to the growth of vital public services in the various states in a manner closely resembling the monetary grants-in-aid of the twentieth century.

There was also a system of federal land grants for education and internal improvements made through the states to private companies, primarily for roads, canals, and railroads, but also for academies and colleges. Under such arrangements, the states became the implementing agencies for the federal government administering the distribution and proper use of the grants.

Finally there were the federal programs designed to dispose of the public domain without formally including the states. These programs in the main consisted of the various homestead, mineral, and tree culture acts; grants to certain Western railroads primarily situated outside of state boundaries at the time of the grants; and some townsite and local improvement grants that generally were made to embryonic towns prior to statehood. Even those programs did not function outside of the sphere of federal-state cooperation, since the states either developed concurrent "matching" programs of their own which were then coordinated with the federal grants or were able to gain a say in the formulation and execution of the federal programs through their influence in Congress.

The real import of cooperative federalism in the second period can best be understood when the full impact of federal-aided programs in a single state is assessed as a unified whole. Minnesota is a case-in-point. Federal land grant programs encompassed almost every field of governmental activity in Minnesota. There were grant programs for education (common school, university, agricultural, and mechanical college grants); internal improvements (general internal improvements, railroad construction, river and harbor improvements, and public buildings grants); welfare (salt spring and public institutions grants); reclamation (swamp and overflowed land grants); and conservation (Itasca State Park grant). In addition, funds from the unearmarked federal land grants were instrumental in the founding and maintenance of almost every public institution in the state.

Though few cash grants were in existence, Minnesota did receive money for internal improvements (from the Five Per Cent Fund);[14] welfare (grants for the support of the Minnesota Soldiers' Home); defense (militia grants); and education (the Hatch Act and the second Morrill Act). Goods and materials were granted to the state for programs in science (weights and mea-

[14] The Five Per Cent Fund was an annual federal grant of five per cent of the proceeds from the sale of federal lands within the state to the state for internal improvements. This grant was originated in 1802.

sures, specimens from U. S. scientific expeditions); agriculture and conservation (seed distributions, fish stocking); education and welfare (distribution and exchange of documents for libraries, schools, and public institutions). Cooperative activities involving coordination of services included the fields of education (exchange of information); science (meteorological reports, geological surveys); law enforcement (cooperation in hunting law violators, jailing of federal offenders); conservation (protection of forests); land settlement (homestead and tree culture programs); and agriculture (cooperation in grasshopper eradication, exchange of experiment station research reports, exchange of information).

The financial impact of these programs on the State of Minnesota was generally greater than that of the mid-twentieth-century grants-in-aid. In the latter third of the nineteenth century, a greater portion of the state's revenues came from federal sources than in any subsequent period. At times, revenues from federal sources, including direct federal payments to the state and income from federal grants, represented over forty per cent of the total annual revenue of Minnesota, and after 1865, never fell below twenty per cent.[15] The analogous percentage in 1959 was 25.3, actually somewhat lower than the apparent annual average in the late nineteenth century.

In the nineteenth, as in the twentieth century, federal aid stimulated matching state contributions. In some cases there were formal matching requirements attached to the federal grants. For example, the first Morrill Act required the states to appropriate funds for construction of buildings for their agricultural colleges in order to retain the principal of the federal grant intact for the support of actual instructional activities. In this way, federal-originated funds involved state funds in the development of joint collaborative programs. Between 1862 and 1900, identifiable cooperative programs claimed an apparent average of fifty per cent of the state's total expenditure, excluding amounts spent by the state in informal collaborative arrangements and for the general expenses of executives, such as the

[15] The percentage of income from federal sources between 1865 and 1900 at selected intervals was: 1866, 37.6; 1875, 38.0; 1880, 38.6; 1885, 41.8; 1890, 22.2; 1895, 30.6; 1900, 30.6.

governor, who were directly and continuously involved *ex officio* in the administration of cooperative programs.[16]

The impact of federal aid was state-wide and federal funds penetrated into every county. The state's major activities were clearly dependent on federal aid. Minnesota's military establishment, important in defending the state's settlers against marauding Indians, relied heavily on federal funds. State and local internal improvements were almost entirely federal-supported. Minnesota's railroads were almost entirely the products of formal federal-state collaboration and even the Northern Pacific Railroad, recipient of a direct federal land grant that ostensibly bypassed the state, was brought into the sharing arrangement in several ways.

At the instigation of the territorial legislature, Minnesota's major roads were constructed by the Army Engineers even prior to statehood and were then transferred to state control, while the federal Five Per Cent Fund furnished most of the money for county roads and bridges before the advent of the automobile. In 1875, for example, the Five Per Cent Fund paid for twenty-seven internal improvement projects in twenty counties. Ten years later, the annual distribution of the Fund was used for fifty-one projects in thirty-eight counties. At the same time, the land grant endowed internal improvement permanent fund was also being used for local roads, bridges, and like improvements.

Minnesota's school system benefited greatly from the semi-annual subsidy distributed from the earnings of the common school land grant. In 1866 schools in forty-two counties with a total enrollment of 50,564 met the state educational requirements and received grants from the permanent school fund. Subsequently, schools in every county in the state shared in the annual distributions from the funds. By 1895, some 276,000 students were benefiting from the federal grant. In addition, the Permanent School Fund was used as a revolving fund to provide capital loans for the construction of elementary and high school buildings in every school district and town in the state. In 1895, loans totaling $224,906 were made to 249 school districts in

[16] The percentage of total state "matching" expenditures between 1862 and 1900 at selected intervals was: 1862, 47.6; 1866, 49.1; 1875, 44.7; 1880, 52.4; 1885, 51.3; 1890, 50.1; 1895, 44.3; 1900, 48.3.

seventy-two counties. The State University's operating costs were almost entirely borne by the earnings of the University land grants and direct federal appropriations, including the budgets of the Agriculture Experiment Station and the State Geological Survey. A major proportion of the operating costs of the Minnesota Soldiers' Home also came from direct federal matching grants. Intermittent but vital aid was also given to the state normal schools and public institutions from the various permanent funds and land grants.

Perhaps the major cooperative effort in nineteenth-century Minnesota, as in all the public land states created after 1816, revolved around the construction of railroads, designed to open up the interior of the state for settlement and to connect the state with the outside world. Between 1857, when the first federal grants were made, and 1907, when the last link in the state's internal railroad network was completed, supervision of the railroad land grants was a major activity of the state government, one which involved almost daily contacts with the appropriate federal officials and departments. On the basis of federal and state legislative authorizations, federal and state administrators shared responsibility for approving the railroads' construction plans; supervising the selection of railroad lands along the federally prescribed rights-of-way; securing federal patents for the selected lands; transferring the lands to the railroads as they met the conditions laid down in the federal and state legislation; harmonizing the interests of the railroads and beneficiaries of other land grant programs when they came into conflict; and supervising the relinquishment and replacement of improperly transferred lands. In each case, the Commissioner of the General Land Office and his deputies in Washington and in the field were required to oversee the actions of the governor and his agents to insure compliance with the conditions set down in the land grant legislation by Congress.

All six major railroads operating in present day Minnesota were beneficiaries of federal-state land grants, receiving, all told, 11,173,920 acres valued at approximately $48,812,000. Even the Northern Pacific Railway, which received 1,905,897 acres in Minnesota from a direct federal land grant, was the recipient of 2,167,918 acres through the federal-state program as it absorbed smaller land grant railroads. In addition, the federal grants were matched with bonds valued at $5,875,000 issued by the state and its local governments. Some idea of the magnitude of the cooperative railroad construction program may be gathered from the percentage of the state's total revenue paid by the railroads in taxes between 1875 (over ten per cent) and 1900 (over fifteen per cent).[17]

The types of cooperative activities and the means of their administration in Minnesota were familiar in the other states as well. All the land grant programs except those designed to aid in the reclamation of arid lands were in operation. Direct federal aids to individuals and groups were subject to state influences much as elsewhere. Cooperative exchanges of goods and services in Minnesota were recognizable as parts of the national pattern. So were the paraphernalia of administration—in land grant matters an *ex officio* State Land Board and its agents; the General Land Office and its local land officers; local school and county officials. Indeed, it seems that very few federal and state offices in Minnesota were not involved in the cooperative programs.

Since the scope of cooperative programs and the administration of sharing were no different from the standard nationwide pattern, it is reasonable to project the Minnesota pattern of fiscal sharing onto other states as well. This does not mean that all states benefited equally from federal financial support. As in the twentieth-century grant-in-aid programs, federal aid provided a proportionately larger share of the budgets of the smaller states, the newer states, and the poorer states, though the differences between states may actually have been less pronounced than in the twentieth century because of greater state reluctance in the nineteenth century to finance local programs with tax money obtained locally.

The central fact that emerges from an analysis of the development of sharing in a single state over several decades is the sheer weight of political time devoted to intergovernmental cooperation. Not only were the administrators heavily involved in cooper-

[17] The land grant railroads' share of the state's total revenue for selected years between 1875 and 1900 was:

	1875	1880	1885	1890	1895	1900
Total state revenue (thousands)	$981	$1,417	$2,078	$3,296	$5,427	$6,903
Land grant railroad tax (thousands)	107	209	673	621	729	1,106

ative activities, but the programs that were most highly developed as shared programs also pre-empted the bulk of the policy-makers' time. Minnesota governors and legislatures together were preoccupied with the cooperative programs throughout this entire period. The already enumerated programs should indicate why this was so, since no aspect of internal improvements, education, or general disposition of the public domain in the state escaped involvement in the sharing process. Furthermore, even defense against the Indians and the recruitment of an army for the defense of the Union during the Civil War became shared functions. By the end of the second decade of statehood, the regulatory functions of government were also being shared, partly because the fields of regulation were tied to already cooperative programs (as in the case of railroad regulation) and partly because it was simply more convenient to cooperate (as in the case of regulating state and federal-chartered banking institutions). A survey of the governors' messages, the legislative journals, the statute books, and the attorney generals' opinions reveals the extent of this concern with programs that were cooperative in character, a concern not over the general theory of collaboration but over the procedural aspects of the various programs. Federal-state cooperation was a fact of life, hence the policy-makers rarely referred to it directly in their deliberations. The system of sharing is all the more impressive because of its implicit acceptance as part of the process of government.

COOPERATIVE FEDERALISM SINCE 1913

The last major land grant program was inaugurated in 1894. Selection of lands under the land grant acts has persisted through the mid-twentieth century and the extension of the traditional grants to Alaska upon its admission as a state in 1958 has revived the land grant era in one state. Nevertheless, since 1913 the cash grant, coupled with the rising impact of cooperation among professionals at all levels of government, has become the dominant form of intergovernmental cooperation. The modern cash grants had their origins in the later years of the land grant period. They rose to predominance with the adoption of the specific programs embodied in Woodrow Wilson's New Freedom and were notably extended with the rise of the New Deal. The third period of American federalism does not fall under the purview of this study. Beginning in 1913, it is generally considered to be the era of cooperative federalism. In this period, formally structured grant-in-aid programs of internal improvement have had to share the center of the stage with the "new federalism" of welfare. The less visible areas of intergovernmental collaboration expanded apace. As government has become more pervasive, so has intergovernmental cooperation, to the point where the twentieth century has been labeled the century of cooperative federalism, while the intergovernmental cooperation of the nineteenth century has faded into obscurity.

THE ROLE OF THE PUBLIC DOMAIN

As long as the land frontier lasted, the public domain served as the greatest single source of national wealth, the foundation of the American economy. Even the development of major industries of the nineteenth century, agricultural implements, railroads and telegraphs, machines for processing the produce of the land, and the like, was directly tied to the development of the public domain. It is not surprising, then, that the land, owned, as most of it was, by the federal government, should have served as the foundation for intergovernmental cooperation in the expanding nation.

The public land states differed from their non-public land counterparts in the nature of their cooperative relationships with the federal government only insofar as the existence of the public domain within their boundaries made it less difficult to justify major cooperative programs under the strict constructionist terms then dominant in constitutional interpretation. Certainly the states without public lands were at no time excluded from the operations of cooperative federalism. Considering only formal grants-in-aid, it is possible that the public land states did receive more benefits than the others, and so it was argued on the floors of Congress when the states possessing no public lands wanted to gain additional benefits from the federal government for themselves. Yet, when the benefits derived from the other forms of intergovernmental cooperation and direct federal aid to localities are included, the balance seems to have been rather adequately redressed and the amount of cooperation generally equalized. To take but one example, the protective tariff was unquestionably a great aid to Eastern manufacturing interests, often to the detriment of the West and the South. It was as much a subsidy as a government defense contract is in 1964, and was so considered by both its proponents and opponents.[18] The Eastern railroad companies coupled benefits gained from the protective tariff (or exemptions from the tariff, as was sometimes the case) with federal mail subsidies (whose cooperative impacts were great, particularly in those Eastern states, north and south, which participated in the construction of their railroads as owners or investors, during the era of railroad building) and more direct state and local subsidies to construct the network of railroads east of the Great Lakes. They began to take advantage of these benefits even before the major railroad land grants were made and continued to do so subsequently as well.

Frederick Jackson Turner, in stating his renowned frontier hypothesis, made a major point of the influence of the West, the states carved out of the public domain, in the development of nationalism and governmental centralization. He maintained that the growth of the federal government was greatly fostered by the demands of the Western settlers and their early experiences with federal officials, who preceded state governments in almost every new territory.[19] Turner's point is generally valid, but it is considerably more accurate to say that not only did westward expansion increase central government activity in Washington, but that it did so primarily by increasing intergovernmental cooperation, formal and informal, thus also increasing the central governmental activities of the states. The public domain served as a vehicle for the development of the role of the federal government in promoting national expansion while at the same time providing a means for the states and localities to share in this task. The pattern of relationships that emerged from the cooperative manipulation of the public domain was carried over into the twentieth-century cooperative programs. It was the prior existence of this pattern that made it possible to integrate the increased velocity of government into the federal-state framework without major alterations in the operation of the federal system.

[18] For a discussion of this aspect of the protective tariff, by one of the men who best understood its nature, see Charles Wiltse, *John C. Calhoun* (New York, 1944, 1949), Vols. I and II.
[19] Frederick Jackson Turner, *The Frontier in American History* (New York, 1920).

Indeed, the newer states developed a tradition of intergovernmental cooperation that antedated their admission to the Union.
If the federal government did not always precede the first settlers
into new territory, it almost invariably preceded the state government. From this arrangement emerged an implicit conception of
the rightness of the role of the federal government as a major
participant in the development of new territories and new frontiers. This conception was carried over within each state after
statehood was achieved and, ultimately, became dominant in a
majority of the states in the Union. The movements to attain
statehood reflected the impact of the land grant and the general
tradition of intergovernmental cooperation upon the newly settled territories of the West. On one hand they were certainly
attempts to gain more power for local self-government. Even
more important, the desire for statehood was linked to the perceived greater ability of states than territories to gain more
benefits from Washington. In almost all cases, land grants were
not available until statehood was achieved. Lack of voting power
in the national elections and full representation in the Congress
meant that a territory would be dependent on favors from Washington over which its citizens had only a minimum of influence
and control. Statehood came to mean the right to participate in
national policy formation as much as the right to manage one's
local affairs.

CONTROL OVER THE GRANT PROGRAMS

The organization of control over the grant programs was
another matter that tended to obscure the nature of the cooperative relationships in the nineteenth century. The evolution of
formal federal controls did not signify changes in the fundamental policy of congressional supervision of the programs, but did
indicate that the Congress and the states represented in it
learned from experience. The principle of federal control existed
from the days of the earliest grants. At first it was assumed that
mere incorporation of certain principles into the state consitu-
tions in order to secure congressional approval prior to achieving
statehood would be sufficient to ensure compliance with the
spirit of the program in question. To some extent, this method
was successful and has continued to be so. If for no other reason

than the continued increase in the scope of government activity, this method came to be too cumbersome. As it was seen that more specific controls were necessary, they were added by the representatives of the very states that would receive the grants. In addition, as administrative complexities increased and new methods of enforcement outside the courts had to be found, they too were added, not as changes in policy but as improvements in method.

The question still arises as to the degree of enforcement of these provisions. There is no doubt that grants were not often revoked, or land often withheld, though enough cases of revocation and withholding lands can be found to indicate that federal control could be carried to its ultimate implications in this manner. The absence of large-scale revocation programs is due less to the failure of the federal government to enforce the terms administratively than to the political power of the states in the halls of Congress. This is no less true in 1964 than in 1864. Students of government have noted that since the rise of the great cash grant programs following the New Deal, little money has been withheld from any of the states for maladministration or violation of the terms of the program in question. Attempts have been initiated by the federal executive to withhold funds from individual states for a number of reasons. In almost every case these attempts have been overruled in the Congress or suitable compromises have been negotiated with congressional help. When state violations of federal regulations do occur, they are dealt with in less drastic ways because the Congress will not often allow the drastic solution and the federal bureaucrats know this.

Only once in American history was massive revocation of federal grants because of misuse even considered. Between 1870 and 1900 the question of revoking some of the unfulfilled transportation land grants became a matter of some political importance. Congressional investigations into the uses of land grants by railroad companies were widespread during this period. Ultimately, federal-state land grants to eight railroad companies were revoked in whole or in part and steps were taken to withhold lands from the great transcontinental railroads as well.[20]

[20] Federal Coordinator of Transportation, *Public Aids to Transportation* (Washington, D. C., U.S. Gov't. Printing Office, 1938), Vol. II, Part I, Sect. A.

While other federal grants to the states were not often revoked, specific lands within the different land programs were frequently withheld by the federal government. Not infrequently, the states were even forced to re-cede lands already patented to them because of conflicts with other federal grant programs or land policies. As the available public domain diminished and the number of land grant programs increased, the amount of control and intensity of supervision grew also, leading to greater exercises of federal authority, subject always to the formal and informal limitations attached by Congress. Ultimately these controls were transferred, modified, and expanded to provide adequate supervision for cash grants-in-aid as they began to emerge.

Cooperative Federalism: The Alternate Hypothesis

Cooperative, or collaborative, federalism can be defined as the sharing of responsibilities for given functions by the federal and state governments. In this sense it is conceived to be the opposite of dual federalism which implies a division of functions between governments as well as a division of governmental structures. While the theory of cooperative federalism assumes a division of structures, it also implies a system of sharing that ranges from formal federal-state agreements covering specific programs to informal contacts on a regular basis for the sake of sharing information and experience.

Even during the nineteenth century, when the ethos of the times called forth a theory of dualism that was based on a functional demarcation between governments, the actual exigencies of the operation of the system of necessity demanded cooperation. Consequently, federal-state cooperation was developed in a wide variety of cases. Though it was usually opposed in theory, it persevered in many forms and under different guises. Its procedures were refined through trial and error, often subtly since it was, in the main, unrecognized. Officially recognized or not, a system of intergovernmental collaboration was evolved to serve the dual purpose of maintaining the federal balance while providing needed governmental services. Where cooperation did not develop and should have, both the system and the programs in question suffered. In a sense, a substantial share of the history of American government has been the search for methods to provide for the necessary collaboration of the various parts of the federal system while at the same time preserving and strengthening those parts as separate bases for such collaboration. Much of what historians have mistaken for rejection of intergovernmental cooperation in the nineteenth century was, in reality, the rejection of certain methods of inter-action as failing to meet one or both of these criteria.

On the basis of this evidence, it would seem necessary to develop a new theory to explain the nature of the American federal system and its character over time, a theory which takes into account the continuous existence of an amount of intergov-ernmental collaboration equal to, and in fact greater than, the amount of separation (as traditionally defined) in the federal system. Within the large area of concurrent powers provided, explicitly or implicitly, by the federal constitution, the federal and state governments have been able either to divide responsi-bility among their separate jurisdictions, with each responsible only for its own share of the divided responsibility ("dual feder-alism"), or to divide the works of government cooperatively, sharing responsibility in specific programs, with all units di-rected toward common goals that extend along the entire chain of concurrent powers ("cooperative federalism") and generally overflow into the ostensibly "exclusive" preserves.

The actual division of responsibility under the concurrent powers is primarily determined anew for each case through the political process, rather than through legal decisions. That is, the decisions as to the distribution of the areas of concurrent powers are made either on the political level or by consititui onal inter-pretations based on political realities. Such decisions are recog-nized in constitutional law either after a political decision has been made or as a result of a constitutional interpretation that, sooner or later, must follow the polls.

In understanding our federal system, there is a basic conflict between simple rationalities and the logic of political experi-ence. Simple rationalities demand a federal structure with a clear-cut division of powers that can easily be measured, while political experience, dealing with reality, demands a concurrent approach to problem solving. While the conflict between rhetoric and practice has to a certain degree obscured the image of federalism, the result has nevertheless been the development of that complex mechanism of intergovernmental relations, charac-teristic of the American federal-state-local partnership, known today as cooperative federalism.

11   *American and German Federalism: Distribution of Powers*

Arnold Brecht

Differences between American and German federalism were not restricted to the number and size of the states and to political traditions. They included wide divergencies in the distribution of powers among the various levels of government. The origin of the latter differences and their gradual modification is illuminating not only for recent American and German history but also for the modern problems of federalism in general, and of decentralized administration even in non-federal countries.

The line of demarcation that in the United States separates governmental powers of the nation from those of the states has always been *vertical*. When power to deal with some subject-matter was given to the federal government, it was as a rule *full* governmental power, including administration and adjudication as well as legislation. This was not so in Germany. The imperial constitution of 1871, while liberally granting the federal government the power to legislate in most fields of general significance, left administrative and judicial functions in almost all matters to the states. While the nation's legislative power was much broader in Germany from the very beginning than it has ever become here, its administrative power was much narrower, at least in the beginning. In other words, the original line of demarcation between powers in Germany was *horizontal* rather than vertical.

To illustrate, the national government in Berlin from the inception of the empire in 1871 obtained almost unlimited power to *legislate* in the fields of commerce and industry, criminal law,

From Chapter 6 in *Federalism and Regionalism in Germany: The Division of Prussia* by Arnold Brecht (Oxford University Press, 1945), pp. 47-52. Reprinted by permission of the New School for Social Research and the author.

223

judicial organization and procedure, the press, assemblies, and associations; and as early as 1873 it obtained that power also for civil law. And all these powers were used. The law of bills of exchange (1848) and the codes of commerce (1861), of industry (1869) and of penal law (1869) were taken over ready-made from the German Confederation and the North-German Federation. National codes of the law of the press (1874), of judicial organization and procedure (1879), of civil law (1896), and of the law of assembly and association (1908) came into being during the imperial period, as well as acts providing for public insurance against sickness (1883), accidents-at-work (1884-7), and disability and old age (1889). No doubt was possible of the constitutionality of these federal statutes. No problematic commerce clause of the American kind forced the legislature to distinguish between interstate and intrastate commerce, or between commerce and manufacture, or to engage in roundabout methods of reaching its goals.[1]

Broad as had been the federal power to legislate before 1919, it was expanded still further by the Weimar Constitution. Several new items were added. Moreover, the federal government obtained the power to establish uniform "principles" in matters in which it had no full legislative power, namely, regarding religious corporations, schools, libraries, state and municipal civil services, agricultural law, land distribution, housing, and burials (*Grundsatzgesetzgebung*, Articles 10 and 11). With regard to two other categories—matters of public welfare and those of public peace and order—the federal government was authorized to legislate "whenever the circumstances required it" (*Bedürfnisgesetzgebung*, Article 9).

In regard to *administration* matters were strikingly different during the imperial period. Federal laws were as a rule administered in the field not by federal agencies but by the states. The federal postal service and the federal navy alone had field agencies of their own at that time, if we except here the federal bank (Reichsbank), which had a number of branches throughout the nation. Since naval field administration was practically restricted to the coastal regions, the only federal field agencies one encountered in urban and rural places outside Berlin prior to the First

[1] See the following chapter.

World War were the local post offices with their inscription "Kaiserliches Postamt," most of their buildings constructed during the poorest architectural period in a pseudo-gothic style. Even these were not to be found in Bavaria and Württemberg, whose sovereign privilege to conduct their own postal administration had been reserved to them.

All other field administrations were run by the separate states or under their supervision by their subdivisions. This was so even in regard to customs duties. Although tariffs were federal, the customs officers who inspected the luggage of the traveler or any other goods imported were state employees — of Prussia, Bavaria, Hamburg, Bremen, etc. The states retained a small percentage of the proceeds as a compensation for their administrative costs, and passed the rest on to the federal treasury.

Law enforcement too was a matter for the separate states. While the federal government in the United States may enforce its own laws by its own courts and through its own district attorneys and investigation bureaus, German federal power — at least during the imperial period — had to leave enforcement to the states. True, the final appeal in important cases lay to the federal Supreme Court, and judicial prosecution for high treason fell under its original jurisdiction. But the states established all other regular courts, and the police; they appointed the judges, district attorneys, and police officers; and they exercised whatever administrative discretion was left in regard to enforcement of the laws.

Not even the military administration was federal. The army was paid for by the federal government, but was subdivided into state contingents. Prussia, Bavaria, Württemberg, and Saxony administered their separate contingents, while the smaller states had military agreements with Prussia. Legislation, budgeting, and certain general regulations in military matters were federal, but not the current administration of these matters in peacetime.[2]

Summing up, in imperial times federal administration as distinct from legislation was restricted to foreign affairs, the navy, the postal services, and a few central institutions, such as the federal Supreme Court in Leipzig, which had no federal district courts below it. In other matters, federal departments in Berlin

[2] See Chapter IV on Bavaria's special privileges.

exercised some central administrative functions, such as research, preparation of legislation, the issuance of "directives" in execution of the federal legislation after discussion in the Federal Council, and a weak sort of surveillance over state administration to assure its conformity with the federal laws. But they had no field agencies. They were, as the slang expression had it, like heads without bodies.[3]

This horizontal division of powers, which permitted the federal government to pass general legislation and to watch over the execution of federal laws but left the execution itself to the states, had obvious advantages. It helped German administration to avoid duplication and triplication in the field. Clarity of jurisdiction, and efficient collaboration under one government only—the state government—distinguished field administration under this scheme.

The basic idea of this arrangement could not be maintained, however, under the force of postwar requirements. Large branches of administration were taken over by the federal government in the democratic period. Bavaria's and Württemberg's separate postal services disappeared. The army, too small to be divided into four contingents, became federal. The care of veterans was put in the charge of a large federal administration with regional and local offices. Furthermore, the financial disaster made it necessary to establish federal financial agencies in the field. To avoid duplication, these agencies took over also the administration of state income taxes and other state revenues, the federal government passing part of the proceeds on to the states, in reversal of the former practice. The railroads, formerly owned by the separate states, were transferred to a federal railroad administration. The navigable streams were likewise placed under federal administration. Finally, when the problem of unemployment was tackled, federal agencies in charge of employment offices and unemployment compensation were established on three levels.[4]

Thus by the middle of the nineteen-twenties a vertical distribution of powers had been added to the horizontal one. The former unity of command over all the public services operating

---

[3] The German saying was "Dame ohne Unterleib," referring to the popular feature in country fairs—a woman with no body below her waist.

[4] See the following chapter.

within a state had disappeared. The traveler now could see federal post offices even in Bavaria and Württemberg. He could find federal railroads, federal finance agencies, federal employment agencies everywhere, and at many places also federal agencies dealing with war veterans, federal army barracks or federal agencies in charge of waterways.

The federal budget clearly reflected these changes. In 1871 it contained only four big items: for the army—and actually these allotments were spent by the four contingent armies rather than by federal agencies; for the navy; for war veterans; and for foreign affairs. By 1913 four more major appropriations had been added: for the colonies; for the Kiel Canal, which was mainly a military affair; for the national debt service; and for old-age and disability insurance. At the end of the republican period the colonial item had disappeared, and the appropriations for the army and navy were considerably smaller. The other items, however, had much larger amounts allocated to them. In addition, there were big items now for many commercial canals; for financial administration; and especially for the various branches of social administration.

But state administration had not vanished. Most important, justice, police, education, and the supervision of municipalities continued to be affairs of the states, and theirs alone, except for some central institutions, such as the federal Supreme Court, and except for temporary interference through federal emergency decrees.

Thus the problems of "administrative federalism" came more and more to the fore in Germany, much as they did ten years later in the United States. Some differences, however, should be noted. The United States is still far from having income taxes assessed and collected by one set of agencies for both federal and state purposes, as has been the case in Germany ever since 1871. Nor is justice here administered by the same set of state attorneys and state courts, irrespective of whether cases arise from federal or state laws. In Germany all judicial administration became federal under Hitler. But even when it was in state hands, there was no duplication of courts—or even triplication, with county and municipal courts added to federal and state courts—such as prevails here. Nor was there duplication or triplication of police authority. Other administrative differences between Germany and the United States existed in the field of social security.[5] But important as these variations are, they should not distract attention from the basic similarities between the United States after 1933 and democratic Germany before 1933 in their administrative problems of federalism.

Much more marked differences between the two countries persisted in the sphere of legislation. When Germany adopted the American principle of a vertical division of power between the nation and the states, she nevertheless continued the old horizontal division. Federal power to legislate remained, therefore, much stronger in Germany than in the United States. In this country federal legislation in matters of business, trade, and commerce has recently increased by leaps and bounds, but there are still constitutional limits to be observed that have never troubled Germany.[6] Furthermore, the United States is far from possessing national codes of civil and penal law; or federal laws for the press, for assemblies and associations, or for judicial organization and procedure in the states.

Not only was the legislative power of the federal government further enlarged in Germany during the democratic period, as has been mentioned above, but Article 48 of the Weimar Constitution provided the federal government also with a temporary power to legislate by presidential decree, or otherwise to become active in any field, by virtue of such a decree, "in order to restore peace and order whenever they were seriously disturbed" (*Ausnahmegesetzgebung*). Only the basic structure of the Constitution was to be indefeasible. This provision enabled the federal government temporarily to take over even state police or other branches of state administration, although this was not done between 1924 and 1932 because of the opposition of the state governments to such encroachment.

[5] See the following chapter.
[6] See the following chapter.

Decision-Making in a Federal System

EDWARD W. WEIDNER

Federalism has been thought of as the golden mean between excessive centralization and excessive decentralization. It has also been thought of as an inherently imperfect and defective form of government that stymies a positive solution to the pressing governmental problems of the twentieth century.[1] At base, both of these viewpoints picture national-state relations as a give-and-take situation in which there is disagreement and possibly conflict. A common assumption is that in this give-and-take situation the interests of state and national governments are competing or opposed. The one school of thought sees such competition resulting in a highly acceptable compromise, while the other sees it as destroying any possibility of a systematic attack on national domestic problems.

It is a thesis of the present discussion that in the federal system in the United States there are relatively few direct clashes or compromises between state and national governments on large issues of national domestic policy. Furthermore, in the administrative sphere positive cooperation is the pattern rather than aloofness or conflict. The disagreements and conflicts that do arise and that may be encouraged by federalism's structural features are not basically clashes between state and national governments. Instead, they are clashes between much smaller groups of people and the opposing groups are located within a single governmental level as often as not.

While this thesis is essentially different from that developed fifteen years ago by Jane Perry Clark in her monograph entitled

---

From Chapter 19 in *Federalism: Mature and Emergent*, Arthur W. MacMahon, editor, Russell and Russell Publishers. Reprinted by permission of the Trustees of Columbia University and the author.

[1] William Anderson, *Federalism and Intergovernmental Relations, A Budget of Suggestions for Research*, Chicago, Public Administration Service, 1946, pp. 32-3.

The Rise of A New Federalism, it is complementary, not contradictory, to it.[2] Jane Clark pointed out that a cooperative federalism existed in which nation and state combined their resources the better to carry out their responsibilities. The presence of cooperative federalism is certainly in evidence today, but certain patterns of disagreement and conflict are with us as well. Indeed they always have been. If an understanding is to be gained of how federalism affects political behavior, it is essential that elements of disagreement be analyzed and understood as well as patterns of cooperation, and that such elements be analyzed in terms of the forces that produce them and their consequences.

A second assumption is implicit in the older view of national-state relations as a give-and-take situation of disagreement and conflict between levels of government as such. A theory of leadership is implied. Political and administrative leaders of national and state governments are thought of as rather forceful and direct. Supposedly they develop and support fairly clear-cut public policies for which they become known. Furthermore, the assumption is that they use all the means at their command to gain acceptance for the public policies they support, including coercive techniques. Given the assumed competing interests of national and state governments, a compromise becomes necessary but only as a last resort. In any event, it is believed that leadership is not based upon the idea of "getting along" with officials of the other level of government at almost any price, nor is a community of interests assumed. A further thesis of the present discussion denies the validity of this view of leadership.

The entire process of agreement and disagreement, of cooperation and conflict, is here viewed as a decision-making process. Put another way, the basic datum in political science is the political act or the individual in an action situation. Each act has its own general environment or ecology varying all the way from factors rather remote from the action situation to the immediate conditioning factors or foci of attention and the actual stimulus that presents a problem to an individual. The problem that an individual faces is essentially a decision-making problem. Something happens that creates tension, frustration, insecurity, or expectations of indulgence. A greater or lesser period of hesita-

[2] New York, Columbia University Press, 1938.

tion sets in and then a choice or decision is made. The decision is made in a value context, that is, the very reason for tension or frustration as the result of a stimulus is the need of or striving for values. Men are essentially goal-oriented although there are wide differences in the extent to which they are conscious of their long-range goals or have a systematically thought-out value framework. There are also wide differences in the degree to which they are able to implement their values or desires, and of course the intensity with which particular values are held varies greatly.

The decision or choice results in one of two kinds of behavior or both. An individual's attitude may change; this is essentially a subjective matter with the individual involving a tendency to participate in a certain way. Secondly, the patterns of participation (that is, human interaction) may be altered; these are overt or external to the individual. Presumably the change in attitude or participation is designed to remove the tension of the individual, and a new state of gratification or equilibrium sets in, a state that the individual hopes will be more compatible with the ends he is seeking.

Unfortunately for purposes of analysis, political acts seldom occur in a separate, neat sequence. The more usual situation is that many of them are occurring simultaneously, often involving a series of individuals in a multitude of decisions. Rather than causes and effects there are a series of interrelations. Before responses can be made to certain stimuli, other stimuli present still further problems. Patterns of attitudes and participation must be adapted quickly and often imperfectly to only a select few of the many stimuli. In national-state relations this pressure of events and pressure of other individuals and groups is an ever-present phenomenon. Decision-making in a federal system thus takes place in the context of many varied groups, formal and informal, large and small.

If attention is concentrated upon areas of agreement and coop-eration on the one hand, and areas of disagreement and conflict on the other, a study of decision-making in a federal system is very suggestive of major factors that affect or are related to political behavior. To study decision-making in a federal system is to study the kind of choices that are made under different circumstances, the factors that may have shaped the choices, and the resulting or related patterns of attitudes and participation. These choices, factors, and patterns vary with the probability of cooperation or conflict; a theory of behavior must take account of such variances. Viewed from the standpoint of public policy, change may take place under conditions of either cooperation or conflict but the secondary effects of these conditions may be quite different. Conflict is normally avoided as much as possible and cooperation sought, but only within a limited frame of reference. Cooperation may come at too high a price. By selecting for analysis a group of decisions concerning which agreement and cooperation are to be found and another group concerning which disagreement and conflict are present, we are limiting our investigation, but in a manner that contributes to its usefulness in building empirical theory while at the same time the enquiry has important policy implications.

I

There are countless causes for disagreement and conflict in a federal system. Personalities play a part. So do bothersome procedures, differences in the age and general background of administrators, poor communication, frequency of contact, and so on. However, all these factors are secondary in importance. They are relatively easy to deal with: procedures may be changed, frequency of contact increased, personnel shifted. This is not to say that such variables are never troublesome, for they are very troublesome on occasion. Rather, they are secondary in the sense that they are not of crucial importance to the participants in federal-state relations. The main concern of these participants, and, for that matter, most men, is to have their values implemented to as great an extent as possible. Hence it is not surprising that the fundamental reason for disagreement and conflict in a federal system is that there is a lack of consensus as to what values should be implemented. This is true in both the legislative and administrative spheres.

While differences on public policy or values are to be expected in a country containing as many heterogeneous elements as are to be found in the United States, it does not necessarily follow that officials in the several states will take one policy position and those of the national government another. Indeed, on an *a priori* basis it would seem surprising if this were the case, given the diversity of conditions in the several states and the fact that the union is made up of all states. "States' rights" is only one of numerous values held by state officials, and it is relatively unimportant to many of them. The prime thing that the states have in common is their existence; it is possible that if an issue were presented that threatened the very existence of the states their political officials might be brought together. In actual fact, a major issue of this kind has not been presented. Consequently, usually national government officials can find many of their state counterparts who support national policy objectives and many others who oppose. And among the states, differences in values are the rule.

The framers of the Constitution clearly expected value or policy disagreements among the states as well as between the central government and one or more states. In his famous essay on faction, Madison wrote:

Hence, it clearly appears, that the same advantages which a republic has over a democracy, in controlling the effects of faction, is enjoyed by a large over a small republic,—is enjoyed by the Union over the States composing it. Does the advantage consist in the substitution of representatives whose enlightened views and virtuous sentiments render them superior to local prejudices and to schemes of injustice? It will not be denied that the representation of the Union will be most likely to possess these requisite endowments. Does it consist in the greater security afforded by a greater variety of parties, against the event of any one party being able to outnumber and oppress the rest? In an equal degree does the increased variety of parties comprised within the Union, increase this security? Does it, in fine, consist in the greater obstacles opposed to the concert and accomplishment of the secret wishes of an unjust and interested majority? Here, again, the extent of the Union gives it the most palpable advantage.

The influence of factious leaders may kindle a flame within their particular States, but will be unable to spread a general conflagration through the other States. A religious sect may degenerate into a political faction in a part of the Confederacy; but the variety of sects dispersed over the entire face of it must secure the national councils against any danger from that source. A rage for paper money, for an abolition of debts, for an equal division of property, or for any other improper or wicked project, will be less apt to pervade the whole body of the Union than a particular member of it; in the same proportion as such a malady is more likely to taint a particular county or district, than an entire State.[3]

[3] *The Federalist*, No. 10 (Modern Library ed., 1937, pp. 61-2).

Thus Madison emphasized that one of the main characteristics of the federal system would be the wide variation in the public policies that would be followed in the several states. To guard against the possible excesses of certain states the central government was given a core of power over matters deemed to be of nationwide concern. The states were expected to disagree among themselves over how the central government exercised its powers, and they were also expected to pursue different policies in matters that were reserved to them for decision.

Federalism implies that there is a variety of political values in a nation for which allowance needs to be made. It is more than a neutral centralizing or decentralizing device. Historically it has been a unifying device that took cognizance of the fact, among others, that agreement was lacking as to political goals and values, and hence single public policies for a society would be developed only in those matters over which the central government was given jurisdiction. State participation in public policy would automatically mean lack of uniformity and recognition of alternative and even competing political values. Viewed in this context, "states' rights" and the division of powers and responsibility for public services between the national and state governments become matters affecting substantive policy. They are matters upon which citizens will disagree in the proportion that their values or goals vary. The appointment of a President's commission to make recommendations on national-state relations may be an excellent political device but by the very nature of the subject with which it deals it cannot be a nonpartisan body whose recommendations will be supported by all or nearly all men of good will.

Given the diverse policy objectives of the several states, it becomes unrealistic and impossible to expect of them any unified approach to important public problems. The United States learned at an early date, under the Articles of Confederation, how true this was. As a result of the experience with the Articles, the framers of the Constitution sought to vest the new central government with effective power over those matters that, in their opinion, required a single, unified policy or that required a minimum standard of performance. Foreign affairs and defense from external attacks were thought to be areas in which a single policy was necessary, while interstate commerce and the preservation of peace in the face of possible internal disturbances were thought to be areas in which minimum standards or assurances were needed.

The experience of 170 years ago is confirmed by contemporary events. The states have been unable to follow a single course even in such comparatively noncontroversial areas as are covered by the so-called uniform state laws. If minimum standards are desired for the nation as a whole in a particular policy area such as health or welfare, it is the central government that must act to assure these ends. To leave the matter exclusively to the states means that there will be a variation in standards from very low to quite high. To set up a system of joint national-state participation means that standards and practices will vary much more than in a system of central action alone. It also means that some disagreement and conflict are inevitable because officials in various states will not all see eye-to-eye with those of the national government in terms of the objectives of the program.

This is not to blame the states in any way for their actions. Rather it is to recognize that public policy is in large part the result of the values that men hold and that these values vary from individual to individual and group to group. It would be unexpected and surprising if the several states followed identical or even similar courses of action on important public issues. The normal expectancy is that they will differ in greater or lesser degree among themselves in regard to policies they enact and in regard to the policies of the national government.

II

As we have already seen, two broad categories of values are immediately noticeable in a federal system. There are those values that attach to units of government or agencies or individuals within the units, and there are those values that attach to programs or types of substantive policies. The latter may be called principled, programmatic, or organization goals; the former may be called expendiency or conservation goals.[4] Pro-

---

[4] The terms "principled" and "expediency" have been suggested by Harold D. Lasswell and Abraham Kaplan, *Power and Society*, New Haven, Yale University Press, 1950, p. 42; the terms "organization" and "conservation" have been put forth by Herbert A. Simon, *Administrative Behavior*, New York, Macmillan, 1947, pp. 112-3 and 117.

grammatic goals are normally those concerned with adequate standards of public service—minimum standards in health and welfare, better public education, a more extensive system of interstate highways, more service to farmers, and so on. Expendiency goals refer to the preservation and extension of influence of individuals, agencies, or units of government—for example, the defense of state government against "encroachment" from Washington, the desire of an individual for more power for its own sake, or the protection of an agency from supervision by those deemed unfriendly to it.

It is in the nature of a federal system that there are many occasions when the one set of values conflicts with the other. The states are not creatures of the national government and thus need not accept many of the programmatic or expediency goals that are put forth by those in control nationally. The constitutionally guaranteed semi-independence of the states lends encouragement to the development of strong expediency values relative to them, their leaders, and agencies. At the same time, the trend toward an increase in national-state relations helps strengthen the hold of programmatic values on many state and national administrators. The inevitable result is disagreement and conflict of three kinds: between competing expediency values, between competing programmatic values, and between expediency and programmatic values. The interplay of these goals is such that it is not unusual to find a programmatic value being defended in terms of expediency objectives and vice versa. Thus many who hesitate directly to attack programmatic values such as the so-called welfare state do so indirectly by defending states' rights since they feel that if welfare services were turned over to the states entirely they would be much less extensive and effective. On the other hand a welfare agency may battle for independence from supervision by the governor in order that it may better pursue certain types of welfare policies in cooperation with welfare personnel at the national level.

The net effect of a federal system is not by any means in the direction of increasing value conflict. Rather, while the system results in increasing the likelihood of certain disagreements over goals, it results in decreasing the likelihood of other and often more basic value conflicts. The federal system of the United States has withstood the shocks of wars and depressions and the changing centuries and meanwhile it has provided an organization that has helped weld a strongly unified nation where formerly there were independent states and unorganized territory. This has been an effective demonstration of the ability of a federal system to contribute toward modifying values and reducing value conflict. The expediency values attached to the several states are not nearly as intensely held as those attached to independent nation-states.

Disagreement or conflict in national-state relations is limited. It is not a matter that normally determines election results or on which there is a clear public opinion. General issues of national-state relations have concerned only a small minority of individuals and groups in recent decades, usually a group of public officials at each level and a few interest groups outside the framework of government. When an important new substantive policy for the national government is under consideration, national-state relations may take on a broader significance, as was the case in welfare and labor policy during the thirties. As a whole, however, interest groups and public opinion have not found states' rights an attractive theme unless by the defense of states' rights they could defend some programmatic value. Nonetheless, for those public officials daily engaged in national-state relations the issues arising therefrom may be crucial.

The values that individuals hold are so diverse that there is no definable "state" point of view in intergovernmental relations as a whole. Even if the forty-eight governors were considered to be spokesmen for their entire states there does not emerge a single state approach to intergovernmental relations. Occasionally all the governors will agree on a minor point or two but they have never agreed that a specific general reallocation of activities should take place between national and state governments. This is understandable since some of them are Democrats, some Republicans; some are liberals, others conservatives; some have national political ambitions, others do not; some come from poor states, others from well-to-do areas. These are only a few of the variables that affect the approach governors take on national-state relations. Much of the publicity arising from recent political events, Governors' Conferences, and the Council of State Governments tends to give the impression that all governors demand that certain functions and tax resources of the national government be turned over to the states. The impression is erroneous. It is true that the governors probably defend states' rights as vigorously as any other group of public officials; they tend to stress expediency values relative to state government. In part this is a function of their role as chief executive and chief party leader. Nevertheless, such a set of values may be subordinate to many other considerations, and consequently consensus is not easily forthcoming.

If the governors as a group cannot produce a state point of view on intergovernmental relations, there is little likelihood that it will be found elsewhere. State legislators or elected state administrators show no more tendency to agree than the governors. Political parties remain rather vague on the subject and public opinion gives no evidence of a state viewpoint. Therefore, the most that can be said is that state political officials who hold elective and/or general executive posts tend to defend state government as such more vigorously than others, but that this expediency value is often secondary to a number of other values these individuals hold.

If any analysis is made of the national government, similar conclusions are reached. Although there is only one unit of government here compared to the forty-eight states, a single approach to national-state relations is never found. Of course, to the extent that the President speaks for the entire government and has a clearly defined policy on relations with the several states, a "national" policy may be referred to. But such a policy is not binding on Congress, and in actual recent practice Congress, the various departments and agencies, and the President have not followed a unified policy on intergovernmental relations. No comprehensive policy has been put forth by the President or the Congress; for the most part a piecemeal approach has prevailed. The reason is not hard to find. A unified policy requires agreement or compromise on basic programmatic and expediency values and such a general agreement is difficult if not impossible to secure even when the President has a large majority in Congress. The major political parties are too diverse in composition, the interest groups too strong relative to special programs, and the determinants of values too varied.

Nevertheless in one way the national situation differs somewhat from that in the states. Since defending the national government per se is usually thought of as centralization and is condemned, the political officials of the nation, at least outwardly, are less oriented toward expediency values than their state counterparts. Within this framework, however, the President is usually more committed to defending the national government than other top officials of his party or of the nation.

To summarize, the states disagree among themselves as to the major public policies they pursue and as to the desirability of particular national policies. They also differ even on smaller issues of national-state relations which may appear to be purely procedural in nature. The explanation is that public policies and even national-state procedures reflect particular values and on these there is lack of agreement. But it is not accurate to speak of the attitudes or policies of the several "states" or "national government." Public policies, and consequent disagreement and conflict, are not the product of entire units of government. Particular individuals, more or less associated in groups and to be found both within a unit of government and without, are the central forces behind the molding of public policy.

Therefore, we turn to an analysis of some of the groups that are playing a crucial role in national-state relations and the kinds of values their members hold. In making this analysis, the concept of an interest group developed by David B. Truman will be especially helpful: an interest group is any group formally organized or not, "that, on the basis of one or more shared attitudes, makes certain claims upon other groups in the society for the establishment, maintenance, or enhancement of forms of behavior that are implied by the shared attitudes."[5] Our concern will be to examine interest groups whose members share values or goals resulting in claims on others relative to national-state relations.

III[6]

While it is not possible to speak of a state or a national attitude on intergovernmental relations, there are many interest

[5] *The Governmental Process*, New York, Knopf, 1951, p. 33; see also chapter 2 generally.

[6] The material that follows in this and the next section is based heavily upon the data collected by Research in Intergovernmental Relations in the United States as observed in the State of Minnesota, a group research project at the

groups that have rather distinct approaches to the subject. It has already been suggested that as a group state elective and/or general executive officials tend to have more intense expediency values relative to state government as a whole than other groups of officials or employees. As part of its regular program the Council of State Governments tries to further these values; on many occasions its leaders have taken the initiative to get the state governors or other top officials to favor particular provisions in legislation before Congress that emphasize the prerogatives of the states or to encourage the President to appoint certain types of individuals—namely those generally considered pro-states' rights—to commissions or other posts. The Council has probably been more states' rights in its attitude than the recent governors of Minnesota. It would seem a reasonable hypothesis that it has been more states' rights than most state elective officials throughout the nation. Put more accurately, state officials find a large variety of values pressing upon them as they carry out their responsibilities, of which states' rights is usually a minor one. The Council, on the other hand, performs a limited number of functions. In addition to its technical assistance activities, its main emphasis has been placed on states' rights.

The most striking interest groups in national-state relations are those of a professional nature. Formally, these interests are evidenced by the many professional associations that have as members national, state, and often local government employees and occasionally members of the profession who are not employed in government. Professionalism has been introduced into almost all the principal services that state and national governments perform. Education was probably the first, soon after the middle of the nineteenth century. There followed such fields as

University of Minnesota from 1946 to 1951. For more complete documentation of some of the points made here, see the series of ten research monographs published by the University of Minnesota Press as the result of the study, particularly the forthcoming analytical volume which will be number nine in the series. William Anderson and the present author were directors of the project.

The functional fields covered are indicated by citing the six volumes in the series which deal with particular activities: No. 1, *Intergovernmental Relations and the Courts*, by Forrest Talbott; No. 2, *Intergovernmental Relations in Highways*, by R. A. Gomez; No. 3, *Intergovernmental Relations in Education*, by Robert L. Morlan; No. 4, *Intergovernmental Relations in Public Health*, by Laurence Wyatt; No. 5, *Intergovernmental Relations in Social Welfare*, by Ruth Raup; No. 6, *Intergovernmental Relations in Employment Security*, by Francis E. Rourke.

agricultural extension, public health, highway administration and engineering, and social work, and more recently airport management, employment security, and others. The process of professionalizing has even gone so far that the professional fields have tended to split. Thus, in addition to a general education profession, there are separate groups interested primarily in vocational education, higher education, secondary education, and so on.

As each professional group has its own peculiar way of organizing it is difficult to generalize about the structure and membership of professional associations. For purposes of analysis, considerable clarity may be gained by thinking of a professional interest group as any group, whether formally organized or not, that shares a professional attitude on the basis of which claims are made on others "for the establishment, maintenance, or enhancement of forms of behavior that are implied by the shared attitudes."[7] In observing national-state relations it is immediately noticeable that there is a marked parallel in the behavior of the members of each of the several professions relative to the type of values held, the occurrence of administrative cooperation and conflict, and the decisions made — all this despite the different functions of government involved and the wide differences in formal organization of professional associations.

One of the basic motivations of a professional interest group is the furtherance of programmatic values. If the profession is social work, for example, it will be concerned with high professional standards and conduct in social welfare and the raising of minimum standards of welfare aid. The secondary effect of such goals is of course to promote the well-being of the social work profession — an expediency consideration that is also an agreed-upon goal — but the genuine programmatic interest is clear. From the moment of entrance into schools of social work to the first inservice training and on to regular employment, social workers are placed in an environment where certain programmatic values are accepted without much question. It is partly a matter of conformity but also a matter of mutual interests. Some of the vocational guidance tests are based upon this idea of mutual interests.

[7] Truman, *op. cit.*, p. 33.

Any group, professional or otherwise, that seeks to implement certain values finds a number of allies in the form of those groups that share some concern for the same goals. Social workers have had ready support on many matters from their clientele, the recipients of welfare services. Liberal and labor groups generally have demanded higher minimum welfare standards and certain segments of the two major parties have indicated their sympathy for action in such a direction. A number of state legislators and congressmen have been favorably disposed, and often the warmest support in legislative bodies will come from those on legislative committees dealing with welfare matters. The position of any one governor or President is less predictable and his policies can be changed more quickly. Also, of all public officials, the chief executives must keep the "general interest" in mind most often.

It is easy to secure the cooperation of those who share the same values. National, state, and local professional officials in social welfare find they see eye-to-eye on most important matters, and consequently their decisions to cooperate reflect basic agreement on welfare programmatic values and agreement on expediency goals relative to their profession. Other values pale in importance to these as far as national-state relations in welfare are concerned. Professional employees do not feel strongly about defending the unit of government for which they work. The states' rights argument is not persuasive, although there may be some expediency values associated with the welfare agency itself. Cooperation not only extends across national, state, and local levels in the administrative work but also includes clientele activities, party and legislative groups, and others who for the moment at least feel that certain welfare programmatic values are especially worthy of their support. The help that the professional welfare group receives from such outside sources is considerable and greatly strengthens its hand.

From the standpoint of social workers, conflicts over social welfare policies are of three types. There is the ever-present tendency for a large profession to subdivide, particularly under pressure from special clientele interests. Thus child welfare and welfare for the aged tend to be separated (or be kept separate) from a general welfare program. Secondly, at the professional or agency level, welfare values must compete with values associated with the other main substantive services of government such as education, health, and highways. Here the social worker comes in occasional conflict with professionals in other fields. The third and main area of conflict is the political. The citizen and the politican must pick and choose among many expediency and programmatic values of which welfare is only one. To convince citizen and politician that welfare values should have a high priority is the task the social worker assigns to himself.

All three areas of conflict affect national-state relations. In a general way all three have the same effect, namely, to lessen direct national-state conflict and to promote conflict among or within the main substantive services of each level of government. From the standpoint of both political leaders and professional employees, the disagreements within and among the professions are probably less serious than those between the professional and citizen and politician. It is particularly in conflicts of a political type that the very nature of federalism presents a special problem. Under a unitary system, the social worker would be involved in a simple direct clash between professional welfare workers and political leaders, be the latter located in the legislative body, the office of the general executive, or in departmental offices. With federalism the clash occurs at both the state and the national levels, and federalism's structural features make available to the combatants additional goals, tactics, and strategy.

In Minnesota the governor and his staff, the budget officer, and the director of the state welfare agency have traditionally been political officials who have not shared the typical programmatic values of professional social workers. The main division in attitude therefore tends to come between the welfare director and his professional employees rather than between the director and the budget office or governor's staff. In general the political officials feel that professional employees engaged in administering national grant-in-aid programs tend to play off supposedly rigid national standards against state political control they do not like. Since a prime objective of professional employees is to further the governmental service with which they are connected and not necessarily policy control at the state level, they tend to read somewhat more into national minimum standards than is actually there. The professionals are also active in appearing before the state legislature from time to time in an attempt to have legislation modified to anticipate changes in national standards. Often they are optimistic in their forecasts of probable national action. Viewing national standards with a different set of values than the professionals, political officials tend to underestimate the demands of the national agency or overestimate the deleterious effects such restrictions may have on the discretion left for state policy-makers. A similar set of circumstances exists at the national level as to the weight national officials give to state demands – the professionals underestimating them, the political leaders overestimating them. The situation portrayed in welfare is equally true of national-state relations in most other functions.

Considerable empirical data exist to support these conclusions. In a mail questionaire sent to a cross-section of officials in Minnesota's state government, counties, municipalities, and urban school districts, the following question was asked: "What is your evaluation of the cooperativeness of public officials in the national government with you? (check): no contacts _____, very poor _____, poor _____, fair _____, good _____, very good _____." At the local government level, comparisons were made between the responses of administrative officials and legislative officials and in every one of the three types of local units in the sample, the administrators were markedly more of the opinion that the national officials were cooperative. A comparison of the responses of 302 municipal administrators (engineers, police chiefs, fire chiefs, assessors, and health officers) with those of 280 city councilmen by means of the chi square test indicated that the difference in attitude was very significant beyond the one per cent level; that is, this difference could have occurred by chance less than once in one hundred times. Comparing the responses of 239 county administrators (engineers, superintendents of schools, sheriffs, county agents, assessors, and welfare executives) with those of 199 county governing body members by the same test also yielded a very significant difference beyond the one per cent level. Furthermore no significant difference appeared between the attitude of state administrators and that of county, school district, or municipal administrators. However, county and state administrators felt that the officials of the national government were more cooperative than their school district and municipal counterparts. They are also the officials who have the most contact with the national government. While the questionnaire was not sent to state legislators, a number of interviews indicate that there is every reason for assuming that these officials would have reacted in much the same way as the local legislators did. Seventy-nine per cent of the 275 national administrators queried by questionnaire thought that state cooperation with them could be rated as good or very good. Only about two-and-a-half per cent thought it poor or very poor.

It is difficult to develop a measure of professionalism so that questionnaire and interview data can be classified on the presence or absence of this characteristic. The closest approximation used in the Minnesota study was the breakdown by type of official, together with general education, professional education, age, and various experience breakdowns. All these groups showed a positive orientation to the cooperativeness question; for example, the more education and the more frequent the contacts the more cooperative the national officals were rated.

Since the data from the Minnesota study are being reported at length elsewhere, our present purposes will be served by summarizing the quantitative data in regard to professionalism drawn from about 650 questionnaires and an equal number of interviews of public officials, national, state, and local. The main findings are these:

1. Administrators rate national-state relations as being more cooperative than do legislators, and within the administrative group those who would commonly be thought of as professional rather than amateur or political lean more heavily in the same direction.

2. Administrative officials think that administrators of other governmental levels cooperate best and legislative officials think legislators do.

3. Professional officials at all levels of government tend to favor more centralization and expansion of their own function than of other activities. Here the programmatic values of professional administrators are revealed. At least state and local professional officials seem to value their activity more than their unit of government.

4. Local administrators are much more critical of the extent of control of their departments by the local legislative body and the executive office than are members of the local legislative body or the executive office; the latter groups would like to see their

control somewhat increased. This is hardly surprising. Moreover, local administrators see much less danger in the existing extent of state administrative supervision over their departments than the local political officials do, and there is even some tendency on the part of the former group to favor an increase in it. Here again is a tendency that cannot be explained in terms of expediency values; expediency values would dictate that local administrators should oppose control of their departments both from within and without their units of government. While by far the majority of administrators are satisfied with the existing levels of control both from within and without, four to five times as many want to increase state administrative supervision as want to decrease it. Also, more favor an increase in state administrative supervision than in local control, and more favor a decrease in local control than favor a decrease in state administrative supervision. Chi square analysis indicates very significant differences beyond the one per cent level.

At this point an apparent contradiction arises between national-state and state-local relations. About two-thirds of the state administrators answering questionnaires agreed that the extent of national administrative supervision was about right, but the remainder split about four to one in favor of decreasing it. A number of factors account for this contrast between national-state and state-local relations. In the first place, quite a few state administrators included in the sample have very few relations with the national government, and it was noticeable that the ratio was cut to about two-and-a-half to one in the case of administrators in such departments as education and welfare where contacts are quite frequent. Secondly, state administrators feel less need for national administrative supervision since within their numbers various technical competencies are likely to be found and since there are enough of them in each department to set up a strong defense for professional standards against executive or legislative interference. At the city level a similar tendency is noted in large cities in contrast to the situation in small cities where more administrative supervision is desired by the semi-isolated professionals. Yet neither of these factors explains the entire difference.

States' rights, outwardly at least, are valued more intensively and extensively than local self-government, and here seems to lie some of the explanation. They are valued more partly because of the superior legal position that states hold in their relations with the national government, compared to that held by local governments in their dealings with the states. A subordinate role for local government is accepted much more readily than a similar role for the states. The states, according to the law and theory of federalism, are permanent partners in governance with a set of powers that cannot be taken away except by constitutional amendment. They are the proving grounds where the loyal opposition gains experience and experiments. To subordinate them to the national government is counter to the tenets of federalism and thus runs counter to customary values, and in the eyes of some officials an increase in national administrative supervision appears to lead in this direction.

In fact, however, the difference in national-state and state-local relations is more apparent than real. The difference shows up almost entirely on general questions or issues such as asking a respondent whether he favors an increase in administrative supervision. As actual case studies of intergovernmental relations are examined, the difference all but disappears. In other words, the difference occurs in reacting to general symbols and not to actual events. For example, the enactment of general regulations and their acceptance by officials of lower levels of government is much the same in national-state and state-local relations. So are the processes of audit and review and the possible consequences of finding officials violating regulations. Intergovernmental relations are at base human relations and require some mutual adjustment if they are to be cooperative in nature in the long run. This adjustment takes place in much the same manner in national-state and state-local relations despite the legal differences of federal and unitary systems. In this adjustment, professionalism plays an important role because participants from both state and national governments share many of the same goals.

5. Administrative and legislative officials alike are of the opinion that the main clash of values occurs within a unit of government rather than between units. This is true even in regard to the issues arising from intergovernmental programs. The professional is especially prone to this point of view.

The conclusions outlined so far, based on both quantitative and case study material, have been largely descriptive. They have indicated that the values and identifications of different types of public officials vary widely, and consequently the decisions they make vary. The two most significant values for purposes of this analysis were found to be the expediency values attached to a unit or level of government and held especially by some political officials, and the programmatic values, attached to the performance of certain governmental services and held especially by professional officials. This is not to deny that there are some who defend states' rights or local self-government through a genuine concern for decentralism and not on the basis of expediency. Nor is it to deny that some professionals develop strong expediency values in connection with their own agencies — the Corps of Engineers is a case in point. Indeed the activity of the Corps of Engineers is a good example of intergovernmental action that promotes intragovernmental discord — in this case, within the national government. However, situations where the programmatic values of professional administrators are overridden by their expediency values are not frequent except as professionals develop expediency values in connection with their entire profession rather than a single agency.

Furthermore, problems arising from intergovernmental programs have been described mainly as problems within units of government rather than between levels. Professional administrators are especially prone to perceive the situation in this manner. Yet there are those who perceive the situation in opposite terms — as a national-state conflict — and they may act upon their perceptions. Some political officials, expecially a few governors, respond in this manner.

Explanatory conclusions can be drawn as well. As has already been emphasized, professionalism creates a powerful set of programmatic values the existence of which explains much of the behavior of professional and nonprofessional public officials in intergovernmental relations. But there is a larger point. To use the suggestive terminology of John M. Gaus,[8] we are in an era of

---

[8] *Reflections on Public Administration*, University, University of Alabama Press, 1947, p. 9.

vastly increased physical and social technology, an era in which the catastrophes of war and depression can strike quickly. As a result, new programmatic values have been emphasized by those who want to take advantage of services that are now available because of the advances in physical and social technology and by those who demand governmental activities designed to lessen or avoid the ravages of wars and depressions. The technicians themselves have become attached to and encourage the creation of programmatic values. In such a situation, the cry of states' rights sounds a hollow note. The stronger the programmatic values, the less states' rights and federalism can become important independent values even for state public officials. States' rights come to be judged by the programmatic values that are implemented by the states and not by a set of independent expediency values.

IV

In a clash of values involving national-state relations some individuals try to affect and succeed in affecting the policies of others. Such political acts are acts of leadership, and leadership plays a central role in decision-making in a federal system. By definition leaders try to influence others; the idea of manipulation is present. But manipulation is not sufficient; some success or influence must result.[9] We have already noted in discussing programmatic and expediency values some of the patterns of leadership in the federal system of the United States and some consequences flowing therefrom. We now turn to an analysis of the methods of leadership and the motives underlying their use.

Leaders, or those who perform acts of leadership frequently, have available to them two general methods, namely, authoritative means and nonauthoritative means. Authority is the formal and effective power "to make decisions which guide the actions of another." This means that the individual affected "sets himself a general rule which permits the communicated decision of another to guide his own choices (i.e., to serve as a premise of those choices) without deliberation on his own part on the

[9] Influence is here defined as effect on policies of others (Lasswell's and Kaplan's "exercise of influence"). Leadership is a subset of influences involving purposive manipulation. Compare Lasswell and Kaplan, *op. cit.*, pp. 71, 74-75, 152.

expediency of those premises."[10] In contrast, nonauthoritative means do not involve an abdication of choice. "Persuasion and suggestion result in a change in the evidential environment of choice which may, but may not, lead to conviction."[11]

In a unitary system, the political and administrative leaders of the central government are vested with a rather complete set of authoritative means to use in their relations with subordinate units of government. Often there is the power to remove local officials and even appoint others in their place if they do not perform in an acceptable manner; there are powers to issue orders and make general rules that govern the very minute details of local action. Furthermore, the officials at the higher level can substitute, if they wish, direct central legislation and administration. Federalism sets severe limitations on the authority of central government officials in dealing with the lower governmental units. Constitutionally they are forbidden to alter in any way the power of officials in lower units to act. This means they cannot expand or contract such power, and they therefore cannot substitute central administration for local administration on matters that are within the authority of the lower units to perform. Today most national-state relations are based on grants-in-aid or the voluntary exchange of technical information and assistance. Most state-local relations, legally at least, are based upon the state's constitutional unitary authority over local government; there is no formal dependence on local officials accepting state policy decisions voluntarily.

However, when a comparison was made of national-state and state-local relations as observed in the State of Minnesota, no important differences were found in the frequency of use of authoritative and of nonauthoritative means by the two supervisory levels. Both national and state administrators stressed nonauthoritative means. Advice, consultation, technical assistance, information—these were the devices that had an appeal alike to the state and national administrator in charge of state-local or national-state relations, be the program in the field of welfare,

[10] Simon, *op. cit.*, p. 125. Compare David Easton, *The Political System, An Inquiry into the State of Political Science*, New York, Knopf, 1953, p. 132: "A policy is authoritative when the people to whom it is intended to apply or are affected by it consider that they must or ought to obey it."

[11] Simon, *op. cit.*, p. 127.

education, health, highways, or in some other field. The more authoritative devices went unused, or were used only with the advice and consent of the officials to whom they were to apply, or were used as an unwelcome last resort in one or two rare cases.[12] Occasionally, strong statements and hot words were used by the supervised in describing the supervisors, particularly if one was a professional and the other a nonprofessional official. Almost never was the reciprocal found true.

There are a number of explanations of this phenomenon. "Pulling rank" or flaunting authority are not devices that win many friends, and most individuals with experience in human relations became accustomed to dealing with others in a more friendly, permissive manner. So it is in intergovernmental relations. The more experience an official has, the greater the likelihood that he has cooperative relationships with those of other levels of government. Political and administrative realism lead to other factors of explanation. The success of a program depends in most instances on the lack of use of authoritative devices in carrying it out. Politically, the superior unit of government is open to attack. If a national administrative official were to offend unduly the administrators from a state, there might be immediate repercussions in the congressional delegation of the state as well as official protest from the governor to the President. State officials have powerful political levers over national action just as local officials have a real check over state administrative supervision through the legislature and governor. These checks are enough of a threat to make frequent use of authoritative means of supervision unlikely. Yet administrators as a group are less concerned with the possibilities of such an attack from the flanks than they are with direct conflict or cooperation with their counterparts on the other governmental level. Here administrative realism enters. No program involving national relations with the forty-eight states is going to be successful if the national officials have to be checking up constantly on the states to see if they are complying with every detail of national standards. Nor is it going to be successful if the national administrators have to

[12] For an analysis of the devices of administrative supervision and their persuasiveness in actual practice, see Edward W. Weidner, "State Supervision of Local Government in Minnesota," *Public Administration Review*, Vol. 4 (1944), pp. 226-233.

make all the important decisions through the use of authoritative methods. A national-state program must be based on the assumption that the great majority of states are going to cooperate to the best of their ability without close supervision, and that therefore the prime role of the national government is to assist the states and to help them carry out the program more effectively. To follow any other course is to increase the cost of administration and decrease its effectiveness. State administrators would rebel against a system that was apparently based on a lack of trust in them, although they do not object to occasional audits to see if their agencies are in accord with national policy. Similar considerations affect state-local relations.

The use of nonauthoritative devices by political and administrative leaders in national-state relations is supplemented by a further practice, namely, the cooperative development of program policy.[13] State and national administrators almost never develop rules and regulations or program changes by themselves without consultation with and participation by local and state officials, respectively. The practice is quite standardized. For example, a problem-area arises either in the minds of state or national officials involving a national-state program. Within a short time, the problem finds its way to the agenda of a meeting of state administrators from the several states, a meeting at which national officials will probably be present but withhold much comment. If it is a problem of large proportions, it may be referred to a special committee of state administrators and a report brought in at a subsequent meeting. It will be discussed and debated informally around the country and in regional or state meetings of administrators. Appropriate clientele or other

[13] In the discussion of the fiscal aspects of federalism, not specifically in connection with the material in this chapter, John E. Burton presented a somewhat different picture of national leadership in grant-in-aid programs, as a phase of his plea for procedures that would "establish the minimum service in various fields that we want a state to perform, and on the basis of general compliance which can be audited on a much broader basis than the detailed audit that now goes on by federal administrators." In developing his point of view about a more broadly-based system of grants with compliance on a broader basis, he contrasted it with "compliance set in detail and in the back room, as it were, as now — a field agent of a federal bureau works with some deputy or department head in the state government and receives compliance. Many times what he achieves is no part of the law, no part of the regulation. But because the state is on the receiving end, a sort of attrition goes on and finally they agree to certain conditions." (Editor)

interest groups are likely to be consulted. Finally, the state administrators will recommend a course of action to national officials, usually with prior knowledge that their suggestion will be acted upon without substantial change.

This practice of developing policy from below is based upon much the same line of reasoning as the preference for nonauthoritative devices. In a national-state program, more cooperation will be forthcoming from the several states if their officials have taken an active part in the framing of the regulations and the making of decisions that outline the main course of national policy. State administrative officials must accept part of the responsibility for national policy, and this makes the task of the national official easier when it comes to enforcing minimum standards. It may also place the state administrator in a peculiar position if top state political leaders object to a policy he had a part in developing. In order to defend himself, the state administrator may blame the national government for a policy he helped write.

In thus decentralizing decision-making on public policy, national administrators are acting in accord with rather vague and undefined notions of democracy and therefore receive support from traditional cultural values. At the same time, they are not risking much in terms of lack of control over the direction of public policy because professionalism is prevalent in the states and leads to agreement on many values between national and state officials. To be sure, many of these national-state relations occur essentially between national professional and state political officials, since the heads of state agencies tend to be political rather than professional in orientation. But to a considerable extent the political heads of agencies must rely upon their professional subordinates for advice and help, and consequently the influence of professionalism is not without its effect.

V

The conclusions reached and the hypotheses for future research put forth in these pages are of a very limited nature. They refer to conditions within the United States and many of the data have been confined to national-state and state-local relations as observed in Minnesota. In the United States with a particular tradition of freedom and democracy patterns of political behavior may be present that are not duplicated elsewhere. Our federal system and political party structure present many unique features. In like manner the State of Minnesota has many political patterns that are not found in some states. In recent times it has never been a boss-ridden state but rather one of loosely organized political parties and independent voting. It has been neither a very well-to-do state nor a poor state. And over all, its state administration has been of a fairly high quality from the standpoint of professional standards.

Under the conditions that prevail in the United States and in Minnesota, public officials who would be leaders in national-state relations must base their acts on the idea of getting along with officials of the other level of government by using voluntary, nonauthoritative methods. In particular, two theorems are suggested. The more the administrative leaders of the national government use nonauthoritative methods in their dealings with the states and, secondly, the more decision-making related to national-state programs is participated in by state officials, (1) the more cooperative will be the continuing relations, (2) the less chance there will be of the program being seriously curtailed or altered in a direction contrary to the values of the national administrators, and (3) the greater will be the probability that the values of the national administrators will be implemented in the long run. The converse of these propositions is likewise true.

Power as a value and expediency values in general have less hold on those engaged in national-state relations than various programmatic values. The picture of a power-mad individual seeking to strengthen his personal influence over his associates by every means at his command because he values power so highly is a false picture, or at least not a typical one, in national-state relations. This is especially true of administrative leadership in an era of professionalism but the tendency is observable among political officials as well. Program values are the usual goals for which power is sought with expediency values supplemental or subordinate thereto. Perhaps in an era of contracting governmental services expediency and power values would be prized more highly. Since such conditions did not prevail at the time the observations reported here were made the present data do not deny or confirm this possibility.

In conclusion, some comments are ventured on current suggestions for "improving" national-state relations. One of the most popular suggestions is that national-state relations be coordinated by the national government so that a single policy would prevail in all fields. If this idea were followed, national-state relations in highways would follow the same general policy and procedure as national-state relations in welfare, and so on. A second proposal is that the success or failure of intergovernmental relations be judged by the degree of harmony and cooperation that prevails between each set of national and state officials. Thirdly, particularly since the Eisenhower Administration took office, there has been much talk of the desirability of decentralization and a movement "back" to the states.

A common difficulty besets all these suggestions. Coordination, harmony or cooperation, and decentralization or states' rights are not necessarily good or bad in and of themselves. They are usually neutral concepts and are good or bad only in relation to other and more fundamental objectives an individual or group is seeking. To the extent that they are valued in and of themselves, they almost always hold a secondary place in the value framework. A program may be highly successful yet not present a picture of harmony and cooperation between state and nation. This often happens in the early years of a program when program goals remain unanswered or not agreed upon. Complete harmony is simply not possible if there is conflict over program goals. On the other hand, harmony may come at a high price. The professional administrators of national and state governments may have very harmonious relations but this good feeling may be a means of masking their fundamental disagreement with the general political officials of both levels and of suppressing policy issues that the latter would prefer to have brought to light.

As for coordination, all national-state relations cannot be coordinated until policy goals are agreed upon. The important problem is not coordination but coordination *for what*. The President and Congress have found it impossible to give a single answer. The policy and procedures in connection with national-state relations are not coordinated because no one in authority can agree on a single set of goals or objectives. Similarly decentralization. Decentralization for what and with what policy results? Decentralization cannot be considered apart from programmatic values that are affected thereby, particularly with an increase in the nationwide economic and social problems confronting government. Decentralization or states' rights, if applied to a number of activities, would mean virtual elimination of effective governmental action. Decentralization is thus often advocated by those who oppose governmental activity in a particular area and believe that decentralizing it would make action ineffective; it is also frequently supported by those from rich states as opposed to those from poor areas, by those not in political power nationally, and by those voicing a general political philosophy rather than by those confronted with very detailed and practical problems.

The patterns of national-state relations can be changed or "improved." But since these patterns reflect the values of individuals engaged in these relations, any change in the patterns is likely to heighten value conflict, at least temporarily.

13   *The Federal System**

MORTON GRODZINS

Federalism is a device for dividing decisions and functions of government. As the constitutional fathers well understood, the federal structure is a means, not an end. The pages that follow are therefore not concerned with an exposition of American federalism as a formal, legal set of relationships. The focus, rather, is on the purpose of federalism, that is to say, on the distribution of power between central and peripheral units of government.

From *Goals for Americans*, © 1960, by The American Assembly, Columbia University, New York, New York, pp. 265-282. Reprinted by permission of Prentice-Hall, Inc., Englewood Cliffs, New Jersey.

*This paper is the product of research carried out in the Federalism Workshop of the University of Chicago. I am indebted to the workshop participants, particularly Daniel J. Elazar, Dennis Palumbo, and Kenneth E. Gray, for data they collected. I profited greatly in writing Part III of the paper from Mr. Elazar's prize-winning dissertation, "Intergovernmental Relations in Nineteenth Century American Federalism" (Chicago, 1959).

THE SHARING OF FUNCTIONS

The American form of government is often, but erroneously, symbolized by a three-layer cake. A far more accurate image is the rainbow or marble cake, characterized by an inseparable mingling of differently colored ingredients, the colors appearing in vertical and diagonal strands and unexpected whirls. As colors are mixed in the marble cake, so functions are mixed in the American federal system. Consider the health officer, styled "sanitarian," of a rural county in a border state. He embodies the whole idea of the marble cake of government.

The sanitarian is appointed by the state under merit standards established by the federal government. His base salary comes jointly from state and federal funds, the county provides him with an office and office amenities and pays a portion of his expenses, and the largest city in the county also contributes to his salary and office by virtue of his appointment as a city plumbing inspector. It is impossible from moment to moment to tell under which governmental hat the sanitarian operates. His work of inspecting the purity of food is carried out under federal standards; but he is enforcing state laws when inspecting commodities that have not been in interstate commerce; and somewhat perversely he also acts under state authority when inspecting milk coming into the county from producing areas across the state border. He is a federal officer when impounding impure drugs shipped from a neighboring state; a federal-state officer when distributing typhoid immunization serum; a state officer when enforcing standards of industrial hygiene; a state-local officer when inspecting the city's water supply; and (to complete the circle) a local officer when insisting that the city butchers adopt more hygienic methods of handling their garbage. But he cannot and does not think of himself as acting in these separate capacities. All business in the county that concerns public health and sanitation he considers his business. Paid largely from federal funds, he does not find it strange to attend meetings of the city council to give expert advice on matters ranging from rotten apples to rabies control. He is even deputized as a member of both the city and county police forces.

The sanitarian is an extreme case, but he accurately represents an important aspect of the whole range of governmental activities in the United States. Functions are not neatly parceled out among the many governments. They are shared functions. It is difficult to find any governmental activity which does not involve all three of the so-called "levels" of the federal system. In the most local of local functions — law enforcement or education, for example — the federal and state governments play important roles. In what, *a priori*, may be considered the purest central government activities — the conduct of foreign affairs, for example — the state and local governments have considerable responsibilities, directly and indirectly.

The federal grant programs are only the most obvious example of shared functions. They also most clearly exhibit how sharing serves to disperse governmental powers. The grants utilize the greater wealth-gathering abilities of the central government and establish nation-wide standards, yet they are "in aid" of functions carried out under state law, with considerable state and local discretion. The national supervision of such programs is largely a process of mutual accommodation. Leading state and local officials, acting through their professional organizations, are in considerable part responsible for the very standards that national officers try to persuade all state and local officers to accept.

Even in the absence of joint financing, federal-state-local collaboration is the characteristic mode of action. Federal expertise is available to aid in the building of a local jail (which may later be used to house federal prisoners), to improve a local water purification system, to step up building inspections, to provide standards for state and local personnel in protecting housewives against dishonest butchers' scales, to prevent gas explosions, or to produce a land use plan. States and localities, on the other hand, take important formal responsibilities in the development of national programs for atomic energy, civil defense, the regulation of commerce, and the protection of purity in foods and drugs; local political weight is always a factor in the operation of even a post office or a military establishment. From abattoirs and accounting through zoning and zoo administration, any governmental activity is almost certain to involve the influence, if not the formal administration, of all three planes of the federal system.

ATTEMPTS TO UNWIND THE FEDERAL SYSTEM

Within the past dozen years there have been four major attempts to reform or reorganize the federal system: the first (1947-49) and second (1953-55) Hoover Commissions on Executive

Organization; the Kestnbaum Commission on Intergovernmental Relations (1953-55); and the Joint Federal-State Action Committee (1957-59). All four of these groups have aimed to minimize federal activities. None of them has recognized the sharing of functions as the characteristic way American governments do things. Even when making recommendations for joint action, these official commissions take the view (as expressed in the Kestnbaum report) that "the main tradition of American federalism [is] the tradition of separateness." All four have, in varying degrees, worked to separate functions and tax sources.

The history of the Joint Federal-State Action Committee is especially instructive. The committee was established at the suggestion of President Eisenhower, who charged it, first of all, "to designate functions which the States are ready and willing to assume and finance that are now performed or financed wholly or in part by the Federal Government." He also gave the committee the task of recommending "Federal and State revenue adjustments required to enable the States to assume such functions."[1]

The committee subsequently established seemed most favorably situated to accomplish the task of functional separation. It was composed of distinguished and able men, including among its personnel three leading members of the President's cabinet, the director of the Bureau of the Budget, and ten state governors. It had the full support of the President at every point, and it worked hard and conscientiously. Excellent staff studies were supplied by the Bureau of the Budget, the White House, the Treasury Department, and, from the state side, the Council of State Governments. It had available to it a large mass of research data, including the sixteen recently completed volumes of the Kestnbaum Commission. There existed no disagreements on party lines within the committee and, of course, no constitutional impediments to its mission. The President, his

[1]The President's third suggestion was that the committee "identify functions and responsibilities likely to require state or federal attention in the future and . . . recommend the level of state effort, or federal effort, or both, that will be needed to assure effective action." The committee initially devoted little attention to this problem. Upon discovering the difficulty of making separatist recommendations, i.e., for turning over federal functions and taxes to the states, it developed a series of proposals looking to greater effectiveness in intergovernmental collaboration. The committee was succeeded by a legislatively-based, 26-member Advisory Commission on Intergovernmental Relations, established September 29, 1959.

cabinet members, and all the governors (with one possible exception) on the committee completely agreed on the desirability of decentralization-via-separation-of-functions-and-taxes. They were unanimous in wanting to justify the committee's name and to produce action, not just another report.

The committee worked for more than two years. It found exactly two programs to recommend for transfer from federal to state hands. One was the federal grant program for vocational education (including practical-nurse training and aid to fishery trades); the other was federal grants for municipal waste treatment plants. The programs together cost the federal government less than $80 million in 1957, slightly more than two per cent of the total federal grants for that year. To allow the states to pay for these programs, the committee recommended that they be allowed a credit against the federal tax on local telephone calls. Calculations showed that this offset device, plus an equalizing factor, would give every state at least 40 per cent more from the tax than it received from the federal government in vocational education and sewage disposal grants. Some states were "equalized" to receive twice as much.

The recommendations were modest enough, and the generous financing feature seemed calculated to gain state support. The President recommended to Congress that all points of the program be legislated. None of them was, none has been since, and none is likely to be.

A POINT OF HISTORY

The American federal system has never been a system of separated governmental activities. There has never been a time when it was possible to put neat labels on discrete "federal," "state," and "local" functions. Even before the Consititution, a statute of 1785, reinforced by the Northwest Ordinance of 1787, gave grants-in-land to the states for public schools. Thus the national government was a prime force in making possible what is now taken to be the most local function of all, primary and secondary education. More important, the nation, before it was fully organized, established by this action a first principle of American federalism: the national government would use its superior resources to initiate and support national programs, principally administered by the states and localities.

The essential unity of state and federal financial systems was again recognized in the earliest constitutional days with the assumption by the federal government of the Revolutionary War debts of the states. Other points of federal-state collaboration during the Federalist period concerned the militia, law enforcement, court practices, the administration of elections, public health measures, pilot laws, and many other matters.

The nineteenth century is widely believed to have been the pre-eminent period of duality in the American system. Lord Bryce at the end of the century described (in *The American Commonwealth*) the federal and state governments as "distinct and separate in their action." The system, he said, was "like a great factory wherein two sets of machinery are at work, their revolving wheels apparently intermixed, their bands crossing one another, yet each set doing its own work without touching or hampering the other." Great works may contain gross errors. Bryce was wrong. The nineteenth century, like the early days of the republic, was a period principally characterized by intergovernmental collaboration.

Decisions of the Supreme Court are often cited as evidence of nineteenth century duality. In the early part of the century the Court, heavily weighted with Federalists, was intent upon enlarging the sphere of national authority; in the later years (and to the 1930's) its actions were in the direction of paring down national powers and indeed all governmental authority. Decisions referred to "areas of exclusive competence" exercised by the federal government and the states; to their powers being "separate and distinct"; and to neither being able "to intrude within the jurisdiction of the other."

Judicial rhetoric is not always consistent with judicial action, and the Court did not always adhere to separatist doctrine. Indeed, its rhetoric sometimes indicated a positive view of cooperation. In any case, the Court was rarely, if ever, directly confronted with the issue of cooperation *vs.* separation as such. Rather it was concerned with defining permissible areas of action for the central government and the states; or with saying with respect to a point at issue whether any government could take action. The Marshall Court contributed to intergovernmental cooperation by the very act of permitting federal operations where they had not existed before. Furthermore, even Marshall was willing to allow interstate commerce to be affected by the states in their use of the police power. Later courts also upheld state laws that had an impact on interstate commerce, just as they approved the expansion of the national commerce power, as in statutes providing for the control of telegraphic communication or prohibiting the interstate transportation of lotteries, impure foods and drugs, and prostitutes. Similar room for cooperation was found outside the commerce field, notably in the Court's refusal to interfere with federal grants in land or cash to the states. Although research to clinch the point has not been completed, it is probably true that the Supreme Court from 1800 to 1936 allowed far more federal-state collaboration than it blocked.

Political behavior and administrative action of the nineteenth century provide positive evidence that, throughout the entire era of so-called dual federalism, the many governments in the American federal system continued the close administrative and fiscal collaboration of the earlier period. Governmental activities were not extensive. But relative to what governments did, intergovernmental cooperation during the last century was comparable with that existing today.

Occasional presidential vetoes (from Madison to Buchanan) of cash and land grants are evidence of constitutional and ideological apprehensions about the extensive expansion of federal activities which produced widespread intergovernmental collaboration. In perspective, however, the vetoes are a more important evidence of the continuous search, not least by state officials, for ways and means to involve the central government in a wide variety of joint programs. The search was successful.

Grants-in-land and grants-in-services from the national government were of first importance in virtually all the principal functions undertaken by the states and their local subsidiaries. Land grants were made to the states for, among other purposes, elementary schools, colleges, and special educational institutions; roads, canals, rivers, harbors, and railroads; reclamation of desert and swamp lands; and veterans' welfare. In fact whatever was at the focus of state attention became the recipient of national grants. (Then, as today, national grants established state emphasis as well as followed it.) If Connecticut wished to establish a program for the care and education of the deaf and dumb, federal money in the form of a land grant was found to aid that program.

If higher education relating to agriculture became a pressing need, Congress could dip into the public domain and make appropriate grants to states. If the need for swamp drainage and flood control appeared, the federal government could supply both grants-in-land and, from the Army's Corps of Engineers, the services of the only trained engineers then available.

Aid also went in the other direction. The federal government, theoretically in exclusive control of the Indian population, relied continuously (and not always wisely) on the experience and resources of state and local governments. State militias were an all-important ingredient in the nation's armed forces. State governments became unofficial but real partners in federal programs for homesteading, reclamation, tree culture, law enforcement, inland waterways, the nation's internal communications system (including highway and railroad routes), and veterans' aid of various sorts. Administrative contacts were voluminous, and the whole process of interaction was lubricated, then as today, by constituent-conscious members of Congress.

The essential continuity of the collaborative system is best demonstrated by the history of the grants. The land grant tended to become a cash grant based on the calculated disposable value of the land, and the cash grant tended to become an annual grant based upon the national government's superior tax powers. In 1887, only three years before the frontier was officially closed, thus signalizing the end of the disposable public domain, Congress enacted the first continuing cash grants.

A long, extensive, and continuous experience is therefore the foundation of the present system of shared functions characteristic of the American federal system, what we have called the marble cake of government. It is a misjudgment of our history and our present situation to believe that a neat separation of governmental functions could take place without drastic alterations in our society and system of government.

DYNAMICS OF SHARING: THE POLITICS OF THE FEDERAL SYSTEM

Many causes contribute to dispersed power in the federal system. One is the simple historical fact that the states existed before the nation. A second is in the form of creed, the traditional opinion of Americans that expresses distrust of centralized power and places great value in the strength and vitality of local units of government. Another is pride in locality and state, nurtured by the nation's size and by variations of regional and state history. Still a fourth cause of decentralization is the sheer wealth of the nation. It allows all groups, including state and local governments, to partake of the central government's largesse, supplies room for experimentation and even waste, and makes unnecessary the tight organization of political power that must follow when the support of one program necessarily means the deprivation of another.

In one important respect, the Constitution no longer operates to impede centralized government. The Supreme Court since 1937 has given Congress a relatively free hand. The federal government can build substantive programs in many areas on the taxation and commerce powers. Limitations of such central programs based on the argument, "it's unconstitutional," are no longer possible as long as Congress (in the Court's view) acts reasonably in the interest of the whole nation. The Court is unlikely to reverse this permissive view in the foreseeable future.

Nevertheless, some constitutional restraints on centralization continue to operate. The strong constitutional position of the states—for example, the assignment of two senators to each state, the role given the states in administering even national elections, and the relatively few limitations on their law-making powers—establish the geographical units as natural centers of administrative and political strength. Many clauses of the Constitution are not subject to the same latitude of interpretation as the commerce and tax clauses. The simple, clearly stated, unambiguous phrases—for example, the President "shall hold his office during the term of four years"—are subject to change only through the formal amendment process. Similar provisions exist with respect to the terms of senators and congressmen and the amendment process. All of them have the effect of retarding or restraining centralizing action of the federal government. The fixed terms of the President and members of Congress, for example, greatly impede the development of nation-wide, disciplined political parties that almost certainly would have to precede continuous large-scale expansion of federal functions.

The constitutional restraints on the expansion of national authority are less important and less direct today than they were in 1879 or in 1936. But to say that they are less important is not to say that they are unimportant.

The nation's politics reflect these decentralizing causes and add some of their own. The political parties of the United States are unique. They seldom perform the function that parties traditionally perform in other countries, the function of gathering together diverse strands of power and welding them into one. Except during the period of nominating and electing a president and for the essential but non-substantive business of organizing the houses of Congress, the American parties rarely coalesce power at all. Characteristically they do the reverse, serving as a canopy under which special and local interests are represented with little regard for anything that can be called a party program. National leaders are elected on a party ticket, but in Congress they must seek cross-party support if their leadership is to be effective. It is a rare president during rare periods who can produce legislation without facing the defection of substantial numbers of his own party. (Wilson could do this in the first session of the sixty-third Congress; but Franklin D. Roosevelt could not, even during the famous hundred days of 1933.) Presidents whose parties form the majority of the congressional houses must still count heavily on support from the other party.

The parties provide the pivot on which the entire governmental system swings. Party operations, first of all, produce in legislation the basic division of functions between the federal government, on the one hand, and state and local governments, on the other. The Supreme Court's permissiveness with respect to the expansion of national powers has not in fact produced any considerable extension of exclusive federal functions. The body of federal law in all fields has remained, in the words of Henry M. Hart, Jr. and Herbert Wechsler, "interstitial in its nature," limited in objective and resting upon the principal body of legal relationships defined by state law. It is difficult to find any area of federal legislation that is not significantly affected by state law.

In areas of new or enlarged federal activity, legislation characteristically provides important roles for state and local governments. This is as true of Democratic as of Republican administrations and true even of functions for which arguments of efficiency would produce exclusive federal responsibility. Thus the unemployment compensation program of the New Deal and the airport program of President Truman's administration both provided important responsibilities for state governments. In both cases attempts to eliminate state participation were defeated by a cross-party coalition of pro-state votes and influence. A large fraction of the Senate is usually made up of ex-governors, and the membership of both houses is composed of men who know that their re-election depends less upon national leaders or national party organization than upon support from their home constituencies. State and local officials are key members of these constituencies, often central figures in selecting candidates and in turning out the vote. Under such circumstances, national legislation taking state and local views heavily into account is inevitable.

Second, the undisciplined parties affect the character of the federal system as a result of senatorial and congressional interference in federal administrative programs on behalf of local interests. Many aspects of the legislative involvement in administrative affairs are formalized. The Legislative Reorganization Act of 1946, to take only one example, provided that each of the standing committees "shall exercise continuous watchfulness" over administration of laws within its jurisdiction. But the formal system of controls, extensive as it is, does not compare in importance with the informal and extralegal network of relationships in producing continuous legislative involvement in administrative affairs.

Senators and congressmen spend a major fraction of their time representing problems of their constituents before administrative agencies. An even larger fraction of congressional staff time is devoted to the same task. The total magnitude of such "case work" operations is great. In one five-month period of 1943 the Office of Price Administration received a weekly average of 842 letters from members of Congress. If phone calls and personal contacts are added, each member of Congress on the average presented the OPA with a problem involving one of his constituents twice a day in each five-day work week. Data for less vulnerable agencies during less intensive periods are also impressive. In 1958, to take only one example, the Department of Agriculture estimated (and underestimated) that it received an average of 159 congressional letters per working day. Special congressional liaison staffs have been created to service this mass of business, though all higher officials meet it in one form or another. The Air Force in 1958 had, under the command of a major general, 137 people (55 officers and 82 civilians) working in its liaison office.

The widespread, consistent, and in many ways unpredictable

character of legislative interference in administrative affairs has many consequences for the tone and character of American administrative behavior. From the perspective of this paper, the important consequence is the comprehensive, day-to-day, even hour-by-hour, impact of local views on national programs. No point of substance or procedure is immune from congressional scrutiny. A substantial portion of the entire weight of this impact is on behalf of the state and local governments. It is a weight that can alter procedures for screening immigration applications, divert the course of a national highway, change the tone of an international negotiation, and amend a social security law to accommodate local practices or fulfill local desires.

The party system compels administrators to take a political role. This is a third way in which the parties function to decentralize the American system. The administrator must play politics for the same reason that the politician is able to play in administration: the parties are without program and without discipline.

In response to the unprotected position in which the party situation places him, the administrator is forced to seek support where he can find it. One ever-present task is to nurse the Congress of the United States, that crucial constituency which ultimately controls his agency's budget and program. From the administrator's view, a sympathetic consideration of congressional requests (if not downright submission to them) is the surest way to build the political support without which the administrative job could not continue. Even the completely task-oriented administrator must be sensitive to the need for congressional support and to the relationship between case work requests, on one side, and budgetary and legislative support, on the other. "You do a good job handling the personal problems and requests of a Congressman," a White House officer said, "and you have an easier time convincing him to back your program." Thus there is an important link between the nursing of congressional requests, requests that largely concern local matters, and the most comprehensive national programs. The administrator must accommodate to the former as a price of gaining support for the latter.

One result of administrative politics is that the administrative agency may become the captive of the nation-wide interest group it serves or presumably regulates. In such cases no government may come out with effective authority: the winners are the interest groups themselves. But in a very large number of cases, states and localities also win influence. The politics of administration is a process of making peace with legislators who for the most part consider themselves the guardians of local interests. The political role of administrators therefore contributes to the power of states and localities in national programs.

Finally, the way the party system operates gives American politics their over-all distinctive tone. The lack of party discipline produces an openness in the system that allows individuals, groups, and institutions (including state and local governments) to attempt to influence national policy at every step of the legislative-administrative process. This is the "multiple-crack" attribute of the American government. "Crack" has two meanings. It means not only many fissures or access points; it also means, less statically, opportunities for wallops or smacks at government.

. If the parties were more disciplined, the result would not be a cessation of the process by which individuals and groups impinge themselves upon the central government. But the present state of the parties clearly allows for a far greater operation of the multiple crack than would be possible under the conditions of centralized party control. American interest groups exploit literally uncountable access points in the legislative-administrative process. If legislative lobbying, from committee stages to the conference committee, does not produce results, a cabinet secretary is called. His immediate associates are petitioned. Bureau chiefs and their aides are hit. Field officers are put under pressure. Campaigns are instituted by which friends of the agency apply a secondary influence on behalf of the interested party. A conference with the President may be urged.

To these multiple points for bringing influence must be added the multiple voices of the influencers. Consider, for example, those in a small town who wish to have a federal action taken. The easy merging of public and private interest at the local level means that the influence attempt is made in the name of the whole community, thus removing it from political partisanship. The Rotary Club as well as the City Council, the Chamber of Commerce and the mayor, eminent citizens and political bosses — all are readily enlisted. If a conference in a senator's office will expedite matters, someone on the local scene can be found to make such a conference possible and effective. If technical information is needed, technicians will supply it. State or national professional organizations of local officials, individual congressmen and senators, and not infrequently whole state delegations will make the local cause their own. Federal field officers, who service localities, often assume local views. So may elected and appointed state officers. Friendships are exploited, and political mortgages called due. Under these circumstances, national policies are molded by local action.

In summary, then, the party system functions to devolve power. The American parties, unlike any other, are highly responsive when directives move from the bottom to the top, highly unresponsive from top to bottom. Congressmen and senators can rarely ignore concerted demands from their home constituencies; but no party leader can expect the same kind of response from those below, whether he be a President asking for congressional support or a congressman seeking aid from local or state leaders.

Any tightening of the party apparatus would have the effect of strengthening the central government. The four characteristics of the system, discussed above, would become less important. If control from the top were strictly applied, these hallmarks of American decentralization might entirely disappear. To be specific, if disciplined and program-oriented parties were achieved: (1) It would make far less likely legislation that takes heavily into account the desires and prejudices of the highly decentralized power groups and institutions of the country, including the state and local governments. (2) It would to a large extent prevent legislators, individually and collectively, from intruding themselves on behalf of non-national interests in national administrative programs. (3) It would put an end to the administrator's search for his own political support, a search that often results in fostering state, local, and other non-national powers. (4) It would dampen the process by which individuals and groups, including state and local political leaders, take advantage of multiple cracks to steer national legislation and administration in ways congenial to them and the institutions they represent.

Alterations of this sort could only accompany basic changes in the organization and style of politics which, in turn, presuppose fundamental changes at the parties' social base. The sharing of functions is, in fact, the sharing of power. To end this sharing

MORTON GRODZINS

process would mean the destruction of whatever measure of decentralization exists in the United States today.

GOALS FOR THE SYSTEM OF SHARING

The goal of understanding. Our structure of government is complex, and the politics operating that structure are mildly chaotic. Circumstances are ever-changing. Old institutions mask intricate procedures. The nation's history can be read with alternative glosses, and what is nearest at hand may be furthest from comprehension. Simply to understand the federal system is therefore a difficult task. Yet without understanding there is little possibility of producing desired changes in the system. Social structures and processes are relatively impervious to purposeful change. They also exhibit intricate interrelationships so that change induced at point "A" often produces unanticipated results at point "Z." Changes introduced into an imperfectly understood system are as likely to produce reverse consequences as the desired ones.

This is counsel of neither futility nor conservatism for those who seek to make our government a better servant of the people. It is only to say that the first goal for those setting goals with respect to the federal system is that of understanding it.

Two kinds of decentralization. The recent major efforts to reform the federal system have in large part been aimed at separating functions and tax sources, at dividing them between the federal government and the states. All of these attempts have failed. We can now add that their success would be undesirable.

It is easy to specify the conditions under which an ordered separation of functions could take place. What is principally needed is a majority political party, under firm leadership, in control of both Presidency and Congress, and, ideally but not necessarily, also in control of a number of states. The political discontinuities, or the absence of party links, (1) between the governors and their state legislatures, (2) between the President and the governors, and (3) between the President and Congress clearly account for both the picayune recommendations of the Federal-State Action Committee and for the failure of even those recommendations in Congress. If the President had been in control of Congress (that is, consistently able to direct a majority of House and Senate votes), this alone would have made possible some genuine separation and devolution of functions. The failure to decentralize by order is a measure of the decentralization of power in the political parties.

Stated positively, party centralization must precede governmental decentralization by order. But this is a slender reed on which to hang decentralization. It implies the power to centralize. A majority party powerful enough to bring about ordered decentralization is far more likely to choose in favor of ordered centralization. And a society that produced centralized national parties would, by that very fact, be a society prepared to accept centralized government.

Decentralization by order must be contrasted with the different kind of decentralization that exists today in the United States. It may be called the decentralization of mild chaos. It exists because of the existence of dispersed power centers. This form of decentralization is less visible and less neat. It rests on no discretion of central authorities. It produces at time specific acts that many citizens may consider undesirable or evil. But power sometimes wielded even for evil ends may be desirable power. To those who find value in the dispersion of power, decentralization by mild chaos is infinitely more desirable than decentralization by order. The preservation of mild chaos is an important goal for the American federal system.

Oiling the squeak points. In a governmental system of genuinely shared responsibilities, disagreements inevitably occur. Opinions clash over proximate ends, particular ways of doing things become the subject of public debate, innovations are contested. These are not basic defects in the system. Rather, they are the system's energy-reflecting life blood. There can be no permanent "solutions" short of changing the system itself by elevating one partner to absolute supremacy. What can be done is to attempt to produce conditions in which conflict will not fester but be turned to constructive solutions of particular problems.

A long list of specific points of difficulty in the federal system can be easily identified. No adequate congressional or administrative mechanism exists to review the patchwork of grants in terms of national needs. There is no procedure by which to judge, for example, whether the national government is justified in spending so much more for highways than for education. The working force in some states is inadequate for the effective performance of some nation-wide programs, while honest and not-so-honest graft frustrates efficiency in others. Some federal aid programs distort state budgets, and some are so closely supervised as to impede state action in meeting local needs. Grants are given for programs too narrowly defined, and over-all programs at the state level consequently suffer. Administrative, accounting and auditing difficulties are the consequence of the multiplicity of grant programs. City officials complain that the states are intrusive fifth wheels in housing, urban redevelopment, and airport building programs.

Some differences are so basic that only a demonstration of strength on one side or another can solve them. School desegregation illustrates such an issue. It also illustrates the correct solution (although not the most desirable method of reaching it): in policy conflicts of fundamental importance, touching the nature of democracy itself, the view of the whole nation must prevail. Such basic ends, however, are rarely at issue, and sides are rarely taken with such passion that loggerheads are reached. Modes of settlement can usually be found to lubricate the squeak points of the system.

A pressing and permanent state problem, general in its impact, is the difficulty of raising sufficient revenue without putting local industries at a competitive disadvantage or without an expansion of sales taxes that press hardest on the least wealthy. A possible way of meeting this problem is to establish a state-levied income tax that could be used as an offset for federal taxes. The maximum level of the tax which could be offset would be fixed by federal law. When levied by a state, the state collection would be deducted from federal taxes. But if a state did not levy the tax, the federal government would. An additional fraction of the total tax imposed by the states would be collected directly by the federal government and used as an equalization fund, that is, distributed among the less wealthy states. Such a tax would almost certainly be imposed by all states since not to levy it would give neither political advantage to its public leaders nor financial advantage to its citizens. The net effect would be an increase in the total personal and corporate income tax.

The offset has great promise for strengthening state governments. It would help produce a more economic distribution of industry. It would have obvious financial advantages for the vast majority of states. Since a large fraction of all state income is used to aid political subdivisions, the local governments would also profit, though not equally as long as cities are under-represented in state legislatures. On the other hand, such a scheme will appear disadvantageous to some low-tax states which profit from the in-migration of industry (though it would by no means end all state-by-state tax differentials). It will probably excite the opposition of those concerned over governmental centralization, and they will not be assuaged by methods that suggest themselves for making both state and central governments bear the psychological impact of the tax. Although the offset would probably produce an across-the-board tax increase, wealthier persons, who are affected more by an income tax than by other levies, can be expected to join forces with those whose fear is centralization. (This is a common alliance and, in the nature of things, the philosophical issue rather than financial advantage is kept foremost.)

Those opposing such a tax would gain additional ammunition from the certain knowledge that federal participation in the scheme would lead to some federal standards governing the use of the funds. Yet the political strength of the states would keep these from becoming onerous. Indeed, inauguration of the tax offset as a means of providing funds to the states might be an occasion for dropping some of the specifications for existing federal grants. One federal standard, however, might be possible because of the greater representation of urban areas in the constituency of Congress and the President than in the constituency of state legislatures: Congress might make a state's participation in the offset scheme dependent upon a periodic reapportionment of state legislatures.

The income tax offset is only one of many ideas that can be generated to meet serious problems of closely meshed governments. The fate of all such schemes ultimately rests, as it should, with the politics of a free people. But much can be done if the primary technical effort of those concerned with improving the federal system were directed not at separating its interrelated parts but at making them work together more effectively. Temporary commissions are relatively inefficient in this effort, though they may be useful for making general assessments and for generating new ideas. The professional organizations of government workers do part of the job of continuously scrutinizing programs and ways and means of improving them. A permanent staff, established in the President's office and working closely with state and local officials, could also perform a useful and perhaps important role.

The strength of the parts. Whatever governmental "strength" or "vitality" may be, it does not consist of independent decision-making in legislation and administration. Federal-state inter-penetration here is extensive. Indeed, a judgment of the relative domestic strength of the two planes must take heavily into account the influence of one on the other's decisions. In such an analysis the strength of the states (and localities) does not weigh lightly. The nature of the nation's politics makes federal functions more vulnerable to state influence than state offices are to federal influence. Many states, as the Kestnbaum Commission noted, live with "self-imposed constitutional limitations" that make it difficult for them to "perform all of the services that their citizens require." If this has the result of adding to federal responsibilities, the states' importance in shaping and administering federal programs eliminates much of the sting.

The geography of state boundaries, as well as many aspects of state internal organization, are the products of history and cannot be justified on any grounds of rational efficiency. Who, today, would create major governmental subdivisions the size of Maryland, Delaware, New Jersey, or Rhode Island? Who would write into Oklahoma's fundamental law an absolute state debt limit of $500,000? Who would design (to cite only the most extreme cases) Georgia's and Florida's gross under-representation of urban areas in both houses of the legislature?

A complete catalogue of state political and administrative horrors would fill a sizeable volume. Yet exhortations to erase them have roughly the same effect as similar exhortations to erase sin. Some of the worst inanities – for example, the boundaries of the states, themselves – are fixed in the national constitution and defy alteration for all foreseeable time. Others, such as urban under-representation in state legislatures, serve the over-represented groups, including some urban ones, and the effective political organization of the deprived groups must precede reform.

Despite deficiencies of politics and organizations that are unchangeable or slowly changing, it is an error to look at the states as static anachronisms. Some of them – New York, Minnesota, and California, to take three examples spanning the country – have administrative organizations that compare favorably in many ways with the national establishment. Many more in recent years have moved rapidly towards integrated administrative departments, state-wide budgeting, and central leadership. The others have models-in-existence to follow, and active professional organizations (led by the Council of State Governments) promoting their development. Slow as this change may be, the states move in the direction of greater internal effectiveness.

The pace toward more effective performance at the state level is likely to increase. Urban leaders, who generally feel themselves disadvantaged in state affairs, and suburban and rural spokesmen, who are most concerned about national centralization, have a common interest in this task. The urban dwellers want greater equality in state affairs, including a more equitable share of state financial aid; non-urban dwellers are concerned that city dissatisfactions should not be met by exclusive federal, or federal-local, programs. Antagonistic, rather than amiable, cooperation may be the consequence. But it is a cooperation that can be turned to politically effective measures for a desirable upgrading of state institutions.

If one looks closely, there is scant evidence for the fear of the federal octopus, the fear that expansion of central programs and influence threatens to reduce the states and localities to compliant administrative arms of the central government. In fact, state and local governments are touching a larger proportion of the people in more ways than ever before; and they are spending a higher fraction of the total national product than ever before. Federal programs have increased, rather than diminished, the importance of the governors; stimulated professionalism in state agencies; increased citizen interest and participation in government; and, generally, enlarged and made more effective the scope of state action.[2] It may no longer be true in any significant sense that the states and localities are "closer" than the federal government to the people. It is true that the smaller governments remain active and powerful members of the federal system.

Central leadership: The need for balance. The chaos of party processes makes difficult the task of presidential leadership. It

[2]See the valuable report, *The Impact of Federal Grants-in-Aid on the Structure and Functions of State and Local Governments,* submitted to the Commission on Intergovernmental Relations by the Governmental Affairs Institute (Washington, 1955).

deprives the President of ready-made congressional majorities. It may produce, as in the chairmen of legislative committees, power-holders relatively hidden from public scrutiny and relatively protected from presidential direction. It allows the growth of administrative agencies which sometimes escape control by central officials. These are prices paid for a wide dispersion of political power. The cost is tolerable because the total results of dispersed power are themselves desirable and because, where clear national supremacy is essential, in foreign policy and military affairs, it is easiest to secure.

Moreover, in the balance of strength between the central and peripheral governments, the central government has on its side the whole secular drift towards the concentration of power. It has on its side technical developments that make central decisions easy and sometimes mandatory. It has on its side potent purse powers, the result of superior tax-gathering resources. It has potentially on its side the national leadership capacities of the presidential office. The last factor is the controlling one, and national strength in the federal system has shifted with the leadership desires and capacities of the chief executive. As these have varied, so there has been an almost rhythmic pattern: periods of central strength put to use alternating with periods of central strength dormant.

Following a high point of federal influence during the early and middle years of the New Deal, the post-war years have been, in the weighing of central-peripheral strength, a period of light federal activity. Excepting the Supreme Court's action in favor of school desegregation, national influence by design or default has not been strong in domestic affairs. The danger now is that the central government is doing too little rather than too much. National deficiencies in education and health require the renewed attention of the national government. Steepening population and urbanization trend lines have produced metropolitan area problems that can be effectively attacked only with the aid of federal resources. New definitions of old programs in housing and urban redevelopment, and new programs to deal with air pollution, water supply, and mass transportation are necessary. The federal government's essential role in the federal system is that of organizing, and helping to finance, such nation-wide programs.

The American federal system exhibits many evidences of the dispersion of power not only because of formal federalism but more importantly because our politics reflect and reinforce the nation's diversities-within-unity. Those who value the virtues of decentralization, which writ large are virtues of freedom, need not scruple at recognizing the defects of those virtues. The defects are principally the danger that parochial and private interests may not coincide with, or give way to, the nation's interest. The necessary cure for these defects is effective national leadership.

The centrifugal force of domestic politics needs to be balanced by the centripetal force of strong presidential leadership. Simultaneous strength at center and periphery exhibits the American system at its best, if also at its noisiest. The interests of both find effective spokesmen. States and localities (and private interest groups) do not lose their influence opportunities, but national policy becomes more than the simple consequence of successful, momentary concentrations of non-national pressures: it is guided by national leaders.[3]

[3]Messrs. Perkins and Redford state:

Professor Grodzins has made a significant contribution. The federal system has contributed to a "mild chaos" both administratively and financially. He accurately assesses the several quite futile attempts to disentangle the administrative and fiscal relationships of the states and the national government.

At this juncture, however, it should be remembered that the present system of shared responsibility confuses rather than fixes responsibility. Ascertainable responsibility for policy, administrative performance, and financing is an essential feature of effective self-government. The possibility of achieving it needs to be explored.

A reduction of the sharing of power would to some degree cause greater centralization of responsibility in the federal government. It would not necessarily result in loss of appropriate administrative decentralization and the loss of influence by the ordinary citizen over the activities of government. This is illustrated by what Mr. Grodzins himself says concerning the influence of the localized party structure on administration of centralized national functions.

The chaos of party processes itself impairs leadership for national functions and national aims. Mr. Grodzins' conclusion that the costs of this chaos are tolerable may be drawn too easily. Whether the centrifugal pulls of party decentralization are so strong as to seriously threaten national leadership and responsibility in our government deserves careful assessment.

Decentralization is an essential goal of American policy. So also are responsibility and leadership. Public concern needs to manifest itself about both of these goals.

YOU'VE GOT TO KNOW HOW TO SELL YOURSELF

Would you like your product or name to be recognized by thousands? Are you trying to build and expand your business to increase sales and profits? Are you looking for ways to reach more potential customers than ever before? Promotion is the crucial key to all these goals.

And you don't need a lot of money, a large staff, or a bunch of specialists to produce advertisements, catalogs, commercials—and results. All you really need is the expert advice you'll find in HOW TO PROMOTE YOUR OWN BUSINESS, the nuts-and-bolts guide to doing it all yourself or learning when and how to have others do it for you.

GARY BLAKE is the director of The Communication Workshop, a consulting firm helping business management to improve writing and communications skills. He has been published in such magazines as *Harper's, New York, The New York Times Book Review,* and *Advertising Age.* He is the author of *The Status Book* (Doubleday).

ROBERT W. BLY is an independent copywriter and consultant specializing in industrial advertising and promotion. He has written articles for such publications as *Direct Marketing, Amtrak Express, Business Marketing,* and *Writer's Digest.* He is the author of *A Dictionary of Computer Words* (Dell/Banbury).

Bly and Blake are co-authors of *Technical Writing: Structure, Standards, and Style* (McGraw-Hill).

HOW TO PROMOTE YOUR OWN BUSINESS

Gary Blake and Robert W. Bly

A PLUME BOOK
NEW AMERICAN LIBRARY
TIMES MIRROR
NEW YORK AND SCARBOROUGH, ONTARIO

NAL BOOKS ARE AVAILABLE AT QUANTITY DISCOUNTS WHEN USED TO PROMOTE PRODUCTS OR SERVICES. FOR INFORMATION PLEASE WRITE TO PREMIUM MARKETING DIVISION, THE NEW AMERICAN LIBRARY, INC., 1633 BROADWAY, NEW YORK, NEW YORK 10019.

SIGNET, SIGNET CLASSIC, MENTOR, PLUME, MERIDIAN and NAL BOOKS are published *in the United States* by The New American Library, Inc., 1633 Broadway, New York, New York 10019, *in Canada* by The New American Library of Canada Limited, 81 Mack Avenue, Scarborough, Ontario M1L 1M8

Library of Congress Cataloging in Publication Data:
Blake, Gary.
How to promote your own business.
"A Plume book."
Bibliography: p.
Includes index.
1. Advertising. 2. Public relations. 3. Small business.
I. Bly, Robert W. II. Title.
HF5823.B59 1983 659.2'81 83-12093
ISBN 0-452-25456-6

First Printing, October, 1983
1 2 3 4 5 6 7 8 9

PRINTED IN THE UNITED STATES OF AMERICA

ACKNOWLEDGMENTS

For those who may think publicity is a thankless task, we'd like to respond by publicly applauding a few of the many people who had faith in this book and who helped contribute to its birth.

Very special thanks to our editor, Channa Taub, who had the sagacity to buy it and the tenacity to help mold it; to Dominick Abel, whose blend of gentleness, tough-mindedness, and patience helped us to do our best; to the small-business owners of the United States, whose creativity in finding new ways to promote their businesses has added variety and fun to this project.

Special thanks also to Eve Blake, Jean Blake, Jack Nathan, Amy Sprecher, and the rest of the "kitchen cabinet" who somehow managed to stay alert even after the tenth time we asked if they'd "mind taking a look at this draft."

We'd also like to thank the following people and organizations for allowing us to use their promotions in our book: Louis Galterio, Abbondanza; Lyla Ward, The Party Place; Tom Okada, Okada Studios; Adele Gross, Bon Bon Travel; Ed Waldman, Ed Waldman Gallery; Bridgford Hunt, The Hunt Company; Philip Magerman, Magerman Associates; Barbara Weinstein, Barbara H. Weinstein & Associates; Contempo Design; Kevin Gormely; Steve Brown; Koch Engineering; Thompson Cigar Co.; Dick and Bert for Weil Olds.

Finally, we thank Alan Cohen at Westwinds for sponsoring the "How to Promote Your Own Business" seminars that provided much of the source material for this book; Jon Isear, who offered numerous helpful comments on many areas of promotion and advertising; and Pauline Yearwood.

Every day is a fishing day,
But every day is not a catching day.
                    —Caribbean saying

Some people make things happen,
Some wait for things to happen,
And then there are those that say—what happened?
                              —Anonymous

CONTENTS

INTRODUCTION

"Why are my competitors the ones who always get written about in magazines and newspapers?"

"How can I write a press release that will get the editor's attention?"

"How can I learn some basics about graphic design, printing, brochure writing, and photography so that when I hire someone I'll know what to look for?"

"How can direct mail and mail order help my business?"

"What's the difference between advertising and publicity?"

"Do I need a newsletter?"

"In my newspaper advertising, should I run a big ad once or a small ad many times?"

"How can I bring in new business quickly on a limited promotion budget?"

* * *

These are just some of the questions that entrepreneurs ask us over and over again. Naturally, you'll add some of your own to the list. *How to Promote Your Own Business* was written to give you the answers.

Whether you're a novice or an old hand at running a small business, effective advertising and publicity can be the key to your success. By planning your promotions carefully, and by taking into consideration what has been tried in the past, you can significantly improve your chances of getting publicity—leads—orders—*money!*

How to Promote Your Own Business is a practical, do-it-yourself guide to advertising, publicity, and sales promotion for the small-business owner or manager. The book's numerous examples are drawn from real promotions carried out by real companies, so you can learn from their successes—and failures. We've written the book for the layman, and we've arranged it in an easy-to-use, easy-to-read format. There are numerous step-by-step case histories, checklists, tips, and lists of promotional "dos and don'ts," plus a number of helpful illustrations showing what a finished ad, brochure, or press release looks like. We've collected these examples and illustrations from a wide variety of small businesses—drugstores, florist shops, restaurants, consultants, publishers, travel agents, photographers, caterers, art galleries, and many, many more.

Here's how the book is organized:

Chapters 1–3 present the basics of promotion. They'll help you plan and budget your advertising and publicity program.

Chapters 4–6 tell you how to create your own promotions. They provide tips on copywriting, graphic design, photography, printing, and working with professionals—ad agencies, PR firms, and free-lancers.

Chapters 7–8 explain how you can influence the media to gain free publicity for your product and your business.

Chapters 9–10 cover the basics of direct mail and mail order —today's fastest-growing area of marketing.

Chapter 11 is devoted to sales literature—the brochures, flyers, circulars, and catalogs that almost every business must have in order to sell its products and services.

Chapters 12–13 tell you how to advertise effectively in newspapers, magazines, and directories, and on radio and television.

Chapters 14–16 cover newsletters, trade shows, expositions, and a miscellany of other useful promotional techniques.

Chapter 17 sums it all up, and tells you how to measure the *results* of your promotions so you'll know whether they were successful or not.

Finally, the Appendix lists some further reading in small-business promotion, management, finance, and start-up.

How to Promote Your Own Business will give you the

know-how you need to turn your ideas into action—action that will produce new prospects, new customers, new sales. Simply add your own imagination—and a lot of hard work.

We believe that the hundreds of examples, ideas, tips, and case histories provided in this book will help you gain the recognition that you and your business deserve. We believe that the quality of your promotions reflects the quality of your business and will, in time, lead to success.

Take a look at the sales letters, ads, catalogs, and brochures that cross your desk every day. Some are sharp, clear, crisp, and original. Others are sloppy, or dull and boring, or ill-timed, or misdirected. We want *your* promotions to be the best. We want *you* to have the edge. And that's why we wrote *How to Promote Your Own Business*.

Now, it's up to you.

• Chapter 1 •

WHAT PROMOTION IS ALL ABOUT

Promotion: A Key to Success for Small Business

Each year, American entrepreneurs start a quarter of a million new small businesses—everything from bookstores and bake shops to computer companies and catering services to restaurants and real estate agencies.

Today, there are more than 10.8 million small businesses in the United States.* These growing companies employ 58% of our work force and account for 43% of the U.S. Gross National Product. Small business provides, directly or indirectly, for the livelihood of more than 100 million Americans.

Now for some bad news: Three out of four of the 250,000 new small businesses that start up each year will fail within their first five years, and nine out of ten will fail within ten years. *Of every ten companies going into business today, only one will make it*.

According to Dun & Bradstreet, 95% of these small-business failures are the result of poor management. Many of them are the result of poorly managed—or neglected—*promotion*.

For the small business, a well-planned, properly executed

---

* The U.S. Small Business Administration defines (for the purpose of making loans) small businesses by their income or number of employees. To be defined as "small business," a service business can take in up to $8 million; retail, up to $7.5 million; construction, up to $9.5 million; and wholesale, up to $22 million. A "small" manufacturer must not employ more than 1,500 people.

promotional program can mean the difference between success and failure.

What Is Promotion?

Promotion is communication. It is you telling your potential customers and clients about your business so they will buy your product or service.

Promotion is providing information about those products and services in a way that *persuades* people that they want, need, can use, and should buy them. Promotion is salesmanship—in person, in print, and on the air.

Why You Should Promote Your Business

For the small business, the bottom line of promotion is greater profit through increased sales. Most small-business people feel that any promotion that does not pay for itself many times over (in the profit it brings in from sales) is a waste of time, money, and effort. Fortunately, many promotions *can* justify their expense.

Promotions can benefit you and your business in several different and exciting ways:

• Promotion can sell products directly and immediately. A price-off coupon for orange juice in the Sunday newspaper is a promotion designed to generate a direct sale.

• Promotion can also build awareness among consumers of a company, product, service, idea, or brand name. When you decide to rent a car, you probably think of Hertz, Avis, and possibly Budget—because they *advertise*. Awareness builds sales and businesses over the long run.

• Promotion can establish or change your image. Through promotion, A&P supermarkets became known for high quality and reasonable prices—"Price & Pride." Coca-Cola is "the real thing," GE "brings good things to life," and Westinghouse is "a powerful part of your life." How many small businesses in your area have built their image and reputation using similar slogans and promotions on a smaller scale?

• Promotion can reach many prospects and bring in thousands of qualified sales leads. Sometimes, promotion does not result in a direct sale, but instead helps salespeople make a sale.

• Promotions remind, inform, and persuade your audience.

The Four Types of Promotions

There are four basic types of promotion: personal selling, advertising, publicity, and sales promotion.

1. Personal selling

"Personal selling" is just what the words imply: selling done person-to-person. It is a presentation made by the salesperson to one or more prospects for the purpose of making a sale. The presentation can be made in face-to-face conversation, over the phone, by personal letter, or by wire. When the Avon lady rings your doorbell, *that's* personal selling.

2. Advertising

According to the textbook definition,* advertising is "any paid form of nonpersonal presentation and promotion of ideas, goods, or services by an identified sponsor."

Unlike a letter from your accountant or insurance agent, a local auto dealer's newspaper advertisement is *not* a personal message created for your eyes only. It is a *mass* communication, designed to reach a broad audience. The dealer is identified as an advertiser (the sponsor of the ad). He created the message. And he paid for the space.

Advertising takes many forms. Print advertisements appear

---

* In this case, the textbook is *Marketing Principles: The Management Process,* 2nd ed., by Ben M. Enis (Santa Monica: Goodyear Publishing Company, 1977), pp. 360–365.

in newspapers, magazines, local shoppers, the telephone book, catalogs, directories, programs, menus, and circulars. Signs appear as highway billboards, posters, on buses and subways, and in train stations. The written word can even be delivered as skywriting. And the spoken word is aired as commercials for television and radio.

3. Publicity

Publicity is a kind of free advertising. By providing editors and program directors with news and other information, you can get your business coverage in the media. You do not pay for the coverage, and are not identified as the source of the story—and you have no control over the timing and content of your free publicity. The basic tool of publicity is the press release, and Chapter 7 tells you how to use it to get your name in newspapers and magazines and on radio and television.

4. Sales promotion

Sales promotion encompasses a miscellany of promotional activities. Sales promotion is everything that is not personal selling, advertising, or publicity. Trade shows, product samples, premiums, contests, demonstrations, coupons, "price-off" deals, dealer incentives, point-of-purchase displays, sales brochures, flyers, and direct mail* are all sales promotion.

What Promotion Is Best for Your Business?

Not every business can profit equally from all the different types of promotion. A dry cleaner would benefit very little from sending out a press release, since dry cleaning is not of great interest to the press. An advertisement in a neighbor-

---

* Some authorities classify direct mail as sales promotion; others call it advertising. While it is true that direct mail is a kind of advertising by mail, it doesn't usually require the purchase of space in any media, and so we have chosen to list it under sales promotion.

hood newspaper, however, could bring new customers to the store.

Below we've listed different types of promotions and a few of the types of businesses that have used them with success.

Newspaper ads:

Health care	Barber
Apparel	Beauty parlor
Restaurant	Home furnishings
Entertainment	Limousine service
Dry cleaner	Gifts
Real estate	Tailor
Tutor	Typing service
Jeweler	Bookstore

Local shopper ads:

Kitchenware	Music lessons
Vitamins	Bookstore
Beauty parlor	Boutique
Exercise clinic	Optician
Car rental	Travel agent
Picture framing	Accountant
Interior design	Liquor store
Clothing	Bake shop
Antiques	Locksmith

Local magazine ads:

Department store	Auto dealer
Real estate	Plastic surgeon
Clothing	Bar or tavern
Hotel	Disco
Furniture	Limousine service
Restaurant	Dating service
Entertainment	Stereo systems
Exercise clinic	Résumé writing
Private club	Personal instruction

Telephone directory ads:

Insurance agent	Stationer
Exterminator	Phone answering service
Printer	Travel agent
Photographer	Mover

Telephone directory ads: (cont.)

Auto dealer	Air-conditioning repair
Take-out food	Locksmith
House painter	Laundry
Physician	Karate instructor
Attorney	Hardware store
Pet shop	Dentist
Roofing contractor	Carpet cleaning
Typing service	Bicycle shop

Television commercials:

Auto dealer	Marine equipment
Stereo systems	Department store
Restaurant	Tires
Racetrack	Mufflers
Vocational training	Record store
Home video equipment	Mail order

Radio commercials:

Furniture	Restaurant
Auto dealer	Health club
Ice cream parlor	Travel agent
Entertainment	Department store
Bank	Home improvement
Accountant	Health care

Direct mail:

Magazine	Coins and stamps for collectors
Newsletter	
Consultant	Clothing
Free-lance artist	Gifts
Office equipment	Driver training
Insurance	Cleaning service
Advertising agency	Public relations agency
Seminar	

Publicity:

Acupuncturist	Boutique
Gourmet store	Handbags
Art gallery	Consumer newsletter
Consultant	Home-cleaning service
Restaurant	Dating service
Gift shop	Interior design

Brochures, catalogs, or flyers:

Medical products	Industrial manufacturer
Consultant	Handcrafts
Travel agent	Mail order
Advertising agency	Engineering design
Typing service	Construction
Computer store	Educational seminar
Office equipment	Publisher

Newsletters:

Management consultant	Gift shop
Bank	Trade association
Publisher	Business cooperative
Art gallery	Engineering firm

Trade shows and expositions:

Craftsperson	Industrial manufacturer
Antique dealer	Farmer
Jeweler	Automobile dealer
Artist	Boat dealer

You, Too, Can Promote Your Business

Promotion can get your message across and bring in business. It can improve your image, build recognition, and increase sales and profits.

You do not need a great deal of money to succeed at promotion. Hathaway Shirts began advertising with a budget of $30,000; Wrigley's Gum began with only $30.

Promotions work best when they are done to achieve some specific sales or marketing goal. That takes some planning, and planning your promotions is the subject of our next chapter.

• Chapter 2 •

PLANNING YOUR PROMOTIONS

Having a Business Plan

Every business begins with a plan—usually an idea that forms in the mind of an entrepreneur. One idea leads quickly to another, and, before long, a sketch of what the business will be, and who the prospects are, begins to take shape.

This initial flow of ideas is invigorating and may spawn numerous other ideas about how the business will run, but, inevitably, the ideas need to be refined, arranged, and acted upon. A business plan helps form the ideas into a workable program, a systematic way of viewing and reaching your prospects, planning promotions, and defining your business goals.

A simple business plan should cover such points as why the product or service is needed, its potential market, competitors, estimated earnings, and so forth.

Our purpose in this chapter is to discuss some of the marketing aspects of an informal business plan. Using several typical businesses as examples—a gourmet food store called Abbondanza, a typing service, a photography studio, a newsletter publisher—we'll look at key areas of marketing that may help you decide how best to promote your business.

Marketing

Marketing is an aggregate of functions involved in moving goods or services from producer to consumer. This important function involves four elements—the four P's of marketing:

product, price, place (distribution), and promotion. Your marketing strategy will depend on how you define each of these P's in terms of your own business.

Owners of small businesses have limited resources to spend on marketing activities. Concentrating the marketing efforts on one or more key marketing segments is the basis of target marketing. The major ways to segment a market are:

• *Geographic segmentation.* People located close to your place of business are more likely to become customers than those who are far away.

• *Demographic segmentation.* You may choose to market to groups of prospects based on age, race, sex, social class, marital status, or income.

• *Type-of-business segmentation.* Your market may be specific types of businesses (car dealers, hotels, steelmakers, restaurants, computer companies) and organizations (hospitals, universities, federal agencies).

• *Product segmentation.* The market for your products may be determined by how customers will use your product, and what benefits they derive from it. For example, beer brewers know that there are "heavy" beer drinkers who purchase 90% of all beer, and light (not "Lite") drinkers who buy an occasional six-pack. The heavy beer drinkers drink for taste and develop loyalty to a brand; light beer drinkers are likely to buy the low-priced brand.

Know Your Customer

Marketing begins with knowing your customer. A *customer* is someone who purchases your product or service; a *prospect* is a prospective customer. And, although luck may play a role in determining the *actual* people who eventually become your customers, you should nevertheless form a detailed picture of your *typical* customer.

For example, a new gourmet store will primarily appeal to people with a refined palate. The owner would be very foolish if he reasoned that since everyone has to eat, my store has thousands of potential customers. Most people, either because of taste or budget, do not include pâté, French roasted duck, smoked salmon, or watercress dip in their daily menu!

A gourmet store appeals to people who are affluent enough to afford luxury food items and who choose these delicacies over simpler (often less caloric) foods. Naturally, a fine presentation of the food will entice even those on a budget to indulge in the occasional Smithfield ham, caviar spread, or Amaretto cheesecake, but these people are not the devotees, the people who a gourmet store owner hopes will be his steady customers.

In the same way, a photographer who is just starting out may stay alive by shooting the occasional photograph of a child or a wedding, but his real market may be commercial customers. In his business plan, he should estimate the numbers of people whom he can reach who are actively engaged in purchasing the services of a commercial photographer (advertising agencies, public relations agencies, corporations, catalog producers).

When it comes to a neighborhood typing service, the "typical" steady customer is harder to define. Businesspeople may stop in to have a report, manual, or proposal typed quickly and accurately; students want term papers and book reviews typed; writers need their book manuscripts, plays, and screenplays typed in proper form. Each of these customers cares only about his particular needs, and your promotion to each group should speak primarily to those needs.

It may be helpful for you to think of these separate markets in terms of their relative value. Students may bring in the most repeat business, but screenplay writers, page for page, may be your most lucrative market. Also, you may wish to think about which of your submarkets is easiest to service. As with so many businesses, the most lucrative business often requires the most time. For a typing service, businesspeople may be a better market than either students or writers.

After you've been in business awhile, you'll come to have a clearer picture of your typical customer, and that information can be used to focus your promotions. So, if the typing service discovered that the office manager typically was the person at each company who brought in the office's reports, manuals, and proposals, the typing service's owner might think about a promotion aimed at reaching office managers throughout the neighboring business district.

A versatile neighborhood photographer who discovers that his work derives from a variety of sources should define his customers in terms of steadiness as well as how lucrative their business is. If he is engaged to shoot photos of an annual banquet, he should know that it is hardly "bread-and-butter" business. Unless he chooses to specialize in doing banquets, he must orient his business to ongoing clients, people who can be counted on for regular assignments.

Think about each type of customer who purchases your products or services. What do you know about your customers? Where do they live? Are they married or single? How much money do they make each year? You don't have to do a sophisticated marketing survey to help make a realistic assessment as to whether the people you need for your business need you. The better you define your customers' "demographics" and "geographics," the less chance you have of kidding yourself into thinking that, to paraphrase Will Rogers, "I never met a person who didn't like my product."

How Can You Reach Your Customer?

Try to outline realistic methods of reaching your customer. Each business reaches its audience in a variety of ways. For some businesses, a sign over the door is the only way in which they let their potential customers know of their existence. However, considering the unlimited ways in which to use advertising, press releases, articles, flyers, brochures, radio, TV, newspapers, and magazines to help us communicate our message to the public, it seems foolish not to at least explore many possible avenues for exposure.

In the case of our fledgling photographer, he may choose to stimulate interest in his work by circulating a press release focusing on one aspect of his work. In his press release (Fig. 2-1), photographer Tom Okada used his past associations as well as the opening of his new studio as "pegs" upon which to construct the release. By circulating the press release to local newspapers and magazines involved with photography, advertising, and the media, Okada was able to generate interest in his work and gain some publicity.

After writing (or having a publicity-minded friend write) the release, Tom must choose places to send it. If his goals were purely to gain recognition in artistic circles, he might send it only to photographic "arts" magazines. But if he is interested in stimulating business, he will select magazines that reach people who have the power to make a decision to hire him for an assignment, such as fashion magazines or women's magazines.

In the same way, a gourmet-store owner has a variety of promotional options, and must decide upon his goals for a particular promotion. A great deal of care must go into a promotional decision, because the goals sometimes conflict with each other. For example, it would be easy to print 10,000 flyers announcing the store's opening and hire high school students to hand the flyers out throughout the neighborhood. That would certainly get the word out, and it might well bring in customers. But an inexpensively produced flyer might tacitly label the store as "cheap" or, worse, as just another "takeout place." So, although you might gain customers, you wouldn't be gaining the "right" customers—people who are motivated to buy good food, not just curiosity-seekers.

A gourmet-store owner may have to take a long-range view. The owner may want to throw a grand-opening party for the press or try to line up corporate catering business, reasoning that in these ways he will be building a continuing market for his store's food. The critics, once they know of the store, may review the food; if the reviews are good, customers will follow. In the same way, a promotion aimed at food-service people at corporations might result in the catering of several business luncheons or office parties. After that, word of mouth might well take over.

A stenography service that has determined that its prime customers are (1) local businesspeople, (2) out-of-town businesspeople staying at local hotels, (3) screenwriters or playwrights, and (4) job seekers who wish to dictate cover letters to accompany résumés has taken the first step toward reaching these people.

Client: Contact:
Tom Okada   THE COMMUNICATION WORKSHOP
45 West 18th Street   207 East 85th Street
New York, NY 10011   New York, NY 10028
                               (212) 794-1144

For Immediate Release:

FORMER APPRENTICE TO MASTER PHOTOGRAPHERS
W. EUGENE SMITH AND ARNOLD NEWMAN
OPENS MANHATTAN STUDIO

NEW YORK, NY—"When you work with a good photographer, you get a lot of good information; when you work with a great one, you receive inspiration." So says Tom Okada, who gained not only inspiration but earned the respect and affection of top photographers Arnold Newman and W. Eugene Smith.

Now, with a versatility and experience few photographers achieve, Okada, 29, has just opened his own photographic studio at 45 West 18th Street in New York.

Since a Newman or a Smith can have his pick of eager photographic assistants, Okada had to prove himself in a number of areas. His portfolio established him as an expert in a number of photographic formats. He's at ease with tungsten as well as strobe lighting; in studio as well as location settings. Okada is also a fine carpenter, and is as exacting building sets as he is in photographing them.

Specializing in "fine-image" still-life photography, Okada hopes to broaden his experience in candid photography, catalog work and general advertising. Says Okada, "A photographer is one artist who can't afford to be a prima donna

—more—

Fig. 2-1   This excerpt from a three-page release shows how a press release arranges thematic material. The central idea (the studio opening) is blended with the photographer's background to give importance to the event.

In the same way, a dating service segments its market by recognizing that there are a number of subgroups within its market, and by approaching each subgroup with a unique angle.

For example, a dating service might wish to send one type of message to gays who are single and a completely different one to senior citizens. Another message could be fashioned for middle-aged singles or recently divorced or widowed singles—assuming that you can separate these people and address them as special groups of people. Mailing lists of people who fit each category may be available from mailing-list brokers, specialty magazines, or associations. By addressing the particular needs of each group separately, you give the impression that your organization specializes in that group's needs. That will go a long way toward making gays or senior citizens or the recently divorced respond to your message.

Direct mail and sales promotion worked for the dating service; a press release worked for Tom Okada; a grand-opening press party helped gain attention for the gourmet store. Other businesses might make use of late-night radio, advertising, or phone calls to prospects. In any case, you should consider the risks, costs, and time demands of all types of promotions before deciding which ones to pursue.

What Do You Want to Say to Your Audience?

The answer: anything that might stimulate them to buy your product or service! You are arranging your product or service's "sales points" in a clear, careful manner. You hope that your customer will seize upon one or more of them and keep them in mind when it comes time to make a purchase.

A dating service that stressed its empathy with being alone and aging might well be remembered by a single senior citizen. On the other hand, a food store or a photography service might have to work hard to truly separate itself from the crowd. Tom Okada drew attention by talking about his unique experience and the singular event of opening his own studio; the food store also uses its opening as an occasion to introduce its products to the public. Perhaps the chef is famous, or the store has a new concept in takeout food. It might be that the store has a dazzlingly beautiful interior or that it specializes in salads or cheesecakes or baby back ribs. To entice the media into writing about the store, the owner must keep in mind that his is one of many similar stores, all craving media attention. Attention will be paid, therefore, to the store that presents itself in the most newsworthy light.

It's not hard to gain publicity for an odd business such as a love-letter-writing service or a breakfast-in-bed catering service that features a strolling violinist, but it is often difficult to gain ongoing publicity for more mundane businesses— beauty parlors, or locksmiths, or plumbers. Therefore, you should consider not just the uniqueness or "sexiness" of the concept of your business, but its ability to grow, to gain new customers, to entice ongoing media coverage or consumer interest.

For many businesses, a sale or a new item or a new location provides the spark for a new promotion. Perhaps a personnel change—a new chef, decorator, or administrator—is noteworthy. The thrust of your promotion remains steady: You are selling quality or service or low cost or all three, and you need to keep reminding the public that you, among your competitors, are best equipped to handle its business. It also helps to just say "thank you" to past customers. A Christmas card is one of the easiest and nicest ways of keeping your name in front of your customers without making a blatant sales pitch.

The Best Way to Say It

Christmas cards lead us to the idea of finding the best way to say what you want us to say. Do you want subtlety or do you want to bang the drum loudly? Subtlety doesn't work for everyone. A new pizza place doesn't want subtle promotion; it wants to tell people that its prices are reasonable, the mozzarella is fresh, and the crust is crusty. A flyer dropped strategically near the mailboxes at a few hundred large apartment buildings in the neighborhood can do the trick. So can posting the flyer at nearby laundromats, supermarkets, and community bulletin boards. Since anyone might crave a pizza, there need not be any targeting of the market, except that the flyers will pull best if they are delivered within walking distance of the pizza place. It would be absurd to spread the flyer to other neighborhoods, because they are likely to have their own pizza parlors.

However, a business selling an expensive service must take great care to hone its promotional messages, and even greater pains to target them to decision-makers. For example, a consultant who sells training seminars in writing or presentation skills must make sure that his written promotions are especially well written, concise, and clear. He, above all others, must avoid redundancy, antiquated phrases, clichés, and self-serving statements. When preparing his promotional message, the consultant must tailor his ideas to fit the interests of his audience.

And who are the audience? They may be training directors who purchase training seminars from outside vendors. Or his message may go to people with similar titles or corporate functions: manager of management development, vice-president of human resources, or vice-president of manpower planning. These people receive numerous sales messages every day, and a consultant must catch attention before he can present his full message. An example of a consultant's sales letter is shown in Fig. 2-2.

How Do You Want Your Customers to Respond?

When a pizza parlor delivers flyers to an apartment house, the pizza purveyor hopes that the flyer will stimulate the reader's appetite, and that the message will translate into the sale of a pizza or at least a meatball hero.

But sometimes sales are not that simple. It would be unreasonable for the writing consultant to expect a person receiving his mailing to pick up a phone and, without gaining more information, order one writing seminar "to go." The writing consultant's package—brochure, cover letter, and return postcard (Figs. 2-3 and 2-4 show a sample brochure cover and return postcard)—aims at stimulating a request for additional information. That's all. There's no expectation of an immedi-

This year, my business writing seminars will save a large insurance company $50,000. Next year, they'll save the company even more.

Here's how:

Recently I designed and implemented a writing program for twelve supervisors at Mutual of New York. Among the many skills they learned was how to edit the "fat" out of their letters, memos and reports.

We figured out that if each of the twelve trainees cut just one paragraph out of each of their communications, MONY would save 2,400 paragraphs per year. Since each paragraph takes an average of 20 minutes to write, edit, type, read and understand, MONY would save 800 man-hours a year.

Since corporate time costs about $60 per hour, the savings could amount to as much as $50,000 in the first year. And that's a conservative figure.

Why? Because <u>extra</u> dividends are paid in an employee's greater confidence, improved productivity and sharper communication skills as well as in a better corporate image.

Next year, these same twelve people will again save their company $50,000 in wasted words, effort and time—and it won't cost MONY another penny. And, if MONY trains another twelve people, they'll probably save an <u>additional</u> $50,000 a year. . . every year.

Insurance companies such as MONY and The American Re-Insurance Company, for whom I designed a similar program, must feel I'm doing something right: they've invited me back to help train new groups of employees.

Please take a moment to review the enclosed brochure. If you'd like more information about how improved writing can make your company more productive, just fill out the enclosed card and mail it.

Gary Blake, Ph.D.
Director

THE
COMMUNICATION WORKSHOP

207 East 85th Street
New York 10028
(212) 794-1144

Fig. 2-2 Aimed solely at training managers at insurance companies, this cover letter attempts to translate improved writing skills into tangible benefits.

ate sale. If the training manager returns the postcard, he is taking the first step in what may be many steps between the first contact and the final sale. Considering that the price of a seminar is several thousand dollars, it would be foolish to expect a purchase to take place before the prospect calls references, sees the consultant in action at another organization, or asks for a proposal. The true value of a return postcard is its help in building a reliable mailing list of qualified prospects.

When a mail or TV solicitation is used solely to generate immediate sales, we call that direct-response advertising. In this type of advertising, products such as subscriptions, records, books, and cutlery are sold directly to a consumer who, upon hearing or reading the solicitation, writes a check. Perhaps he'll be induced to act quickly because he's been promised a "premium" or gift for speedy action. Keep in mind that the more money your product or service costs, the more so-

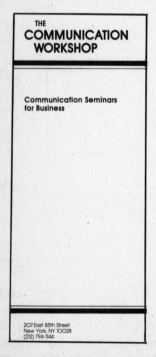

THE COMMUNICATION WORKSHOP

Communication Seminars for Business

207 East 85th Street
New York, NY 10028
(212) 794-1144

Fig. 2-3 This front panel of a consultant's brochure uses lots of white space to attain a "clean" look. White space also helps the eye rivet on the company name.

☐ We are currently offering training in writing.

☐ We are not currently offering training in writing.

Please send me additional information about:

☐ The Writing Audit   ☐ Stress Management

☐ Effective Business Writing   ☐ Persuasive Speaking

☐ Technical Writing   ☐ Successful Business Meetings

Name_____Organization_____

Address_____

Telephone_____

THE COMMUNICATION WORKSHOP
207 East 85th Street
New York, NY 10028

Fig. 2-4   The front and back of a return postcard. This card provides the sender with valuable information about an organization's training needs and at the same time helps build a specific mailing list of prospects.

phisticated the promotion must be, and the more times you'll have to contact your prospect before completing the sale.

Your business plan, therefore, charts a course for your business and your promotions. It makes you face the primary question of your business life: What can I do with limited time and money and unlimited imagination and enthusiasm?

A plan forces you to think carefully about your product and your prospects, and this chapter has raised a few questions that may arise in your own business plan. A plan forces you to evaluate the number of prospects you have as well as to confront the difference between steady customers and the occasional customer. In order for your business to flourish, you'll probably need to build a base of ongoing customers.

A business plan is the foundation upon which your promotions will be built. If you understand your customer, his needs, his spending habits, and his awareness of the competition, you have taken a step toward leading him to your door.

Chapter 3

HOW TO BUDGET YOUR PROMOTIONS

Promotion Is an Expense

You know you will have to spend some money to execute your advertising and publicity plan. The question is: How much?

Promotion is a gamble. You never know for sure that a given promotion will bring in enough new business to justify the time and money spent to execute the project. When you're running a small operation on a shoestring budget, it takes real guts to allocate a large sum for advertising when you've never advertised before.

Without guidance, setting the annual promotion budget is a task fraught with uncertainty. How do you know that you're not spending too much on promotion? How do you know that you're spending enough? Why not just spend as little as you can get away with? What rational basis do you have for this decision? These are the questions which gnaw at the promotional novice.

There is no magic formula that can easily and precisely set the proper promotion budget for your company. There *are*, however, six time-tested methods that other businesses have used throughout the years to plan their promotion budgets.

Below, we list each budgeting method, and describe its advantages and disadvantages. Each has some merit, and at the end of the list, we suggest how to combine the best of several techniques to plan your budget effectively.

Six Methods for Planning Promotion Budgets

1. Percentage of sales

The most widely used budgeting technique is to set your promotion budget as a fixed percentage of your sales.

Let's say you sell $50,000 in handwoven baskets every year. If you set the promotion budget at 2% of sales, you will allocate $1,000 for promotion.

What sales do you base the percentage on? It's up to you. You can base it on past sales (either last year's sales or an average of the past several years), on future sales (as predicted by your sales forecast), or some combination of past and predicted sales.

What percentage of sales should you choose as the promotion budget? It varies from industry to industry. Defense contractors spend very little on promotion—about 0.15% of sales. Some large consumer companies spend 15%—and more. In 1975, General Motors' advertising budget was 0.6% of sales; General Foods', 6.8%; Carter-Wallace's, 31.4%; Revlon's, 9.2%; Pepsi's, 3.9%; Sears', 1.9%; Procter & Gamble's, 7.9%.

Listed below are some types of small businesses and their typical promotion budgets as a percentage of sales: *

Type of Business	Advertising Budget as a Percentage of Sales
Apparel stores	2.5–3.0%
Auto supply stores	0.5–2.0%
Bars and cocktail lounges	1.0–2.0%
Bookstores	1.5–1.7%
Coin-op laundries	0.6–2.0%

* The source for most of these figures is "Advertising Small Business: Small Business Reporter," Bank of America, 1981, vol. 15, no. 2, pp. 10–11.

Type of Business	Advertising Budget as a Percentage of Sales
Gift stores	1.5–2.5%
Hairgrooming/beauty salons	2.5–3.0%
Industrial manufacturers	0.15–3.0%
Printers	0.4–1.0%
Restaurants	0.8–3.0%

As you can see, most small businesses spend between 1% and 3% of their income from sales on advertising and promotion.

The percentage-of-sales method is simple to use, and its major benefit to small business is that these percentage guidelines can tell you whether your budget is reasonable or way out of line.

On the negative side, basing promotional expenditures on sales is somewhat illogical—it implies that promotion is the result of sales when, in fact, sales are the result of promotion.

Also, the percentage-of-sales method does not take into account the economy, the market, the competition, and your own planned sales objectives. Therefore, it is, at best, a rough guideline only—and not the final word.

2. Unit of sales

This variation of the percentage-of-sales method bases promotional expenditures on units of product sold rather than on the gross dollar amount of sales.

Say past experience has taught you that it takes 5 cents worth of promotion to sell one can of baked beans. If your goal is to sell 100,000 cans of beans, you will need to spend $5,000 on promotion.

This method can be helpful when you are selling durable goods of high value, such as television sets and washing machines, or goods of small unit value, such as canned food, toilet paper, and motor oil. It is not a valid approach to setting a budget for a service business.

3. Match the competition

Some companies play follow-the-leader by basing their promotion budget on what their competitors are spending.

It is good business sense to recognize the importance of competition. But, by matching your competitors' promotions dollar for dollar,* you assume they are trying to achieve the same sales and marketing objectives as you are—and that is probably false. Besides, your competitors may not know how to budget and execute promotions effectively, in which case you would be mimicking their errors.

By all means, pay attention to the competition. But don't follow them automatically. Instead, come up with a plan that suits your goals, your company, your products, and your marketing philosophy.

4. All you can afford

With the all-you-can-afford method, you first appropriate money for essential operating expenses: rent, raw material, taxes, insurance, labor, postage, inventory. Whatever is left over is allocated to the promotion budget.

This technique can help fledgling business ventures survive. But if you are past the stage where you're struggling just to pay the landlord, avoid the all-you-can-afford method, because it implies that promotion is a luxury and not an essential part of running a growing business. And chances are, if you are reading this book, that is not the case.

5. Historical

The easiest way to set a promotion budget is to say, "Let's spend what we spent last year—plus 10% for inflation."

This method has essentially the same advantages and disadvantages as the percentage-of-sales method. Use it as a rough guideline only.

---

* Of course, if a competing firm is much larger than you are, you can't possibly match its budget dollar-for-dollar. But you *could* spend what it's spending on a percentage-of-sales basis.

6. Objective and task

This is the most effective method: to define the sales and marketing objectives that promotion should accomplish, and then appropriate the budget needed to achieve these objectives.

Let's say a free-lance graphic artist wants to promote his services, and that his *sales objective* is to earn $30,000 by getting assignments from a dozen or so different advertising agencies.

The *task* that can best accomplish this objective is a direct-mail campaign aimed at ad-agency creative directors. Thus, his simple promotion budget would look like this:

Sales Objective	Task	Cost
To get $30,000 in work from 10–15 different ad agencies	Direct mail to 1,000 creative directors	$500
	Phone follow-up	$50
	Second mailing to 1,000 creative directors	$250
	TOTAL BUDGET:	$800

Methods 1 through 5 set a budget, and then allocate funds for specific tasks. The objective-and-task method takes the more logical approach of building a budget based on the tasks you want to complete. It ensures that promotional dollars are spent on those projects that will most benefit your business.

A disadvantage of the objective-and-task method is that the budget will probably be much more than you can afford. If that happens, you must rank objectives in order of importance, and concentrate on those at the top of your list.

One Sensible Solution

None of these six methods—percentage of sales, unit of sales, match the competition, all you can afford, historical, or objective and task—is the absolute ideal way of setting a promotion budget.

Rather, a combination of several techniques seems to work best. We recommend the following three-step method for budgeting promotions:

1. Use the percentage-of-sales method (number 1) to set upper and lower limits on your budget. An industrial manufacturer with sales of $600,000 should, according to the list given earlier, be spending somewhere between $900 (0.15% of sales) and $18,000 (3% of sales) on promotion.

2. Pay attention to what your competitors are doing, but don't copy them blindly. If one widget maker triples his trade-journal advertising, the others may lose sales to him unless they do something. This something may be an increase in advertising. Or it may be a price reduction, a product improvement, a penetration into a new market or application, or any one of a number of non-advertising items.

3. Now that you know what the competition is doing and have established a minimum and maximum budget, allocate money to complete tasks that will achieve your planned objectives (objective-and-task, method number 6). Be sure not to spend more than you can afford, and don't underspend, either.

More Budgeting Tips

Here are some more helpful hints on how to set a promotion budget:

• *Be flexible*. If the economy fluctuates, if you develop a new product, or if your major competitor goes out of business, you may change your promotion strategy—and your promotion budget—in midyear. Remember, a budget is not a commandment cast in stone; it is a tool to help you control promotional expenditures. Don't be afraid to change the budget to suit your changing needs.

• *Set priorities*. The majority of small businesses can't afford to do even half the promotions they'd like to do. Therefore, you need to rank your objectives, and concentrate on high-priority projects.

• *Make it manageable.* Large promotion budgets can be broken down by product, department, division, store, sales territory, or market. Or any combination of these.

• *Use the calendar.* Some small businesses set budgets by the year; others by the quarter; a few by the month. Don't neglect seasonal promotions when setting the budget. A greeting-card wholesaler would spend more money in December than in any other month, because Christmas-card sales are the lifeblood of that industry.

• *Spend money to make money.* Be prepared to spend more than the usual percentage of sales if you are introducing a new product or trying to break into a new market. It costs more to promote the new than to maintain the status quo. In Holland, a food company coming out with a new salad dressing set a promotion budget that was *three times* the product's projected sales for the next two years.

• *Expect the unexpected.* Put a 10% contingency fund in the promotion budget. It is difficult to estimate all promotion costs precisely, and many companies find themselves going over budget by as much as 10%.

Promotion Budgets in a Down Economy

When money is tight, it is only natural to cut back on expenses; after all, the employees must be paid and the shelves filled with merchandise before you can indulge in a costly radio campaign.

However, *Magazine Age* reports that in 1982, a year of severe recession, nearly 60% of all industrial manufacturers planned to *increase* their advertising budgets by an average of 27%. Only 6% of the manufacturers planned to cut back on their advertising expenditures.

Although it is tempting to panic at the first sign of a slump in the economy, there is wisdom in not slashing the promotion budget when money becomes tight. Consider, for example, these findings from some recent articles in the *Harvard Business Review:*

• Increased advertising during a recession will still result in increased sales. The increase in sales will be greater than that of competitors who do not increase their ad budgets.

• If you choose to reduce your advertising budget, your sales will probably fall off *even more sharply than the sales of those firms which do no advertising at all!*

• Promotion can stimulate consumer demand for products even in hard times.

Surprisingly, the nation's total "disposable income" (the amount of money consumers can spend on products and services) does not fall more than a percentage point or so during a recession.

• • •

Should it become necessary to cut the budget, eliminate low-priority items. Concentrate on the promotions vital to your continued sales success. Stick with proven promotions you know will work, and save experimentation for better times.

Also, see if you can find a less expensive way of doing things—a thinner paper stock for your brochures, a smaller newspaper ad, a shorter television commercial.

Chapter 4

WHEN TO HIRE A PROFESSIONAL—AND WHEN TO DO IT YOURSELF

Few of us in small business have the time to become expert in the many skills needed to produce effective advertising and promotions, and so the question is raised: Should you hire an advertising agency or public relations firm to handle all this, or can you do it yourself?

There are some small businesses that use such agencies to handle their promotions. Other entrepreneurs create the bulk of their promotions in-house. Most small businesses, however, use a combination of staff and outside services. These outside services are provided by advertising and public relations agencies, graphic design studios, and free-lance writers, artists, photographers, and publicists.

Advertising Agencies

Advertising agencies provide advertisers with a wide range of communications services: copywriting, art, production, media planning and buying, market research, sales promotion, and public relations.

The very words "advertising agency" are a turn-off to most small-business managers. They conjure up images of Madison Avenue at its worst: three-martini lunches, plush conference rooms, elaborate creative presentations, golf-playing account executives, and other evils that waste clients' time and money.

Yes, it's true that Madison Avenue agencies probably aren't for you. For starters, their "creative time" (copywriting, artwork, planning) goes for about $125 an hour and more. (Even medium-size New York agencies are getting $75 an hour.)

Worse, your company will get lost in the shuffle at a large agency. Let's say the agency does $20 million a year. Assuming the agency would even talk to you, how much attention will you get if you spend $200,000 or $20,000?

(As an interesting aside, industry sources note that major advertising agencies will devote three members of their staff to your account full-time for every *million* dollars you spend.)

This doesn't mean that there isn't an ad agency out there that's right for you. The advertising business has more than its fair share of entrepreneurs—small agencies ranging from one- or two-person shops to those with perhaps a dozen or so employees. Many of these small advertising agencies do work that rivals the creative excellence of Madison Avenue—and costs far less. A six-man agency in New York, for example, bills creative time at $60 an hour, while a one-man shop in Akron charges $20 an hour. In addition, small agencies often distinguish themselves from their giant competitors by specializing in a particular area such as medical, financial, dental, corporate, retail, fashion, or industrial advertising. A small specialty agency can be ideal for a small business.

Should You Use an Advertising Agency?

Do you need the highly professional and somewhat costly services of an advertising agency? Or can you do things less expensively and better yourself? Here's a list of dos and don'ts to help you decide:

• *Do* use an agency if effective advertising is crucial to your success, and if you feel you can afford the going rates.

• *Do* consider using an agency if you spend $10,000 or more a year on promotion. That's probably the minimum amount it will take to interest even the smallest agency in handling your account.

• *Don't* hire an agency because you're trying to cut costs. Getting outside help is almost always more expensive than doing it yourself.

• *Don't* hire an agency solely because "you don't have time to do it yourself." Yes, the agency will free your time for other tasks. But when you hire an agency, you're hiring creativity coupled with marketing expertise—and not just another pair of hands.

• *Do* hire an agency if your company is marketing-oriented.

• *Do* hire an agency if you intend to use its services to full advantage.

• *Do* hire an agency for fresh thinking, outside objectivity, and a more creative approach to promotions.

• *Do* hire an agency if you need help planning promotions, introducing new products, and selecting target markets.

• *Do* hire an agency to do things "first-class."

• *Don't* hire an agency if you are certain that only *you* know the best way to promote your business, and that outsiders can *never* make useful suggestions in this area.

• *Don't* avoid hiring an agency because you want to save its 15% commission by placing your ads and commercials with the media yourself. Studies show that after taking into account administrative and staff costs, buying media yourself saves only 4.5%—not 15%.

• *Don't* feel you must hire an outside agency for prestige when your company becomes big. Ralston Purina, General Electric, Pfizer, Scott Paper, and Lever Brothers all have sizable in-house advertising departments.

If you decide to hire an agency, you need to know how to select the one that's right for your business.

How to Select an Advertising Agency

Here are six useful tips for selecting the advertising agency that can best serve your company:

1. Choose an ad agency with expertise in your area.

Accountants, brokers, and banks should select an advertising agency that specializes in financial accounts. A manufac-

turer of globe valves for petroleum refineries should choose
an agency with industrial-advertising expertise. A designer of
men's swimwear would do best to seek counsel from an
agency with other fashion accounts.

By insisting that your agency already be somewhat expert
in your industry, you save yourself the costly and time-consuming process of educating its staff from scratch. One warning: Make sure the agency does not have any of your
competitors as clients. A conflict would surely arise.

2. Do not hire an agency with more capabilities than you need.

Do you really need an agency with overseas branch offices,
television-production capabilities, a market research department, and clout with nationwide print and broadcast media?
All of an agency's clients pay to support its complete operations—so, to save money without sacrificing service or quality, select an agency that offers only those communications
services you need. Which, at the very least, will likely be
copywriting, print production, and media buying.

3. Make sure the agency is the right size for you.

A $20,000 account represents only 0.1% of a $20 million
agency's income, and consequently will receive only 0.1% of
its management attention and 0.1% of its creative effort. Make
sure your agency is small enough to consider your account
profitable and worth its best efforts.

4. Ask to see the agency's work.

Examine a prospective agency's portfolio of ads, brochures, and catalogs. Do you like what you see? Is it the kind
and caliber of work you want done? Avoid agencies whose
work is either too shabby or too elegant for your market,
business, and taste.

5. Make sure the agency is sympathetic with the needs of small business.

Explain to prospective agencies that your goal is to create promotions that increase sales—and not to win advertising awards.

Tell them your money is limited. Tell them you want an ad to pull inquiries or generate sales, not to look pretty on the page or read like a poem.

Let them know what you expect. If you want the agency to design and produce letterhead, business cards, signs, brochures, price sheets, mail stuffers, and flyers, say so. Not every agency will handle these small assignments.

6. Check out the price.

Most smaller agencies collect a 15% commission for placing ads with the media, and charge a flat project fee for creating advertisements and other promotions. This fee is usually based on some hourly rate for agency time.

Ask what they typically charge to produce a quarter-page black-and-white newspaper ad, a four-page brochure, a 30-second radio commercial. It may be more than you want to pay.

Public Relations Agencies

Public relations agencies are the professionals to turn to when you want to get coverage in the media.

Now, sending out a press release or calling up a local editor are two things anyone can do—you don't need to be a specialist to practice public relations. So why hire a PR agency? Here's what you buy when you contract for their services:

• *Media contacts.* Frequently, a PR man will wink slyly and promise that he can "get you" the *Wall Street Journal* or the *Boston Globe*. This is an unprofessional attitude and an exaggeration; editors are not tools of PR agents, and no PR pro can guarantee favorable coverage of your story in the press. Nevertheless, most PR professionals do have relationships with members of the press, and they can use their contacts to place stories in the media. This is what makes them valuable to you, the client.

• *Expertise*. Public relations agents are expert at writing, planning, timing, and executing publicity campaigns. While novices tend to be unstructured and haphazard in their PR efforts, professionals can plan and execute a campaign that supports marketing strategy.

Most public relations firms charge their clients a monthly retainer for their services; a typical monthly retainer can be $1,000 and up. Therefore, most small businesses are better off finding a small PR agency to do work on a project basis, or handling public relations in-house.

Graphic Design Studios

Most small businesses rely on print promotions—posters, signs, pamphlets, ads, point-of-purchase displays, coupons, and brochures—to reach their customers and prospects.

Graphic design studios do not, as a rule, offer media, marketing, writing, and PR services. They are simply the experts in designing and producing print material. (For more information on producing print promotions, see Chapter 6.)

Some small-business managers have a good grasp of sales and marketing, know their business well, write lucid copy, and understand the basic promotional tools. They just need help turning their ideas into polished print material, and the graphic design studio can provide that help.

Graphic design studios usually offer two hourly rates: a "design" rate for the creative work of designing the format and special look of your promotions, and a lower "mechanical" rate for the more straightforward task of physically pasting up type, illustrations, and photos for the printer.

The rates vary according to where your business is located. In Manhattan, a city that may have more working graphic artists than anywhere in the United States, the design rate ranges from $40 to $60 an hour and up and the mechanical rate from $10 to $25 an hour or so.

Free-lancers

Many creative types in promotion—especially writers, artists, photographers, and publicists—work as free-lancers serving both advertisers and advertising agencies.

Free-lancers are capable of delivering the same high-quality work as advertising and PR agencies at a fraction of the cost. Using free-lancers can be the least expensive way of getting professional help to create your promotions.

Before hiring a free-lancer, check his résumé, portfolio, and client list. Find out his rates, and get a written estimate in advance. Most important, make sure you like (or at least can tolerate) the free-lancer *as a person*. With advertising agencies, an account executive separates you from the writer or artist. With free-lance help, you deal with the creator of your promotion directly. If you are to have a successful collaboration with the free-lancer, you must be able to work well together.

How to Work with Professional Help

You've looked at your checkbook, looked with dismay at your current promotion campaign, and made a major decision: You want your promotions to be first-class, and you've decided to get professional help—an advertising agency, a PR firm, a graphic design studio, or a free-lancer.

Here, then, are some helpful hints for getting the best work out of your outside supplier with the least amount of trouble:

1. Brief your agency.

The more your advertising agency knows about your product, your company, and your markets, the better. Tell your agency what makes your product unique. Explain its advantages over the competition's products. Explain your marketing strategy. Provide background material in the form of current ads and press releases, brochures, articles on your industry, and market-research reports. The best clients prepare comprehensive agency briefings *in writing*.

2. Do not compete with your agency in the creative area.

Certainly you can disapprove of the brochure copy your copywriter turns in. Make helpful criticisms, and turn it back to him for a revision. But do not tell outside talent how to do the job. If you can write better than the writer and take better pictures than the photographer, then fire them and do it yourself.

3. Don't strain your promotions through many layers of approval.

You, and possibly your business partner, should approve or disapprove the work submitted by the outside agency. But don't look for approval from your purchasing agent, your accountant, your cashier, and your mother-in-law. Too many levels of approval will muddy clear writing and water down the impact of the message. Worse, it will dampen the creative spirit of your writers or artists so that the next thing they do will be mediocre enough to get your company's approval *instantly*.

4. Be reasonable about paying.

It is difficult to make a good profit in advertising, and many agencies and free-lancers have gone out of business waiting for late payments from their clients. Be fair to your agencies and free-lancers, and pay them promptly.

By all means, watch expenses carefully and don't pay for something you never asked for in the first place. On the other hand, too much haggling over money can cause your outside professionals to put forth less effort on your account. You will get, then, a competent promotion, but not a great one.

Where to Find Help

You want to hire an agency or free-lancer, but don't know where to turn. The following mini-directory of creative talent should be of some assistance:

• *Standard Directory of Advertising Agencies: The Agency Red Book,* published by the National Register Publishing Company, Inc., 5201 Old Orchard Road, Skokie, IL 60077. This directory lists 4,400 advertising agencies here and overseas. For each agency, the *Red Book* reports agency income, number of employees, key accounts, and the addresses and phone numbers of its offices. There is also a useful index listing agencies by state. The *Red Book* is available in most libraries.

• *O'Dwyer Directory of Public Relations Firms,* 271 Madison Avenue, New York, NY 10016. Lists 1,200 PR firms. Available in most libraries.

• *The Creative Black Book,* published by Friendly Publications, Inc., 401 Park Avenue South, New York, NY 10016. Lists thousands of photographers, illustrators, graphic designers, printers, TV producers, ad agencies, and other creative resources. Available by mail order through the publisher and in some major bookstores.

• *Adweek Creative Services Directories,* published by *Adweek,* 820 Second Avenue, New York, NY 10017. Similar in scope to the *Black Book,* the *Adweek Creative Services Directories* list photographers, artists, illustrators, designers, printers, and other creative resources. The *Adweek Directories* are published in five regional editions (East, Southeast, Midwest, Southwest, and West), and can be purchased from the publisher.

• *Public Relations Journal,* a monthly magazine published by the Public Relations Society of America, 845 Third Avenue, New York, NY 10022. Many PR agents offer their services each month in the classified ads section of this journal.

• Also, check your local Yellow Pages for listings under "Advertising Agencies," "Public Relations Agencies," "Graphic Design Studios," "Illustrators," "Writers," "Copywriters," "Artists," and "Photographers."

• Chapter 5 •

HOW TO WRITE COPY THAT SELLS

What Is Copy?

The word "copy" refers to the text of an article, advertisement, press release, brochure, flyer, or almost anything else that is written.

Copy is writing. It is used to inform, to entertain, to persuade, and to sell. Although advertising copywriters are paid to write copy that will catch attention and sell products, they do not have a monopoly on copywriting skill. In fact, with a little practice, you can write copy for your promotions.

Good copy sets your promotions apart from the crowd, and therefore it's easy to understand why professionals are often needed to add their talents to a commercial, a brochure, a solicitation letter, or a flyer. Yet, if you are willing to take a look at what makes for good copy, and are willing to learn to distinguish effective copy from uninteresting, sloppy, or boring copy, you'll be taking the first long step toward creating your own promotions.

In this chapter, we'll concentrate on how style, taste, structure, and human insight—as well as the specific sales points of your product or service—can be united to make exciting, original copy that helps motivate people to buy whatever you're selling.

All of the hints and ideas we'll discuss are mentioned in the context of persuading people to take an interest in a product or service. Although one could spend a chapter focusing solely on beer-advertisement headlines or press releases announcing sales at retail stores, this chapter attempts to discuss elements of persuasive writing as they apply to a wide gamut of promotions.

The Sales Sequence

Meeting a person, dating, and getting engaged are parts of a sequence of activities resulting in a wedding. In the same way, a sale is the final step in a sequence of activities. Recognizing this fact, we should attempt to understand just what steps compose the sequence, and how one step leads to another. The steps usually involved are:

1. Getting attention for your product or service
2. Showing that a need exists for it
3. Convincing prospects that your product or service satisfies the need
4. Requesting action or belief for the ideas you've set forth

Let's examine each part of this sequence:

1. Getting attention

People get attention in a variety of ways. Some ask questions; others shout. Other people say startling things, or use humor, conflict, sex, or suspense. Your job is to capture the attention of your reader, suggest an element of your sales message, and motivate the reader to continue reading. It would certainly capture attention if an air-conditioner manufacturer used a semiclad woman to gain attention for his ad, but it would also be irrelevant and perhaps even tasteless.

However, a bold thought or a "teaser" may well "hook" a reader. A travel agent used the following headline in a flyer: "When You Travel, You Don't Need a 'Super-Saver,' You Need a Super Travel Agent." That headline caught people's attention and led them naturally to the *body copy* (text following the headline). Another headline that is bound to catch attention is "You've Just Taken Your Last Food Binge." It practically compels the reader to read on and learn more about the diet plan being advertised.

2. Showing a need

After you've gained attention, you need to show your readers that they have a need for your product. You do this by empathizing with their situations, their feelings. A public relations firm found a way to gain attention and show a need in the opening passage from the letter to an executive search firm (Fig. 5–1).

This opening waves a red flag in front of the executive recruiter, a person who is probably sensitive to the word "headhunter." Using this highly charged word, the writer carefully allies himself with the reader. After accomplishing that, he can then pose, subtly, a hypothetical question, one which he'll delight in answering.

3. Convincing Prospects

Once you've pointed to a customer's need—for a book, a subscription, a pizza, photographs, anything—you must be prepared to step forward and *convince* him that you can *satisfy* the need. In simplified form, here is how a pizza parlor's flyer convinces you that Tony's pizza will satisfy you:

(Attention)	TONY'S PIZZA—OLD-FASHIONED FLAVOR YOU'LL LOVE
(Showing a Need)	Tired of pizza with soggy crust, skimpy cheese, and too few pepperonis?
(Conviction)	At Tony's, you'll love our pizza because the crust is thick. So's the cheese. And the pepperoni!

You have stepped forward to answer a need and to help the reader better visualize how your product will meet the need. Tony's pizza answers his neighborhood's need for good pizza, but it also paints a picture of how his pizza achieves perfection.

Similarly, if you were applying for a job, your cover letter would go beyond stating your belief that you could do the job. You'd probably point out several things you could do that would make you an asset to the employer. It gives the em-

Dear Mr. Thomas:

Some people think of all executive search firms as "headhunters." They're wrong. The only heads you search for are attached to people who have talent, experience, and the will to succeed. But how do you tell corporate recruiters, job-seekers, and other professionals that your firm is a cut above the rest?

Sales letters are a simple, inexpensive, attention-getting method of keeping your name in front of the people you want to reach. And that's where we come in.

We're Mann & Mann, a publicity and sales promotion company with special expertise in direct mail for executive search firms. We know that whether you're sending a cover letter to accompany a recent article in Business Week or a "keep in touch" letter to current clients, every word counts—as you can see by reading this letter and our flyer.

If you'd like to see samples of our work, call us. We think you'll like our style.

Sincerely,

Fred A. Heyward
Director of Sales

Fig. 5-1   This letter follows the sales sequence and culminates in a call for action: "Call us."

ployer an image of exactly how you would help him solve his business problems.

The sales points of a typing service's flyer were selected, arranged, and bulleted to allow the customer to make a mental picture of each service:

- Work guaranteed when promised
- Pickup and delivery
- Experience with proofreaders' marks
- Typists who specialize in financial and legal typing as well as in tape transcriptions

The public relations agency that was pitching its services to the executive recruiting firm used the following passage to help the reader gain an image of the writer's potential value:

. . . whether you're sending a cover letter to accompany a recent article in *Business Week* or a "keep in touch" letter to current clients, every word counts . . .

4. Requesting action

Practically every flyer, TV commercial, sales letter, or catalog ends with an appeal to take action. A sales letter from a consultant may ask the reader to send for more information. A TV ad for a set of recordings or books might end with the phrase "Call this toll-free number." A magazine solicitation letter might ask you to fill out a coupon and place an order. Other promotions may call for other responses, but the message is the same: Believe us! Take action!

Just as a wedding invitation ends with an RSVP, an ad for a restaurant might conclude: "Come tonight and let us make your dinner a real feast!" A brochure for a new directory might be more abrupt: "Complete the reverse side of this form and mail to . . ."

Headlines

Just as a newspaper headline catches our attention, the headline of an advertisement, flyer, or direct-mail piece is meant to capture the prospect's attention. The only difference is that advertising headlines may use a wide assortment of interesting gambits that would be inappropriate for gaining attention in the non-advertising sections of newspapers.

After capturing our attention, an effective headline will make us want to read further. It will make us hungry for more information.

Also, a headline selects prospects; it sends a signal to your customer. A headline involving "The Great American Cannoli" will whet the appetite of pastry-lovers. A dating service will attract a single person's attention with a headline like "Need a Date?" A newspaper scored a success with the inventive headline: "You can't judge a book by its cover but you should judge a newspaper by its coverage." Not every headline focuses on a particular type of prospect, but many concentrate on specific purchasers: women, children, smokers, beer drinkers, swingers, housewives, business people.

Here are a few generic types of headlines:

1. The how-to headline

A how-to headline offers the promise of specific, practical information: how to eat and still stay slim, how to choose a writing consultant, how to turn your old coins into new gold. The how-to headline need not contain the words "how-to." A how-to headline might be phrased: "Five Secrets of Successful Pasta," "The Secret of Solar Power," or "Advice to Halloween Party Givers."

The how-to headline is informational, even educational, and it offers the reader the allure of real information instead of ballyhoo.

2. The question headline

Just as rhetorical questions help a speaker gain attention, a question headline pulls the reader into the ad copy.

You're probably familiar with headlines that go "Tired of the Same, Boring Breakfast Cereal?" or "Would You Like to Make $500 Per Week Operating a Word Processor?" If the headline raises a question that will be explored in the body copy, and if the headline is not designed to mislead the reader, a question headline can be very effective.

3. The reason-why headline

"Three Reasons Why Small Businesses Avoid Public Relations Firms" is an example of the reason-why headline. This type of headline is effective for new companies that must explain their product or service in short order. It is also wise to use this type of headline when you are trying to distinguish your service from those of your competitors.

Essentially, this is the same type of headline as those that guarantee a service. Take the famous Lee Myles slogan "You'll Never Pay for Another Muffler as Long as You Own Your Car." The ad goes on to explain the reasons why Lee Myles can make this claim, and the reasons why you should choose Lee Myles.

4. The command headline

The command headline commands you to take notice by telling you to take action. A hair stylist might use a command headline such as "Take Care of Your Hair and It Will Take Care of You"; a copy shop announces, "Be a Copy Cat"; a dental group's headline reads, "Save Your Teeth."

5. The direct headline

This type of declarative headline has a news feeling to it, and it promises the reader something fresh and important. It can be as simple as "Sale! Everything Marked Down 50 Percent" to "Wait! You Can Earn Money in Your Spare Time" or "The Future Card: Never Spend Cash Again."

6. The indirect headline

As the name suggests, the indirect headline sneaks up on you. It could be a predicament: "You're alone in a city and you've lost your wallet . . ." Or it could be a word play such as that used by the co-authors of a book on technical writing: "When It Comes to Technical Writing, We Wrote the Book."

Characteristics of Good Headlines

How do you know when you've written a good headline? You'll know. You'll know through experience and through instinct. You'll know because the people you show it to will respond well to it.

Let's recapitulate some of the characteristics of good headlines:

Good headlines send a signal to particular prospects for the kind of product or service you are advertising. They also promise the reader that he will benefit from your business; they do this by building a bridge to your reader's self-interest.

If possible, you should include the selling promise in your headline ("Are You Sick and Tired of Being Sick and Tired?") and you should try to end your headline with a lure to read on ("An Effective Business Writing Program Will Save Your Organization Time and Money. Here's How:").

Avoid "blind" headlines—the kind that mean nothing unless you read the body copy underneath them. (Examples of blind headlines are "Britannia Waves the Rules" and "What's Black and White and Read All Over?") Studies show that 80% of your readers will read only the headline and not the body copy. Therefore, ads with blind headlines waste 80% of your advertising dollars.

Headlines are usually stated in the affirmative, and for good reason: Negative words, no matter what they are leading up to, set a negative tone. Examples of negative headlines are "Don't Rely on Just Any Security System" and "We Have Never Had a Complaint About Our Food."

Finally, keep obscure references out of your headline altogether. Here are two examples of obscure headlines, or, at least, headlines that test a reader's knowledge of a particular allusion: "See Rodney Dangerfield—the Mouth That Roared" and "At LeDisco, You Can Always Depend Upon the Kindness of Strangers" (a reference to the last line of Tennessee Williams' play *A Streetcar Named Desire*).

Body Copy

Body copy can take a variety of approaches; it can be factual, or fanciful, or descriptive. It can rely on testimonials, or it can tell a story. It can even be written in dialogue. It all depends on what you're selling, who your audience is, and what approach will catch attention and be persuasive.

Body copy has no predetermined length, but conciseness is always a virtue.

You can't afford to waste the impact of the headline by taking your time to get to the point in the body copy. As you would in other writing, it's wise to be as specific and concrete as possible, putting an enthusiastic, factual, and friendly tone into the words and ideas.

As for gaining believability, your promotions may be helped by the use of testimonials. When Joe DiMaggio speaks up for Mr. Coffee or for New York City's Bowery Savings Bank, he is lending his personal persuasion to the product. Why Joe DiMaggio for a bank? Perhaps it's because DiMaggio seems prosperous thirty years following his retirement from baseball. The reader or listener makes the subtle connection that Joe saved wisely for his golden years . . . at the Bowery. Also, the Bowery is a part of New York City, while Joe DiMaggio also has a strong identification as part of New York City.

Finding that best person to give a testimonial for your product or service is an art. There is no rule of thumb, except that the person must be trustworthy and be recognized by your prospects. Joe DiMaggio would not make a good pitchman for candy because the youngsters today might not know his name half as well as they know the names of Reggie Jackson, George Foster, and Sugar Ray Leonard.

Three other tips on writing effective body copy: Don't try to be entertaining (it often doesn't work); write your ads in everyday language (so that everyone understands), and give the reader advice that is both helpful and useful.

CASE HISTORY: The Travel-Agency Flyer

A travel agency commissioned a small PR firm to write a flyer to help stimulate new business. The one-page flyer had one purpose: to attract business. But how could the agency make itself distinctive when all travel agencies offer the same basic services?

When the public relations people started learning about the breadth of those services, they decided to write a flyer stressing the services. They designed a flyer that made no outrageous claims, nor did it try to distinguish the travel agency from its competitors. What it did do was concisely list the main services provided by good travel agencies, and then end the flyer with the travel agent's name, company name, address, and phone number. It was felt that an upbeat, specific, and educational flyer would prompt people to hold on to it, to tack it to bulletin boards and keep it in desk drawers.

The flyer (Fig. 5-2) shows an effective use of a headline, and a thoughtful arrangement of sales points, even though the sales points pertain to all agents. The flyer relies on short sentences and short paragraphs to keep the reader reading.

The flyer has yielded dozens of responses.

Ten Tips on Copywriting Technique

The following tips will help you sharpen your copywriting skills and create more effective promotions:

1. Have a "you" orientation.

Copywriters know that the word "you" may well be the most important word in their vocabulary. By thinking of the *reader's needs* first, a good copywriter never confuses his own biases or irrelevant sales points with appeals that will touch the lives of his audience. An acting teacher who, in a sales flyer, goes into a detailed description of where he studied acting before even describing the class he's offering is hardly taking a "you" orientation. He's simply flexing his ego. In the same way, when a school for reflexology presents a program called "Diagnoses East/West," it has lost sight of the fact that people need to be *introduced* to what reflexology is before they can absorb the implications of the program's title.

2. Slogans help readers and listeners remember.

"Pan Am Makes the Going Great," "GE: We Bring Good Things To Life," and "American Express: Don't Leave

When You Travel, You Don't Need A "Super-Saver," You Need A Super Travel Agent.

Here's Why:

1. **Their service is free.**
   You don't pay one penny more for your trip when you let a travel agent arrange it. Travel agents earn their fees from hotels and airlines, not travelers.

2. **They'll take the confusion out of complex fares.**
   Their job is to help you understand your travel alternatives, and discover which is truly the most economical and convenient.

3. **They save you time and money.**
   They make all your reservations. You save time and don't run up your phone bill. They'll contact the hotels, arrange for a car and even help you choose a cabin on a cruise ship.

4. **They're travel experts.**
   They know about most destinations because they've been there themselves. So they'll help you decide what to pack, where to stay, what to see, and where to eat.

5. **They're aware of money-saving travel plans.**
   They have up-to-the-minute information about mid-week excursions, night flights and a variety of special "package" vacations.

6. **They do the ticketing.**
   A travel agent can write your ticket for you—whether you're going to Madison, Wisconsin or Madagascar. They can also arrange for a pre-paid ticket to be left for you at the airport.

7. **They'll arrange for special service.**
   Don't feel limited to the usual airline menu. If you like, a travel agent will arrange a vegetarian, seafood, dietetic or kosher meal, as well as arrange for a seat in a smoking or non-smoking section.

8. **They're sensitive to special business needs.**
   They know that executives of each industry have specific travel requirements. Travel agents are able to provide the type of V.I.P comforts busy travelers demand.

9. **They accept all major credit cards, and are available during business hours.**
   Like your lawyer or your doctor, your travel agent is a consultant, someone you can trust with the personal details of your travel arrangements.

"We believe in going the extra mile"

BON BON TRAVEL, INC.

Roger Smith Hotel • Suite 205 • 501 Lexington Avenue • New York, N.Y. 10017 • (212) 752-7384

Fig. 5-2   This flyer takes a low-key, informative approach. By giving the reader useful information instead of mere sales talk, the flyer suggests that the owners of the agency are not just travel agents but highly informed spokespeople of the travel industry.

Home Without It" are examples of catchy slogans. These pithy phrases have permeated our minds, becoming part of a national idiom, while reminding consumers of each company's spirit and services.

A clever slogan continually reverberates in the mind. The phrase "Coffee-er coffee" came to Savarin in a verse submitted by a free-lance writer (who, by the way, is still writing and editing at age ninety). The simplicity and directness of phrases like "I Love New York" or "You Deserve a Break Today" help make them memorable.

The phrase "Perfect Typing" became a slogan for a typing service, and the slogan was used on all of the typing service's promotions. The owner of the service even became known as the "Perfect Typing" lady. Sometimes a slogan will be more a byword than a fancy phrase. A paperhanger in New Jersey uses the phrase "All work done with craftsmanship and integrity" on his flyers. A gourmet shop has imprinted the phrase "catering with an Italian accent" on its letterhead. These phrases, when repeated through advertising and sales literature, provide a uniformity and unity to your promotions. They not only help your customers remember you, but they help form a single, identifiable symbol in their minds. Just as a logo is unique, a slogan attempts to capture the essence of what you do in a single, succinct phrase.

3. Carefully arrange your selling points.

It is not just the sales points that are important, it's their arrangement. You must develop a feel for which points deserve top billing, and which are extra added attractions. The typing-service owner knew that "Perfect Typing" was a more important idea than "24 Hours a Day" and so she put them in just that order on her flyers. To help readers absorb more than a few sales points, you may wish to use "bullets," numbers, or subheads (as we do in this book).

4. Avoid sexism.

The women's liberation movement has had a great impact on our language. For one thing, we can no longer blithely use the word "man" as a stand-in for "person." Since women

share almost all occupations with men, writers must be ready
to search for ways to recast sentences so that they do not
have sexist connotations. When you reach for a phrase like
"the man who sells ice cream," or "an advertising man's
salary," an alarm should sound in your brain. "The person
who sells ice cream" is more generic, since the field isn't
limited to males, and should be used unless you are describing
a particular male ice cream sales*person*. "Ad man" is one of
a storehouse of stock phrases that now must be rethought and
reworded. You might recast the phrase to read "an advertising professional's salary."

How about a sexist phrase like "the doctor uses *his* car"?
Using the plural form is one way to avoid the male pronoun
"his." The phrase would then read, "doctors use their cars."

5. Be tasteful.

No one can teach you about taste; you either have it or you
don't. But you can become more sensitive to exactly what
constitutes bad taste by studying the ads you see all around
you. We once saw an ad for a beautician specializing in elec-
trolysis. The ad featured a line drawing of a ballet dancer in a
spotlight. The copy read, "Why share the spotlight with unwanted hair?" Something about hair in the spotlight strikes
us as unfortunate . . . the kind of image you want to forget,
not remember. Taken literally, it's not a very pretty picture.

6. Use graphics.

Don't be dissuaded from using graphics. Photographs, line
drawings, charts, maps, tables, and other illustrations attract
the reader. Graphics should be of high quality and should
blend harmoniously with the body copy. Don't just use a
graphic because it's handy or free; use it when it will communicate an idea well. A photo of two people dancing helps
communicate the nature of a dance studio as well as or better
than any copy.

7. Avoid jargon.

Technical advertisements and promotions speak to technical people and therefore require the use of technical terms.

Indeed, technical terms such as "CPU," "binomial theorem," or "biodegradable" seem hard to avoid under such circumstances. What you should avoid are the catch phrases, the words that have been bandied about in the media: *stagflation, meltdown, feedback, state of the art, hands-on, on-line, supply-side economics*. Use your best judgment. Many people, for example, have some understanding of the word "cholesterol," but how many truly understand terms like "polyunsaturated," "emulsified," or "rack-and-pinion steering"?

8. Keep sentences and paragraphs short.

People are scared off by lengthy sentences and paragraphs; they view them with the trepidation with which a light eater views a 12-ounce sirloin. The words seem to blend into a formidable chunk of type. The solution? Loosen it up. Break up lengthy sentences and paragraphs. Allow the reader to grasp your message in short, easy-to-understand blocks.

Very brief sentences (two or three words) and paragraphs (one sentence or two), if used sparingly, can add a touch of drama to your copy.

9. Don't forget the obvious.

Sometimes you're so busy writing an ad or a press release that you forget to include obvious information. You may remember to put your telephone number in an ad but neglect to put in the area code. Similarly, you may give your address but forget the zip code. If your address is one that does not readily conjure up a specific locale—even to people who live just across town—you can sometimes clarify things by adding more information. For example, instead of just putting "1665 Second Avenue" on your business cards, you might say "1665 Second Avenue (between 79th and 80th Streets)." And don't forget store hours, prices, branch locations, and other essential information.

10. Add an additional inducement.

Just as a P.S. adds an additional thought to a letter, a flyer or ad is sometimes enhanced by a "bonus" sales point, another reason to buy the product or service. On TV commercials for various kitchen appliances, a voice excitedly tacks on, "And, if you act *now,* you'll receive, free of charge . . ." These added inducements do tip the scales in favor of the sale.

Your company's added inducement may take the form of mentioning an award you've won ("Voted One of the Five Best Seafood Restaurants in the County"), or a brand-new service you're offering ("Free Delivery"), or a premium item that you'll give away along with another product or service (a shoe store that offers a free shoeshine kit with all repairs over $20). Other examples: "Now available in the New Economy Size," "Special Discount for Newlyweds," and "10% Off for New Customers."

Effective Body Copy: A Checklist

When you write copy, make sure it is:
- *Interesting.* Does it keep your attention and make you want to keep reading?
- *Specific.* Specificity is the heart of all effective writing. Don't ever settle for general or vague words when you can be specific and concrete.
- *Simple.* A good ad uses simple language because, in a world of advertising messages competing for attention, simplicity reaches people on a "gut" level. It doesn't overburden them.
- *Concise.* As in all types of writing, there should be no wasted words. Economy of words is as much of a virtue as using the right words.
- *Believable.* People are skeptics when it comes to promotion. They've been burned many times and they don't like to be plied with phony claims. You have to earn the reader's respect and credibility in every bit of copy you write.
- *Relevant.* Your product or service may have a variety of selling points, but you should try to keep your copy focused on matters that pertain to the particular audience you're trying to reach. One promotion may stress economy, while another stresses status. Keep your ideas consistent by

remembering that you should not be trying to please everyone at once.

• *Persuasive*. Your copy must motivate readers to take an interest. It must present compelling evidence that will show consumers how products and services meet their most vital needs. According to Yale University researchers, the twelve most persuasive words are: *discovery, easy, guarantee, health, love, money, new, proven, results, safety, save,* and *you*.

· Chapter 6 ·

PRODUCING YOUR
PROMOTIONAL MATERIAL

The Graphic Arts

This chapter will tell you how to take the copy you've written and turn it into a brochure, a flyer, a poster, or any other print promotion.

We don't expect you to design and illustrate your print material yourself. Most of us can't draw well enough to do the job professionally. And frankly, we're too busy running our businesses to take the time to become skilled graphic artists.

Fortunately, there are many places to turn to for help. Advertising and PR firms, graphic design studios, free-lance artists, local art schools, and even the corner print shop can handle most of the graphic work you need done.

This chapter presents the basics of graphic design and production: type, layout, photography, illustration, printing, and binding. By knowing something about graphics, you can work with the experts more effectively and gain a realistic sense of what can be accomplished within your budget.

The Elements of Graphic Production

There are five basic elements that go into the making of any print promotion:

1. Type—the text, including headlines, body copy, and captions

2. Layout—positioning of the components of a printed page (headline, body copy, art, and blank space)

3. Art—illustrations and photographs
4. Printing—reproduction of an original printed page
5. Folding or binding

Type

Type is text to be reproduced by the printer. When you buy type, you buy words.

Today, most type is produced or "set" by electronic photo-typesetting machines. The typesetter takes your typescript and transcribes the copy onto an electronic CRT terminal, and the machine produces the words as black images on strips of white photographic paper. A graphic artist will then take the type and arrange it on an "art board" for reproduction on the printing press.

There are more than 8,000 different styles of type to choose from; a few of these are shown in Fig. 6–1.

Specifying type is a complex procedure that requires a knowledge of such esoteric things as point size, letterspacing, line spacing, line length, and type justification. But don't worry about it—that's what the printer or graphic artist is for. All you need to recognize in type are two things: style and readability.

1. Style

Take another look at the typefaces in Fig. 6–1. Megaron Light has a clean, modern look. Souvenir medium has a warmer appearance. Eurostile Extended looks futuristic and technical. And Nuptial Script seems just right for a wedding invitation.

Obviously, type style is an important design element in the overall look of your advertising and print promotion campaign. Select a type that fits your image—elegant or plain, high-tech or old-fashioned, corporate or folksy, loud or quiet. Try to stick with the same type in all your promotions; a consistent graphic style will help build your image and recognition of your company.

This is Megaron Light
This is Megaron Light Italic
This is Megaron Medium
This is Megaron Medium Italic
This is Megaron Bold
This is Megaron Bold Italic
This is Souvenir Medium
This is Souvenir Medium Italic
This is Souvenir Demi-Bold
This is Souvenir Demi-Bold Italic
This is Times Roman
This is Times Roman Italic
This is Times Bold
This is Times Bold Italic
This is Colonial
This is Colonial Italic
This is Eurostile Extended
This is Eurostile Bold Extended
This is Friz Quadrata Medium
This is Friz Quadrata Bold
This is Bauhaus Light
This is Bauhaus Medium
This is Bauhaus Demi-Bold
This is Bauhaus Bold
THIS IS ENGRAVERS ROMAN
THIS IS ENGRAVERS BOLD
This is Caslon Openface
This is Univers Light
This is Univers Light Italic
This is Univers Light Condensed
This is Univers Light Condensed Italic
This is Univers Condensed Medium
This is Univers Condensed Medium Italic
This is Univers Condensed Bold
This is Univers Condensed Bold Italic

This is Avant Garde Extra Light
This is Avant Garde Medium
THIS IS COPPERPLATE GOTHIC LIGHT
THIS IS COPPERPLATE GOTHIC HEAVY
This is Stymie Light
This is Stymie Medium
This is Franklin Gothic Condensed
This is Bodoni Medium
This is Bodoni Medium Italic
This is Bodoni Bold
This is Bodoni Bold Italic
This is Highland Medium
THIS IS ALSO HIGHLAND MEDIUM
This is Highland Medium Italic
This is Highland Bold
THIS IS ALSO HIGHLAND BOLD
This is Gothic Outline
This is Helenna Script
This is Kaylin Script
This is Park Avenue
This is P.T. Barnum
This is Murray Hill Bold
This is Broadway
This is Broadway Bold
THIS IS BROADWAY ENGRAVED
This is Hobo
THIS IS KARTOON
This is Wedding Text
This is Commercial Script
This is Formal Script
This is Nuptial Script
This is Wintergreen
This is Bernhard Fashion
This is Brush
This is Francine
This is Bernhard Tango
á è ï ô ü ñ ç å œ ß

Fig. 6-1   Typefaces. (Credit: Emery Printing Co.)

2. Readability

Your message will be lost if an ad or brochure is difficult to read. Make things easy on your readers by following these simple dos and don'ts of typography:

• *Do* select a typeface that is easy to read. There are two basic kinds of type: *serif* types have little crossbars on the tops or bottoms of certain letters; *sans serif* types do not. Most graphic artists feel that serif type is more readable for body copy. Headlines are set in either style.

• *Don't* SET TYPE IN ALL CAPITAL LETTERS. ALTHOUGH IT MAY GET ATTENTION, IT IS DIFFICULT TO READ IF USED IN BODY COPY.

• *Do* set type large enough to read. Type size is measured, from top to bottom of the letters, in *points* (a point is 1/72 of an inch). This book is set in 11-point type. The body copy of your promotional material should be set in 9-point type or larger.

• *Don't* set any promotional body copy in type that is less than 8-point; it will be difficult to read.

• *Do* set type in narrow columns. On an 8½-by-11-inch flyer, for example, the type should be broken up into two or three columns. Columns should generally not exceed 40 characters (letters and spaces) in width; most newspapers use columns of approximately 26 characters. Wider columns cause the eye to wander across the page.

• *Do* leave plenty of blank space ("white space") on the page. A page jam-packed with solid copy scares readers away.

• *Do* leave space between the paragraphs. It will increase readership by as much as 12%.

• *Do* leave sufficient spacing between individual letters and between lines in a paragraph. A little breathing space will make things easy on the reader.

• *Don't* set long sections of body copy in reverse (white text on black background), and don't set it over a colored tint. Occasionally, black or colored type on a colored paper can be attractive and elegant, and white copy on a black background can be attention-getting. But more often than not, the old standard—black print on white paper—is best.

• *Don't mix typefaces*. For variety, you can use several typefaces in the same family—for example, you might use Megaron Bold for headlines, Megaron Medium for subheads, Megaron Light for body copy, and Megaron Light Italic for captions. But don't mix typefaces from different families (Megaron with Souvenir or Times Roman with Colonial) in the same document; it would result in a jumbled, amateurish appearance.

Alternatives to Type

Typesetting is far more expensive than producing text on an ordinary typewriter. To typeset 100 words of 10-point body copy, for example, could cost between $10 and $75, depending on the typeface. Therefore, the budget-minded entrepreneur is tempted to ask his graphic designer, "Isn't there a way to produce my flyer *without* a fancy typesetting charge?"

The answer is: "Yes—*but* . . ." *Yes,* because there are several techniques—hand lettering, rub-on type, and typewriter type—that can yield reproducible text. And *but,* because in most instances these methods are not satisfactory substitutes for the style and reproduction quality of phototypesetting.

Let's take a quick look, then, at these three options:

1. Hand lettering

Writing headlines and body copy in freehand is time-consuming work that usually produces unsatisfactory results: Freehand writing looks amateurish and reproduces poorly. It can be appropriate for certain signs and posters, and a fine handwriting such as calligraphy will add a touch of class to menus, business cards, letterhead, and invitations. In general, though, it is best to avoid hand lettering.

2. Rub-on type (also known as transfer type)

Rub-on lettering is transferred from a plastic sheet to the page by pressure; rubbing causes the ink to adhere to paper or art board. Using rub-on type is a slow, tedious process, and the letters often develop cracks that cause them to reproduce poorly. Aside from an occasional headline, rub-on type is best used in items that will not be reproduced at the printer's—signs, posters, quickie flyers, and other "throwaway" pieces. Rub-on type can be purchased at any art supply store.

3. Typewriter

An electric typewriter with a fresh black ribbon can produce text that will reproduce cleanly. Unfortunately, even the most sophisticated electric typewriter is limited in choice of type size and style. Typewriters are ideal for producing sales letters, press releases, newsletters, and simple flyers (especially if it's a flyer for a typing service!). For more sophisticated print promotions—advertisements, brochures, and catalogs—typesetting is the better choice.

A Glossary of Graphic Arts Terms

Like doctors, lawyers, and engineers, graphic arts people have a jargon all their own, and words like *comprehensive, mechanical, score,* and *cut* take on entirely new meanings in their lingo.

Half the battle in working with graphics people is learning to understand their language. The glossary of terms presented below should get you off to a good start:

Art   an illustration or photograph

black-and-white   originals or reproductions in a single color, as opposed to multicolor

blue-line (blueprint or blues)   a photoprint used as a final proof to check the position of layout elements before reproducing the piece on the press

color separation   the process used to prepare color art for full-color printing

comprehensive (comp)   an artist's drawing of the layout of a printed piece. The comp is used for review purposes and as a guide for the printer.

copy   headline, body, and caption text, usually set in type

cut   a photograph

design   the creative process of putting together a print piece to achieve some specific look, style, or effect

dummy   a sample brochure or other piece made of blank pages. The dummy is used to indicate the weight and feel of the finished piece.

four-color printing   there are four primary colors in printing: black, magenta (red), yellow, and cyan (blue). A four-color printing job uses all four color inks to reproduce art in natural full color.

halftone   reproduction of continuous-tone artwork (such as a photograph) through a screen which converts the image into dots of various sizes

layout   the positioning of the elements of the print piece

line art   art suitable for reproduction without using a halftone screen

logo (logotype)   the name of a company or product in a special design used as a trademark in promotion

mechanical   camera-ready pasteup of artwork. The mechanical includes type, photos, and illustrations all on a single piece of art board.

rough   a crude sketch of the layout, used for showing the basic idea

score   to impress a mark with a rule in the paper to make folding easier

stock   the paper on which the piece will be printed

Fig. 6-2a The *rough* is a crude sketch of the print piece. It is used to approve the basic concept.

tissue a thin, translucent paper placed as an overlay on the mechanical. Used for protection, and to indicate colors, corrections, and other special instructions.

white space blank area on a page

Ten Tips for Better Layouts

Your artist is the expert in art; you are the expert in your business. Here are ten tips on layout that will help both of you produce effective print promotions:

1. Always ask to see a rough sketch first.

Steve Brown, a free-lance graphic artist, designed and produced the ad "A Prescription for Profits" for Magerman Associates, Incorporated. First, Steve submitted a *rough* (Fig. 6–2a) to his client for approval of the basic concept. Then he created a *comp* (Fig. 6–2b) to show the exact positions of the headline, body copy, illustrations, and logo as they would appear in the final version. After the comp was approved, Steve bought type and produced the finished ad (Fig. 6–2c).

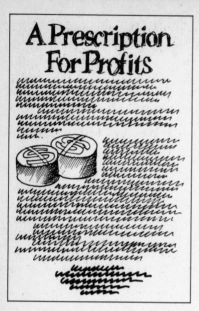

Fig. 6-2b   A *comprehensive* or *comp* is a "fine-tuned" version of the rough. It shows the exact positions of the headline, body copy, art, and logo as they will appear on the final print piece.

Fig. 6-2c   The finished ad. Note how closely it follows the layout of the comp.

A Prescription For Profits

Dear apparel manufacturer:

Do you have pre-tax profits of 10% to 17%?

Do you ship 90% to 95% of your customer orders complete and on time?

Do you produce what you sell and sell what you produce?

Do you have minimal surpluses of garments and piece goods or yarn at the end of each season?

Does your computer or manual system give you the critical information to anticipate:

    A. Total seasonal sales potential.
    B. Total seasonal fabric, yarn or purchased garment needs.
    C. Total seasonal manufacturing needs by style, and the capability to create a new set of requirements weekly based on any changes in the seasonal sales goal or selling mix.

Finally, if you are computerized, does your computer or computer service give you the timely and critical data so that you can manage your business profitably or is it just a very expensive record keeper?

If the answers to the above are a resounding "yes," congratulations.

However, if your answers are more "no" than "yes" with a few sprinklings of "maybe's," then I offer my credentials and track record of proven accomplishments with many of your peers and competitors who would not settle for less than the best in developing the system from which consistently superior decisions are made.

When you enlist my services, you receive the following:
    A. An apparel executive with over 25 years in the field who understands your business and informational needs.
    B. One who can develop for you a total apparel management program utilizing your computer or other forms of information to generate the critical data that spells profits and success.
    C. One who will give you the competitive edge.

Philip Magerman
Magerman Associates, Incorporated
225 West 34th Street, Room 918
New York, N.Y. 10001
(212) 279-4845

"I always show my client a sketch of the layout first," says Steve. "That way, the client knows what I'm going to do before I spend his money to do it."

Ask to see a rough. It helps you avoid costly surprises.

2. Make the headline big.

Be bold. Set the headline in large type to capture the reader's eye and attention.

3. Illustrate your writing.

Good illustrations can add interest to print promotions. And photographs are even better than drawings—they're more real, more believable (provided the quality of the reproduction is good). Using photos instead of drawings can increase reader recall of your brochure by up to 26%.

4. Make the artwork big.

A single large photo gains more attention than several smaller ones. Also, a page with one large halftone is less expensive to produce than a page with multiple halftones.

5. Use captions.

Put a caption under every photo and drawing, and write captions that make a selling point. The readership of captions is twice that of body copy.

6. Find a consistent style.

Give all your promotions a uniform graphic look. Consistency is the key to building recognition in your prospects' minds.

7. Make the design portray your image.

Typeface, layout, art, and paper stock can create an image of your business in the mind of the reader.

Graphic arts novices don't realize that a one-color piece does not *have* to be black ink on white paper. You could, for example, use a dark-brown ink on a textured, off-white paper to convey a warm and friendly yet dignified image—perfect for an art gallery or small accounting firm. A supermarket, on the other hand, might use black ink on brightly colored stock —orange, blue, red, or yellow—to make its coupon sheets stand out.

8. Leave plenty of white space.

Pages crammed with words and pictures fatigue readers. Large, unbroken chunks of text intimidate them.

Plenty of open ("white") space will make your brochure inviting, attractive, and easy to read.

Koch Engineering used white space in its brochure (Fig. 6–3) to make highly technical information seem less formidable. The blank space, headline, table, photo, captions, and body copy blend together to make a handsome page that's a pleasure to look at—and to read.

9. Make the logo big.

A logo helps readers to tune in quickly to what a promotion is all about. Why not make the logo big enough to be noticed?

10. Design with the reader in mind.

If you are opening a health clinic in Spanish Harlem, print your flyer in English and Spanish. If you market to senior citizens, make the type larger on all your promotions. Always design print promotions with the special needs of your audience in mind.

Photography

There are three ways to obtain photographs to use in your promotions: buy them, hire a photographer, or take them yourself.

Stock photo houses will sell you photographs they already have on hand. Tell the stock photo suppliers what photos you need—a fighter plane, a mountain range, a sunset—and they'll supply it, for a price.

HEAT EXCHANGERS

In an empty pipe, the thermal boundary layer that builds up along the pipe wall inhibits heat transfer. The Koch SMXL static mixing unit induces a strong transversal flow that virtually eliminates this boundary layer, raising the heat transfer coefficient. And by inducing radial flow, the SMXL unit maintains a uniform temperature over a given cross section of pipe. This prevents "hot spots" caused by exothermic reactions and insufficient cooling at the center of the pipe.

The Koch viscous heat exchanger achieves efficient heat transfer with a minimal surface area. So it takes less space, reduces residence time, and offers significant savings in construction costs for units fabricated from exotic materials.

Some applications of this unique viscous heat exchanger include:
• Food—pasteurizing temperature-sensitive foodstuffs
• Plastics—heating and cooling polymer melts, e.g. cellulose acetate, polystyrene, PVC
• Adhesives—heating and cooling at various process stages in adhesives production
• Chemical—removing heat from exothermic reactions in laminar flow

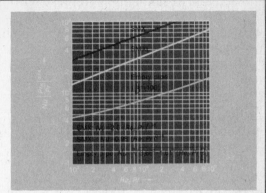

FIG.14 Heat transfer is boosted by a factor of three to six when Koch SMX or SMXL elements are placed in an empty pipe.

FIG.15 The Koch multitube viscous heat exchanger is used for large volumetric flow rates where space and residence time must be kept to a minimum.

FIG.16 The Koch monotube heat exchanger is the simple, low-cost solution to viscous heating or cooling problems.

Fig. 6-3 Page from a technical sales brochure showing how white space can be an effective element in a layout. (Credit: Koch Engineering Co., Inc.)

Retailers, manufacturers' representatives, insurance agents, and other middlemen can obtain photos (and many other advertising support materials) from the companies whose products and services they sell.

Hiring a professional photographer is the surest way of obtaining high-quality photographs. Day rates for photographers range from $100 to $500 and up. A simple black-and-white publicity shot may be commissioned for as little as $50, while a sophisticated fashion shot can cost several thousand dollars. Your needs will probably fall somewhere in between.

If you are the do-it-yourself type, you may elect to take your own photographs. Purchase a 35mm camera and a good book on basic photography. We recommend Tom Grimm's *The Basic Book of Photography* (Revised Edition, Plume, 1979).

What makes for a good promotional photo?

First, the photo should make a selling point. A photograph of a slim bikini-clad girl has no relevance to a piece of industrial equipment. It can, however, make a selling point about a health spa, a beach resort, or a fashion boutique specializing in swimwear.

Second, *people* add interest to photographs. If you are selling a luxury car, put a driver behind the wheel in the photo.

Third, keep the photo simple. Photos are often reduced in reproduction, and fine detail will be lost.

Fourth, use photographs that arouse the reader's curiosity. When the photo raises a question in the reader's mind, he will read your copy in search of an answer.

Illustrations

Can you draw? If not, you can obtain drawings for your print promotions from one of three sources: a commercial art studio, a local art school, or a "clip book."

Commercial artists can draw or paint whatever you need. Their services are apt to be expensive, so get a firm price quotation in writing before you commission a piece of art.

Students at local art schools can provide excellent illustrations at a fraction of the cost of a professional illustrator.

Look over the student artist's portfolio to see if he or she can indeed handle the assignment.

Art supply stores sell "clip books" containing a wide variety of drawings you can cut out and use in your promotions. Clip-book art is inexpensive, but it is unlikely that the clip book will contain a drawing directly related to your product. Clip art is no substitute for custom-made art.

Illustrations can enhance print promotions in many ways. A cutaway drawing grabs an engineer's attention and makes the message of a technical brochure immediately clear. A map in a hotel brochure guides tourists to the resort. A series of bar charts sums up an annual report at a glance. The cover of a mailer for "YOUR MAGIC BODY: A Health and Science Magic Show" (Fig. 6–4) uses an illustration that tells the whole story and lures you into the body of the piece. (The Magic Show uses magic and other entertainment techniques to teach children about science and the human body.)

It is best to avoid abstract art in promotion. Abstract art

Fig. 6-4   The cover illustration graphically tells the story of this mailer on a health and science magic show for children. (Illustration by Gary Allen. Credit: Kevin Gormley.)

does not communicate selling messages quickly and directly enough to be effective in an ad, brochure cover, or mailer.

Pulling It All Together

Let's review briefly the steps the artist takes in creating print promotions:

1. The artist produces a rough sketch of the proposed layout.

2. Upon your approval of the rough, the artist sets the type and produces the necessary art.

3. Type and art are pasted up on the mechanical—a single art board with all the elements of the print piece in place.

At this stage, the job is ready for the printer. But before you send it off to have hundreds (or thousands) of copies made, look over the mechanical thoroughly to make certain it is as you want it to be. The checklist presented below covers ten items you should check for.

A Production Checklist

Before you release a mechanical to the printer, ask yourself:

• Has all type on the mechanical been proofread against the original manuscript?

• In proofreading, have you checked for punctuation, spelling, and capitalization?

• Are the logos properly drawn, sized, and positioned?

• Have all logos, trademarks, and proprietary names been given registration marks or trademark designations where appropriate?

• Have all addresses and phone numbers been checked for accuracy?

• Have all form numbers, dates, and copyright lines been set and placed according to requirements?

• Have all elements been securely mounted on the mechanicals?

- Have all smudges, pencil marks, and excess rubber cement been removed?
- Are all elements properly sized and positioned?
- Does the tissue overlay indicate the proper instructions for the printer?

Printing Tips

Printing can be an expensive proposition. To make sure you pay a fair price, get bids from at least three different printers.

In order to ask for bids, you should put, in writing, the exact specifications of your job—number of pages, weight and type of paper stock, number of halftones, number of colors, type of folding or binding, number of copies to be printed, and any other special instructions.

There are dozens of variables in the printing process. Be as precise as possible in your specifications to eliminate any chance of misunderstanding or error.

Order as many copies of the piece as you think you will need. It is better to order too many rather than too few, since the biggest expense in printing is creating the plates, and running off extra copies is a simple and inexpensive matter.

For example, 1,000 copies of a pamphlet might cost $300 to print—30 cents each. Now, 2,000 copies might run you $350 —17½ cents each. Ordering an additional 1,000 pamphlets added only $50 to the bill and reduced the unit cost considerably.

A Quick Paper Primer

Your printer or graphic artist will guide you in the selection of the paper stock used in your printed pieces. This section will help you understand the basics of paper selection.

Paper is graded by weight. Heavy papers are stiff and thick, lighter papers are thinner.

Paper weight is measured using the term "pound." Newspapers are printed on 30-pound stock. "Quick print" shops use 50- or 60-pound stock to run off letters, résumés, and flyers. Magazines are printed on 80- or 90-pound stock.

Paper may be smooth and uniform in composition, or it may have an interesting weave or texture running through it.

The surface of the paper may be dull, highly glossy, or somewhere in between.

Below, we list a few of the grades of paper commonly used in printing, along with some of their applications:

• *Bond papers* are used in stationery and business forms. Bond paper is easy to write on.

• *Coated stock* has a glossy finish. It receives ink well, and is used for high-quality printing jobs such as sales brochures.

• *Text papers* have a rich texture and feel to them. They are used in booklets, brochures, and other print promotions.

• *Cover stock* is a heavier paper used mainly for brochure covers. It is easy to cut, fold, and emboss.

• *Book stock* is a less expensive grade of paper used for trade books and textbooks.

• *Offset* is similar to book stock and is used on most small offset lithography presses.

Although it helps to know the lingo, do not spend your time fretting over the complex world of paper. Instead, ask for the recommendation of your printer or artist, and *ask to see samples of the various papers he suggests*. Then select a stock you like—and can afford.

Printing Techniques

There are five basic reproduction techniques to choose from: copier, offset lithography, letterpress, gravure, and silk screen.

1. Copier

Copiers make what we call a *xerox** or *photocopy*.

This technique is simple and inexpensive—copies cost between 5 and 10 cents apiece at your local library or copy

---

* Actually, the word *xerox* is a trademark of the Xerox Corporation and should *not* be used to refer to any kind of photocopy, even one done on a Xerox copier.

center. And many small businesses can afford to own their own copiers.

Copiers can make adequate reproductions of black-and-white line art and type. But most can't handle halftones or color reproduction.

Use copiers to reproduce small quantities of press releases, reports, proposals, announcements, and day-to-day correspondence. The quality of photocopy reproduction is inadequate for brochures, pamphlets, and other promotion material.

2. Offset lithography

Most local print shops handle small runs of offset printing at reasonable prices. Printing a one-page 8½-by-11-inch sheet costs around $5 per 100 copies.

Offset is rapidly becoming the most popular method of reproducing print promotions. It is likely that 90% of the jobs you have will be handled on an offset press.

The process is termed *offset* because material is not printed from the plate directly. Instead, the plate deposits its design on an intermediate rubber roller which, in turn, acts as the printing surface. *Lithography* means that prints are made from a flat surface—printing ink is transferred chemically, not mechanically.

Offset printing produces extremely clear impressions. It is used for books, folders, flyers, catalogs, print advertising, press releases, and brochures.

3. Letterpress (relief printing)

In letterpress, the printing occurs as the raised surface of the printing plate gives up its ink to the paper. (This is the way a rubber stamp works.)

Although letterpress is losing ground to offset lithography, it is still used in some package and specialty printing, and for printed matter that is mainly text—price lists, parts lists, schedules, and directories.

4. Gravure (intaglio)

Gravure is the opposite of letterpress; in gravure, the printing surface is depressed, not raised. The ink lies in the depressions.

Gravure is used primarily on large runs, because the plates are expensive to produce.

Its main advantage is high-quality reproduction of illustrations and halftones on cheaper grades of paper. It is used to print Sunday magazines for newspapers, color advertising preprints, and large mail-order catalogs.

5. Silk screen (screen printing, serigraphy)

In silk screen, an ink or other pigment is pressed through a fine silk screen to create a design.

Because silk screen can be done on virtually any surface, it is used for trade-show display panels, decals, posters, billboards, and menu covers.

Folding

To save money on paper and binding, smaller pieces can be printed on a single sheet of paper and folded to form pages or "panels." By using the folding techniques illustrated in Fig. 6–5, you can turn a single sheet of paper into a four-page, six-page, or eight-page booklet.

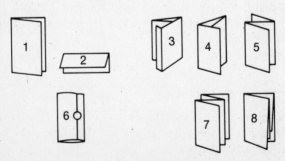

Fig. 6-5   Some popular folding styles are shown here: (1,2) four pages; (3) six pages with flap; (4,5,6) six pages; (7,8) eight pages.

Binding

On large jobs, several sheets of paper must be mechanically bound together to form the printed piece. Fig. 6–6 shows a variety of common binding techniques.

Saddlewire stitching (saddle stitching) is the simplest and least expensive binding method for brochures, small booklets, programs, and catalogs. In saddlewire stitching, staples are forced through the backbone of the booklet to hold the pages together.

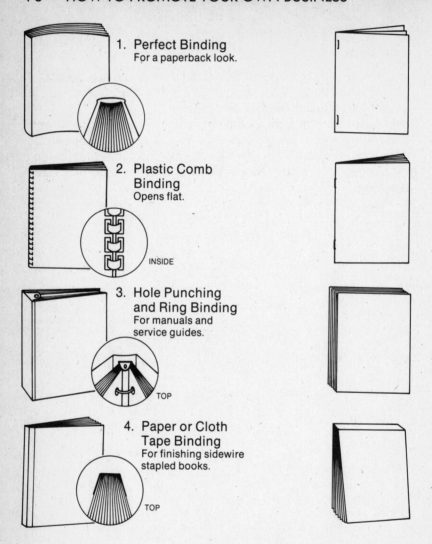

1. **Perfect Binding**
   For a paperback look.

2. **Plastic Comb Binding**
   Opens flat.

   INSIDE

3. **Hole Punching and Ring Binding**
   For manuals and service guides.

   TOP

4. **Paper or Cloth Tape Binding**
   For finishing sidewire stapled books.

   TOP

Fig. 6-6   Binding techniques.

5. **Sidewire Binding**
   For scientific reprints
   or business reports.

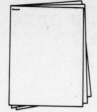

9. **Collating and
   Corner-Stapling**
   For research notes,
   newsletters and
   presentations.

6. **Saddlewire
   Stitching**
   For small booklets and
   brochures.

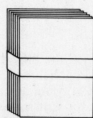

10. **Paper Banding**
    For securing loose
    pages.

7. **Shrink Packaging**
   For loose pages that
   require handling or
   shipping.

11. **Duo-tang**
    For protection for all
    printed matter. To
    allow pages to be
    added at a later date.

8. **Padded Material**
   For memo pads,
   telephone messages,
   order forms, and
   specification sheets.

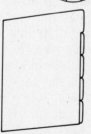

12. **Tabs**
    Can be added for
    easy division of
    categories in most
    binding processes.

• Chapter 7 •

REACHING THE PRESS: PUBLICITY

In Chapter 1, we defined the difference between advertising, sales promotion, and publicity:

• *Advertising* is a paid communication in print or broadcast media in which the sponsor is identified. A McDonald's TV commercial, a billboard on a highway, and a "help wanted" classified in your town paper are all advertisements.

• *Sales promotion* encompasses a broad range of activities that support advertising, publicity, and person-to-person selling. Brochures, cents-off coupons, point-of-purchase store displays, and trade-show exhibits all fall under this category.

• *Publicity* is a *non*paid communication in the media in which the sponsor is *not* identified. If we were to send a copy of this book to Phil Donahue and he talked about it on his show, that would be publicity. A mention on the Donahue show would probably sell many copies of the book. Clearly, we would have prompted the event by sending Mr. Donahue the book and bringing it to his attention. But we would not have had to pay for the air time, nor would we be a sponsor who has control over the time. Mr. Donahue would be allowed to say anything he wished about the book, complimentary or otherwise, and wouldn't even be obligated to mention it at all.

Why the Media Need Your Help

Publicity, then, means generating news and feature stories about yourself, your organization, and your product in newspapers, newsletters, and magazines and on radio and television. This news may be anything from a one-line mention in a fashion column to a full-page feature story in a trade publication.

To say that business "generates news" may sound shocking and somewhat unethical to novices in business and journalism. But the media, especially small newspapers, local radio stations, and specialty trade magazines, cannot always find enough information on their own. Newsworthy items help them fill their publications and broadcasts, while providing a form of "free advertising" for you.

There are several techniques for getting your story to Phil Donahue and other TV and radio shows as well as newspapers and magazines. The basic technique is the press release.

What Is a Press Release?

Generally, a press release is information released to the press, in written form, usually from a source outside the media.

It may be a brief announcement about a change in personnel, a January white sale, or a new branch of a restaurant or bookstore; or it may cover the details of an upcoming speech, graduation ceremony, new Broadway opening, or sporting event.

In a way, a press release makes its writer a potential journalist, because one need not be a professional writer or member of a public relations firm to write, distribute, or place a press release. *Anyone can do it . . . for any purpose.* If your message is newsworthy, accurate, and well written, it stands a chance of being picked up—or "run"—by a newspaper, magazine, or radio show, or even a TV talk or news show.

What does a press release look like? Very much like any typed story: double-spaced, neatly typed, wide margins, paragraph form. A look at a sample release (Fig. 7-1) will show you the generally accepted format.

First, most releases identify the person or organization (or both) the release is about. Generally, the name of this person or company appears in the upper left-hand corner of the page, although this may vary.

If the release is prepared by a professional public relations agency, it also identifies the "contact:" the person or public relations firm responsible for writing the release as well as for responding to any inquiries it may generate. The name of the contact is generally found in the upper right-hand corner of the release.

Client: Contact:

For immediate release:

ABBONDANZA, MANHATTAN'S FIRST ROSTICCERIA, OPENS ON UPPER EAST SIDE—ABUNDANT DELICACIES WITH AN ITALIAN ACCENT

NEW YORK, NY, May 18th—In Italian, Abbondanza means abundance. And Abbondanza is the perfect word to describe Manhattan's first "rosticceria," which officially opens on May 18, 1981.

A rosticceria is a store which features cooked foods prepared on the premises, along with a variety of other entrees which may be purchased for eating at home.

Abbondanza offers—for the first time—truly authentic Italian dishes prepared in an open kitchen for all to see. Owner Lou Galterio explains his concept this way: "People think of Italian food as just pizza, pasta and provolone. I want them to see that Italian food is just as sophisticated as French food—if not more."

To ensure that Abbondanza's offerings would be Italian—and not Italian-American—Lou Galterio imported a chef who spent more than 30 years heading up the kitchens of Italy's finest hotels.

Chef Giuseppe Allegra has forged an international reputation at such hotels as the Riviera Grand Hotel in Messina, the Ritz Carleton in Montreal and the Four Seasons in Toronto, where he was sent on special assignment by the Italian government.

In Abbondanza, Chef Allegra works in a kitchen that is in full view of the customers. Since the main kitchen is an integral part of the store, the aromas surround you. And browsers are invited to ask the staff about any of the food preparation.

Like a fine pantry, Abbondanza is decentralized, with sections of the store devoted to cheeses, coffees and teas, Italian desserts, meats and pastas. Each department is staffed by people who are delighted to offer suggestions for meal-planning, serving and entertaining. For example, they'll suggest an unusual menu for a romantic supper or a tempting meal for those who want to eat at home and not cook. Also, Abbondanza is able to prepare a complete buffet for any special occasion.

In addition to the Italian appetizers, entrees and vegetables prepared in the store by Chef Allegra, Abbondanza offers a variety of specialty items. Freshly prepared mozzarella plus tortellinis and gnocchis are available at the pasta department.

The meat department is replete with Italian sausages made on the premises as well as a variety of salamis and hams.

The breads and rolls are baked daily by Frank Vermonti, owner of Vermonti's, one of Greenwich Village's most highly-regarded bakers.

The coffee department, where the beans are displayed in their burlap shipping sacks, boasts a truly Italian espresso, ground to each customer's specifications.

Via closed-circuit television, patrons upstairs can view dishes being readied in the preparation kitchen downstairs. While browsing, customers can watch ice cream, cheesecake, quiches, pastas or Italian pastries being created.

Abbondanza's not a stuffy place where you're too intimidated to ask questions or ask for samples; it's a place with hot food and warm surroundings. Abbondanza is a grand Italian kitchen where you'll discover many joys and bring those joys from our kitchen to your table.

Abbondanza, 1647 Second Avenue (between 85th and 86th Streets), is open 10 a.m. to 10 p.m., seven days a week. Telephone: (212) 879-6060.

Here are a few of the many Italian specialties served at
Abbondanza:

> Vitello Aurora Tonnato (Veal with Tuna). Veal stuffed
> with cooked prosciutto, baked in a tuna, vegetable and
> sardine sauce.

> Impanata di Pescespada (Swordfish in Puff Pastry).
> Swordfish, cooked in a casserole, with anchovies,
> artichoke and zucchini. Wrapped in a flaky, brown
> pastry shell.

> Chicken ville Roy (Chicken in Cheese). Breasts of
> boned chicken, cooked in a blend of melted cheeses.

> Flan di Spanaci (Spinach, Mushroom and Cheese
> Pâté). This unusual vegetarian dish has a mushroom
> and vegetable sauce in its center.

> Fillet of Beef Brasalla. Beef, coated with a layer of pâté
> de foie gras and sealed with a light shell of puff
> pastry.

And these special desserts:

> Mandarin Orange Ice Cream. With morsels of fresh
> mandarin oranges.

> Pesche all'Imperiale. Peeled peaches, marinated in
> champagne and mixed with strawberries and
> maraschino liquor.

> Ricotta alla Romana. Tart with ricotta cheese and
> assorted fresh berries.

●

Fig. 7-1   This press release uses the word *rosticceria* as a "hook." It
stresses the store's atmosphere and originality as much as the food itself.
The release became the basis for stories in all of New York City's major
daily newspapers.

A press release is not an immediate "turn off" to an editor
unless he works for a publication that makes it a policy never
to use press releases. Very few of this country's print or

broadcast media ever discard all releases unread. *The Today Show, The Tonight Show,* the *New York Times,* and *Time* magazine have all used numerous stories which grew out of press releases.

Your release should be typed on a plain piece of 8½-by-11-inch typing paper. If you wish, you may use paper—usually found at stationery stores—which already has the words "News Release" or "For Immediate Release" printed across each sheet. Your release may be written on letterhead, or it may have the logo of your company. Some releases show the logos and addresses of both the client and the PR firm representing the client.

Usually, as you look down the first page of a news release, you'll see the words "For Immediate Release" close to the top of the page. Many releases are written to be timeless, and the phrase "For Immediate Release" means that the release may be run at any time. Naturally, if your release concerns an event that is timely or carries an element of surprise, you may wish your release to carry a phrase indicating the specific date and time when the release may run. Press releases on grand openings, sales, and other special events are usually dated.

The Headline

A press release, like a news story, should have a headline. A good headline will succinctly announce or describe the main idea of the release, but it must also be written for impact, to gain immediate attention.

The press release's content will be the chief factor in determining just how specific, spicy, or succinct the headline should be.

If, for example, you were to send a press release to announce the opening of a new store, you would probably want to specify the store's name in the headline. The challenge would be to find a new, interesting angle to the store's opening.

For instance, when Abbondanza opened on the Upper East Side of New York City, we had to write a release which would try to suggest this store's unique qualities without playing into the public's perception of Italian takeout food as limited to "pizza, pasta, and provolone." In the course of conversations with the store's owner, we kept hearing him refer to a type of Italian food store called a "rosticceria." We asked him to explain exactly what a rosticceria was, and he went into a detailed description of how in Italy the term "rosticceria" connoted a type of food store where meats, game, and other fresh delicacies were cooked on the premises and sold fresh. Knowing how food journalists love to seize upon new food concepts, we decided to play up the idea of the store as a rosticceria. In fact, we said it was Manhattan's *first* rosticceria. The headline ran: "Abbondanza, Manhattan's First Rosticceria, Opens on Upper East Side—Abundant Delicacies with an Italian Accent." By the way, the release was picked up or served as the basis for stories in all the major New York newspapers, and it even led to a mention on the front page of the *Wall Street Journal*.

How to Write a Release

A well-written release, like a well-written news story, conveys information concisely, tending to capsulize the story in its opening paragraphs. This "lead" carries the who, what, when, where, why, and how of the story. Succeeding paragraphs elaborate on the story stated in the opening paragraph or paragraphs.

Unlike a news story, a release may vary its lead in an attempt to capture the reader's attention and interest before focusing on the facts. The first two paragraphs of the Abbondanza release capture the attention and then swiftly proceed to the facts. They also have the additional task of defining two words—*abbondanza* and *rosticceria*—which must be understood before the facts of the release will make sense.

The rest of the release addresses itself to subordinate ideas such as the store's unique approach to Italian food, the chef, the various departments in the store, and the store's physical layout. It ends with the store's address and phone number, as well as the hours and days it is open.

Naturally, press releases will vary greatly, depending upon the product or service being written about, the publicist's style, and the particular media for which the release is being prepared. However, there are a few tips on writing releases which we feel will help make your release the best release it can be:

- Keep it short.
- Use many quotes (when applicable).
- Keep it factual.
- Keep it focused.
- Keep it neat: no typos, wide margins.
- Offset the release instead of photocopying it.
- Write for the reader, not for yourself.
- Use correct press-release format.
- Single-space the name of the "contact" in the upper right-hand corner along with the person's phone number.
- Before the text of a news release, there is a city and date. It's called a dateline. Every release needs one so that the editor can tell when it was mailed.
- Do not address editorial staff as if they were advertising staff. Even if you are the biggest advertiser in the newspaper, don't put on the bottom, "I advertise frequently in your newspaper." Some editors may be influenced by advertising but most will be affronted. A good story and an interesting angle are your best credentials.

Press Kits

A press kit is an entire package of materials prepared for members of the press. Like a press release, a press kit functions to gain the attention and interest of members of the press. A release is only one part of a press kit. Other elements of a kit may include:

- *Photographs*. Reasoning that a photo is worth at least 1,000 words, some publicists like to circulate a photo or two epitomizing the product or service they are describing. One handsome photograph of savory pasta is far more attention-catching than even a well-written release. A lovely photo of a new handbag will not only be a fitting accompaniment to a release about new handbags, but it may very well illustrate any story which the editor chooses to pursue. Photos can be expensive to have taken and to produce (more about this in our chapter on production), so, if money is tight, you may want to indicate on your release that photos are "available upon request." In the same way, if you circulate a black-and-white photo with your release, you can indicate that color photos are available upon request. Naturally, if the requests pour in, you can then make a judgment about investing in color shots.

• *Fact Sheet*. A fact sheet is a rundown of factual information, usually in tabular form, allowing readers to gain a synopsis of the facts of the story without having to wade through the release. For example, Abbondanza attached a "Food Facts" sheet (included in Fig. 7–1) which mentions a few of the dishes available and gives a brief description of each dish. This information was not derived from the press release; it was additional information—material which, if included in the release, would have made the release too long.

• *Biography*. Occasionally, a press kit hinges on the credibility of a key individual. In these cases, it's appropriate to include a one- or two-page biography of the person. By breaking out biographical information, you aid the editor in separating an individual from the accomplishment or product or service with which the release links him. Also, a biography may serve to reveal additional interesting facts—any one of which could suggest a new angle to the story.

• *Backgrounder*. A backgrounder supplies the history of an event or a company. It may or may not have a news peg. Often it is included in a press kit merely to suggest that a product, person, or service is well established.

• *Client list*. Occasionally, you add credibility to your organization when you include in your kit a list of people or organizations with whom you have done business. A manufacturer of retail clothing might benefit, for example, by enclosing a one-page list of stores carrying its fashions (especially if those stores include names that will be instantly recognizable to editors and shoppers alike).

What News Deserves a Press Release?

You may send out press releases on any topic, whether it's a front-page story or not. However, the more news appeal your press release has, the better its chances of gaining an editor's attention.

Here are just a few of the many events and items that may gain your business some publicity if you send out a press release on them:

- Anniversaries of events such as the opening of your store
- Introduction of new products or product lines
- An improvement on an existing product or service
- Changing your company name
- Opening a new business, store, or branch
- Personnel changes (new employees and promotions)
- Special events—sales, parties, demonstrations, open houses, plant tours, charitable acts, other community relations
- Publication of a new brochure, flyer, or catalog
- Expert-opinion stories in which you, as a leader in your business or community, speak out or provide new information on some market trend, controversial issue, or other subject

Why Send Out a Press Release?

There are a number of reasons why you would wish to send out a press release. The first is to gain recognition and acceptance for your business or organization.

People always complain that "the other guy" is always being mentioned in the paper, and that "it isn't fair." True. Being mentioned in the newspaper or on the radio is not an equal-opportunity procedure. Newspapers, like people, have a tendency to reach for whatever is close at hand. If a newspaper or radio show is planning to run a story about new gourmet restaurants and a press release announcing your new gourmet restaurant arrives on the editor's desk that day, you stand a good chance of being included in the article or broadcast.

If a newspaper or a magazine mentions your company in its story, or makes a story out of your release, the public will get to read about *your* business—not the other person's. They'll find out about your offerings, your special features, and where they can find you. If the story has appeal, you may experience a quick and sharp surge in business. The day that the *New York Times* printed its story about Abbondanza, the store was jammed. In fact, Abbondanza had its best day of the year. And what made the day especially welcome was that the article ran in mid-July, a time when most gourmet stores are empty.

Where Do You Send Your Press Release?

The surest way of satisfying every editor's news needs would be to write a customized press release, tailored to his particular editorial requirements.

That's not practical if you want to reach more than one or two publications. That's why we use the press release, a kind of mass-produced news story that each editor can use as the basis for a news item.

Your press release should be distributed to any publication or station that could benefit your business and reach qualified prospects. If you're selling computing systems to small-business people, you'd send your release to *Inc., Venture,* and *Entrepreneur*—three magazines whose readers have a strong interest in small and growing businesses.

But don't stop here. These small-business people are also interested in the complete business picture, not just small business. Pickup of the release in *Forbes, Fortune,* or *Business Week* would help promote your small-business computer.

You begin to get the picture. The bulk of your time and energy went into creating the release; printing and mailing extra copies is relatively inexpensive. So you want to be sure you mail the release to *all* the publications that your key prospects might read. Public relations people call a list of these publications the *media list*.

Most PR novices are surprised and pleased to learn that there is a book that lists most of the major newspapers, popular magazines, and trade journals published in the United States and Canada. The book is *Bacon's Publicity Checker* and it's published annually by Bacon's Publishing Company, 14 East Jackson Boulevard, Chicago, IL 60604. *Bacon's* lists nearly 9,000 newspapers by region and approximately 4,400 magazines by specialty (women's magazines, electronics, computers, and so forth) and has an alphabetical index, too.

Let's say you wanted to send a release on your small business computing system. Here are the steps to take in compiling the media list:

1. Ask yourself, "What kind of publications does my prospect read?" The small-business person probably reads small-business publications, general business publications, and trade publications in his particular industry. If the release was aimed at corporate types, you'd add in-flight magazines to the list, since Fortune 500 managers do a lot of business flying.

2. *Bacon's* lists these publications by specialty. Make a list of the publications, addresses, and the names of the editors who should receive your release.

3. Unfortunately, *Bacon's* is not complete. It doesn't include many newsletters, local newspapers, and other specialized media, such as a weekly TV shopper or advertising mart. If your release has a local flavor, you need to look around to see what people in your town read. Also, there may be specialized magazines, newsletters, circulars, or reports in your particular industry which *Bacon's* doesn't include. Add these to your media list.

4. Some releases may be appropriate for radio and television. While these media are discussed at length in Chapter 13, several major reference books should be mentioned here. The first, *Broadcasting Yearbook* (published by *Broadcasting Magazine,* 1735 DeSales St., NW, Washington, DC 20036) lists 9,000 AM and FM radio stations by state and city. Another section of this book lists the addresses, personnel data,

and other information about shows of a particular format (talk shows, black radio, Top 40). This book will help you compile lists of "call-in shows," radio shows nationwide that, if interested, could interview you via telephone. The interviews, conducted live or on tape, help the show as much as they help you: It's often very difficult for producers to fill up 24 hours of air time each day.

5. For a reference of key network TV shows, consult *New York Publicity Outlets,* a spiral-bound annual reference that includes "key personnel on media located within a 50-mile radius of Columbus Circle." This book, put out by Public Relations Plus, Inc. (Washington Depot, CT 06794; 203-868-0200), also contains information about magazines, news syndicates, radio shows, and trade publications.

6. Time your release for maximum effect. If you know that *Accessories Magazine* has a March issue that regularly features new handbags for spring, make sure that you have your release to the magazine by early December. Remember that the lead time for most monthly magazines is at least three months.

Following Up Your Release

After distributing your release, it's only natural that you'd like to see it picked up in the media. But is it wise to start calling all of the editors and program directors (of radio stations) you've mailed your release to? Do you have the time, the patience, and the telephone budget to make all those calls? And, assuming you do make a few calls, what do you say?

When you send out numerous copies of a release, you may wish to follow up on a *percentage* of them by telephone. For example, if you mailed a hundred copies of a release to editors and program directors, you might wish to choose ten or fifteen of the most valuable media (for your particular product or service) and place calls to the specific individuals who received your release.

If, for example, you're in the handbag industry, you might wish to follow up on a release sent to the accessories editor of *Women's Wear Daily* or *Accessories Magazine.* If you were the owner of Abbondanza, you might wish to follow through on the releases sent to *New York Magazine,* the *Daily News, Gourmet,* or *Food and Wine.*

Obviously, when you call, you don't want to begin your discussion with a plea that the editor use your release. That's a turn-off, as most begging generally is. Perhaps you want first to find out if the material was even received. You'd be surprised how often material arrives later than you could have imagined. Mail moves slowly.

You may then want to ask if the editor has had the opportunity to take a look at the material you sent. That gives the editor a chance to let you know that you're calling too early. If that's the case, simply say that you'll call back later on. Don't reprimand an editor for not getting to read your release as soon as it hits his desk. Your goal is to elicit information, and not to be judgmental.

If—glory be!—the editor has read your release, and is warming up to explain, gently, why the release is (a) inappropriate or (b) poorly timed, maintain your cool. By doing so, you may have the opportunity to turn a negative into a positive. For example, you may point out to the editor that some other details of the story have suddenly made your release even more timely than the day it was sent. If the press release, for example, describes a book you have written, you might be able to let the editor know that your book has received good notices in the interim. Try to show the editor a new angle to a story. Many press releases have been picked up because of the quick thinking of press agents and businesspeople during a follow-up call.

The editor may compliment you on the release and then go on to talk about the timing being wrong. Fine. Make a mental note as to the right timing (or issue) and make sure that your next release is timed to the specifications of the magazine— perhaps a holiday issue or special issue.

If the editor is undecided about your release, it is often best simply to assure him that you're happy to answer any questions or provide additional information. Always have a few ideas or facts at your fingertips when you call, because one of them may set the editor thinking about a new angle for the future. Let the editor know that you'll be happy to research any question he may have about your release, and that you'd be happy to send over more material—by messenger, if need be.

Remember that follow-up calls are a great opportunity to sharpen your promotional talents. If you can find out why a particular release was not accepted, you can begin to home in on the best media for your releases, as well as focus even more sharply on which media have specific issues or features most apt for your service or product. Timing and knowledge of the media are your tools for successful placement.

• Chapter 8 •

SPEAK UP FOR YOURSELF—AND YOUR BUSINESS

There are times when you need help in promoting your own business and there are other times when *you* are your own best spokesperson. Recently, corporate presidents and chief executive officers have taken to the airwaves to promote their own products. Lee Iacocca talks about Chrysler, Orville Redenbacher talks about his popcorn, and the wife of the largest Cadillac distributor in the United States has become a household name in New York City.

But what if you can't afford to pay to be the star of your own TV commercial or radio spot? Perhaps you've never looked into the possibilities of free publicity via articles in magazines, speeches to associations and clubs, and community relations. There are, literally, millions of dollars in free publicity that go a-begging each day in the United States. There are thousands of opportunities to give talks, write articles, go on the radio, and tap local resources. Many people don't know about them because they don't take the time to look for them.

Radio and TV: The Not-So-Impossible Dream

Tonight, all across America, hundreds of authors will be guests on radio and TV shows. Will they be there because they are famous people with best-selling books? No, they'll be there because public relations people—or the authors themselves—contacted the program directors at the radio and TV stations and *asked* to be on the shows.

Radio and TV shows face an overwhelming problem: They must fill up hour after hour of air time. And although their staffs may be adept at conceiving of program ideas, they depend heavily on outsiders to suggest segments and to fill up the remaining time. Even a show as popular as *The Tonight Show* leans heavily on publicity people to supply them with guest stars, ideas for segments, and topics for discussion. The publicity people are, naturally, eager to help out. They know how valuable it is to have a client seen by nine million viewers. They know that an author who holds his book up to the camera will, in one second, create a demand for that book which can result in crowded bookstores the following morning.

If authors can get themselves on local shows, news shows, and even network programs, perhaps you can get on radio and TV too. If you have a product or service (or some type of clever, humorous, or timely "gimmick") that is unique or indicative of some trend or fad, you might qualify for a few minutes of local air time. First, you need an idea.

Certain ideas are a "natural"; they reach out to thousands of people because they are universal, entertaining, and timely. The recent boom in the erotic-apparel industry has given rise to dozens of TV stories about these garments and how they are sold, usually by women, in the home. The story has media appeal, and, as a thank-you for suggesting the story (and sometimes even providing videotape coverage of the event) the show's host may not be averse to mentioning the brand name of the products shown. He may even interview the head of the company, who can then sprinkle in some choice remarks about her products and her business while commenting on the industry at large. It's done every day. The local show gets a story and the enterprising entrepreneur gains exposure for her products.

What can you do to attract media attention to your product or service? First, you can become media-minded. Take notes when you watch the local news, talk shows, and magazine-format shows. How often are products mentioned? In what context? Who gets interviewed? How often is the interview tied in with an upcoming event or book or film?

It will soon become apparent which segments were inspired

by newsworthy events and which were inspired by newsworthy promotions. Newsworthy promotions will ultimately mention a product, service, or company in a favorable light.

People love fantasy, and it would be easy to get TV exposure for a "sexy" service business, such as one that provides breakfast in bed (complete with personal maid, butler, caviar, Dom Pérignon, smoked salmon, and a dozen roses). If you offered this service, a press release or letter sent to assignment editors, program directors, or producers at local TV shows might be enough to get attention.

Naturally, the less intriguing or innovative your product or service, the more difficult it is to get it noticed by the media. It may be that you consider your product or service too mundane to rate TV coverage. Fine. Ask yourself, "How can I make it less mundane?" Think of ideas that might appeal to the media's thirst for the special, the unusual, the romantic, the refreshing. Suppose you owned a flower shop. And suppose the local baseball team had a superstar with a hitting streak. You might wish to create a promotion focusing on the hitting streak—perhaps sending the star's wife a rose for each day the streak lasts. Then let the press know about your civic- and sports-minded gesture. You can almost bet that the promotion will be covered. Don't be surprised if the station sends a camera crew to cover the delivery of the roses.

You can also try to appeal to the public's need for useful information: This type of imaginative thinking can be applied to almost any business, product or service. The promotion need not be obvious, noisy, or gauche; it should be well timed, clever, and low-key.

Radio: The Listening Audience

There are hundreds of radio talk shows across America.* Many of the shows have half-hour, hour, and even all-night formats, and many originate in towns of fewer than 20,000

---

* For the names, addresses, and program directors of radio talk shows, consult *Broadcasting Yearbook*.

people. These shows are constantly on the lookout for new interviewees, new ideas, and new approaches to old ideas. A "pitch" letter sent to the program director of each talk-show program—even if the letter is only a personally signed form letter—should bring some response for any interesting idea.

Recently, the enterprising young publisher of a small newsletter in the sweepstakes field decided that he wanted to gain radio exposure for his newsletter. In order not to seem to be tooting his own horn, he asked a friend who was in public relations to help him write a pitch letter aimed at radio producers throughout the country.

Since the letter did what it was supposed to do—attract attention—we're reprinting it, in slightly altered fashion, in its entirety:

Dear Program Director:

A house in the country, a new Jaguar, a 60-foot yacht—are these the things that dreams are made of? Yes, but some people are doing more than dreaming.

Millions of people compete for these and thousands of other prizes by entering sweepstakes and contests. And they're not just casual entrants either. With 14% inflation and $1.30-a-gallon gas, men and women are approaching giveaways with newfound respect and with a sense of purpose worthy of a Wall Street investor.

The tremendous demand for sweepstake and contest information—as well as tips—has given rise to a publication aimed solely at sweepstakes and contest fans.

John Jones, publisher of WIN NEWSLETTER, recently described the founding of his newsletter in this way: "I've always loved contests. Because I've won thousands of dollars in prizes, people were always asking for my advice. Last year, I decided to make my avocation into a vocation. I started WIN NEWSLETTER."

John Jones has spent many years perfecting techniques for cashing in on contests and sweepstakes. He has literally dozens of wonderful stories and hints for would-be contest winners.

John is 31 years old, and works by day as an investment banker. He is extremely articulate and is quite enthusiastic whenever he displays his contest and sweepstakes savvy. He's at ease on the radio, whether he's answering questions from the host or listeners. He'll be delighted to share his expertise with your audience at your convenience.

We're sure that John would make an excellent guest for a telephone interview—with or without phone-in questions. If you'd like to talk to John in person, just give me a call or drop me a line and we'll be in touch with you.

Sincerely,

Fred Ryan, President
Ryan Public Relations Co., Inc.

The letter worked. During the next four months, the publisher was a guest on nearly forty radio call-in shows. On some shows, he was on the air for five minutes; on others, he was on the air for as long as two hours! During that time he chatted with the host, took calls from listeners, and gently tried to weave his own publication's name into the conversation. The shows yielded more than 500 inquiries for a tip sheet suggesting how listeners could improve their chances of winning sweepstakes and contests. The names that were acquired from this free offer became a mailing list of highly qualified prospects for the newsletter itself. In fact, more than half the people on the list eventually became subscribers.

Let's assume *your* letter gets results, and program directors ask you to be on their call-in radio shows. Here's how to handle it in a way that will get you some free publicity:

1. Help construct and plan your own interview.

Very often, talk-show hosts have little time to study the subject you are presenting. Although they are professionals, they can use your help in selecting some areas of interest within the field under discussion. Don't be shy about asking the person who interviews you to ask questions about a particularly noteworthy aspect of your subject. Obviously, these areas can't be self-serving. No radio-show host will permit you to go on the air and give what amounts to a free commercial for your business. However, if you're clever, you can construct pointed questions that emphasize areas of interest that will lead naturally to a discussion of what you are doing.

We know of a particularly assertive retail merchant who was given the opportunity to appear on a local radio show. The merchant took the time and trouble to write a list of sample questions that she could handle easily. Many of the questions were indirect lead-ins to topics that would allow her to mention her experience in a variety of areas.

As it turned out, the show's host arrived late and hadn't prepared to conduct the interview. The host was delighted when the merchant presented the list of possible questions (it was done in a way that did not seem intimidating or threatening to the host—e.g., "Here are a few questions you may wish to use, since they touch upon interesting aspects of what I do"). Because of the questions, the merchant, who had been scheduled for a ten-minute segment, got half an hour of air time. And because of the subtlety of her "sample questions," she was able to show her products and her business off to best advantage. It was as if she had had a job interview and knew what questions the interviewer was going to ask—she was able to relax, and to concentrate on planning her "spontaneous" responses.

2. Set up a time and a date for the interview.

Many call-in shows interview you while you are at home. The show is either taped for later broadcast, or it goes out "live" as you speak. The sweepstakes publisher scheduled times and dates for each radio show to call him at home. He made sure that he chose dates that assured him of privacy, quiet, and lots of time. Sometimes, because of time differences throughout the United States, mistakes are made and calls come in later than expected. Do not expect everything to work like clockwork. A time may be arranged and then reset for an hour later; a show that was supposed to last ten minutes might decide to keep you on for an hour.

3. Keep an eye on the clock.

Five minutes of "air time" is not quite the same as five minutes of regular time: it goes by quickly. Why? Because talk-show hosts are trained, like actors, to keep the pace lively. Unless you're forewarned, you may miss any available opportunities to say what you want to say. Therefore, you should be aware of the passage of time, decide on the points you wish to mention on the air, and try to bring the conversation back to those points. This need not be done abruptly or impolitely. It can be accomplished by just keeping the interview's purpose—and your own business purposes—in the front of your mind. And it takes a willingness to be assertive.

4. Thank the host.

An obvious but important point. Thank the host both immediately following the show and, later on, by letter. It leaves the door open for a return engagement. It also may, in some cases, persuade the host to mention you or your business again, even after the interview ends. There are lots of cases of an interviewee's gaining thousands of dollars in residual publicity because he made an impression on the talk show's host, and the host mentioned the product or person months after the segment was aired.

By-lined Articles: The Recognition Game

Even sophisticated peopel put halos around writers. Having an article printed—even if the article is poorly written and says little that is new—adds to the author's reputation as an authority in his field.

For the promotion-minded person, there are two basic types of articles that will help advance his promotional goals: by-lined articles about a facet of his business and articles that are written by a publication's staff reporters and editors.

An optometrist who sells an article titled "How to Choose Eyeglasses" to his local newspaper will usually receive a by-line ("By John Peterson") and an identification at the conclusion of his piece ("John Peterson is an Albany optometrist and the author of *The Eyes Have It!*"). The by-line and ID give Peterson exposure in the community, and label him an expert in eye care.

If John had decided not to write the piece but to suggest it as an idea, he'd still write or call an editor or reporter, but he would not ask to write the article himself. He might send a press release on the subject of eyes and leave it to the editor to choose a particular angle for the story. His goal might simply be to be mentioned in the article or interviewed by the writer who is assigned to work on the article.

The Query Letter

We have discussed how press releases are written, but have not yet mentioned either the type of letter that is used to sell a story to a magazine or newspaper or the type of letter that one writes to suggest an idea.

Free-lance writers and journalists refer to letters pitching article ideas as "query letters." The letters "inquire" about the editor's interest in a specific subject, event, or idea (see Fig. 8-1).

Whether you wish to sell an idea based on some facet of your business or merely to generate an "impartial" news story that could mention you or your business in passing, you should understand the elements of a query letter. In a way, the letter resembles the type of pitch letter sent to radio program directors.

The letter should contain material about the following: your specific idea, the approach to the subject, a sense of enthusiasm, details about your sources, word length, and due date.

The specific idea

A florist queried the *New York Times* about the idea of a flower shop for browsers. The shop was unique because it displayed its flowers in the open instead of behind the doors of a refrigerator. The idea resulted in a three-column story which showed the owners of the store, and even mentioned the store's address and business hours. Hard news? No, but

Dear _____

Almost everyone in business writes letters or memos, yet few people find any joy in putting pen to paper. Business writing, despite the influence of best-selling books such as <u>Strictly Speaking</u> and <u>A Civil Tongue</u>, remains mired in mediocrity. Poor writing costs American business tens of millions of dollars in lost productivity every year.

I'd like to suggest a 1,500-word piece titled "LETTER PERFECT: Six Ways to Give Your Letters Clarity, Conciseness and Clout." Using lively examples, this how-to article will help business and non-business travelers improve their writing and make the chore, if not a joy, at least less stressful.

As an executive recruiter, I'm aware that good writing skills are high on the list of criteria for top managerial positions. That's why I feel that most of your readers will find this article lively, informative, and relevant to their lives.

I can have the finished manuscript on your desk within two weeks. Would you care to have a look?

Sincerely,

Bridgford Hunt

P.S. By way of introduction, my articles have appeared in <u>Mainliner</u>, <u>Pace</u>, <u>American Way</u>, <u>Advanced Management Journal</u> and <u>Iron Age</u>.

Fig. 8-1   This query letter, written by the president of an executive search firm, is specific, crisp, and enthusiastic.

a clever idea for a brief story, and one which brought over-whelming reader response. Because the idea was good, and because it caught someone's eye, the owners received thousands of dollars in free publicity.

When a writer actually proposes writing the article himself, he is usually interested in establishing himself as an authority rather than just being mentioned in a reporter-written story.

For example, a career counselor might benefit from having a story written about her, but she might gain even more prestige if she herself wrote an article about some aspect of career counseling. In the by-lined article, the career counselor may be restricted from describing her own business or its location, but she has the advantage of being perceived as an impartial authority in the field. Ultimately, the ability to provide factual, reliable information will lead to business.

Naturally, there are some businesses that simply don't lend themselves to articles, and even if they did, an article would not result in tangible prestige or sales. Articles are effective promotional tools for businesses selling sophisticated products, products on which the more information given, the better the possibility for sales. However, a flower shop can be helped immensely by an article that "positions" it as different from its competitors.

There are many cooking instructors who publish articles with recipes. This type of recognition of one's creativity and versatility is a first step in the chain of events leading to people willing to sign up for cooking classes.

Finally, publishing articles and papers is a surefire way to gain prestige and acceptance in just about any technical field, from aerospace and automotive engineering to plastics and petroleum to textiles and communications. Technical prospects (engineers, scientists, and industrial managers) are often more receptive to a reprint of a technical publication than to sales brochures.

The approach

"Approach" is defined as your attitude or "slant" toward a subject. If you were writing about restaurants that literally "float" on bays and lakes throughout the United States, your approach might be the joys of physically being on the water while eating. The wrong approach would be to suggest a piece about *your* floating restaurant. In the same way, if you owned an all-night pharmacy, you might wish to generalize the subject by suggesting an article on all-night pharmacies in your city. You might elaborate on your idea by pointing out that it would cover well-established pharmacies which cater to people in emergency situations. It could include anecdotes about some of the emergencies that arise late at night.

Enthusiasm

There's a difference between enthusiasm and drum-beating. Your query letter should suggest your enthusiasm for writing about a subject that intrigues you, in the same way a scientific proposal will show signs of a scientist's eagerness to grapple with a scientific problem. Your enthusiasm should be for the universality, intrinsic interest, and value of your idea, not for its potential as a self-promotion.

Sources, Word Length, Due Date

The willingness to use sources, to go beyond your own experience, is the earmark of a professional. An editor expects you to go to the source of your story and not settle for secondhand or merely convenient information about it. As for word length, try to judge whether the article merits brevity (500 words) or extended treatment (more than 2,000 words). Let the magazine's format and past articles help you in deciding how lengthy a piece to suggest.

Finally, suggest a due date (if you are to write the piece yourself), telling the editor when he might reasonably expect to have the piece on his desk.

Need some ideas as to which magazines or newspapers to query? A stroll to the local newsstand may give you some ideas. Also, you may wish to check *Bacon's Publicity Checker* and *Writer's Market. Bacon's,* as we mentioned in Chapter 7, is the "bible" of public relations. It groups magazines by category and tells which are open to by-lined articles by nonstaffers. *Writer's Market* (Writer's Digest Books, 9933 Alliance Road, Cincinnati, OH 45242) is available at libraries as well as at most bookstores, and it describes approximately 5,000 publications, giving editorial requirements, subject matter, and addresses as well as other helpful details of each periodical's requirements for articles, artwork, and reviews.

One more thing: Keep trying! It takes a while to break into print. Writing a clear, well-organized article takes time and innumerable drafts. Your first efforts may go awry. Perhaps you can ask help from a friend who has editorial skills. Start small: Write a brief piece (for free) for a small magazine or newspaper. After all, a small, well-written article in a local newspaper may do more for your business than a lengthy piece in a magazine with a national audience. It depends on your business, the market you are trying to reach, and the location of both.

Speaking Up for Your Business

Some surveys have shown that people regard public speaking as slightly more frightening than flying . . . or even dying. We may all have memories of wobbly knees and stage fright from the time in high school when we were asked to give a speech in front of the class.

Speaking in front of a group requires skill and more than a drop of courage, yet we can reach unbelievable heights of eloquence when we are asked to speak about something we identify with—like our own business.

We've seen the most inarticulate people suddenly speak in torrents about the latest accomplishment of a five-month-old grandchild. Why? Because the subject captivates the speaker. And when the speaker is committed, enthusiastic, and concerned, audiences quickly warm up to the subject matter.

By arranging speaking engagements throughout the community—or country—you'll be able to enhance your business or your image. There are many opportunities. But first, think of your goals.

If an author wishes to speak at a meeting of his local MENSA society in order to tout his book and perhaps even sell copies, he may not accomplish both goals. He may motivate a few people to buy the book later on, but may not sell a single book at the meeting itself. Why? Because the program may be a prelude to an event or social activity, and not the focus of the evening. In other words, the speaker may only be a prelude to an evening of music and good fellowship. So, if his book is a somewhat somber tome, he may be catching his audience at the wrong time. If he simply wanted to get his name in the MENSA bulletin, gain some recognition, practice his speaking skills, and distribute his promotional materials, then he could be said to have met his goals.

An eminent psychologist once turned down the opportunity to appear on *The Tonight Show* because he found out that his segment was to be preceded by a circus act. The psychologist felt that the carnival atmosphere engendered by the circus act would be detrimental to the mood he wished to create when speaking about his theories.

In any free demonstration or speech, you must be able to identify your ultimate aims. If you are a politician, your goal is to meet voters, and it would be absurd to fill up your schedule with lecture dates at grammar schools. In the same way, you are searching for prospects or, at least, people who can tell prospects about yourself and your business. It is important to target your audiences with the same accuracy and meticulousness with which you choose an advertising medium.

Where Can You Speak?

Almost anywhere. Associations, clubs, religious organizations, civic organizations, charitable groups, chambers of commerce, community centers—any might be open to a program that would be both entertaining, informative, and relevant to its members.

You need not be a Winston Churchill, Erma Bombeck, or Orson Welles to succeed as a speaker. A florist can demonstrate the art of flower arranging; a karate instructor can demonstrate the art of self-defense; an art-gallery owner can give pointers on buying sculpture; a dentist can talk about saving money on major dental work.

Make a list of societies and neighborhood groups you belong to, adding the names of local clubs that might be attracted to what you have to say. The next step is to contact the program chairman and propose your program.

Don't expect to be paid for your efforts. Comparatively few speakers are paid. Of course, if you were being paid, you'd probably be restricted from mentioning your own business—no one likes paying for a commercial. As a speaker who is not being paid, you should ask yourself several questions:

1. *How many people will attend?* The more people, the more prospects. Make sure that if your speech has visual elements, they can be seen by everyone.

2. *What else is on the club's agenda?* As we mentioned, the event may be the incorrect forum for your product or service. You want to speak to people who want to hear what you have to say, not just people who happen to be members and are showing up merely to socialize with other members.

3. *Do you expect to take orders after the speech?* At some gatherings, it is perfectly acceptable for a speaker to hand out promotional information after a speech. However, many organizations feel this is too blatantly commercial, and will forbid you to hand out promotional material or even refer to your business directly. Find out how the program chairman of the organization you're interested in feels about your blending information with salesmanship.

4. *Remain factual.* Never take a swipe at the competition or indicate that only your product or service can answer people's needs. Good speakers try to remain factual, even when a person requests a comparison between the speaker's service and a competitor's. Try to be a spokesperson for your field, and, in that way, you rise above petty squabbles and are perceived as an authoritative source of information, not just another person with something to sell.

Community Relations

*"This program has been presented through
a grant by the Mobil Corporation. . . ."*

Just as big business has learned the value of being a participant in the "community," so too small businesses should never miss an opportunity to create goodwill and public recognition as well as be better citizens.

If no man is an island, then certainly businesses are even more closely related to their surroundings. Businesses exist within the framework of a community, and simply cannot afford to ignore the political, social, and cultural changes that surround it. Business people who just curry favor with their suppliers and their biggest customers will soon find themselves isolated, and that can spell financial as well as social disaster.

Take the local store on the corner. Is it the type of place that announces, "No Children, No Bicycles, No Cones, and No Baby Carriages" on the door (thus setting up a feeling of intimidation), or is it the type of place that says "Hi!" to everyone who walks in, offers a cup of tea or a piece of candy, and provides Bach or the Beatles on the radio or stereo? Good community relations begin with having a good feeling about everyone who approaches our business, regardless of whether or not he becomes a customer. A person who regards the public in much the same way W. C. Fields regarded children and dogs just shouldn't be in a business that depends on face-to-face encounters.

On the other hand, a storeowner or other business person soon realizes that it is prudent and often enjoyable to participate in community activities.

Is it opportunism or Good Samaritanism? Only you can answer that. Only you can say whether you should buy an ad in the school yearbook or donate a product to a charity raffle or become a scout leader willingly. No one is suggesting that you should let your enthusiasm for community functions outstrip your enthusiasm for your own business, but you should understand that the best community relations come about when you do things for other people without expecting to be rewarded for your efforts.

Contributing to the United Way or to your local hospital's clothing drive may not catapult your business's name into the pages of your local newspaper, but it will make you feel good and it will earn you the respect of your neighbors. In the same way, working with a neighborhood group, becoming a block watcher, getting involved in helping the political candidate of your choice, or volunteering to man a booth at your church bazaar won't make you rich, but it will add richness to your life.

Realistically, it may have more tangible benefits, too. By banding together, business people can help improve their community, and the more neighbors, politicians, and civic leaders you know, the better. If you're trying to get a permit to open an outside café or trying to close down a nearby rowdy video-game parlor, your community relations may be as helpful to you as your business acumen.

Keeping your name in front of the public is another realistic benefit of community involvement. Whether you're sponsoring a local bowling or Little League team or donating samples of your product to a worthy cause, you're gaining exposure in the community. Theaters are in the habit of giving free tickets to disabled and disadvantaged people. While it is a noble gesture, it does help publicize shows, build a new audience for the theater, and fill up empty seats. In fact, one theater, the Trinity Theatre in Providence, has set such a fine record of community involvement that Marion Simon, the public relations director, was recently granted an honorary Doctorate of Public Service from Rhode Island College for her outstanding contribution to "one of Rhode Island's prime cultural assets . . . the Tony-winning Trinity Company."

So whether you consider yourself a "joiner" or not, you must remember that your business is not isolated and neither are you. Groups such as a chamber of commerce, a mayor's action committee, or a neighborhood association offer a network of contacts as well as a spirit of involvement. As long as you keep your business ambitions in tune with the community you are servicing, you won't run across a conflict that makes you sacrifice one commitment for the other.

Teaching: A Textbook Example of Publicity

We are living in an age of adult education, and with it has come an age in which teachers are offering their students "relevant" courses taught by people with "hands-on" experience in a variety of fields. With this trend toward adult education, it is not uncommon to find courses taught at vest-pocket colleges (informal adult-education centers) in subjects like interviewing, stress management, networking, meeting a lover, public speaking, and auditioning for commercials. In general, the teachers are poorly paid, but they do it for—you guessed it—the publicity.

For many teachers, the class provides an endless flow of qualified prospects. It's an ideal way for businesspeople to talk about what they do in front of a group of people who view the information as educational. The only thing to bear in mind is professionalism: never slight the competition, and never use your prestige as a teacher to blatantly solicit business instead of providing factual information. After the class has formally ended, you may wish to briefly mention your business or pass out a brochure or business card, but this "pitch" should be clearly segregated from class time.

Adult education, with its mass distribution of catalogs, flyers, and brochures, helps give visibility to those who are willing to suffer short pay. It can give you recognition in the community, and it can help direct people to you. For many entrepreneurs, adult education is the best low-cost promotion in their entire promotion campaign.

Chapter 9

ADVERTISING BY LETTER: DIRECT MAIL

What Is Direct Mail?

Direct mail is mail consisting of advertising matter, sent individually to large numbers of people. Some people refer to this type of mail as "junk mail," because so many solicitations for so many products are mailed each year that most hit the wastebasket within moments of being received.

And yet, advertisers persist. In fact, the use of direct mail is growing. That's because direct mail can work; it can be highly profitable, and it fits the growing American trend toward specialization of interests.

Advantages of Direct Mail

For many small and large businesses, direct mail is the preferred way of reaching customers. It offers great selectivity, since businesses can choose to send mail to people of a particular age, occupation, sex, special interest, marital status, or locale. There are mailing lists available that are remarkably specific, and the more accurately you pinpoint your potential customer, the better the chances that each of your pieces of mail will be read carefully.

Direct mail also gives you complete control over your schedules. You can mail whenever you choose, in whatever quantity your choose. And you can adjust your mailing schedule as you learn more about how many inquiries are being generated over a specified period of time.

Direct mail is perfect for small businesses because of its simplicity. You can create an effective direct-mail package with a typed, offset letter. Total cost? About $30 per 100, including postage, printing, paper, and envelopes.

If your business is slow, you can step up your direct-mail program. When things get busy, you can cut back. Once you've created the elements of a direct-mail program, you can keep them on hand and send them out on the spur of the moment whenever the time is right.

Another advantage of direct mail is that you control what you spend: Your costs are only at the mercy of rising postal rates. And, of course, it is your choice whether you wish to create a simple package like a typed, offset letter or one that is elaborate, such as several full-color brochures, and a reply envelope. If you wish, you can do limited runs of 1,000. Or even 100. This makes direct mail particularly attractive to new and expanding businesses with limited promotion budgets.

Finally, direct mail allows you to evaluate the success of your promotional program quickly. In general, you receive 70% of whatever responses you are going to get within two weeks, and 90% within four weeks. If your response rate is low, you may wish to change a particular element in your mailing or try another mailing list. Testing different forms of mailings is the only way to learn how your audience will respond to your business; almost everyone in direct mail advocates a program of never-ending testing—"test, test, and test again." With direct mail, you can create a separate mailing for each of your target markets, even if those markets are comparatively small.

Uses of Mailings

Direct mail has a number of specific uses in business. Perhaps its most common use is in mail-order selling. A number of products such as books, insurance, clothing, food, and magazines are sold by direct mail. Your prospects need not live in a rural setting to respond to a direct-mail offering of an unusual food or even a new book. Witness the success of the Fruit-of-the-Month Club and the Book-of-the-Month Club.

Many people enjoy shopping by mail (see Chapter 10 for more information on mail order).

Naturally, direct mail is also an important source of leads for your salespeople. It helps them eliminate cold canvassing for prospects. By generating real leads, direct mail helps salespeople make the most cost-effective use of their prospecting time.

Direct mail is a personal form of communication, and it is the appropriate form of communication for inviting people to see your place of business. Many direct-mail campaigns aim simply at getting people to see a new store or visit a brand-new business. The direct-mail campaign can center around an opening-day party, an exhibit, or any special event. In any case, it alerts people to a specific happening that may persuade them to think of you. An author autographing his new book, for example, is an event that can serve as the basis of a direct-mail letter aimed at bringing book buyers into the store.

There are other uses of direct mail, including:

• *Keep-in-touch mailings*. These "cordial contacts" serve to remind clients and contacts of your existence. Fig. 9-1 is an example of this type of letter. It was sent as an accompaniment to a recent reprint of a pertinent article.

• *Building mailing lists for future promotions*. Fig. 9-2 shows this type of letter. It was sent to people at corporations for the purpose of building an accurate mailing list of people in charge of corporate catering.

• *Image-building*. This type of letter keeps your name in front of your prospects.

• *Advertising*. This type of letter or package is used to get information out to a selected audience.

Elements of Direct Mail

From the moment your prospects pick up a piece of direct mail, they are the audience for an array of elements and effects that has taken days, weeks, or even months to create. Energy and talent have been put into that one piece of mail, despite the knowledge that ninety-eight out of every hun-

THE HUNT COMPANY
A Division of Hunt Management, Inc.

Are all executive search firms "headhunters"? No. At The
Hunt Company, we realize that it doesn't matter how good a
head you have if your heart isn't in your work.

This is especially true for those whose only affiliation
with a particular company is that they sit on the board of
directors. In "The Changing Role of Outside Directors",
which recently appeared in <u>Enterprise</u>, I focused on the
changing role of outside directors, people who must be as
sensitive to the interests of consumers and environmental-
ists as they are to shareholders and employees. The best
outside directors are those who aren't afraid to voice their
opinions and do battle with corporate complacency.

By now you must know that at The Hunt Company, we're keyed into
the top managerial talent in the United States. The only
"heads" we hunt for are those attached to people who have
talent, experience and the will to succeed. They're people
who view the future with eagerness instead of anxiety, and
who know that a little change is good for the corporate
soul.

We hope that you'll think "Hunt" the next time you search
for an outside director or for anyone with the type of
head -- and heart -- well-run businesses demand.

274 Madison Avenue at 40th Street • New York, New York 10016 • (212) 889-2020

Fig. 9-1 This cover letter, used to transmit a recent article, helps reinforce
the article's ideas as well as keep the author's name in front of his clients.
In this case, the letter writer is also the author of the article.

Catering with an Italian accent

Why choose a caterer out of habit when we can send you food that's out of this world?

Now you have an opportunity to discover for yourself what the food writers of *The New York Times, The Wall Street Journal, The News* and *The Post* have been writing about.

In Italian, Abbondanza means "abundance." And we offer an abundance of entrées, cheeses, breads, salads, meats, desserts and drinks for any occasion.

Whether you're interested in box lunches or sumptuous sit-down meals, we're ready with more than 100 different specialties.

All of our dishes are prepared in our own kitchen. You're welcome to drop in at any time, sample our array of specialties and even talk to our chef. We're sending along our brochure which describes our catering services. Of course, words are no substitute for tasting our food.

Please take a moment to fill out the enclosed card so that we may arrange a visit for you to experience Abbondanza first-hand.

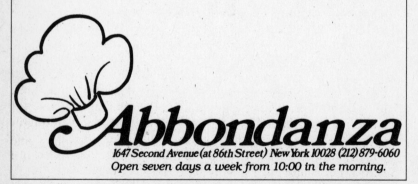

Abbondanza

1647 Second Avenue (at 86th Street) New York 10028 (212) 879-6060
Open seven days a week from 10:00 in the morning.

Fig. 9-2 Sent to food-service managers as well as office managers, this cover letter helped Abbondanza introduce itself to the potentially lucrative corporate catering market, and also helped Abbondanza build a mailing list for future promotions.

dred people who receive it will throw it away, in a split second, without even a backward glance.

As we have stated, the elements of a direct-mail package will depend upon your business and your budget. You may send a simple sales letter or you may send an array of colorful literature. Here are some of the elements that are most common to direct mail:

Envelope

Naturally, every piece of direct mail needs an envelope (except for self-mailer brochures or flyers). Direct-mail professionals like to begin the sales process by putting an arresting message right on the envelope. One such message is "Stop!" (in the shape of a stop sign). The rest of the message may be "Don't throw this away unless you want to lose a chance at making millions!" Since the envelope is the first thing a reader sees, direct-mail professionals feel that the crucial moment is the instant that the reader first looks at the envelope. That's when the sale must begin. For small businesses, however, printing envelopes with specific sales messages can become rather expensive.

Letter

Solicitation letters are an art. If they are well written, they can persuade thousands of customers to purchase goods and services. No wonder leading professional direct-mail writers can earn as much as $7,500 from creating a single direct-mail letter!

Letters are integral to direct mail and are also considered sales literature. They lead the reader to take action, and direct his attention to other elements in the mailing. The letter, sometimes spiced with testimonials or factual claims, conveys a sense of the personal relationship between prospect and seller. The letter must awaken a need within each reader if it is to move many people to read it and respond to it.

Fig. 9-3 shows a letter that generated a 7% response and $15,000 in business in just six months. Fig. 9-4 shows a letter that effectively distinguishes one writing consultant from his competitors. This letter led to assignments from a half-dozen

An effective business writing program will save your organization time and money.
Here's how to find the right one.

1. An effective writing program defines your writing problems before training begins.

The first step in improving writing is to identify the specific problems that need to be solved. Ask a consultant how he plans to uncover stylistic, organizational, and job-related writing problems prior to training.

2. Choose an authority.

Your managers will listen closely to consultants who have achieved recognition in their field. Ask a consultant, "What have you written lately? Any articles or books on writing?" There is no substitute for publication.

3. Business writing experience is important.

In addition to having written letters, memos, reports, and proposals, a business writing consultant should also have written successful sales, marketing, or promotional literature aimed at consumers or clients.

4. Look for versatility as well as experience.

Select a consultant who has designed and implemented writing programs for top organizations in both the public and private sector.

5. Pay for imagination, not image.

The person who conducts your writing program is half the program. You should be paying for time, talent, and expertise—not paneled walls, four-color brochures, or other frills.

If these ideas make good sense to you, call or write us. We make even better sense in person.

Gary Blake, Ph.D.
Director

THE
COMMUNICATION WORKSHOP

207 East 85th Street
New York 10028
(212) 794-1144

Fig. 9-4   Aimed at training directors, this letter takes a low-key approach. It attempts to make logical suggestions rather than sales points, hoping that the sense of the suggestions will sell itself.

Fig. 9-3   This letter, mailed with brochures to prospects in advertising and public relations, led to a 7% response and about $15,000 in business in six months.

Bob Bly
Copywriter/Consultant

How an Engineer and Former Ad Manager Can Help You Write Better Ads and Brochures.

For many ad agency people, industrial advertising is a difficult chore. It's detailed work, and highly technical. To write the copy, you need someone with the technical know-how of an engineer and the communications skills of a copywriter.

That's where I can help.

As a freelance industrial copywriter who is also a graduate engineer, I know how to write clear, jargon-free, technically sound copy. You'll like my writing samples—ads, brochures, catalogs, direct mail, PR, and AV. And you'll like having a writer on call who works only when you need him—by the hour, by the day, or by the project.

Here are my qualifications:

I have an engineering background (BS, chemical engineering, University of Rochester). I started out writing brochures and AV scripts for the Westinghouse Defense Center. After I left Westinghouse, I became advertising manager for Koch Engineering, a manufacturer of chemical process equipment.

In my freelance work, I've handled projects in a wide variety of industries including computers, construction, chemical equipment, electronics, telecommunications, and many other areas. My articles on business communication have appeared in Industrial Marketing, Writer's Digest, Chemical Engineering, and Audio-Visual Directions. And, I'm the author of two books: Technical Writing: Structure, Standards, and Style (McGraw Hill) and the forthcoming How to Promote Your Own Business (New American Library).

Now, I'd like to help *you* create ads, brochures, and other promotions. Call me when your creative team is overloaded, or when the project is highly technical.

If it sounds like I can be of service, please complete and mail the enclosed postcard.

Sincerely,

Bob Bly

major corporations planning to institute a business-writing program. It has also led to very profitable repeat business.

Brochures

Brochures give detailed descriptive information about products and services. Their format is conducive to gaining product knowledge quickly, concisely, and with a minimum of formality. Not every direct-mail package contains a brochure, but many do. While a letter can be tailored to a specific person, or group of people, a brochure or flyer conveys a more general—and more timeless—type of information about your business.

Reply envelope, postcard, coupon, or order form

A reply element is a major element of almost every direct-mail package. A return postcard helps you gather information on prospects, gain feedback, and build a mailing list, just as an order form or coupon allows readers to purchase a product. A reply enclosure persuades the prospect to take action now.

Tips on Writing Direct Mail That Pulls

Everyone—or so it seems—has had a say on what makes direct mail successful or unsuccessful. If anyone had a fool-proof formula for getting people to respond, they would have, by now, found a way to bottle it, sell it, and become rich enough to retire to the French Riviera.

Still, there are a few bits of advice that seem to us to be useful. Keep in mind that probably you are the person who knows your customer best, so don't ever be afraid to go against the ''experts'' or against supposedly ''time-tested'' theories.

One advertising professional says there are three rules in direct mail: Make it short, make it clear, and make it count. Yet, as we've mentioned, short copy may not always be adequate for describing high-priced or sophisticated products or services.

Most people agree that your direct-mail piece must quickly

show the reader the *benefits* of what you are selling, and that your mailing piece should reflect the personality of your business. It's generally a good idea to put your product's chief benefit right in the first paragraph of your brochure or letter.

Many professionals agree that you need to back up your statements with proof. It may be a testimonial from a famous person, or from someone known in your field. Ads or direct mail promoting new books lean heavily on "blurbs" praising the book, especially blurbs from people who have solid reputations and are well known.

There are other tips that may work for you, such as indenting paragraphs or enclosing a postage-free business reply card. Reply cards stimulate a greater response than order forms that require the consumer to affix postage.

Perhaps the greatest cliché of direct mail is the "Act NOW!" closing of the letter or brochure. Subscriptions for magazines and other types of direct mail in which a check is being elicited try to provoke action by promising you a "premium" or gift for sending your check quickly. These premiums are often the deciding factors in making the sale. If you can purchase a book, calendar, or novelty at low cost, you may be able to offer it to your prospects as an incentive to buy what you are selling. But be careful: Most premiums seem "cheap" to sophisticated readers, and most people are wise to the gimmick of offering a low-priced premium as an inducement.

Like all other promotions, direct mail works best when your product has relevance to a person's life, when it is something that he considers vital. Good copy, handsome packaging, carefully timed mailing, and pretty graphics all help, but nothing makes up for the persuasion that goes into convincing people that your product is going to enrich their lives.

Selecting Mailing Lists

Some people are good prospects for your business, yet many are not. That simple fact is the cornerstone of the mailing-list business.

At some point, many businesses come to the stage at which

they require expansion. Mailing lists help you reach prospects efficiently. Of course, you can begin by creating your own mailing list, simply keeping records of present customers as well as anyone who may have inquired about a particular product or service. Don't miss the opportunity to add a name to your own mailing list. You can never tell when you will want to send that person information about a new product or service.

Compiling your own list is not necessarily difficult. Stores, galleries, and boutiques sometimes keep "guest books" prominently displayed so that browsers can sign their names and addresses. This appeal to one's ego is a subtle way of collecting names for future mailings. Other businesses simply check their sales slips or credit-card receipts when they want to pull together a mailing list of recent customers. Responses to advertisements and PR provide other valuable names of prospects or past customers.

At some point, however, you may need outside help in identifying new prospects for your business. There are a number of sources of potential prospects. The following are the most common:

The telephone book

Don't ignore the obvious. The Yellow Pages of your phone directory lists businesses by category. If you are marketing a product or service to a particular industry (or if you wish to identify certain companies by location) the Yellow Pages is valuable . . . and free.

Subscription lists

Magazines have become more specialized over the past decade, and their lists of subscribers are usually highly focused. You may wish to try to identify a particular magazine that is read by people who might also be good prospects for your business. Then, contact the magazine and ask to rent its mailing list (lists are rarely "sold"; they are "rented" for one-time use). Sometimes a magazine's subscription list will be valuable simply because the magazine is read by affluent people and your product appeals to that market. If you sell products to the teenage market, one of the teen magazines might provide a valuable list for your business.

Club and service organization lists

Using the same logic, you may wish to buy or rent the membership list of a club or service organization whose members are prospects for whatever you are selling. The membership list of the Society for Technical Communication, for example, would have great potential value to a publisher of a book on technical writing. A cooking-utensil maker would certainly see the value of buying a mailing list of the students of a gourmet cooking school. In the same way, professional-organization and trade-association directories can be valuable to a business. Some people join organizations for the sole purpose of receiving the group's membership directory.

Newspaper listings and town-hall records.

To people who sell products to newlyweds, the newspaper's wedding announcements are a perennial source of prospects. Similarly, you are welcome to go to the county clerk, town hall, or state motor vehicle department and find out public information about land ownership or car registration—a boon to businesses trying to reach those people.

Mailing-list brokers

The renting of mailing lists is a large, sophisticated industry, and list brokers (people who compile and rent mailing lists) have become known for the reliability, type, and number of lists they rent.

Business and consumer lists are culled from phone books, credit organizations, newspapers, magazines, directories, trade-show registrants, people in the news, and buyers of products and services.

These lists can be compiled and sold by industrial classification (SIC*), company size (number of employees, sales

---

* Standard Industrial Classifications are code numbers used to define different industries for advertising and marketing purposes.

volume, net worth), home vs. branch office, city size, geography (state, metro, city, 3- or 5-digit zip), and job title. With the advances in computer technology, mailing lists can be merged or divided in such a way as to provide astoundingly specific sublists. If you want to reach apparel executives who are 30–35 years old and who live in the suburbs of northern New Jersey (and who smoke Pall Malls), somewhere there's probably a list broker with just such a list!

Many small list compilers supply segments such as insurance, banking, churches, schools, and professionals by discipline. For example, all physicians at office addresses are available from the American Medical Association.

Although you can find the names of mailing-list brokers in the Yellow Pages, you should also "think lists" whenever you hear of a magazine, association, club, or newspaper that serves your market. All may be sources of prospect lists.

To determine the quality of any list, determine what percentage of the names you are buying will truly be good prospects. How many have the right title, fall within the right age group, or live within the vicinity you can most easily serve? No list will ever have 100% of the precise types of people you want to reach, but the best lists are those that most closely match the demographics of your business. Good lists are accurate (correct addresses, correct titles), up-to-date (corrections are made frequently), and well targeted to contain a high percentage of the type of people you've determined to be your best prospects.

If you're selling computers, your prospect may not be the data-processing manager. There may not even be such a title in a prospective organization. It could be the president in a small company, the vice-president of data processing, the administrative VP, the director of management information systems (MIS), the treasurer, the controller, the operations manager, or the general purchasing agent.

So, as you thumb through mailing-list catalogs, list the basic Standard Industrial Classification (SIC) categories that could use your item based on the research you've done. A business catalog offers you a choice of hundreds of such categories.

It is only by shopping extensively and making innumerable comparisons that you can choose between lists, all of which may contain drawbacks. Some lists will include people who are not really qualified prospects, others will take in too wide a geographic sweep, others will take in too wide an economic or age grouping. Finding good lists is a result of learning precisely whom you wish to reach, finding out what is available and at what price, and then making your decision based upon which list will yield the most qualified prospects for the least money.

And speaking of money, renting mailing lists will cost $50–$100 per 1,000 names. Most lists are available printed on labels, making them convenient for pasting directly on envelopes. Since list brokers want you to use the list only once, labels inhibit you from making a permanent record of the names. Names are available on either pressure-sensitive labels (labels that peel off by hand, and can be affixed to envelopes) or "cheshire" labels, which can be affixed automatically by machine.

Other list sources include *Direct Mail List Rates and Data* (Direct Mail Lists Rate and Data, 5201 Old Orchard Road, Skokie, IL 60076), the "Standard Rate and Data" of mailing lists. It contains about 25,000 indexed lists. Also, the Direct Mail Marketing Association (6 East 43rd St., New York, NY 10017) has information on list sources.

Keeping Your Own Lists

If you rely on list brokers, they will maintain the lists and you may rent them when necessary. If you compile and maintain your own lists—lists drawn from advertising, publicity and direct-mail-generated sales leads—you take the responsibility for updating them, keeping them accurate, and making the addition and deletion of names a simple procedure.

Both Xerox and Avery put out 8½-by-11-inch sheets designed to keep the names and addresses on your mailing lists. These sheets, known as "label matrices," are available at many business supply stores and stationery stores. Each matrix is divided into 33 equal rectangles; guidelines are drawn in nonreproducing blue ink. By typing directly onto the matrices, you can keep a permanent mailing list, ready, at any time, to be photocopied directly onto pressure-sensitive labels. The matrices are easy to store, prepare, and change.

Doing the Mailing

Sending the direct-mail package presents almost as many challenges and decisions as creating it. Should you send all the packages at once, or stagger them? Should you send them bulk mail? First class? Third class? Does your mailing have the required postage for its class and weight? How do you create a business reply card? Do you need a permit for a business reply card?

Many of the answers to these questions can be found at your local post office. Generalities won't help, so the best we can do is to refer you to post-office publications that may.

Publication No. 113, for example, tells you every regulation pertaining to first-class, third-class, and fourth-class bulk mailings. This publication defines the eligibility requirements for mail sent via each class.

Bulk mail

Your direct-mail package may be forwarded via third class, first class, or airmail. Detailed information on these classifications of mail and the postage rates applicable for each are given in the Postage Manual and in Post Office Publication No. 3, titled "Domestic Postage Rates and Fees."

Third-class bulk mail costs substantially less than regular third-class mail, first-class mail, or airmail. For this reason, most direct mail is forwarded via third-class bulk mail.

In order to qualify for the third-class rate, the contents of the mailing must be printed—not handwritten or typewritten. Third-class mail is subject to inspection by the post office. Check your local post office for conditions under which third-class mail may be forwarded at bulk rate.

The bulk-mail permit

A bulk-mail permit can be obtained at your local post office on completion of the appropriate form and payment of an annual bulk-mail fee. The permit is valid only at the post office at which it is issued and is good for the calendar year of issue. The mailer must pay the annual bulk-mail fee each calendar year before he sends out his first bulk mailings for the year.

Reply envelopes

Reply envelopes make it easy for customers to place an order. It saves them the addressing of an envelope and having to search for a stamp.

The reply envelope may be a regular self-addressed envelope with or without postage affixed, or it may be a business reply envelope which can be returned by the recipient to the mailer without affixing postage.

The most convenient and cost-effective type of reply envelope is the business reply envelope. Not only does it save a search for stamps, but it also saves the mailer postage because he pays only for those envelopes that are returned—presumably with the names of prospects or with the orders themselves.

In order to use business reply envelopes, the mailer must first obtain a permit from the post office. Application must be filed at the post office to which the envelopes will be returned. The permit is annual and costs under $50. The business reply envelope must have the mailer's permit imprint and the phrases "Business Reply Mail," "Postage Is Not Necessary if Mailed Within the United States," and "Postage Will Be Paid by" followed by the return address printed on the face of the card. Postage on returned envelopes is payable to the mailman on delivery of the envelopes.

For further details on business reply envelopes, take a look at the Postal Manual or Post Office Publication No. 13, titled "Mailing Permits." The latter may be obtained from your local post office.

Direct-Response Postcards

A direct-response postcard is not an element of a direct-mail package; it is a special type of direct mail (Fig. 9-5). Typically, a trade journal will offer advertisers three or four postcard mailings a year. For $600–$1,200, your company's postcard can be included in a packet of cards (usually wrapped in plastic) sent to all of the magazine's subscribers.

Direct-response postcards are a low-cost alternative to space advertising. Their only mission in life is to generate sales or leads. A typical card contains reply-card information on one side. The other side contains a simple advertising message and invites the reader to fill in the card and drop it in the mail to receive a brochure, catalog, or other offering.

Response rates vary, usually hovering at about 0.5% to 1%. Not bad, considering that the cost is usually less than that of running an ad. A 0.5% response rate to 50,000 people still yields 250 inquiries. They'll come directly to you, and most will have a name and address. If the card costs $900, that's about $3.60 per sales lead.

Cards have generated excellent response for companies as diverse as a window-blinds manufacturer and a maker of specialized machine parts. Color and frequency are not factors in success.

Here are some tips on getting the most out of response postcards.

• *Don't run a card unless you are able to handle the response*. Whether you turn leads over to a sales force or handle them yourself, you must be ready to answer many responses quickly. There's nothing colder than a dead sales lead.

• *Be selective*. You have only 3 by 5 inches of space, and about a third of that is space where prospects can fill out their name, title, address, and phone number. If your product or service has seven or eight key benefits, you may have to settle for mentioning only the two most important ones.

• *Don't be cute*. There's no room to make connections between odd headlines and the product itself. Keep the ideas simple.

Is stress robbing your company of productivity?

Teach your people to manage stress with

The Stress Mess

a valuable training film that

• Teaches how to reduce and manage stress.
• Reveals many common signs of stress.
• Explains important time management techniques.

Color, 24½ minutes – Order #C316G

☐ *2-Day Preview (16mm only)* . . . .$ 50.00*
☐ *5-Day Rental* $100.00*
☐ *5-Year Lease or Purchase* $565.00*
☐ *16mm* ☐ *Video* ☐ *Send me more information!*

Shipping and handling additional. Prices subject to change without notice.

Name _____ Position _____

Organization _____

Dept. _____ Phone _____

Address _____

City _____ State ____ Zip _____

Signature _____

Barr Films
P.O. Box 5667
Pasadena, California 91107
(213) 793-6153

Fig. 9-5 This direct-response postcard is typical in its brief, self-contained sales message.

TAP 9/82

BUSINESS REPLY CARD
FIRST CLASS PERMIT NO. 2285 PASADENA, CA

POSTAGE WILL BE PAID BY ADDRESSEE

Barr Films
3490 E. Foothill Boulevard
P.O. Box 5667
Pasadena, CA 91107

NO POSTAGE
NECESSARY
IF MAILED
IN THE
UNITED STATES

• *Line art is often preferable to photos.* When photos are reduced to small size, they often lose quality. The subtle distinctions blur and the photo looks "muddy." On the other hand, line art can usually be reduced without losing too much quality or impact.

• *Keep the card as clean-looking as possible.* White space adds to a postcard's "clean" look. Don't try to fill every available inch of the card.

• *And, most important, offer something:* a brochure, a demonstration, a free sample. Cards are an inquiry medium, and all efforts should be directed toward that one objective.

Measuring the Response

Mr. Mutsakis sends 1,000 direct-mail packages to prospects and receives twenty return postcards. Mr. Birch also sends 1,000 packages and gets three return postcards. Did either campaign "succeed"? It's impossible to say unless we know how much each program cost to create, how many strong leads were developed, or how many sales were made, and the profit per sale.

It is one thing to design a direct-mail program that yields response, and quite another to design one that gets people to send checks. To measure your success, you must first set goals, set a budget, and set up reasonable expectations for converting leads into sales.

Naturally, if your direct-mail program cost $1,000 to launch and any one sale would gross $100, you need to make at least ten sales to meet your expenses. And you've not added to the equation the "cost" of your time or the energy you've spent on the program.

Measuring a response, of course, is more than bookkeeping —counting inquiries, true leads, and sales. Anyone who can add can count return postcards or telephone calls. Anyone can be trained to calculate the costs of the mailing program and decide whether the effort was worthwhile. You should concern yourself with a broad look at the effect of direct mail on your business.

Direct mail has publicity value. It lets your prospects know that you exist. There is no telling when a prospect might pull your direct-mail piece out of a file and give you a call. Therefore, never assume that a direct-mail campaign is dead if it doesn't yield immediate results.

Direct mail should also be weighed against the cost of other advertising. Since direct mail is easier to pinpoint than advertising, you may want to try it for its experimental value alone.

If you believe that your direct mail has yielded a *low* response rate (1.4% is a figure often mentioned as an *average* response rate), or if you find that the people who respond are not, on the whole, people who can make the decision to buy your product, you may wish to find a better list of prospects or change one of the elements in your package.

Through marketing research, Procter & Gamble discovered that when a product is put on eye level in a store (instead of foot level), sales increase by as much as 200%! Same product, same price, different position on the shelves. Similar benefits might be gained by changing a headline or a reply postcard or even the color of an envelope in your direct-mail package.

• Chapter 10 •

SELLING BY LETTER: MAIL ORDER

Mail Order: A $100 Billion Market

In Chapter 9, we talked about direct mail—a kind of "advertising by letter." In this chapter, we'll see how products can actually be bought and sold through the mail—something called mail order. Since the two terms *direct mail* and *mail order* are often confused, we'll start with some definitions.

Like television commercials, catalogs, and coupons, direct mail is a type of promotion, a mass communication used to inform prospects about your products and services.

Mail order, on the other hand, is a type of *selling*. As the name implies, mail order is the offering of a product through the mail. In mail order, there is no personal selling involved. The promotion, purchasing, and delivery are conducted entirely through the mail.

In some cases, direct-mail sales letters or catalogs serve as the promotional vehicle for advertising mail-order products. But newspaper ads, magazine ads, free publicity, and TV commercials are also used to move mail-order merchandise.

The mail-order market is *tremendous:* Nearly $100 billion worth of mail-order merchandise is sold each year. And it's a growing market: Mail-order sales are increasing twice as fast as sales through stores.

For some small businesses, mail-order sales may supplement wholesaling, retailing, and other selling techniques. Other entrepreneurs may find it cost-effective to start *mail-order* businesses—companies in which 100% of the business is conducted by mail. This chapter will tell you how to select and sell mail-order products, and how to measure the results of your mail-order promotions.

What Sells by Mail?

Not everything is appropriate for sale by mail. A lawn-mower is too large, a bottle of soda pop too easily purchased at the corner store, a legal service too important and expensive to buy without meeting the lawyer face-to-face.

Why do people buy through the mail? Convenience, for one thing. People use mail order to buy what is not readily available at the local department store or town shopping mall. Privacy is a second incentive for using mail order; mail is an easy way of purchasing items you'd be embarrassed to buy in public: a seductive negligee, a lotion to prevent baldness, or an especially racy romance novel. Sometimes, mail-order houses offer items you can't get in *any* store, such as unusual collectibles or odd-size shoes. And finally, shopping through an L. L. Bean or Neiman-Marcus mail-order catalog is just plain *fun*.

According to the *Mail Order Industry Annual Report,* published by the Maxwell Scroge Company, *insurance* is the leading mail-order product, with sales of mail-order insurance policies hitting $4 billion in 1980. The other leading mail-order product categories include general merchandising, home furnishings, housewares, gifts, magazine subscriptions, books, ready-to-wear clothing, collectibles, sporting goods, crafts, foods, and records and tapes.

In addition, we looked over our "junk mail" this month and found offerings for a variety of other products, including appliances, home decorations, health and beauty aids, business stationery, auto accessories, toys, pet products, lawn and garden items, cigars, cigarette holders, needlecraft kits, costume jewelry, watches, radios, and home-study courses.

How to Select Mail-Order Merchandise

It's a relatively simple matter to determine whether your own products are suitable for mail-order sales. Selecting mail-order merchandise is like playing the game "Twenty Questions." And here are the twenty questions to ask:

1. *Can you buy it in a store?* If buyers can find the product on the store shelves, there's no need for them to send for it by mail.

2. *Do people want it?* Products with broad appeal stand a better chance for success. Make sure the potential market is large enough.

3. *Will it appeal to well-defined segments of the market?* With your limited small-business budget, you can't possibly advertise to every man, woman, and child in the United States. Make sure the product appeals to specific market segments so you can target your promotions.

4. *Does it have sales appeal?* Mail-order advertisements for unique and interesting products stand a better chance of being noticed (and acted upon) than advertisements for dull, mundane ones.

5. *What's the competition like?* The marketplace can't bear too many similar products. Make sure your product is just a little bit different, a little bit better, than the competition's.

6. *Is it too big?* What size and weight is the product? Can it be shipped economically? A small business may not have the capital or the facilities to handle large mail-order merchandise.

7. *Will it survive shipping?* Fragile and perishable products do not make good mail-order merchandise.

8. *Can I make a good profit on it?* To sell profitably, the price should be at least twice, and probably four or five times, your cost. Can you make this markup and still sell at a price your prospects will pay?

9. *Are sales seasonal?* With some items, such as Christmas cards, swimwear, and back-to-school supplies, sales are seasonal. Most mail-order marketers prefer items that will sell well all year round.

10. *Can I count on repeat sales?* Repeat sales are the backbone of the mail-order industry. Is yours a one-shot product, or will the customer need a refill or replacement later on? High-potency vitamins are a classic example of a mail-order product that can pull replacement orders again and again.

11. *Does it work?* Consumers today are wary indeed of

products that don't live up to their promise—especially in mail order, where they never get to meet the salesperson face-to-face. Mail-order products should live up to any claims made in the advertisements. Beware of baldness lotions, instant weight-loss programs, pills that claim to increase sexual potency, and other "miracle" products. All too often, they spell s-c-a-m to the buyer.

12. *Is it simple enough?* Products that must be assembled, installed, or operated should come with a set of clear, easy-to-follow instructions. Nothing infuriates mail-order customers more than products that turn out to be too complicated to use.

13. *Is it a good product?* Is this something you yourself would buy? Or is it substandard? Mail order is not the place to unload junk merchandise.

14. *Is it interesting?* Does descriptive copy about the product make you yawn or make you smile? Pick products with unusual selling features that, if highlighted in an ad or catalog description, will make for compelling reading.

15. *Does it look good?* Mail-order buyers are at a severe disadvantage—they can't actually see or touch the merchandise until after they've purchased it. Products that can be illustrated or photographed in an interesting fashion will stand out in an ad or catalog and catch the buyer's attention.

16. *Can one or two models satisfy all customers?* If too many different sizes and colors of a single product are required, inventory can become a problem.

17. *Does it tie in with your other mail-order items?* When a group of similar items appeal to the same market, they can be promoted together at far less cost than a single item.

18. *Have similar items succeeded in the past?* Does the success of similar products indicate that this one will succeed? Or does the track record say that this product won't sell? Mail-order marketers are a close-knit community, and the competition will often be glad to chat with you about successes and failures.

19. *Does the product fill a void in the marketplace?* Is there a crying need for the product that has, until now, gone largely unfulfilled? Select products because there's a demand for them—and not solely because you like them.

20. *Can you handle it?* Is mail order worth the time and trouble? Or are you content with your normal methods of selling the product?

How to Promote Mail-Order Merchandise

With mail order, no salesman calls, no store opens its doors. The promotion does all the selling. Traditionally, mail-order marketers use the following types of promotions:

Direct-mail letters

You see this one at least three or four times a month. It's the long-winded, chummy letter from the company president asking you to join the Book-of-the-Month Club, subscribe to *Business Week,* apply for the American Express Card, or take out a life insurance policy.

To you it's junk mail, but to the mail-order people these solicitation letters mean big business, and they'll pay professional copywriters $2,000, $4,000, and even $7,500 for a well-written letter that will bring in orders.

At these prices, you might want to take a crack at writing the direct-mail letter yourself. Here are a few hints to help you write a better letter:

● Make it long. For some strange reason, a two-page letter pulls better than a one-page letter. And a four-pager does better than two pages!

● But don't pad it with clever copy and fancy phrases. You want a letter crammed with reason-why-they-should-buy copy. A letter that sells from the first word—to the last.

● Use indentations, underlining, and capital letters for added emphasis. Letters with indented paragraphs pull twice as well as letters without them. Note how the Thompson Cigar Company uses these techniques in its sales letter (Fig. 10-1).

Fig. 10-1 (opposite page) Direct-mail solicitation letter from the Thompson Cigar Company.

Thompson Cigar Company

Promise me one thing.

Before you light up your first cigar from the
box of 50 I want to send you to sample free --
promise me you'll examine it carefully.

In particular, I want you to feel the smooth
texture of its exquisite brown wrapper. And smell
the rich aroma of its expertly cured tobaccos.

Unless I miss my guess, you will realize immediately
that you are scrutnizing no ordinary cigar.

Indeed, it is quite possible that you have never
seen -- much less smoked -- a cigar such as this
in your life. Why? Because the seeds from which
its tobaccos were grown once flourished in the sun-
drenched fields of Pinar del Rio -- perhaps the
finest tobacco-growing region of all Cuba.

Yes, I said Cuba.

You see, the cigars I want to send you are all
genuine Cuban seed leaf cigars -- blended and crafted
in the old Cuban way from tobaccos whose seeds were
literally smuggled out of Cuba from under Castro's
beard! To discover the incredible story of these
magnificent cigars -- and to receive a box of 50 to
sample free -- please read on . . .

Dear Fellow Cigar Lover:

    With this letter -- and with your O.K. on the enclosed card -- I'm
going to break the great, ironclad "law" of cigar-smoking. You know:

                "You gotta buy 'em BEFORE you smoke 'em!"

Not with this remarkable invitation from the Thompson Cigar Company.

    If you'll send me the enclosed Reservation Card as soon as possible
(before my supplies run out), I'll send you one of my "Victory Sampler"
boxes of 50 superb Cuban seed leaf cigars -- a tempting selection of
Panetela Extras, Corona Chicos, Juniors and Plazas. Each cigar is factory-
fresh and ready to smoke -- direct from our temperature and humidity
controlled humidor.

    Now, here's how we break that "law" . . .

• Be personal. Note the use of the personal pronouns *me, you, your,* and *I* in the cigar letter. Talk to the reader— as one human being talks to another.

• Be friendly. Win the reader's confidence.

• Use short sentences.

• Write in a relaxed, conversational style. This is the secret of all successful mail-order letter writing. Read your writing aloud; your ear will help eliminate half of your errors.

• Ask for the order—today. Not tomorrow.

Direct-mail catalogs

While letters are used to sell a single item, catalogs offer many different products and are a favorite promotional tool of mail-order houses. For more information on catalogs, see Chapter 11, "No Fear of Flyers—and Other Sales Literature."

Newspaper and magazine advertisements

Print advertisements are another way to sell single mail-order items. Mail-order advertisements are the most difficult to write, since no salesperson can step in and explain the ad or answer the consumer's questions. A good mail-order ad tells what the product is, shows a photograph or illustration of the product, highlights the key features, explains the benefits the reader will derive from the product, and includes testimonials to the product's superior performance.

In newspapers, mail-order ads can be seen anywhere, in any section. Some magazines, however, have special sections for advertising mail-order products.

Free publicity

The mail-order sections of magazines often run free publicity items on new products. To obtain this free publicity, send the editor a press release (see Chapter 7) and photograph of the product. Some editors will ask to see a product sample before they decide whether it's worthy of mention in their publication.

Television and radio commercials

Recently, television (and less frequently, radio) has been used to advertise a wide range of mail-order items—everything from record collections and kitchenware to exercise machines and costume jewelry. These commercials usually end with a request to "send check or money order" or to call a convenient toll-free number and place an order COD or with your credit card.

Fifteen Tips for Effective Mail-Order Promotions

It doesn't matter whether you're writing a letter, catalog, ad, or commercial—these fifteen tips will help make *any* mail-order promotion get better results. Each tip is designed to get prospects to send you a check or order. (Remember, the goal of mail order is immediate sales, not long-term image-building.)

1. Offer a premium.

A premium is a bonus. It's a gift you give the prospect just for sending in his order promptly. A supplier of mail-order vitamins offers a free booklet on diet and nutrition with each purchase. The Literary Guild, a book club, used to offer a free tote bag to each new member.

Often, mail-order promotions close the sale by offering the reader just one more reason why he should buy, just one more added incentive for writing out that check. A thoughtfully selected premium, one with real value to your prospects, can be that added incentive.

2. Give first-time buyers a low introductory price.

Welcome prospects to the ranks of customers by giving them a break on their first order.

3. Make charter offers.

In a charter offer, your ad or letter lets prospects know that the product is being offered for the very first time, and that they are among the carefully selected list of people chosen to receive this special offer. In a sense, charter offers appeal to a person's ego by saying, "You can be the first on the block." And really, that's the whole secret behind any successful advertising—to make people feel good about buying your products.

4. Use temporary price reductions.

This tactic urges prospects to send in the order immediately, because, after a brief period of time, the price will go up or the supply will be depleted. Most mail-order shoppers respond to a promotion as soon as they see it; few people hold on to them to make a later purchasing decision. So, there is every reason to add incentives for sending in the order *now*.

5. Offer special discounts to repeat customers.

Here's how a sales letter from the ACME Office Supply Company uses discounts to reward its steady customers:

> Dear Mr. Banner:
>
> Thank you for trusting ACME to fill your office equipment and supply needs during the past year.
>
> It's the steady business from valued customers like you that has made us the nation's leading direct-mail office supply distributor.
>
> And, Mr. Banner, I believe that one good turn deserves another. That's why we're offering you a 50% DISCOUNT on your next order of business cards, letterhead, or envelopes!

Price breaks and special offers for repeat customers help make them *feel* special and build loyalty to your company.

6. Guarantee the offer.

Because of its "sight-unseen" nature, there's a certain risk to ordering products by mail. Mail-order shoppers live in fear of receiving shoddy merchandise, not getting the right merchandise, or not getting any merchandise at all.

Put your customers at ease. Guarantee the quality of the product. And promise a speedy refund if they're not satisfied. Here's how the sales letter from Thompson Cigar puts the buyer's fears to rest:

> When your sampler arrives, put my cigars to your own test:
>
> Examine them with a critical eye. Smoke several of each of the four shapes. Then decide. If you are not completely delighted, return the bill unpaid, along with the remainder of the box. You'll owe me not a cent.

With this paragraph in the sales letter, the customer can't lose. (In fact, one of the favorite phrases of mail-order copywriters is "You can't lose!")

7. Include testimonials.

McDonald's, the *New York Daily News,* and *Reader's Digest* all promote their sweepstakes with commercials showing big-money winners talking about their newly won wealth. Nothing sells like a satisfied customer, and testimonials add believability to all promotions—including mail order.

8. Leave adequate space on the coupon.

Few things are as infuriating or as difficult as trying to write your name, address, city, state, zip code, and phone number on a horizontal line that's only half an inch long. Coupons and reply cards should contain adequate space for filling in this information. Make it easy, not difficult, for prospects to respond to your mail-order promotions.

9. Use an actual object in the mailing.

Today's consumers and businesspeople are bombarded every month by dozens of unwanted direct-mail solicitations. By including an actual object in the mailing—a penny, a postage stamp, a product sample—you can make your promotion stand out from the crowd. And breaking through the clutter, getting noticed, is the first and most vital step in making the sale.

10. Make a personal promise.

Most people do not trust corporations, and so a mail-order offer should come from an individual, not a faceless corporate entity. Make the copy as personal as possible. And above all, assure the reader that a real live human being will take the responsibility for making sure the order is processed promptly and correctly, and filled with quality merchandise. Examples of this personal style of writing are given below in the column at right; note how much more encouraging it is than the corporate we-are-not-responsible tone in the column at left.

Corporatese: No-One-Responsible-Here	Personal: We're-Here-to-Help-You
Your current situation with regards to marketing, accounting, and management will be analyzed carefully and expertly. Based on the results, you will receive a written recommendation on which system of hardware and software is optimum for the application.	We'll take a look at how you run your business, and then furnish a clear, concise report on what computer system would best meet your needs.
Unfortunately, the deadline for this offer cannot be extended.	Much as I'd like to, I can't extend the deadline.
The assorted cheeses will be shipped in a humidity-proof container.	I'll send your selection of cheeses in a special package designed to keep the food fresh and delicious.

11. Add a touch of drama to the copy.

Mail-order customers like to think they're getting something a little bit out of the ordinary for their money . . . something you can't buy at the local department store. Adding a dash of drama to your copy reinforces this feeling and gives your prospect more pleasure in his purchase. Here's how the Thompson Cigar Company added excitement and intrigue to a box of cigars:

> A Cuban tobacco farmer, sympathetic to American cigar lovers, managed to smuggle 12 pounds of the finest Pinar del Rio seed out of the country—in the diplomatic pouch of an ambassador stationed in Havana. The precious contraband was now in our hands!

Be careful not to overdo it when using this approach. There's an awfully thin line separating the credible from the cornball.

12. But don't be absurd.

Mail-order copywriters know that to sell, they have to tell prospects the whole story about their products: how they're made, where they come from, why they're the best on the market.

By all means, describe your product in detail. Add flourish and fancy to the package. But don't let your descriptive prose go overboard.

13. Make the package foolproof.

Avoid, whenever possible, using order forms that force prospects to calculate sales tax and handling charges. Include a self-addressed business reply card or envelope. Explain the exact terms of the offer as clearly as possible. And make sure the offer itself is simple to follow. Orders won't come through if the mail-order package is needlessly complex.

14. Call for action.

Mail-order promotions always ask for a check—or at least an order. Here are some closing lines from recent solicitation letters:

To avoid disappointment, better send in your order today, using the enclosed postage-paid envelope.

* * *

Surely it would be a shame to let this opportunity slip by. So send in the token to receive the next three issues on trial.

* * *

Why wait when you can begin enjoying the privileges of membership now?

15. Get feedback.

Test your offer. Your mailing package. Your advertisements. Your mailing lists. Keep track of which promotions bring in the most orders. And which ones flop. As with all promotions, measure the results.

Measuring the Results of Mail-Order Promotion

David Ogilvy, founder of Ogilvy and Mather, one of the world's largest advertising agencies, points out that it's fairly easy to gauge the results of mail-order advertisements.

"Either the reader clips the coupon, or he doesn't," writes Ogilvy in his book, *Confessions of an Advertising Man*. "A few days after his advertisement appears, the mail-order writer knows whether it is profitable or not."

And that's the beauty of mail order—the cost of the promotion can be weighed directly against the profit from the orders it brings in. The results aren't influenced by outside factors such as in-store displays, shelf position, service, sales meetings, and business lunches. As Ogilvy says, the mail-order ad pays for itself . . . or it doesn't.

How soon can you expect the orders to start rolling in? Well, for a mail-order ad in a daily newspaper, you'll get about 70% of your orders within the first week, and the rest within two months.

By comparison, an ad in a weekly magazine or Sunday newspaper will pull only 40% of the orders in the first week, 65% by the second, and 80% after a month has passed. Surprisingly, orders may still come in for several months after the ad has run.

With an advertisement in a monthly magazine, orders roll in even more slowly—which shouldn't come as much of a shock, since a monthly periodical is kept around longer than a daily or weekly publication. If you advertise a mail-order product in a monthly magazine, expect 10% of your orders within the first week, 22% within the second, 50% after a month has passed, 75% after two months, and the remainder within half a year.

Direct-mail letters generate 35% of their orders in the first week, 50% in two weeks, 71% in a month, and 90% in two months. The remainder will trickle in over the next four months or so.

How many orders can you expect the letter to pull? The average direct-mail letter persuades between 1% and 2% of the prospects who receive it to send in orders. Therefore, if you mail 10,000 letters, expect between 100 and 200 orders.

Like most mail-order entrepreneurs, you'll probably experiment, varying the copy and layout of your ads and letters to see what works best. The problem then becomes: How can you tell which ad or letter a given order came from? The solution: *Key the address*.

By keying the address, you're inserting a code that lets you know a prospect is writing in response to a particular promotion. For example, advertisement A for your mail-order T-shirts may ask readers to send their orders to "Tease Shirts, Inc., Dept. 101-A, Fair Lawn, NJ," while a second advertisement, ad B, directs inquiries to "Tease Shirts, Inc., Dept. 101-*B*." This way, you can see how many inquiries the A ad pulls and how many the B ad pulls. Compare the two, and select the version of the ad which yields the best results.

Chapter 11

NO FEAR OF FLYERS—AND OTHER SALES LITERATURE

Why You Need Sales Literature

A housewife walks into her local deli and says, "I'm having a party next week for fifty people—do you have a catering menu?"

A businessman calls a word-processing service with which he's unfamiliar and asks, "Do you have any literature you can send me about your company?"

A consultant visiting a major insurance company is asked for his business card, brochure, and a list of his clients.

We live in a world of documentation, of paper, of establishing "credibility." A friendly smile and the appearance of competence aren't enough. We like to feel that we are doing business with people who are established in business, in the same way we prefer a name brand over Brand X. Of course, no amount of fancy brochures, business cards, streamlined logos, well-crafted sales letters, or colorful catalogs will guarantee that a job will be done well or that a product won't stop working five minutes after it has been purchased. Still, sales literature does go a long way toward setting a professional business tone, one that adds a sense of credibility and stability to our enterprises.

It isn't surprising to find that some of the best-established businesses have the most uniform and attractive sales literature. A certain sureness of tone and style comes with practice. For example, one of the finest old inns in the United States, the Publick House in Sturbridge, Mass., has a folder in each guest room containing no less than twelve brochures

—each dealing with a service or element of the inn's features. The brochures contain the Publick House logo, and each is characterized by a similarity of tone and a warm-spirited, low-key approach.

The Publick House has been in business for 200 years. Not every business has had the opportunity to hone its image for that period of time. Yet almost every business requires some form of sales literature to help keep products and services in the customer's mind, to distinguish itself from the competition, and to answer a prospect's basic questions about who, what, and where you are. Sales literature has a variety of specific uses, among them:

"Leave-behind"

Long after the details of your eloquent sales presentation have been forgotten, a brochure, flyer, or catalog that has been "left behind" continues to keep the sales message alive in your customer's mind. Sales literature recapitulates the highlights of your business as well as the usual information about address, telephone, and business hours. If a leave-behind is well executed, it gives you a second chance at a sale, and serves as a permanent reminder whenever it is viewed.

A response to inquiries

Not every prospect comes to you with money in hand. Many people respond to ads to get more information, and that information is a necessary step toward making the sale. A person answering a telephone-directory advertisement for a local airport limousine service may have several questions on his mind before actually placing an order for a limo. Some people answer ads because they anticipate needs far into the future. For these people, a ready-made brochure or flyer saves you the time of creating an individual response to each inquiry. If you are competing with a service that does not have sales literature, you put yourself in a preferred position to make the sale when the prospect is ready to place an order. After all, your literature will be on hand. A flyer with your phone number on it saves the prospect the need to start his research all over again.

Mailer

Flexibility is the key to sales literature for the small business. After all, a brochure or flyer that is presentable as a leave-behind may also have to serve as a mailer to new prospects. That's one reason why brochures are created to be as timeless as possible. The moment you start specifying prices or other transitory details, you date the piece, and are then put into the awkward position of having to explain the price increases to everyone who has the old brochure.

Naturally, there are times when naming a price will be proper (for example, when you're selling a low-cost service or a service or product whose price is not due to change for a long time). When you create a piece of sales literature to be mailed, you do have to consider several things that did not matter with leave-behinds. You'll have to consider the weight of the mailer (if it exceeds one ounce, the postage will increase) and you'll have to consider whether it is better to send the piece as a self-mailer (designed to be sent through the mail without an envelope) or in an envelope. If the brochure is of an unusual size, then you'll need envelopes to match, and they may well have to be custom-made.

Display in a store

Almost every supermarket or other type of food store has sales literature on the counter. The literature reminds customers of various sales, and sometimes provides recipes that, conveniently, make use of items in plentiful supply in the store. Almost every enterprise can use some type of sales literature within a store. A bookstore, for example, may post the current best-seller list, thus transforming that list into a piece of sales literature. Of course, a travel agency is the essence of a business surrounded on all sides by sales literature—a permanent display of multicolored travel brochures and flyers. So many new brochures come in through the mail every day that it would take a full-time employee in every travel agency just to keep the brochures current.

Sales support

Salespeople rely on literature to give the full story of each of their products or services. No *Encyclopedia Britannica* salesperson lugs the whole encyclopedia around with him, nor is an Avon lady likely to carry every conceivable eye shade, mascara, or nail polish. Catalogs, product sheets, and brochures help educate salespeople and help them make presentations. At the end of these presentations, these sales pieces may be used as "leave-behinds."

Types of Sales Literature

Even though terms such as *flyer, brochure,* and *catalog* are probably quite familiar to you, let's take a moment to define these pieces of sales literature, and possibly even expand our concept of each.

Flyers

Flyers—also spelled "fliers"—are small handbills. They are perhaps the simplest form of sales literature, unless you consider business cards a form of sales literature. Flyers can be as primitive as a handwritten message on a piece of note paper or as elaborate as a four-color, expensively illustrated announcement. Generally, a flyer is relatively inexpensive to produce and easy to distribute. It can be a one-page menu for a Chinese restaurant, or a rack-size—about 4-by-9-inch—slip of paper with your name, logo, a few lines of copy, and, if you're not easy to find, a simple map or directions to guide readers to your place of business.

In tourist areas, rack-size flyers for every circus, zoo, theme park, restaurant, furniture store, inn, museum, and hotel proliferate. In urban areas, flyers for a variety of businesses and services cluster around places and events that attract crowds: photocopy stores, supermarkets, outdoor concerts, and street fairs.

Since flyers are usually mass-produced and mass-distributed, many will not find their way to qualified prospects. However, since flyers are relatively inexpensive (5,000 8½-

by-11-inch flyers, typeset, and offset, could cost as little as 3 cents each), there's a comfortable margin for waste.

Brochures

"Brochure" is a difficult word to define, but most dictionaries consider it a synonym for "pamphlet." Generally, a brochure is a free piece of sales literature that has more than one page. Typically, it is folded, dividing a sheet of paper into several "panels." Brochures have a look of permanence or at least semipermanence; they are usually designed and typeset. A brochure need not be fancy, but it does present a "face" to the world, and its style and tone epitomize the unchanging aspects of your business in a more comprehensive way than any flyer could.

Brochures come in all shapes and sizes. One company that specializes in reducing the width of neckties created two small brochures, one which tells readers the fine points of tying neckties, and the other a cleverly illustrated, more sales-oriented brochure titled "How to Take Care of the Ties You Treasure." Both brochures contain an abundance of information, but the second brochure discusses prices and guides the reader to the details of the service being offered.

While many of the descriptive details of a brochure could also apply to flyers, they are more often associated with brochures: captioned photographs, layout created by a designer, identification of products and prices, typeset copy, at least one "fold" that serves to separate sections of the brochure.

While flyers can be produced inexpensively, it should be clear that even a relatively simple brochure can cost hundreds of dollars to produce. A brochure requires copy that has a "timeless" quality to it, and may require graphics and design that, once created, will serve as the epitome of the very best elements of your business.

A flyer, with its "here today, gone tomorrow" feel to it, need not involve elaborate copywriting or design, but a brochure that may describe your business to prospects and customers for years to come, and that may reach prospects by mail as well as by hand, requires thoughtfulness about everything—down to how much postage it will cost to mail, and whether it should be a self-mailer.

Circulars

Circulars are intended for mass distribution, and usually detail the prices and product information of a particular retail business. A supermarket may print a circular containing that week's food prices and specials. Even though the circular may be printed as a tabloid or as a flyer it is still considered a "circular," because it is intended for wide circulation.

A photographic supply store might also find a circular beneficial, especially if it has different types of films or printing services available at different prices on a regular basis. A drugstore also may use circulars to alert customers to specials on certain cosmetics, drugs, or sundries.

Catalogs

Catalogs have always held a mystique for Americans. In their pictures, we have seen glimpses of a new, sleek way of life, a fashionable, elegant, forever-young grouping of people, places and things.

Whether it meant gathering around a crackling fire and seeing Sears Roebuck's image of next spring's garden tools and home accessories, or peering at Neiman-Marcus's status-laden offerings, catalog reading has never really gone out of vogue. Pick up almost any magazine and you'll see dozens of ads ending in the familiar words "Send for our free catalog." Of course, some of the fancier catalogs, replete with full-color photographs of watches, rugs, and jewelry, are no longer free.

Catalogs are lists of offerings, usually labeling each piece of merchandise, illustrating it, and attaching a price to it. Catalogs make the best sense for businesses that have numerous lines of products: a clothing manufacturer, a large jeweler or department store, a cosmetics manufacturer, a boutique. They are usually expensive to produce, and are justified only when you expect to distribute them to thousands of prospects who request them.

Some of the most famous catalogs are those of L. L. Bean,

Sears, Bloomingdale's, Brooks Brothers, and Neiman-Marcus.

A catalog is generally larger than a brochure. In fact, it resembles an extensive booklet. It presents your products to either the public or to business clients or both.

Bill stuffers

Bill stuffers are a type of literature included with invoices, monthly statements, and other routine correspondence. Because they enjoy a "free ride" in the same envelope carrying bills, they give companies like Consolidated Edison of New York, American Express, and a variety of telephone companies the opportunity to sell new services or merchandise. These bill stuffers sometimes simply serve to reinforce sales messages or to pass along useful information. Their size, typically, is 9 by 3 inches or 6 by 3 inches, depending upon the size of envelope you plan to use.

Other types of sales literature

There are a variety of types of sales literature. *Case histories* briefly describe product success stories; *price sheets* give the latest price information on available services or products; *product data sheets,* like press-release fact sheets, boil down the essentials of particular products. *Business cards* may be the most common type of sales literature. They sell you as well as your business.

Eleven Tips for Creating Better Brochures

Now that you're familiar with the various types of sales literature, here are some tips on making your brochures more effective:

1. Make sure the cover tells your story.

The front panel or page of your brochure is the first thing that your customer sees. That cover should communicate the basics of what you are selling. This need not be an elaborate explanation of what you are offering, but simply a statement of what you do. A barber shop has a barber's pole, a doctor may have a sign on his door identifying him as an "M.D." Similarly, a brochure or catalog or flyer should state *your* business. It can be terse (e.g., "career counseling," "publicity," or "oil paintings") but it should be there.

A catalog may also use a brief description on the cover (e.g., "Gourmet Cookware," "Books for Direct Marketers"), for without such an identification, the prospect may lose interest immediately, and never open the catalog to see what is inside.

2. Let the quality of the sales piece suit its purpose and audience.

Although sales pieces should always look neat and clean, they need not always be printed on fine paper stock or illustrated with photographs. These decisions depend on the nature of your business and of your audience.

A slick catalog may well be needed to sell fancy gift-items, but a slim, serviceable black-and-white catalog may be all that is required to sell any of a number of special-interest books. Why? Because some catalogs are selling status and glamour in addition to the product, while other catalogs replace style with practical, much-needed products: tools, equipment, utensils. That's not to say that style doesn't matter. One of the most beautiful brochures we've ever seen is the one for the newly revived Orient Express. This fully illustrated piece is handsomely produced and colorful, and it exquisitely captures the elegance and mystery of this fabled train. There would be no way to sell this luxurious trip without permitting readers to enter into a fantasy world, and fantasy is often expensive and time-consuming to create.

3. Acquaint the reader with your service or product.

One of the purposes of sales literature is to make common ground with prospects—telling them who you are and what you have to offer. A cover may communicate this information, but you may need to spend a few lines of copy describing specifically what you do. You may also wish to use your brochure to set forth a description of your company's purpose. What distinguishes your company? What are the principles upon which it has been built? Most of the rest of the brochure details, in restrained, factual language, what you can do for your customer. The brochure's style must take its lead from your business and the industry of which you are a part.

4. Don't promise what you can't deliver.

Without lying and without exaggerating, you can produce a brochure that is impressive. If you're a one-person business, you can create a brochure that gives the impression that you're a medium-size business. But don't lie. Keep your brochure defensible. Don't list clients you don't have or products you know you can't deliver.

5. Make benefits meaningful to customers.

A charming inn sells coziness, and its brochure might emphasize features such as fireplaces, sleigh rides, hospitality, and hot mulled cider. These features translate into customer benefits such as comfort, warmth, and a chance to get away from urban pressures. Put yourself in the reader's position. Does he need a car to get to town? If you're five minutes from town, let the customer know it. That way, he can develop a trip in his mind that does not require using a car. An indoor pool? That's going to appeal to those people who want to feel that they'll have some exercise to rid them of the extra calories that the hot mulled cider will add!

6. Keep a uniform look in all of your literature.

Not everyone can afford to furnish a living room or bedroom all at once: Therefore, people are often forced to settle for a more random, catch-as-catch-can decor—at least until they can afford to complete the room. With sales literature, the advantage of maintaining a similar graphic look to all literature is not just the uniformity, but the cumulative effect thereby produced. By seeing the same logo, the same typeface, the same paper stock, and even the same packaging, customers come to develop a Pavlov-like response to your product or service even before they see the name of your company. Think, for example, of the pride and uniform look that attaches itself to particular brands of ice cream, chocolate-chip cookies, and perfumes.

7. Always put informative captions on photographs.

Research indicates that photos capture our interest, so that we're likely to look at a photo in a brochure before—and even *in lieu of*—reading the copy. Since people are drawn to photos, they read captions. Therefore, make sure your captions are informative and highlight the benefits of what you are selling. In other words, don't just *identify* the photo as one of a tennis court or pool; *tell* the reader about the benefits of each facility.

8. Let the copy run as long as necessary.

While brevity is usually a plus, there are times when readers exhibit a preference for lengthy copy. You should be concise, but you should also include all of the important information. When you're selling an expensive product or service, like a condominium or car, you may have to write lengthy copy to be comprehensive and persuasive.

9. Don't rush!

Creating excellent sales literature sometimes takes hours of meticulous detail work. It involves checking and rechecking the work of copywriters, designers, and printers. It means deciding whether to use photos, which photos to use, and when reshooting a photo may be required. A good phrase, a fine photo, the right paper stock, the appropriate typeface—they may be worth the wait. So, before you start compromising on troublesome elements of the piece, ask yourself: "How can I make the piece even better?" Remember, you'll be living with the sales literature for a long, long time, so be a perfectionist about everything—from how the headlines and subheads read to the texture of the paper stock and how the color of the ink will look when it touches that paper.

10. Make your brochure worth keeping.

If your brochure tells people something they don't know or something that they feel is practical, they may want to keep it around. Try to find ways to make your brochure the kind of piece that people will want to keep. Whether your brochure gives tips on tying ties or your calendar helps people keep track of holidays, try to make the piece *valuable* to your customer. A brochure that tells people ways to tie a necktie, or of the services of a travel agent, or tips on improving the chances of winning sweepstakes, may be kept simply because it provides factual information which, in the reader's mind, might come in handy someday.

11. Tell the reader what to do next.

A brochure should not leave the reader hanging. Generally, it should lead the reader to take action. In most cases, a catalog, flyer, brochure, or sales letter will request an order. They provide everything necessary for completing the sale. A brochure might contain a coupon for the reader to use in responding, although this might not be proper form for a brochure that aims at simply describing a company or service. The final line of many sales brochures asks the reader to write, to call, to send for more information, to fill out a coupon, to enclose a check—direct action. Brochures and catalogs cannot be vague about how the sale will be consummated. Generally speaking, sales literature should spell out exactly what the reader has to do to obtain the product or service.

Chapter 12

ADVERTISING IN PRINT: NEWSPAPERS, MAGAZINES, DIRECTORIES, AND THE GREAT OUTDOORS

Newspapers: The Number-One Advertising Medium

Despite what we may read about the decline of literacy in an era of cable TV, personal computers, and home video games, newspaper advertising remains the number-one medium for promoting products and services: In 1981, American business invested an estimated $17.4 billion to run advertisements in newspapers—more than was spent on radio and TV advertising *combined*.

Newspapers have long been the backbone of retail promotion. Typically, retailers run what is called "price and where-to-buy" advertising—simple display ads that emphasize the price of a featured item of merchandise, and then direct local consumers to a nearby retail outlet to make the purchase. The effectiveness of the ad is easily measured by keeping a tally of the next few days' sales.

In addition to retailers, newspaper ads are used by restaurants, nightclubs, beauty salons, home-improvement contractors, and many other types of businesses. Small businesses prefer to advertise in newspapers because newspapers provide an intensive local coverage that's rarely available in magazines or TV. Newspapers get *read*—by almost seven out of every ten consumers in the United States. Daily newspapers allow advertisers to time ad campaigns to the specific day of a particular sale, opening, or other event. And finally, newspapers give advertisers the flexibility to quickly and inexpensively change ad layout, size, and position.

Running a Newspaper Ad

Okay. Let's assume you want to do some newspaper advertising, but don't know how to go about it. We think we can guess your questions:

How can I write an ad that will get noticed?

The first thing your ad must do is get the reader's attention. And getting attention is the job of the headline.

Because the most important goal of newspaper advertising is usually immediate sales rather than long-term brand recognition or image-building, the headlines are pithy and direct. Nothing fancy here—just a short statement of the sale. As an example, take a look at these headlines from a recent issue of the New York *Daily News:*

BE ENERGY WISE! MAKE FUEL-SAVING IMPROVE-MENTS (American Window System)

DIAMOND SALE (Lader & Weisberg Inc. Diamond Importers and Cutters)

BIG SALE! (Kaye Wholesalers)

AS SEEN ON TV/QUALITY COVERS/WHY PAY MORE FOR SLIPCOVERS!!! (Quality Covers)

WHY ARE PEOPLE FLOCKING TO OUR SAME-DAY DENTURE SERVICE? WORD OF MOUTH. (The Denture Center)

The old standbys—headlines like SALE!, SAVE, GRAND OPENING, 50% OFF, and FOR A LIMITED TIME ONLY —are used again and again for one simple reason: *They work.*

What other information should I include in the ad?

First, the basics: Your store locations. Phone number. Dates of the sale. Store hours. Credit cards accepted. Product descriptions. Prices. Etc.

Then, go beyond the nuts-and-bolts information to tell readers the *benefits* they will derive from buying the product. Again, reread Chapter 5 for a refresher course on how to write copy that sells.

Should I include a photo of the product in the ad?

Photos can make ads more appealing to the readers. But beware: the quality of photo reproductions in newspapers is notoriously poor. If the photo contains a great deal of detail, or if it must be greatly reduced in size to fit the ad, you're better off with some simple line art or no visual at all.

How many words will fit in my small display ad?

The number of words you can fit into a given space depends upon the size of the lettering; the larger the *type size* (see Chapter 6), the fewer words the ad can hold. Listed below are type sizes and the maximum number of words of each size that can fit in a 1-inch-square display ad: *

5-point type—69 words

6-point type—47 words

7-point type—38 words

8-point type—32 words

9-point type—28 words

10-point type—21 words

11-point type—17 words

12-point type—14 words

14-point type—11 words

How do I put together a newspaper ad?

The newspaper's advertising department will help you create the layout and mechanical for your ad. Some newspapers

---

* Ted Schwarz, *The Successful Promoter* (Chicago: Contemporary Books, 1976), p. 102.

will charge a small fee; more often the service is given to advertisers free of charge. Although the newspaper's advertising department may make suggestions on headlines and copy, it is not an advertising agency, and *you* are responsible for writing the ad.

As for illustrating the ad, the newspaper may be able to supply simple clip-book art. But you will have to provide any product shots or other photographs.

How is newspaper space sold to advertisers?

Newspaper space is sold in units called "column-inches." A column-inch is 1 column wide by 1 inch deep. A "3 col. × 6 in." ad is 3 columns wide by 6 inches deep—a total of 18 column-inches.

Some newspapers charge by what is known as a "line rate." For example, a "2 col. × 70 line" ad takes up 2 columns in width and is 70 lines deep. An inch is equal to 14 lines, so you can easily convert line rates to column-inches.

How do I choose which newspapers to advertise in?

You can quickly and easily evaluate which newspapers are best by using the "cost per thousand" or "CPM" formula. When you buy an ad, CPM tells you how much money it costs to reach 1,000 of the newspaper's readers.

CPM is equal to the cost of the advertising space divided by the newspaper's total circulation in thousands. Thus, the CPM of a $100 ad in a paper with a circulation of 40,000 would be

$$CPM = \frac{\text{cost of the ad}}{\text{circulation in thousands}} = \frac{\$100}{40} = \$2.50$$

That is, you spend $2.50 to have your ad seen by 1,000 people. The lower the CPM, the more cost-effective the newspaper as an advertising medium.

Any other criteria to consider besides CPM?

Sure. A CPM only compares the *cost* of reaching a news-paper's readers. But you also care what *kind* of readers you reach. For example, if you are selling a mail-order book on tax loopholes for the well-to-do, you'd be better off advertising in the *Wall Street Journal* than the *National Enquirer,* regardless of what the CPM is. Remember, a promotion must be targeted to the *right people*—not just the right *number* of people.

I'm running a small display ad. Where on the page is the best place to put it?

Right-hand pages are better than left-hand pages; top of the page is better than bottom of the page; and the outside column is better than an inside column. Thus, the best position for your ad is the upper right-hand corner of a right-hand page.

However, a choice spot like this is what's called a "preferred position," and if you want it, you'll pay a premium. Otherwise, you'll be given a "run-of-page" position, which means the ad will appear wherever there's room for it.

In addition, it helps if your ad is positioned next to some editorial matter—in other words, next to an article. Ads completely surrounded by other ads are, in advertising lingo, "buried." And buried ads are like buried treasure: hard to find and unlikely to pay off.

What about running in a special section of the paper, such as sports or the society page? Any advantage in this?

Yes—depending on the product being advertised. A book-store could benefit greatly from running its ad in the book-review section. And a marriage counselor might choose to place her ad next to "Dear Abby." Usually, requesting placement in a special section will result in the higher "preferred-position" rate. But the results are often well worth it.

Does it pay to run the ad more than once?

Not only does it pay, but it is *vital* to the ad's success. Research has shown time and time again that most readers can't be moved to action with a single ad. Readers forget ads. Repetition helps them remember.

So repeat your ad—every day, every other day, every week, every two weeks, every month. But, of course, don't repeat ads that fail. Instead find out why the ad failed, and replace it with one that will work for you.

Am I better off running a few large ads or many smaller ones?

Size helps get attention, but *repetition* is the key to success. So, schedule many repeat ads and run them as large as your budget will permit. In general, it is better to run fifty 10-inch ads than it is to run ten 50-inch ads. An exception to this is advertisements for especially newsworthy events, such as the grand opening of a store or the introduction of a new business to the community. These ads should be as large as possible— a full page if you can afford it.

What about running an ad in a pennysaver?

"Pennysavers" or "shoppers" are newspapers that are distributed free through blanket coverage of most households in a neighborhood or community. Pennysavers contain mostly advertising material and exist mainly as an advertising medium. Some are considered "junk mail"; others may be well read. It really depends on the individual publication serving your area. Many neighborhood retailers and small service businesses have gotten good results from pennysaver advertising.

Magazines: The Medium for On-Target Advertising

Magazine and newspaper ads often *look* pretty much the same. But in many other respects, the two are not at all alike.

To begin with, newspapers are read by the general public, not specific groups of people. Magazines, on the other hand, are written for specialized audiences. There are women's magazines and men's magazines. Magazines for parents and magazines for singles. Technical magazines and travel magazines. Whatever group you're selling to, you can be sure there's a magazine published just for them. Magazines deliver a loyal special-interest audience, while newspapers give advertisers a consumer-oriented readership.

Newspapers have a highly local flavor. Magazine readers are more spread out. Some magazines do have regional editions covering the East Coast, West Coast, South, and Midwest. And many metropolitan areas such as New York, Philadelphia, and Dallas are served by city magazines. But if you want to reach the people in a small town or a particular neighborhood of the city, newspapers, not magazines, are the tool to use.

Magazines generally have a longer life than newspapers. A daily newspaper may go out with the next morning's trash. But ads in monthly magazines have been known to pull inquiries *six months* after the date of publication. Magazine ads get their message across and build an audience over a prolonged period of time.

Because of the specialized readership and longevity of each issue, magazine advertising can accomplish different objectives than newspaper advertising. Newspapers, as we've said, generate next-day sales. Magazine advertising has a more far-reaching effect. It can support the sales force. Open doors. Build a company's image and reputation over the long term. Build brand recognition. Change your image. Keep your name in front of your customers—in effect, keeping them sold on you, your company, and your products.

This is not to say that magazine advertising does not generate valuable sales leads. On the contrary, small magazine display and classified ads can pull dozens of inquiries. And experience shows that at the very least, one of every three of these inquiries is a response from someone actively in the market for the type of product being advertised.

Like newspapers, magazines are a good media buy because they are read. Research shows that 89 percent of the adults in this country are avid magazine readers who read an average of eight different magazines each month. For small businesses such as restaurants, entertainments, specialty shops, and mail-order companies, magazine advertising can provide a good return on investment.

Anatomy of a Magazine Ad

Print advertising can serve two basic functions: generating inquiries, leads, and sales; and building buyer awareness and recognition. Newspaper advertising accomplishes the former; magazine ads concentrate on the latter.

While newspapers are eager to help you produce your ad, most magazines prefer to receive your ad in "camera-ready" form, meaning the layout and mechanical are prepared by the advertiser or his agency. A camera-ready mechanical can be sent directly to the printer for reproduction in the magazine.

What will it cost to produce your own ad? According to *Adweek* magazine, production costs for a full-page black-and-white ad run about $2,800 and for a full-color ad about $7,700. But more realistically, if you work with a free-lance graphic artist or print shop, you can produce an effective black-and-white magazine ad for as little as $150 or so.

Magazine ads are generally more sophisticated than newspaper ads in layout and copy. Rather than motivate a consumer to come to a store, they try to convince qualified prospects that a company and its products are superior to the competition.

Magazine ads will often omit price information altogether, and instead work to present, in an interesting and compelling fashion, information that will tell the reader how buying the product advertised can improve his or her life—what the *Harvard Business Review* calls "the shock of personal recognition."

A good magazine ad's headline reaches out to prospects the same way a catchy book title reaches out to bookbuyers. When Writer's Digest Books titled a book on free-lance writing *How You Can Make $20,000 a Year Writing (No Matter Where You Live),* the publisher knew that the title would strike a responsive chord in struggling free-lance writers—the primary market for the book. In the same way, a magazine ad with the headline "Cut Your Summer Electric Bills in Half!" immediately arouses the interest of consumers faced with skyrocketing utility bills and sweltering homes or apartments.

Unlike newspapers, magazines have a reproduction quality

that is quite high, and magazine ads can use more sophisticated photos, illustrations, and other graphics. Most magazines also offer full-color reproduction. While color ads have
a 40% higher readership than black-and-white, the cost of
producing and running them is usually beyond the budgets of
most small businesses.

Display advertising space in magazines is sold in fractions
of pages, and not by column-inch or line rates. The most
popular units are two-page spreads, one page, half page, two-
thirds page, one-third page, quarter-page, and sixth-page.
Smaller units are available. For a monthly magazine, you
have to reserve space at least one month before the publication date of the issue in which your ad will appear.

Positioning of a magazine ad is not as crucial a factor as it
is for newspapers. However, if you're running full-page ads,
the cover positions (inside front, inside back, and back) are
"preferred positions," and with good reason—they get 31%
higher readership than "run-of-book" ads. (In advertising
lingo, magazines are known as "books.")

For small businesses with bigger budgets, a full-page ad is
the best buy. The price is not necessarily prohibitive; a full-
page ad in some highly specialized trade journals can cost less
than a small fractional-page ad in a major newspaper. Surprisingly, a two-page spread is generally *not* a good investment:
Two pages cost twice as much as a single page, but deliver
only a third more impact.

Selecting the Magazine

CPM—cost per thousand—is a useful technique for buying
newspaper space, where you're evaluating several local papers that claim to reach the same audience, more or less. CPM
can be a consideration in selecting magazines, too. But it's
less important, since magazines deliver special markets, not
general consumers. So, even if *Law and Order* and *Lawn and
Garden* did, by some strange coincidence, have identical
CPMs, they would in no way be comparable or competitive
advertising media—one deals with felonies, the other with
fertilizers!

Need to know more about a magazine? Consult *Standard Rate and Data*. For each publication it provides the address of the local advertising sales office, plus all sorts of useful information including circulation, rates, mechanical requirements, closing dates (the closing date is the last day you can reserve advertising space in a given issue), discounts for frequency (each insertion becomes less expensive the more times you run the ad), and a description of the magazine's editorial thrust.

Standard Rate and Data is indexed by category, e.g., magazines for funeral directors, magazines for horse enthusiasts, magazines for hospital administrators, etc. Make a list of the publications in your area of interest. Contact each, and ask for a sample issue and a *media kit.*

The media kit is a package containing detailed information on a particular magazine's readership. By studying this information, you can learn what percentage of a magazine's total readers are potential customers for your business . . . and what percentage are what advertising people call "wasted circulation" (nonprospects). Naturally, you will want to advertise in the magazines that give you the most qualified prospects at the lowest CPM.

The Yellow Pages and Other Directories

There's a *big* difference between directory ads versus newspaper and magazine ads, and the difference is this:

People reading newspapers and magazines are reading articles for information or entertainment, and they tend to pass over the ads. (The average person reads only *four ads* in a magazine.) Therefore, to be effective, a newspaper or magazine ad must forcefully grab the reader's attention through a novel, interesting presentation—a fascinating photo, a distinctive layout, a compelling headline.

But when people turn to a directory, they are prime prospects, *ready to buy and looking for suppliers*. They do not have to be persuaded to buy: they merely have to be persuaded to buy *from you*. As a result, directory advertising is appropriate for nearly every type of small business—manufacturers, retailers, service businesses, and even wholesalers.

According to the Thomas Publishing Company, publishers of *Thomas Register,* a leading industrial-products directory, the surest way to get your directory ad to generate inquiries is to have the biggest ad on the page. The largest ad generates 40 times the response of an ordinary name-and-phone-number listing. And *any* ad is better than no ad—just printing your company name in boldface type will double the response you'd get from a regular listing.

Obviously, it's best to have your ad at the front of your section of the directory, since readers generally start with the A's and end with the Z's. Normally, you won't have much control over this. But if directory advertising is your primary source of new business, you might seriously consider choosing a company name beginning with A just to get your ad up front.

Another time-tested gambit is to list everything you sell or do in your directory ad. One New Jersey insurance agent begins his Yellow Pages ad with the direct headline "INSURANCE" and goes on to list the more than thirty different types of items he insures, reasoning that if he is the only agent to list snowmobiles in his advertisement, then anyone turning to the Yellow Pages with a snowmobile to insure will be hooked by the ad. As a result, his small (2-column-by-2½-inch) display ad generates one or two telephone inquiries on just about *every business day of the year.*

Almost every small business can benefit from an ad in the Yellow Pages. Directory advertising is another story. In some industries, a directory ad is a "must." In others, the standard directories are not often used by customers, and advertisers would be better off putting their money in trade-magazine advertising or direct mail. When you have to decide whether it is worth advertising in a given trade or professional directory, consider these four points:

1. *Completeness.* Does the directory contain enough real information to be useful to buyers? Or is it just one big advertising supplement?

2. *Ease of use.* Is the directory well organized, indexed,

and cross-referenced? Are manufacturers listed by geography, company, *and* product category?

3. *Reputation*. How long has the directory been around? Is it well respected and well used? Check to see if you find it on your customers' desks. Is it considered the leading directory in its industry? Or is it a Johnny-come-lately?

4. *Circulation*. How many people does it reach? Does this circulation include the majority of your potential customers?

Outdoor Advertising: Billboards

If you run a hotel, restaurant, gift shop, recreational facility, or other business buried in a remote area bypassed by the major highways, billboards can guide travelers to your door.

To passing motorists, your billboard remains in view for about five seconds—barely enough time to read a single sentence. Therefore, don't fill your billboard with lengthy copy. Just make sure your name and a capsule description of your business ("diner," "children's zoo," "miniature golf") are visible at a glance. And don't forget to include directions ("Take exit 17 ½-mile ahead and turn right").

Standard billboards are 14 feet high by 48 or 25 feet wide. Billboard graphics should be simple: strong, pure colors; realistic artwork or photography. Legibility is the truest test of a billboard design.

Aside from directing prospects to places off the beaten path, billboards can do little else to tell people about your products or services because of the limited number of words their messages contain. Therefore, for most small businesses in urban and suburban locations, billboards are not an effective promotion.

To find out more about billboard advertising, write to the National Outdoor Advertising Bureau, 711 Third Avenue, New York, NY 10017.

Transit Advertising

Don't look down your nose at writing ads for buses, subways, and commuter trains. If such leading literary lights as F. Scott Fitzgerald and Ogden Nash wrote transit ads, then you can, too.

Actually, for small businesses located in metropolitan areas, transit ads can ensure that your prospects see your message. "Interior" ads—those posters plastered on the insides of buses and trains—are especially effective because they have a captive audience: The ads stay in front of the passengers for as long as they're riding in the vehicle. The average transit rider spends 22 minutes inside the vehicle on each ride and takes 24 rides a month. So chances are your transit ad will be well read. Again . . . and again . . . and again.

But few riders will give up a seat on a crowded bus to walk across the aisle and read an ad on aluminum siding. Keep the copy short so the type will be large enough to be easily read from the opposite side of the vehicle.

Simplicity is also a virtue in transit advertising. As we've mentioned, readers seldom remember advertisements. And the rider can't take a transit ad with him, unlike a newspaper or magazine ad that he can clip and save. (At least not if there's a transit cop around!) Therefore, your message should be short and sweet. Include the name of your business, a brief description of what it is you're selling, and your address and phone number in large, legible lettering.

To increase inquiries, we recommend the use of "Take-ones" in your transit advertising. "Take-ones" are the reply cards you see attached to some transit ads and point-of-purchase displays. The ad copy urges the reader to send for a free brochure or other literature using one of the reply cards. On the card, which is usually postage-paid and addressed to the advertiser, the reader can fill in his name, address, phone number, and request. "Take-ones" are so-named because they often bear the headline "FREE: TAKE ONE!"—urging transit riders to do just that.

The standard interior transit ad unit is 11 inches high by 28 inches wide. But you can't rent a single ad on one vehicle: Transit advertising space is sold on a number of vehicles for a set period of time. You might, for example, pay anywhere from $4,000 to $8,000 a month for a standard unit on 2,200 buses. For the rates in your area, contact the local transit advertising company or sales organization.

Other Print Media

Consider church bulletins, newsletters, company magazines, club and association bulletins, programs, playbills, school papers, and community bulletin boards when planning your print-advertising campaign. Small publications may be diverse, limited in circulation, and difficult to evaluate, but they offer one crucial advantage to small businesses, and that's low cost. Try out some of these media options and see what they do for you. Don't be afraid to experiment; after all, the price is right.

Cooperative Advertising

Cooperative (co-op) advertising is a kind of cost-sharing promotion between a manufacturer and a retailer. Here's how it works:

The retailer agrees to advertise the manufacturer's product (a product that the retailer sells). In return, the manufacturer pays for all or part of the cost of running the ad. The manufacturer may also help the retailer create the ad, or may provide the retailer with ad "mats" or "slicks"—finished, ready-to-run ads with a space for the retailer to insert his name and store location.

Co-op programs often give the retailer free advertising. In return, the manufacturer is spared the time and trouble of executing advertising programs on the local level, since the retailer is scheduling and placing the ads.

Each year, $6 billion in co-op funds is available from manufacturers. Co-op advertising is an excellent way for small retailers to stretch their ad budgets, and you might inquire of manufacturers to see what co-op funds they will make available to you. Be sure to find out how funds are allocated, and what the method of reimbursement is.

Although co-op advertising is traditionally a manufacturer/retailer promotion, other types of businesses are now taking advantage of it. For example, several consumer and industrial trade associations are making co-op funds and promotional materials available to the manufacturing companies that compose their membership.

Chapter 13

BROADCAST ADVERTISING: RADIO AND TV

Radio

Suddenly, radio is "in" again. From tiny transistors to sophisticated Sony Walkmans to huge "boom boxes," radios are everywhere—the streets and the subways, the beach and the park, the bedroom and the bathroom. And where radio goes, advertisers follow.

All fads aside, radio has always made it easy for broadcasters and their sponsors to reach the masses. Today, 99% of all households and 95% of all automobiles have radios. More than 7,800 AM and FM stations broadcast music, news, sports, and talk shows daily to some 458 million radios across the country. People *listen* to radio—the average man or woman has his or her radio turned on about 3½ hours a day. And 88% of these listeners say they are listening to radio as much as or more than they always have.

Although radio doesn't dominate our lives the way television does, as an advertising medium it has two major advantages over the tube. One is comparatively low cost; the other is *selectivity*.

How Radio Reaches Listeners

In order to compete with television, radio stations became specialized in their programming, reaching out to certain select audiences. There are many different types of radio stations: easy listening, religious, Top 40, news, talk, sports, country and western, jazz, hard rock, "middle-of-the-road," Hispanic, black, soft rock, oldies, classical, disco. Each type of station reaches a specific segment of the market—and this is what the stations sell to their advertisers. As a result, radio advertising is extremely effective for businesses catering to specific groups: teenagers, commuters, housewives, college students.

For example, research shows that teenagers are the audience for Top 40 and disco rock-and-roll stations. But the big-band stations, featuring the music of Benny Goodman, Glenn Miller, Count Basie, and Harry James, attract a more mature crowd—60% of their listeners are between 45 and 64 years old.

A recent study by Robert E. Balon and Associates reveals that the listener's *mood* is a crucial factor in what station he or she selects. As one would expect, people in their mid 20s to early 30s prefer news, weather, and soft music when they get up to go to work in the early hours of the morning. But coming home after a hard day's labor, they like to hear mostly music—shows featuring familiar oldies, with little talk in between. Teenagers and young adults like to hear a fast-talking DJ like Don Imus or Dan Ingram early in the morning; after school or work they prefer straight rock.

Naturally, you want your radio spots to reach the right audience at the right time. Here, then, are a few helpful hints on buying radio time.

First, make sure you buy time on the right type of station. As we've mentioned, radio stations are narrowly targeted to specific audiences—primarily on the basis of age, and sometimes by race, ethnic background, and income, too. Find out which stations in your area appeal to your particular market. If you own a sporting goods store, for example, you may wish to sponsor a sports show. If your theater is pushing tickets to a highbrow play, the classical-music stations would be the place to advertise.

To find out if a local station reaches *your* market, call the station's advertising sales department and explain what you're selling and who you're selling it to. If the station's listeners don't match your target market, the sales department may recommend another station.

If, however, the station represents a potential advertising vehicle for your product, ask the station to send you a *media kit*. This package is similar to the kit you'd get from a magazine and contains the following items:

• A coverage map that indicates the geographic area the station reaches. Some powerful stations broadcast to people too far away to be potential customers for your business; other stations broadcast signals that are too weak to cover your area adequately.

• Market-research reports that show how well the station competes with other stations in the area when it comes to attracting listeners.

• Descriptions of the DJs and their shows. In some areas, certain DJs can become minor celebrities, and as a result, more people listen closely to their shows.

• A list of other businesses in the area that have advertised on the station.

• A rate card that tells you the cost of buying air time. Rates vary with the time of the broadcast (morning, afternoon, early evening, late night) because the size of the audience varies with the time of day.

Radio delivers its largest audience during "drive time"— the times when listeners are driving to work (6:00 to 10:00 A.M.) and from work (3:00 to 6:00 P.M.). Naturally, drive time is the most costly time—radio's equivalent to television's "prime time." The least expensive radio spots run from midnight to 5:00 A.M. During this "graveyard" time, few people besides insomniacs and the third shift at the factory are tuned in to their sets.

Rates vary with time, number of commercials, and type of station. Prices for a 60-second spot to air once a week range from $5 in some rural areas to $400 for drive time in a metropolitan area. Sixty-second spots are by far the most popular, but 30-second and 10-second chunks of time are also available. Radio stations will offer "bonus" spots free to advertisers who buy a number of spots at one time. In addition to spot buying, advertisers can elect to buy sponsorship of certain program segments such as the weather, sports, news, or the traffic report. As a sponsor, your name and product will be plugged by on-air personalities at certain points during the broadcast.

Thousands of small businesses have successfully promoted themselves through radio advertisements; these include auto dealers, accountants, banks, boutiques, bars, clubs, lounges, restaurants, theaters, health clubs, and hairdressers, to name a few. If you wish to join them, ask the advertising sales departments of your local radio stations for help in planning your radio advertising. They can set up a schedule and budget, help you plan advertising strategy, recommend an ad agency to produce the commercial, and even help with the writing of the commercial. Best of all, this free service comes with the price of the air time.

Depending on the nature of your business, the radio salespeople may recommend drive-time spots, late-night commercials, sponsorship of program segments, or a combination of several alternatives. Naturally, as with newspaper and magazine radio advertising, you want to reach the greatest number of *qualified* prospects at the lowest possible cost per thousand.

Eight Tips for Writing Radio Commercials

Two major advantages of radio are its short lead time and its minimal production costs. While television spots have to be performed in a studio, recorded on film or videotape, and sent to the station to be aired, a radio commercial can be written, handed to the announcer in script form, and read live on the air—all in the same day.

Some companies do hire advertising agencies to produce more elaborate radio spots using professional narrators, actors, singers, musicians, and sound effects. But for most small businesses, a well-written "live" commercial—one read by the announcer from a script—can get the word out . . . and eliminate production costs altogether. Often, the radio station's advertising sales department can help you write the script.

Chapter 5 presents many helpful hints on how to write effective advertising copy—but it deals mainly with *print* promotions. Broadcast advertising is a little different from magazines, newspapers, and direct mail. Here are eight additional copy tips specifically designed to help you write better radio commercials:

1. Make it sound the way people talk.

Radio, after all, involves talking and listening, not reading and writing. By controlling the volume, tone, and inflection of his or her voice, the radio announcer can emphasize certain points, and communicate in ways a printed page cannot. A natural, conversational style in radio helps keep listeners interested; awkward or stiff monologue sounds false and turns them off.

2. Repeat the product name and the store name.

Ever since Pavlov rang a dinner bell for his hungry dog, we've known that repetition aids the memory. To get listeners to remember your product or your store, repeat the name. We recently heard a 30-second radio spot repeat the advertiser's name *eight times!*

3. Use short words and short sentences.

Two reasons for this. First, although grammarians hate to admit it, people do *talk* this way. They use short sentences. Sentence fragments. And sentences beginning with the conjunctions *and, or,* and *but.*

Secondly, short words and sentences are easier to understand and remember. Listeners cannot grasp long, convoluted arguments and complex terms.

4. Supply the visual.

The major disadvantage of radio versus newspapers, magazines, and television is that *radio has no pictures.* It is a medium of words and sound. The listener's imagination supplies the visual based on what the ear takes in.

So, if it's important that the listener know what your product looks like, you must describe it in the copy. For example, in a radio spot advertising a line of home-baked pies that are packaged in red aluminum foil, end the commercial with a line like: "So, ask for the pie in the bright-red wrapper at your favorite supermarket or grocery store today."

5. Use sound effects.

A lifeguard's whistle, children laughing, the tinkling of the bell on an ice cream truck—these are the sounds that can add warmth, drama, and believability to radio advertising. Promoting stock-car races at the local speedway? Your commercial should include the roar of engines revving up for the big race. Selling mufflers? Let listeners compare the sound of an auto before and after the new muffler is installed.

One important note: Adding sound effects to your spot means you will have to pre-record your commercial . . . and that, in turn, adds considerably to the cost of your radio advertising.

6. Identify with the listener's situation.

In print advertising, you can use hundreds of words plus photos and diagrams to explain the benefits of your product in great detail. In radio and television, you have only 10, 30, or at the most 60 seconds of time to hook the listener's interest and explain your selling proposition. Radio and television are better for eliciting an emotional rather than a logical response from consumers. One way to make this a positive response is to create a situation that empathizes with the listener's own life, to get the listener to say, "Oh yes, that's me." The well-known radio-comedy team of Dick and Bert uses humor to accomplish this in the opening of a spot they wrote for Weil Olds auto dealers:

SHEILA: Sam, you are ready for any pushy car salesman they've got here.

SAM: But I'm still practicing my answers.

SHEILA: Okay, okay. When the car salesman first comes up you say what?

SAM: *I'm just looking!*

SHEILA: Okay, and when he comes around a second time you say what?

SAM: *I haven't made my mind up yet!*

SHEILA: And when he comes up to you a third time you say what?

SAM: *Beat it, buster, before I break your nose!*

SHEILA: Ooo, you're going to be perfect.

SAM: (laughs) Okay!

SHEILA: Ooo, this time no salesperson's gonna talk you into the first car you see. You'll see . . .*

7. Ask for the order.

Don't forget to mention your phone number or address. Most stations will also allow listeners to write to you, the advertiser, care of the station, and you can mention this, too —just in case listeners forget to jot down your number.

8. Experiment.

"Don't be afraid to experiment," says Burt Manning, vice-chairman of J. Walter Thompson, one of the world's largest advertising agencies. "Radio's lower production costs are an invitation to do that. And if you make a mistake, you'll know about it fast, and you can fix it." †

Try a variety of different approaches in your radio scripts —drama, dialogue, humor, warmth, hard sell. Run the spots that do work; rewrite the ones that don't.

• • •

In one sense, radio is the *easiest* advertising medium to succeed in. Readers will turn the page on a dull or boring ad. TV watchers use commercial breaks to run to the refrigerator. But according to a recent study on radio audience listening habits, only 4% of radio listeners change the station when

---

* © 1981 The DOCSI Corporation.
† From *Advertising Age*, Sept. 13, 1982, p. M-10.

they don't like the commercial.* So practically any commercial you write and broadcast will be heard. The trick is to get people to listen—remember—and act.

Television

These days it seems as if the president of every company, big *and* small, is starring in his own TV commercial. Lee Iacocca pitches for Chrysler; Frank Purdue, a tough man, extolls the virtue of his tender chickens; Tom Carvel articulates the benefits of giving Carvel ice cream cakes as Father's Day gifts.

Armand Schaubroek, musician and entrepreneur, achieved status as a minor celebrity in Rochester, N.Y., by starring in self-produced TV commercials for his House of Guitars music and record store. While most advertising textbooks pooh-pooh the practice, Schaubroek feels that being your own TV spokesperson can help bring in business because "it gives the customer something to look for when he comes to the store." Schaubroek's home-grown 15-second TV spots helped to transform the House of Guitars from a basement operation into Rochester's largest musical outlet, a thriving business grossing upward of $5 million a year.†

Small wonder that the House of Guitars and thousands of other small businesses put their advertising dollars in television. TV is undeniably the dominant form of mass communication in the United States today: 98 out of every 100 homes have television, and the average adult watches TV for *6½ hours every day*. Radio and print simply do not have the impact or the mass appeal of television. And that's why TV advertising appeals to record stores, auto dealers, vocational training institutes, mail-order marketers, restaurants, and other businesses trying to reach a broad audience of general consumers.

---

* The study applies to listeners of *car* radios only.

† Andrew Helfer, "A Lot of People Would Like to See Armand Schaubroek—Dead. An Interview," University of Rochester *Campus Times,* February 1, 1978, pp. 6–7.

Television advertising is expensive, and small businesses cannot compete with national advertisers and their Madison Avenue ad agencies in terms of either coverage or quality. To run a single 60-second spot on certain national prime-time programs can cost more than $10,000—a sum that exceeds the entire year's advertising budget for many small companies. And production costs for the commercial can run anywhere from $40,000 to $100,000 if you hire an agency to produce the spot.

David Ogilvy laments that television is "an infernally difficult medium to use." That's certainly true—especially when you can't afford the services of an advertising agency or professional director to guide you in the use of storyboards, answer prints, voice-over tracks, mixing, dubbing, transferring, and other technicalities. Certainly, we advise you to get professional guidance if you can afford it. But, realizing that, like Armand Schaubroek, you may have to do it yourself, we offer the following five tips on producing television commercials:

1. *Read a good book on the subject*. We recommend Hooper White's *How to Produce an Effective TV Commercial,* available from Crain Books, 740 N. Rush St., Chicago, IL 60611.

2. *Demonstrate the product*. Television is a visual medium. Take advantage of it by showing how the product works. If the product doesn't lend itself to demonstration, at least feature it prominently in the picture. Show off the product, its function and its packaging so your viewers will remember it.

3. *Make it lively*. Use action, dialogue, testimonials, and drama to make your commercial interesting to watch. Television programs provide viewers with pure entertainment, and they expect as much from the commercials.

4. *Make it memorable*. The average consumer sees thousands of commercials each month. Make yours memorable so that it sticks out from the crowd. Do not fret if viewers say they do not *like* your commercial; research shows that there is no correlation between people's *liking* commercials and their being *sold* by them.

5. *Repeat the product name and the selling proposition*. Broadcast advertisements come and go quickly—in 60 sec-

onds or less. Help consumers remember your message by repeating it at least twice.

When to Use Television

Radio, like magazines, delivers narrowly targeted audiences. Television is more like newspapers, in that it reaches a broad consumer-oriented audience.

Print can accommodate detail; television cannot. For one thing, there's not enough time in a commercial spot for a lengthy explanation of a product's features and benefits; for another, a television can't handle complex visuals such as tables of prices, long lists of retail outlets, and complicated graphs. As a result, television is good for advertising simple products and services that the average consumer can buy: hamburgers, soap, records, chickens, clothing, rugs, automobiles, soft drinks. Highly technical products and services which require a great deal of explanation generally do not lend themselves to promotion through TV commercials. And television has too broad an audience to be useful as a tool for industrial or business-to-business selling.

When you buy television time, you should understand how the television advertising salespeople price the spots. Generally, air-time price varies with audience: The more people watching, the more expensive the spot. Shows are rated according to "gross rating points" (GRP) and "shares." GRPs measure the percentage of all the television sets that a show can reach in a given market area. A share is the percentage of these sets actually in use and tuned to the program. Therefore, a show of "rating 1, share 16" reaches 1% of the homes in an area . . . but only 16% of the families living in these homes actually watch the broadcast.

Standard commercial lengths are 10, 30, and 60 seconds; many local stations also offer 15- and 20-second spots. Ask the advertising sales department of your local station for a schedule of programs including information on share, rating points, market penetration, cost per thousand, and other data to help you make a buying decision.

One way to save money in television advertising is to buy

what is known as "preemptible time." As the name implies, a commercial scheduled during a preemptible slot can indeed be preempted if another advertiser wants to pay the full rate for the spot. In exchange for giving up the certainty that your commercial will run at the appointed hour, preemptible time will be sold to you at a greatly reduced rate.

How long should a commercial run? Most experts agree that a commercial should stay on the air until it doesn't sell anymore. For some spots, this has turned out to be years . . . and sometimes *decades*.

Finally, in answer to your question "What about cable TV?" we reply, "It sounds good—but it's too early to tell for sure." Despite the thousands of articles written on the cable industry, cable stations are just beginning to provide advertisers with the hard numbers (market penetration, cost per thousand, share, rating, and so forth) they need to evaluate cable as an advertising medium. Cable is a local, fragmented medium, and one that does not easily lend itself to sweeping generalizations.

One thing we *can* say with certainty is that big business is beginning to invest in cable; during the first three months of 1982, more than $31 million was spent on cable TV advertising over four major cable systems (CNN, ESPN, USA, and WTBS). Whether this advertising is effective remains to be seen.

Nonbroadcast Commercials

Next time you're standing in front of a store with TV sets displayed in the window, observe the people who pass by. Inevitably, some will stop to watch the television for minutes on end—*even though they can't hear the sound!*

Go to the neighborhood bar when the ballgame is on the tube. Count how many of the people seated at the bar have their heads turned to the set—again, even though they can't hear the sound.

Novelist Jerzy Kosinski tells of a classroom experiment in which a teacher, lecturing to a class, set up a television monitor on the other side of the room; the monitor showed the teacher speaking. Even though there was a live teacher present, *the students watched the television image!**

If these experiments prove anything, it is that people become mesmerized in front of a TV screen. They're lulled by it, hypnotized by it, captured by it. As a businessperson, why not take advantage of the fact that a film or videotape doesn't have to be broadcast over network TV in order to grab the viewers' attention and get them to watch?

There are many nonbroadcast uses for commercials and films. One manufacturer of designer jeans produces 10-minute spots that run in department stores on movie projectors and videotape monitors. Many industrial manufacturers make films about their equipment and use the films as tools for sales, recruitment, employee communications, public relations, and trade-show displays. An automatic slide show set up in a kiosk at the local airport can make your hotel's advertising stand out from the rest. The list goes on and on, and the message is clear: Even if your film or tape is never aired over regular television channels, it can still sell effectively as an on-location promotion or audiovisual support for the sales force.

Now, about the cost. Hiring a professional director or audiovisual production company to produce nonbroadcast videotapes will cost between $400 and $600 per minute of finished footage; to produce a 10-minute show would cost $4,000 to $6,000. Film is even more expensive: about $1,000 to $1,500 per minute of finished footage.

However, these hefty fees include cameramen, lighting assistants, scriptwriting, actors, and professional editing. Suppose you just want to get the company president to sum up the annual report on a short video program. You can hire a videotaping service to hold the camera in front of him for about $50 to $75 an hour. These taping services don't *produce* shows the way AV production houses and ad agencies do;

---

* Harlan Ellison, *Strange Wine* (New York: Warner Books, 1978), pp. 24–25.

they merely rent you a camera and a technician to squeeze the trigger by the hour. (Mostly, their services are used by people who want a videotape record of a wedding, bar mitzvah, birthday party, or other special event.) For some simple presentations, this may be all you need.

• Chapter 14 •

MAYBE YOU SHOULD BE A PUBLISHER: NEWSLETTERS

What Is a Newsletter?

Newsletters are printed sheets, pamphlets, or small newspapers that contain news or information of interest to a particular group. Generally, they are mailed to a regular list of paying or nonpaying subscribers and are published on a regular basis—daily, weekly, monthly, or quarterly.

In recent years, newsletters have become a popular form of communication, primarily because they are concise, easy to read, focused, and, from a publisher's point of view, inexpensive to start and to produce.

Types of Newsletters

There are a variety of styles of newsletters, but they are usually one of three basic types:

Company newsletters exist to inform people about the activities of others in the organization. These newsletters are usually distributed free to members of the organization. A corporation, hotel, apartment house, or charitable institution may put out such a newsletter to communicate its activities to its own members as well as to have a vehicle for stating policy, reminding people of upcoming events, or noting changes in the organization's structure or functions. It may contain community announcements, regular columns, photos, and features.

An *industry newsletter* is generally sold, at a profit, to people within a particular industry. People buy the newsletter because they want to be well informed about a particular subject. Financial newsletters such as the *Kiplinger Letter* or the *Ruff Report* appeal to people who require fast-breaking information about investments. A newsletter such as *Platt's Oilgram* commands a high price because it gives readers in the petroleum industry vital information about that industry's happenings.

The third type of newsletter—and the one that most concerns us in this chapter—is the *free newsletter* that is distributed by a business as a "soft-sell" self-promotion. A retail store may decide to put out a free newsletter, distributing it either through the mail or at the store itself. In it, customers and browsers may find a blend of tips, hints, and new ideas relating to the products or services offered by the store. An art gallery's newsletter may give helpful advice on framing watercolors or choosing sculpture. But the letter is primarily a promotional vehicle for the store. By blending objective information with articles relating to items that may be purchased at the store, people are inclined to save the newsletter, read it at their leisure, and learn more about your offerings.

For example, The Party Place, a highly successful party-goods store in Stamford, Conn., puts out a newsletter (Fig. 14-1) that alerts its customers to seasonal party items and new ideas for celebrating holidays. It also offers creative ideas for planning successful parties. The blend of specific, useful information about parties and information about the latest party goods never fails to bring about a surge in business soon after the letter has been distributed.

TIMES TO CELEBRATE

Mother's Day May 9
Memorial Day May 31
Father's Day June 20
Graduations May–June

TIMES TO CELEBRATE

Showers April–September
Weddings April–October
Cookouts-Picnics-Swim
  Parties May–September

Dear Friends and Party-Lovers,

If you've seen our new Spring windows, you know pastels are high on our excitement list this season. All those luscious ice cream shades in gift wrap, tableware and stationery and not a calorie in them!

Inside, The Party Place is even more brimming than usual (and you know we can brim) with super gifts for the special days coming up ... Mother's Day, Father's Day, Graduation, Bat and Bar Mitzvahs and Confirmation.

We have desk accessories blooming with soft rose tulips on a blue background and Oriental prints by Caspari covering photo albums, pad holders and picture frames. For a handsome tailored look, there are blotters and accessories in navy or grey suede, while hearts and rainbows are hands down favorite with the younger set. Rainbows continue to star (if that's possible) on diaries, address books, scrapbooks and new memo pad and pen sets in clear boxes . . . a wonderful birthday gift or party favor.

Strawberries, not pastel, but luscious, are on paper plates, napkins and notes by Gordon Fraser, as well as the whole kitchencaboodle by C. R. Gibson: recipe books, memo pads and coupon holders. And for the male saver, how about a coupon holder with Chef Kliban Cat on it?

On the off chance you do not know we personalize stationery and napkins right on the premises, we are again offering free personalizing on any box of stationery or 50 pack of napkins you buy. This includes the fabric covered catchall boxes filled with notes or letters, Matagiri's handmade Indian paper, Mary McFadden and the full range of soft colored Crane sheets, notes and correspondence cards.

We also have a super selection of personalized stationery, social and business, printed by other good people: Crane, Ten Bamboo Studio, Consortium, Buening, Hampton, Lallie, James Aridas, to name a few. Hurry in if you want delivery in time for graduation.

April means showers, wedding, that is, and we have all the fixings . . . matching paper tableware with foldout centerpieces, parasols, garlands, favors in the new lavender and pink shades. We also rent a wishing well and shower umbrellas. You can call to reserve. Personalized toasting glasses, albums and bridal files are popular shower gifts. Allow at least two weeks for delivery on these.

Spring and Summer is wedding time for some, parties for all! Here are just a few of the newest of new things at The Party Place:

. . . A sturdy wicker buffet caddy . . . Fill it with napkins and cutlery and carry to the table or to a friend's house as a great hostess gift.

. . . Chinese food containers . . . three sizes . . . in a brightly colored floral design. Use for picnics, gifts or favors. The same petit fleur is on tissue paper, gift bags and totes.

. . . The Smurfs . . . paper napkins, plates, cups, tablecovers, balloons . . .

. . . Garfield . . . all of the above plus stickers, memo pads, shoelaces . . .

. . . Asparagus and tomatoes to burn . . . candles for your summer tables and garden torches to light your guests' way . . .

. . . Pam Marker's Museum Collection . . . unbelievable reproductions on dinner, dessert plates and three size napkins. English rose . . . a new solid color in plates, cups, napkins joins the family of 15 other solid colors we carry.

Postage being what it is, we'll have to temper our enthusiasm and let you make your own discoveries. But one more thing. If you see a store floating through the air some Saturday, it will be The Party Place aloft with helium-filled balloons: silver, gold or rainbow hearts, stars, Smurfs and Smurfettes, etc. etc. We do so many balloon bouquets sometimes we get an inflated picture of ourselves.

Fig. 14-1   This informal newsletter is circulated by The Party Place, a party-goods store in Stamford, Conn. It's a chatty blend of product information, party ideas, and tips on successful party planning.

Newsletters carry with them the aura of objectivity, and they are helpful to small businesses that welcome the role of industry spokesman. Newsletters are ideal ways of saying ''Hello, again!'' to prospects who are not as yet ready to make a purchase. They also identify you as an expert in your field, or at least someone willing to take the time and trouble to communicate ideas as well as sales literature throughout the marketplace.

How to Decide If a Newsletter Is Right for You

For most businesses, a newsletter is simply too unwieldy, inappropriate, or sophisticated to be worthwhile. Imagine a garage, barbershop, delicatessen, or drugstore putting out a newsletter. Even if the newsletter is free, who will want to read it? A bar owner who puts up a sign saying, "HAPPY HOUR—5–7 P.M." is communicating with his customer better than any newsletter ever could.

However, a fancy gift shop, like the party-supplies store, might help spur business with a newsletter. An art gallery certainly could profit from communicating with its customers via newsletter, especially if the newsletter is targeted to those people who have signed a "guest book" at a previous art exhibition at the gallery.

Your business may be right for a newsletter if you have an identifiable audience in need of specific information, and if you have the time, inclination, and resources to provide that information on a regular basis.

How to Publish a Newsletter

1. Identify your audience.

Some businesses know just where to find their customers —by looking at the addresses on sales slips, by going to mailing lists, or by inventive methods such as guest books. If you can identify the people with whom you'd like to communicate, make a record of their names and addresses. You can either type each name on a "master" sheet (and then reproduce the names on pressure-sensitive mailing labels) or, if you have a word processor, simply store the names, thus automating the process for repeat mailings.

2. Decide on a format.

Most newsletter formats are simple. All that's needed is a clear layout, a title and date, and headlines to introduce the stories. There is no set form. The simplest newsletters are typewritten and offset; they are often no more than two sides of a single 8½-by-11-inch piece of paper.

The newsletter's "look" should match its intended audience. Typewritten newsletters are fine when the information presented is vital. But sometimes, image may be as important as the information itself. If your business is concerned with image, it may pay to make your newsletter graphically distinctive, and to spend money reproducing the information on fine paper. In any case, let a designer lay out your first issue and help you to choose typefaces and paper stock.

3. Keep your purpose in mind.

Ask yourself, "What is the compelling reason to read my newsletter?" List the benefits of your newsletter, translating those benefits into practical actions that will be *vital* to your readers' lives. If you deal in coins, stamps, antiques, or fine art, a newsletter may provide a handy way of staying in touch with infrequent customers. By telling them of trends, sales, and news events, you are reinforcing your image as an expert in the field and putting your name in front of them on a regular basis.

4. Are there additional prospects for your newsletter?

If your newsletter deals with gourmet food, maybe it would be of interest to cooking schools and the food industry as well as to the gourmet who visits your store. A store that sells decorative paperweights may be surprised to find that coin buyers, antique buyers, and Americana enthusiasts would also like to read about paperweights.

5. What makes your newsletter special?

If your newsletter is competing with others, it must have a distinctive angle. Ideally, a newsletter offers inside information, news that would be hard to find elsewhere. Perhaps your method of distribution is unique. Or the frequency with which you publish. Or perhaps it's your method of offering discounts.

How to Write a Newsletter That Will Be Read

Newsletters help people answer problems and meet their needs. Most of our needs are basic—to live, to be healthy, to be loved, to be secure, to be well informed, and to be ahead of the crowd. The following case history tells briefly about an entrepreneur who met the specific needs of a special group of people by appealing to their profit motive.

A Long Island lawyer wanted to start a newsletter that would bring in income and also stimulate new business for his law practice. He came up with an idea based on a need that was going unfulfilled.

He saw opportunities for profit in mortgage-foreclosure purchases. The problem, he reasoned, was that the average person had difficulty uncovering these sales. Foreclosure sales are rarely well publicized; legal notices are printed in obscure local newspapers. And most notices don't provide basic information needed for making a purchasing decision, such as the types of properties involved or the amount of default on each property.

The lawyer met this challenge by publishing a newsletter which gave weekly notices of foreclosure sales of real estate located in the New York City metropolitan area. His newsletter was pitched to real estate brokers as "the only authoritative source of useful foreclosure information available." It would provide a way for people to screen hundreds of properties without ever leaving their offices.

He sent out a solicitation letter in which he described his newsletter as giving the "basic information an investor requires before further investigating a property." He sent it to real estate dealers in the area.

His newsletter met a need: the growing market for moderately priced "distressed" conventional properties. He used the "testimonial" technique when his letter noted that "all the popular how-to-get-rich-through-real-estate books advise purchase of property at foreclosure sales.'' He was offering people an opportunity to acquire property at bargain prices, property which might later be sold at a significant profit.

The foreclosure newsletter is an example of a well-thought-out, highly specific idea that can be marketed to a defined readership. In this case, the newsletter functions as a stimulus to the lawyer's business as well as a money-making proposition on its own. The rationale for this newsletter shows the type of specific thinking and targeting that all successful newsletter ideas require.

Tie-ins with the Newsletter

One of the ways in which a newsletter can support itself or bring in additional revenue is through the promotion of products and services that tie in with the newsletter's main thrust. A dating service that circulates a newsletter about where singles meet may wish to advertise for mail-order sale a new book about being single. (Or the newsletter can sell advertising space to advertisers promoting related products or services.) Since the book will be of interest to the same people who wish to read about singles spots, it makes a natural tie-in, complementing the newsletter as well as other promotions (e.g., singles weekends, dances, etc.) which may also appear in the newsletter.

Almost every business that lends itself to a newsletter has a variety of other products or services that could easily be tied in to the newsletter. The most common tie-in promotions are those involving books, clothing, vacations, novelties, records, and insurance.

A stamp dealer who circulates a newsletter may sell a wide range of tie-ins, including stamp catalogs, stamp albums, stamp books, magnifying glasses, and, of course, the stamps themselves.

How Newsletters Fail

Failure to be timely, failure to be accurate, failure to find an audience, failure to be objective, and failure to be news—

these are a few critical problems that doom newsletters. Even if the newsletter has a pleasing package (format, graphics, paper stock), as well as timely, informative copy, a built-in audience, a reasonable price, and good promotion, there are no guarantees that it will succeed.

To succeed, you need to have a realistic idea of exactly how many people will want to read the newsletter and of how many of these people are potential customers for your business. For more information about making a go of newsletters, contact the *Newsletter on Newsletters,* 44 West Market Street, Rhinebeck, NY 12572.

Case History: An Art Gallery Newsletter

A small New York City art gallery specializing in Oriental art decided to promote itself by putting out a two-page newsletter. The gallery owner did not want to be committed to publishing the newsletter on a regular basis, so each issue was undated.

The newsletter was printed in a lavender ink on a beige paper stock. The name of the newsletter was handsomely lettered and designed. The newsletter made no pretense at objectivity, since each issue was signed by the gallery owner, a person who spent part of the newsletter describing art treasures he had accumulated while touring the Orient. Included in the newsletter were several photographs clearly illustrating several unusual pieces.

The articles were a mixture of information and "invitation": information about Oriental art, correct ways of framing art, etc., and a subtle invitation to visit the gallery to view new arrivals.

The newsletter continues to be distributed free to interior designers and other regular customers.

The newsletter (Fig. 14-2) is easy to produce, informative, and yet keyed totally to the particular art gallery that publishes it. People enjoy reading it because it is well-written, colorful, and brief. It provides the gallery owner with a handy reason to contact interior designers—who are the gallery's prime market—and yet does not commit the publisher to a

Buddha sits on a stepped, waisted throne in contrast to the Thai and Indian Buddha who sits on a single or a double lotus throne.

Towards the end of the 18th century a more naturalistic style of Buddha, the Mandalay developed. The eyes of the Mandalay Buddha have a Mongoloid slant and the large mouth is set in a Mona Lisa smile. The fingers and toes are occasionally of unequal length. Instead of thin clothing, the Buddha's robes are set in thick folds, suggestive of Chinese drapery. Whether of metal, stone, lacquer or wood, the predominant style of Burmese Buddha figure is the Mandalay Style.

Constant in the tradition of Buddha sculpture is the sense of serenity which eminates from the sculpture. This sense of all-pervading calm may explain the attraction of the Buddha sculpture for homes throughout the world.

Rare Finds

Ancient Holy Book

We found a beautiful, rare Holy Book in Burma. The books' two wooden covers enclose 16 pages of palm leaf decorated with lac and gold. The Burmese calligraphy is black lac on a cinnabar-colored ground. This is in striking contrast with the very fine gold work decorations. Each page is 6 inches by 24 inches. Properly framed, this 18th century rarity would be a highly decorative piece for the focal point of a room. The total book would make a smashing large piece on the wall.

Antique Screens

We were fortunate to acquire an extraordinary pair of antique Japanese screens. Painted in sumi, go-fun, colors and gold leaf on paper, these beautiful screens illustrate scenes from the Tales of Genji. They are composed of six panels each 67½ inches by 24 inches, for a pair of screens that is 12 feet wide. These museum quality screens can grace the finest home.

Exhibiting Art

Mounting Sculpture

Just as good framing compliments and protects a painting, good mounting enhances and protects a piece of sculpture. The design considerations of framing and mounting are similiar: Where will the piece be displayed? What is its size? What is its color and texture? The answers to these questions help determine the base on which the sculpture is mounted.

Sculpture - whether six feet or six inches - is usually mounted on a base or plinth. Whether the plinth is wood, stone, metal, or acrylic, the choice is governed by the size, material and color of the object. Often, the sculpture is not attached directly to the plinth but is wired in place. The sculpture with its plinth may now be placed on a table or on its own pedestal to bring the object to a convenient and safe viewing position.

A playful piece may be suspended in the air for an effective display. In one technique, an acrylic rod would be attached to the artwork - perhaps a puppet - and anchored to an appropriate base. The result, a floating sculpture.

Objects in relief are sometimes most effectively displayed when hung on a wall. They make a firmer statement when they are appropriately mounted. A mask could be mounted on a complimentary backing of linen, wood, mirror or other suitable material. The whole could then be hung on the wall. If more protection were needed for a

Thai Musician

fragile or valuable piece, or if design considerations required it, the object with its backing could then be placed in a clear box and hung.

Pre-Columbian terra cottas, contemporary American sculpture, African masks, etc. all benefit from appropriate mounting. Ed Waldman's framing department would be glad to advise or assist you with your mounting and framing needs.

Recent Arrivals

From Northern Thailand

We just received a six-piece teak orchestra from Northern Thailand. The musicians are seated and 20 inches high. They are hand carved and painted and decorated with gold leaf. In the same shipment is an orchestra of six standing musicians, 36 inches high. These 12 pieces represent a full year's work for one of Thailand's most talented artists, whom we discovered on our annual buying trip to Southeast Asia. Used singly or as a group, these musicians can make a dramatic statement in any room.

Around Town

The *Japan Society* features "Treasures of Asian Art from the Idemitsu Collection" from Jan. 28 through March 14. This exhibit includes Japanese and Asian paintings, pottery, bronzes, calligraphy and lacquer ware from one of Japan's great private collections.

The *American Museum of Natural History* just published a glorious book featuring treasures from the museum's vast collections of Asian Art. "Asia: Traditions and Treasures" by Walter A. Fairservis, Jr. presents the delicate ivories of Japan, the translucent jades of China, the wrought brasses of India, the terrifying demons of Tibet and much, much more!

Fig. 14-2 This graphically sophisticated newsletter mirrors the artistic taste of its creator, an art gallery owner. It blends tips on displaying art with a roundup of personal notes about the gallery's recent acquisitions.

regular publishing schedule, high printing and production costs, or the need to keep increasing circulation. The newsletter accomplishes its purpose: to remind customers of the continued interest in serving their needs.

Chapter 15

ON WITH THE SHOW: TRADE SHOWS AND EXPOSITIONS

Trade Shows: A $7 Billion Industry

Every year, industry spends more than $7 billion to exhibit its wares at trade shows and expositions throughout the country. There are more than 9,000 shows each year, so you can be sure there's a show specializing in whatever it is you do; there are shows for everything from chemicals to construction, from farm equipment to pharmaceuticals, from textiles to telecommunications.

At first glance, it seems as if exhibiting at trade shows is too expensive for a small company. And there's some truth to that—at least where the major national shows are concerned. For example, when you consider the cost of travel, lodging, shipping, space, and materials, a manufacturer in Wichita could easily spend $10,000 on a 10-foot booth at the Computer Sales Exposition in New York City. Obviously, continent-hopping is beyond the budgets of most small businesses. (And it makes little sense for a Kansas-based firm to exhibit in New York, unless the company is large enough to distribute nationwide.)

But there are alternatives. Regional shows. "Table-top" shows. County fairs. State fairs. Public shows. Chamber of commerce exhibitions. And thousands of other small, local shows that make sense for small business.

The questions are: Where do you find out about these shows? And how do you pick the ones that are right for you?

Selecting Trade Shows

Choosing the right trade show is like selecting advertising media or publicity outlets. You pick the places that let you reach the most prospects at the lowest possible cost.

Begin with a comprehensive listing of local and national shows. One such listing is *Exhibit Schedule,* published by *Successful Meetings* magazine, 1422 Chestnut Street, Philadelphia, PA 19102. Another is *Trade Show Convention Guide,* available from Budd Publications, Box 7, New York, NY 10004. Trade journals and business publications will include monthly listings of shows and conferences in your particular industry. And your local convention and exhibit bureau can give you the latest information on fairs and expos in your city or town.

From these listings, you'll glean perhaps a dozen or so shows—shows you might exhibit in because they're local, or because they are applicable to your type of business.

Write to the management of each of these shows, and ask for a prospectus or other literature. You'll want to know how many people are expected to attend the show, how many have attended past shows, where these people come from, what industries they represent, what job titles they hold. In short, are they the type of people that want, need, and can afford to buy your products?

Are your competitors exhibiting? That's one sure sign that the show may be worth attending.

Is the show a new one, or is it well established? Select shows that have proved their worth. Too many fly-by-night expos spring up one year and are gone the next. And the companies that invest in them are usually thousands of dollars poorer for their efforts.

What to Show at a Show

Assuming you do sign up for one or more of these shows, what will you display there? And why?

The most compelling reason for your company to participate in a trade show is to introduce a new product to the marketplace. According to studies by the Trade Show Bureau, 50% of the people attending any given show are there to see new products and services. So if you've invented the better mousetrap, motor, or metal detector, a trade show may be the place to show it off. But if you're selling the same old thing, avoid trade shows and try some other promotion, such as a trade ad or direct-mail campaign.

The best way to get people to notice your new product? Demonstrate it. To your prospects, seeing new products in action is the main reason for going to shows. Live action is the one thing that separates a show from print promotions.

At the show, attendees can see your product. Touch it. Feel it. Smell it. Compare it with the competitor—whose booth may be right next to your own.

Prospects can't discuss product features with an advertisement; printed pages don't speak when they're spoken to. But at the show, buyers see whether your orange-juice machine really *can* squeeze 5 gallons an hour. Or whether it filters out the pulp. And if they want to know what kind of price break they can get if they buy juicers in bulk, they can get a straight answer from a real live salesperson—right then and there.

Unfortunately, straightforward demonstrations can produce more yawns than inquiries, since most products and equipment are—let's face it—just plain boring. (Ever hear of someone flying 300 miles to see a sump pump in action?)

If your product is nuts-and-bolts, make the demonstration a little less mundane by adding a touch of flair to the display. For example, a defense contractor was exhibiting helicopters at an Air Force show. In the middle of the display area was the hull of a chopper that had been struck point-blank by an enemy missile. Its windshield was cracked, its armor plating buckled by the impact . . . but that was all. The helicopter had survived the attack. And so, a huge sign taped to the windshield told us, did its two pilots. A most impressive display, combining drama with convincing product demonstration.

You don't have to be selling weapons to set up an interesting, unusual product demonstration that will bring the crowds swarming to your booth. One small manufacturer of scuba equipment built a huge Plexiglas "fishtank" for his booth. The tank was about 8 feet high and 6 feet wide, and inside it swam a bikini-clad beauty who stayed underwater all day, aided by—you guessed it—the exhibitor's marvelous scuba gear. Cost of the tank? About $800—less than a third the cost of placing a full-page ad in a trade journal. The results? A booth jam-packed with prospects; a demonstration that was the hit of the show.

Want to get people to take a look at your orange-juice squeezer? Offer a glass of fresh-squeezed OJ to everybody who stops by to take a peek. Are passersby passing by your display of home video games? Get them to stop and take notice by challenging them to beat the highest score on Pac-Man or Space Invaders—and by giving free game cartridges to the top ten players. Selling a minicomputer that works like magic? Have a professional magician on hand to demonstrate its features in a magical way.

As with any promotion, the first step in successful trade shows is getting the prospect's attention. Product demonstrations, giveaways, contests, and entertainment are four attention-grabbers that will pull people from the aisle into your booth. And that's where the selling starts.

Successful Trade-Show Selling

Retailers may take orders at the show, but the bulk of trade-show exhibitors—manufacturers—don't. Instead, they use shows to introduce new products or new applications of old products. They use shows to make contacts. Build prospect lists. Be seen by decision-makers. Talk to customers. And distribute sales literature.

Trade shows are an unusual hybrid of advertising and personal selling. Advertising, because you pay for a space (in the case of a show, it's an actual space on the floor). And personal selling, because once the display attracts the prospect to the booth, the salesperson has to do the rest.

So . . . although this is a book on promotion, not salesmanship, we're going to take a brief look at personal selling as it applies to the trade show.

To begin with, picture this scene: The prospect, attracted by the flashing lights, bells, whistles, and sirens of your product demonstration, walks toward the booth. You say, "May I help you?" The prospect's reply? A hastily muttered "No thank you" followed by a quick exit away from your booth.

"May I help you?"—the standard department-store lead-in—is the worst way to introduce yourself. If the prospect isn't intimately familiar with what you're selling—and chances are, he's not*—he'll feel threatened by this challenge. It will scare him off.

Instead, draw the prospect into conversation by asking a friendly, nonthreatening question about business. A general question. If you're selling globe valves to petroleum engineers, don't say, "Are you thinking of buying our model X-100 valve?" Ask: "Do you specify valves in your work?" A "no" answer means you're not talking with a qualified prospect; a "yes" tells you to keep the conversation going. Then find out the prospect's problem. And show him how your product can solve it. Get chummy—glance at the prospect's badge or ID tag so you can address him by name. Be personal. Friendly. And helpful. But not pushy.

A cardinal rule of trade-show selling: Stay on your feet. People will not disturb you if you're resting your rear in a chair—in other words, you can't sell if you're seated. So stand. If you need a rest, have someone take your place while you walk around the exhibit hall or stop at the snack bar. But no napping in the booth, please.

Another cardinal rule of trade-show selling: Don't gab with friends and fellow employees when you're manning the booth. Strangers will not interrupt a conversation between friends; instead, they will pass you by and stop at a display where the sales help isn't so occupied. Need to chat with the boss or your assistant for a few minutes? Find a nice quiet corner *outside* of the display area.

---

* According to the Trade Show Bureau, four out of five show attendees will not have known of your company or product prior to visiting your booth.

A question we get asked frequently is: "Should we hand out our brochure to everyone who asks for it?" Well, there are pros and cons to this practice. The *pro* of having literature on hand is that you can quickly satisfy a prospect's hunger for more information. And the brochure serves as a permanent reminder of his visit to your booth. On the *con* side, sales literature is costly to produce, and handing out a fancy four-color brochure to thousands of people, regardless of whether they're serious sales prospects, can be an expensive proposition.

The alternative—not having literature at the show—also has its pros and cons. Without a large supply of brochures, you will have to take down the names and addresses of the people who request information in order to mail the literature at a later date. (Many shows issue each attendee a plastic show card much like a credit card. When the attendee hands you the card, you use a special imprinter, also supplied by show management, to instantly record the sales lead on pre-printed forms.) This technique can work to your advantage, allowing you to build a list of prospects who have expressed interest in your product. A negative is that you've now got to mail thousands of brochures, where before, literature was there for the taking. Also, this system delays getting the brochure into the buyer's hands—and that could hurt sales if the buyers are in a hurry.

Here's our solution: Keep a small sampling of your literature on a table or in a display rack in open view for everyone to see. If a prospect wants a brochure, take down the information and mail it later—*if,* in your judgment, the prospect means business. If you think the person's just collecting brochures, then you can note this on the lead form or his business card, and mail the literature or not, as you choose. Behind the display or under the table, you'll have a surplus supply of several hundred brochures on hand. These are to be distributed to hot prospects who are really serious about your product and want to get down to business right away. With a little practice, you'll be able to tell the buyers from the brochure collectors without a second glance.

Finally, a few more tips to improve your trade show selling:

1. Develop a schedule for manning the booth.

Even Supersalesperson will get tired, cranky, and bored after eight hours of standing in a 10-by-10-foot display filled with file cabinets or fishing poles. Let your salespeople man the booth in two-hour or four-hour rotation shifts, so prospects are always greeted by a salesperson who's relatively fresh and lively.

Naturally, the busier the traffic (flow of people through your booth), the more booth personnel you'll need. Plan the booth duty roster accordingly.

Experience teaches us that shows are busy during the middle days, and slower during their start and finish. As an example of this, take a look at the attendance figures for the 1981 Exposition of Chemical Industries:

day one—4,341 attendees
day two—5,417 attendees
day three—6,016 attendees
day four—2,850 attendees

2. Reduce prices on products sold at the show.

The opportunity to pick up merchandise at reduced cost gives prospects a reward for having taken the time and trouble to visit your display.

3. Use preshow promotion to build booth traffic.

Use advertising, publicity, and direct mail to get prospects to come to the show. For a nominal cost, show management will provide artwork, stickers, mail stuffers, and invitations you can use in your own promotions; this material can easily and inexpensively be imprinted with your company logo and the number of your booth. Include an imprinted show invitation with invoices, literature mailings, personal letters, and other day-to-day correspondence. And don't forget to mention the show in your ads.

Trade Shows vs. Expos: Some Definitions

We've been using the terms *trade show, exposition,* and *fair* interchangeably in this discussion. But they're really not the same thing, and we need to clarify our terms before we go any further.

By strict definition, a *trade show* is limited in attendance to those who meet certain qualifications by virtue of their occupation or industry. Some major national trade shows include the Farm Progress Show, the National Restaurant Show, the Association of Operating Room Nurses Congress, and the National Computer Conference.

An *exposition,* on the other hand, is open to the general public. Anyone can go, provided he is willing to pay the price of admission (usually less than $10). The two types of expositions are outdoor state and county *fairs,* which focus on agriculture, and *public shows,* which include garden shows, automobile shows, boat shows, and other hobby-related shows.

At trade shows, the audience is more select. If you sell products to highly specific markets—engineers, doctors, chemical plants, restaurant owners—concentrate your exhibit efforts on trade shows. However, for small businesses whose prospects are bound by geography and not by profession or industry, the best bet is local expos.

Producing the Display

If you look around at any show, you'll see that most exhibitors have some kind of display in their booths. This display can be as simple as a few photo blowups hung on a curtain, or as complex as a custom-made exhibit constructed out of 26d, plastic, or metal and equipped with overhead signs, rear-projection screens, illuminated photo displays, animated graphics, movable walls, Plexiglas™ product-display cases, and removable graphic panels.

Cost increases with complexity, and anything more involved than the simplest portable display is far beyond what

90% of small businesses can afford. But simple does *not* necessarily mean cheap or ineffective, and a practical working display can be had for under $2,000.

To begin with, you need to purchase a basic exhibit system —the self-standing structure that will contain the product photos, copy, and other graphics of your display. You will probably want a *portable display*—that is, a display that can fold up into an oversized suitcase or other container and be carried by *one person*. If you can't carry it, you'll have to ship it, and with freight, drayage, labor, storage, and insurance costs what they are today, shipping will eat up your budget in no time flat. So avoid it. Get a display you can lug around in the back of your station wagon or company van. If you exhibit in out-of-state shows, be sure the display can be carried on a plane as ordinary luggage.

Purchase a portable display that is easy to carry, easy to pack, and can be set up and dismantled quickly and with a minimum of time and trouble. See a demonstration before you buy. If a trained salesperson can't set up his company's display in the showroom, you can bet that *you'll* have trouble, too.

Avoid displays made of wood; they're heavy and easily damaged. Prefer lighter, more durable displays made of extruded plastic or a lightweight metal, such as aluminum.

When it comes to trade-show graphics, we have just three rules: Keep it simple, keep it big, keep it bold. Grab people's attention with bright colorful photo blowups and bold color graphics. Incorporate your company name and logo into the graphics—and make the logo *big*. Headlines should be short, pithy, and large enough to read from the aisle without eyestrain.

Don't cram your graphic panels with every available piece of technical information about your product. The type will be too small to read, and the customer won't spend enough time in your booth to get through it all. (According to Trade Show Bureau research, the average trade-show attendee spends only *3 minutes* at any given booth.) Besides, the purpose of a trade-show display is to attract customers to the booth, not do the whole selling job. If people want more detailed information, hand them a brochure.

Consult a professional trade-show-exhibit designer if you can, and see what materials and techniques are available. For example, product samples and graphic panels can be easily mounted on the display structure using Velcro, a kind of fabric tape that allows you to "hook" solid objects together. Transparent Plexiglas™ panels can be used to cover and protect pictures and graphics that could otherwise be damaged in handling. Carpet and cloth are frequently used on graphic panels to give displays a warm "homey" look and feel. Go to some trade shows. Take a look at what works. And what doesn't.

For additional information on the design of trade-show displays, write Exhibit Designers and Producers Association, 521 Fifth Avenue, New York, NY 10017.

A Checklist for Exhibit Managers

Much of handling trade-show exhibits can only be learned by doing. It's a trial-and-error business, and one where mistakes are inevitable.

There are *so* many little niggling details that must be attended to when you're in charge of your company's trade-show display. Did we order the right color carpet? Are there enough ashtrays? *Any* ashtrays? How can we fit our 12-foot-high display in an exhibit hall with a 10-foot-high ceiling? Can show management provide us with the right kind of electricity to run our imported electric motor—which is designed for Japanese outlets?

Are there enough brochures in stock to cover us for the show, or must we print more? Who's going to come in to man the booth on Saturday? Do we have up-to-date releases and photos for the press? Can we get our computer through the door of the exhibit hall? The list goes on. And on.

Slip-ups, goofs, lost shipments, and other problems are standard fare for even the most seasoned trade-show pros; there are just more tasks involved than any one person can keep an eye on all the time. To help you get through this ordeal, we've compiled a checklist of things to do that should help you plan effectively and cut down on errors. Trade shows do require much advanced planning, and you should look over this checklist at least three months before the opening of the show.

Here, then, are the things to do before you go to the show:

• Visit the show hall, if possible. Check out the display area for space limitations, plumbing and electrical supplies, and overall appearance.

• Set a budget for the show. Include exhibit construction, shipping, drayage, storage, plumbing, carpenters, electrical, labor, furniture and carpet rental, printing, models, product demonstration, travel, food, lodging, and the cost of the space.

• Look over the show regulations carefully. Don't base your display around a demonstration of your firecrackers only to find out on opening day that loud noises are forbidden in the exhibit hall.

• If you can't carry it with you, work out the details of shipping and storage for your display, literature, and products.

• Build shipping crates for exhibit material. Be sure the crates are marked so they can be identified at a glance. Crates are often misplaced at shows, and painting your crates with odd colors or distinctive markings can help make finding them easier.

• Order any special services you'll need for the booth—electricity, running water, drainage, compressed air, lighting, or signs. Also order carpets, furniture, and any labor you may need.

• Check your inventory of sales literature and product samples. Do you have enough, or will more have to be ordered?

• Work out a booth duty roster. Obtain badges or entrance passes for booth personnel, other employees, and your customers.

• Plan publicity, direct mail, and advertising to support the trade-show effort.

• Order premiums you'll be giving away at the show.

• Order invitations, stickers, logos, and other promotional material from show management.

• Make hotel and travel reservations.

Fig. 15-1   A 20-foot trade-show display unit for Argon Medical Corp. (exhibit designed and built by Contempo Design Inc., Northbrook, Ill.).

• Construct your display. If you already have a display, take it out of the case and inspect it. Are the graphics up-to-date and reflective of what you're selling at this particular show? Also check for damage and make any necessary repairs.

• Hire models, magicians, demonstrators, and any outside talent you need.

• Set up a system to handle inquiries and literature distribution at the booth.

• Check all details with show management and outside vendors, including freight handlers, printers, van lines, and hotels.

A MISCELLANY OF PROMOTIONS

This is our "odds-and-ends" chapter—a miscellany of promotions that don't fit in under any of the broad topics we've discussed in previous chapters. Chapter 16 will cover four topics in brief: sales promotions, business gifts, store displays, and personal selling.

Sales Promotion

As the name implies, sales promotions are programs used for promoting the sale of a product. Most often, these promotions are devised by the manufacturers of nationwide brand-name products and carried out in conjunction with local retailers. Sometimes, however, small retailers and service businesses create and execute their own sales promotions without the help of larger companies. In 1981, American marketers spent more than $58 billion on sales promotion. A few of the basic types of sales promotion are outlined below:

Cents-off packs

Cents-off packs consist of several of the same product bundled in a package with a label announcing a price-off discount for the quantity purchase. Cents-off packs are often used with soap and other health-and-beauty products.

Sampling

A sampling is an offering of a trial-size version of a product for the purpose of introducing it to the marketplace. Small samples can either be delivered free to the home or sold at a nominal cost in the stores. New powder and liquid detergents, toothpastes, and a variety of health-and-beauty products are often launched this way.

Coupons

There are two kinds of coupons. *Manufacturer's coupons* are distributed by the manufacturers of various consumer products. Consumers receive discounts on these products by redeeming the coupons at the retailer's cash register. Coupons are used in print advertisements, newspaper inserts, circulars, and other promotions. More than 100 billion manufacturer's coupons are distributed each year for a wide variety of products including cigarettes, coffee, pet food, cereal, fruit juice, bathroom tissues, and many others.

Retailers receive two benefits from manufacturer's coupons: an increase in sales of the product because of distribution of the coupon, and a small handling fee paid by the manufacturer to the retailer for each coupon redeemed.

Handling coupons takes a great deal of paperwork, and many small retailers find that the handling fee doesn't justify the time and trouble. These retailers often elect the second kind of coupon, where the *retailer creates his own cents-off coupons,* to be distributed through local advertising or circulars. A coupon can generate sales for any business in which price is a key consideration to buyers, and drugstores, groceries, supermarkets, opticians, and restaurants have all used their own coupon promotions with success.

Refunds

Refund deals require that the buyer mail in some sort of proof-of-purchase (usually a seal on the package or a receipt from the store) in order to receive a refund by mail from the manufacturer. Refunds generally carry a higher dollar value than coupons. Recently, the auto makers began offering $100 (and even $1,000) refunds on the purchase of new cars. (Detroit calls this kind of refund a "rebate.") The typical slogan for a refund deal goes something like "Buy three, get one free!"

Contests and sweepstakes

These generate excitement and sales by offering consumers a chance to win prizes. By definition, sweepstakes are games of luck (raffles, drawings, lotteries, etc.) and contests are games of skill. Because they require no special effort or intelligence to enter, sweepstakes are by far the more popular of the two.

Although the most publicized events are those sponsored by major manufacturers, sweepstakes and contests can work on a local level, too; a drawing for a color TV or stereo never fails to draw people to the stores. Sometimes the drawing can even tie in with the product being sold. For example, a tobacconist recently ran a small sweepstakes offering a year's free supply of tobacco to the winner—a prize that surely interested pipesmokers in the promotion and drew them to the store to fill in entry blanks.

Tie-in promotions

In a tie-in promotion, two or more products share an ad and a promotional hook such as a coupon or refund. Tie-ins work well when there is some logical relationship between the two products—hot dogs and mustard, milk and chocolate syrup, shoes and socks.

Point-of-purchase displays

These colorful cardboard constructions serve to hold and display a product while extolling its virtues with headlines, illustrations, graphics, and some short copy. A point-of-purchase (P-O-P) bookstore display for the horror novels of Stephen King bears a sign welcoming readers to "Stephen King *Terror*-Tory." The classic P-O-P display is the egg-shaped rack for L'eggs pantyhose and stockings.

While many national manufacturers supply retailers with ready-made P-O-P displays, stores may also choose to create their own display materials. This allows them to carry the theme of their own advertising and sales literature through to the point of sale, and adds continuity to the look of the store. The famous David's Cookies of New York has built its reputation on what are reputed to the world's best chocolate-chip cookies, and to sustain this image, David's logo appears everywhere at the point of sale: store windows, in-store signs, boxes, bags, and cookie tins.

Premiums

Premiums are gifts that serve as an incentive for buying a product. Classic examples of premiums include the prizes in Cracker Jacks, the toys that come in boxes of children's breakfast cereals, and the free sets of glasses gas stations used to give you when you filled up your tank.

Remember the barber who gave you a comic book after every haircut? Or the pediatrician who handed you a lollipop after a particularly painful mumps or measles shot? In a sense, these rewards were premiums—kind gifts that dried your tears and warmed your mom's heart to future visits to that barber or doctor. Other premiums are more blatant sales pitches—ball-point pens with the phone number of your insurance agent or accountant imprinted on them, or free bottle openers or corkscrews used as giveaways by the local supermarket or liquor store.

Ideally, the best premiums have some tie-in with the business's product or service. An example of this is when the New York Mets have "Bat Day" or "Cap Day" and give away a free baseball bat or Mets cap to every youngster who buys a ticket to the game that day.

• • •

In all cases, the best sales promotions are those that get their point across to consumers quickly and simply; shoppers do not have the time to digest complex promotional schemes.

Promotions should not be used alone, but should tie in with advertising, publicity, direct mail, and other sales efforts.

There are legal restrictions governing sweepstakes, contests, and similar promotions. You might check with a lawyer to make sure your plans comply with the law, which usually varies greatly from state to state. Or you can query the Promotion Marketing Association of America, 420 Lexington Avenue, New York, NY 10017, (212) 867-3990.

To learn more about sales promotion, we suggest you read *Sales Promotion Essentials* by Don E. Schultz and William A. Robinson (Crain Books, 740 N. Rush Street, Chicago, IL 60611).

Business Gifts

Giving business gifts is one of the best ways to get your customers and prospects to like you; after all, everyone enjoys getting presents.

Companies give gifts for a variety of reasons that all make good sense. Business gifts help develop new business. Build goodwill. Say "thank you" to loyal customers. And motivate employees. A recent survey showed that the majority of business people feel that giving gifts does indeed accomplish all of these goals.

Although half of all business gifts are Christmas gifts, a present is really appropriate at any time of the year. Some companies time their gift-giving to coincide with a customer's birthday, an employee's anniversary with the company, or some other special occasion. Other businesspeople think that gifts are more appreciated when they're least expected—sort of like Candid Camera.

In general, though, gift-givers agree that business customers should receive gifts they can use at the office, while gifts to consumers should have some application in the home. In this way, the gift remains in front of buyers when they are thinking of making a purchase.

There's a saying that goes, "It's the thought that counts," and this is surely the case as far as business gifts are concerned. Customers are more impressed with the fact that you remembered them than with the cost or size of your gift.

Still, different business situations call for different types of gifts. A 25-cent plastic keychain might be perfect for a locksmith's customers, but not for a $100,000-a-year corporate bigwig who might have been counting on a set of new golf clubs or trip to Bermuda.

Gift-giving requires a special kind of creativity that only mothers and lovers seem to possess. And so, to help the rest of you choose a gift that will please both your customers and your budget, we've compiled some suggestions on suitable business gifts. The lists below divide the various gift ideas by price category to make your shopping easier. You can buy these items from retailers, wholesale outlets, or specialty advertising distributors.

A SAMPLER OF BUSINESS GIFTS

50¢–$1	$1–$5	$5–$20
letter opener	Business card	Set of drinking
balloon	holder	glasses
Yo-Yo™	Pen light	Tote bag
Frisbee™	Coffee mug	T-shirt
coaster	Ashtray	Lucite paperweight
corkscrew	Playing card	Board game
desk calendar	Tape measure	Cigarette lighter
sewing kit	Plastic raincoat	Garment bag
poster	Thermometer	Beach towel
	Pocket atlas	Necktie
	Mini-tool set	Windbreaker
	Wallet	Umbrella
	Luggage tag	Wall plaque
	Money clip	Desk diary
	Golf cap	Portfolio
	Pocket knife	Golf balls

$20–$100	Over $100
Pocket calculator	Cruise
Trophy	Furniture
Sportswear	Jewelry
Desk clock	Stereo equipment
Sculpture	Television
Fishing rod and reel	Camera
Desk accessory	Telescope
Golf clubs	
Blazer	
Gourmet food	

Depending on the customer and the type of gift, you may wish to have the item imprinted with your name, logo, phone number, and address. On a fun gift like Frisbees or T-shirts, the logo can be big and bold; on more personal presents—jewelry, a wallet, other luxury items—the imprint should be as small and unobtrusive as possible.

In-Store Displays

How the products look in the window and on the shelves is crucial to a retailer's success. Here are a few tips to help you create displays that sell more effectively.

Window displays

- Design the display around the space you have. Don't make it too crowded—or too empty.
- Keep it simple. Merchandise should be readily visible from afar.
- Display only what you have in stock. Exception: If you have remainders you want to get rid of, put them in the window, advertise them as remainders, and offer a big price break.
- Design the window display around a theme—music, sports, spy novels, Christmas scenes.
- Consider animated or even live demonstrations. One California bookstore specializing in fantasy literature had the well-known writer Harlan Ellison sit in the store window while he wrote some new short stories. Any customer purchasing $10 worth of books would get an autographed copy of one of the stories. This kind of creative window display always gets attention.

On the shelves

- Make sure the product name can be clearly seen by shoppers strolling down the aisle.
- Keep shelves at eye level, whenever possible. Studies have shown that raising a product from knee level to eye level will double its sales.

- Crowd the shelves. Research shows that three boxes of Brand X detergent placed end to end on a shelf will sell 50 percent more detergent than only two boxes.

Personal Selling

Chapter 15 touched lightly on personal selling as it applies to trade shows. As we mentioned then, this is a book on print and broadcast promotion, not salesmanship, and so a lengthy discussion of how to be a great salesperson is beyond its scope.

Still, we wanted to say *something* about how a flair for promotion can help the salesperson succeed at his or her task. And so we'd like to relate the following tale from George Lois's column in *Adweek* magazine:

> The most thrilling story of the marriage of expertise and style involved the art dealer Lord Duveen. Finally receiving an audience with J. P. Morgan, the most important collector of the day, the dandyish Duveen, with his cutaway, spats, top hat, cane and all, sashayed into the presence of Morgan in his luxurious mansion on Fifth Avenue. Without a civil greeting, Morgan pointed to three large vases on his marble floor and told Duveen that one was a 16th-century Ming masterpiece, and the other two exact copies that had cost him a fortune to have made.
>
> He asked Duveen to study the vases and tell him which were the copies and which was the invaluable original.
>
> Lord Duveen strutted up to the three vases, hardly glanced at them, raised his pearl-handled cane and, with two violent strokes, smashed two of them to smithereens.
>
> From that moment, every painting and art object that Morgan collected until the day he died he bought from the great English salesman.*

• • •

---

* George Lois, "Down Lois Lane: The Ethic of Mediocrity," *Adweek*, September 14, 1981, p. 25.

Chapter 17

HOW TO MEASURE THE RESULTS OF YOUR PROMOTIONS

The Purpose of Promotion: Sales

Although it may be fine for an IBM or a GE to use part of its promotional efforts to build its image, small businesses need to get immediate sales. While big business has the luxury of creating a campaign that will pay off over the long term, you need to concentrate on the promotion's cost-effectiveness in the short term.

Your promotions, if all goes well, will result in tangible *sales*—you will transact business with some of the people who heard about your products or services via your promotions. Of course, not everyone who learns about your business or inquires about your business is ready to do business with you. A person may *inquire* about a product or service, and that inquiry may, on occasion, result in business. Sometimes a person inquires about a product or service only to discover that it was not what he had in mind. Perhaps it's too expensive. Any such response to a promotion may be termed an *inquiry*. However, a *sales lead* is someone who has inquired about your product or service and who seems to be in the market for it. Not every inquiry is a true lead.

In the case of a national doughnut chain that offers six doughnuts for $1, and makes the offer good for ten days ("just bring the coupon to the location nearest you"), every inquiry (person holding a coupon) will probably result in the sale of at least $1 worth of donuts.

In the same way, a restaurant offering a $6.95 lobster special on Friday nights may receive some inquiries ("Does that price include the salad bar?'') as well as a number of customers. If the restaurant advertised four different specials on four different days of the week, one could easily determine which special tempted the most bargain-hunting diners.

A store advertising a one-day sale on video equipment may be able to measure the response to its advertising by determining the number of people who show up on the sale day and contrasting it with the number that show up at the store during a regular business day. A comparison of sales figures for both days will also help the manager determine whether his promotion yielded increased sales or just increased browsers.

What Kind of Results to Expect

A good response to your promotions is what you want. But just what does "good" mean? For some products (like a Rembrandt painting) one solid inquiry is all that is needed. For other businesses, a promotion must attract thousands of inquiries or else it must be deemed a failure.

A classified ad that costs $10 aims at making back the cost of the ad in addition to the cost of creating or selling the product or service being advertised. If you were selling your time, for example, at $100 an hour, you would start making a profit with your first sale. If, however, you were selling a product for $2, and it cost you $1 to manufacture, you'd have to sell ten just to make back the cost of the ad.

When you see the back page of a local newspaper filled with images of cowboys smoking a popular cigarette, you are looking at an ad that might be almost impossible to monitor, and one that may not be translatable into immediate sales.

Your expectations must be tempered by many things: potential readership of the magazine (or number of direct-mail pieces sent), competition, timing, the positioning of your ad or article. At best, only a few out of each hundred people exposed to the promotion will read it and react to it. There are just too many things fighting for attention each day.

Let's first consider your expectations toward advertising. When you advertise in a weekly magazine, you get approximately half of your inquiries by the end of the first week, more than three-quarters by the end of the second week, and, generally speaking, nearly all of the inquiries by the end of five weeks.

As for advertising in a monthly magazine, you can expect about half your inquiries after the first month, three-quarters at the end of two months, and just about all of the inquiries within three months following the ad's appearance.

Direct-mail results are measured in terms of leads and generated sales. The cost of the mailing package can be expressed in terms of cost per lead. If you spend $100 on your mailing and it has yielded only one lead, that lead has cost you $100. If you made one sale, the promotion cost you $100 for that sale. If you are selling a product or service priced at $1,000, you've done well with your one sale. Results that pay off lead one to ponder even more ambitious direct-mail or advertising programs. The promotions that fail to earn back what they cost suggest a variety of reasons for their failure. It is only by examining all the elements of the promotion that you may discover what went wrong.

As for direct mail, the average response to it—even to pieces designed by professionals—is about 1.4%. This need not signify success or failure. That can only be determined by knowing how much your product costs, how much your direct-mail program cost, and how many sales were made.

Naturally, there are times when expectations are tied to goals of building goodwill—to image building or public relations—rather than immediate sales. When a store or boutique uses its advertising space to ask readers to send for a gift, it is building a mailing list for future promotions. As in life, identifying realistic goals and expectations is the key to judging your promotion's success.

How to Monitor Your Promotions

After a while, it becomes impossible to keep track of inquiries without writing them down. By keeping a response notebook or file, you can begin to systematize the responses and discern more about your prospects. A sample file might contain a clip of the promotion (ad, direct-mail package, press release, flyer), the name and date of the publication that ran it (or the date you mailed it), and the names (and addresses and phone numbers) of everyone who responded. You should also keep close track of expenses incurred in creating the brochure, the number of responses, and the number of sales.

By deducting your expenses from your total sales, you can determine whether your promotion paid for itself—at least in the short term. There is a residual benefit of name recognition, goodwill, and possible future sales that is hard to calculate precisely.

There are a number of time-tested techniques that help you measure the response to a promotion, and help you keep accurate records. They include the use of coupons, reply cards, keyed addresses or telephone numbers, order forms, keying ads to a specific request, and reader response cards.

Coupons are best exemplified by local shopping circulars. By offering discounts on certain items when they are purchased using a coupon, a store can measure response to a particular promotion.

Reply cards help direct-mail readers take action because they do not require a stamp, and because they are pre-addressed.

Keyed addresses or phone numbers are another way of saying "coding." In effect, by pointing readers to an address, telephone, or box number, you can easily discern how many people responded to a particular promotion or item. Whenever a TV ad asks you to send your check to a "Department" or a special box number, the advertiser is simply trying to determine how many people responded. If the TV spot runs two hours later (with a different "Department" key) and the response is increased, the advertiser has learned something about when is the best time to show his commercials.

Whenever an ice cream parlor offers a free sundae with "a copy of this ad," they are making it easy to determine the response to a particular advertisement. This gimmick works with a variety of businesses that offer premiums to the first people to show up at a sale or opening.

Order forms are standard sales slips that are found in catalogs as well as in many ads and flyers, and *reader response cards* are used by publications to indicate to advertisers exactly what the response has been to a particular ad or press release announcing a new product.

The following case history details how one small-business woman—a handbag manufacturer—monitored her promotion and knew that it worked.

Case Study: The Handbag Promotion

A small wholesaler involved in the manufacturing of handbags realized that she needed promotional literature to give to prospects who would visit her booth at an upcoming fashion trade show. She also found herself talking with the trade press occasionally, and she recognized that a ready-made press kit would help her communicate thoroughly and effectively and would be a great time-saver.

She hired a small public relations firm to help her create the press kit. The PR company presented her with an estimate of the costs involved in creating one hundred press kits for distribution to the trade press as well as to important prospects.

The elements of the kit were the press release, a "fact sheet" containing a list of prestige accounts, and a sheet containing product descriptions and prices. These pieces of literature were to be accompanied by black-and-white or color photos of several of her handbags. (The color photos were reserved for magazines that run color.)

Costs were broken down as follows:

Fee for writing and supervising project	$750
Photographer (½ day, including film and processing)	300
Printing	50
100 8 × 10 black-and-white prints	75
100 8 × 10 color prints	175
Clerical	90
Postage	40
50 2-pocket folders, 50 envelopes and supplies	$25
	Total: $1505

The press release was sent to fashion editors in each city where the handbag manufacturer had a distributor or sales office. It also went to fashion trade magazines and style editors, as well as to important general-interest magazines throughout the United States. At last count, two of the people receiving the release via mail had called for additional information. One magazine ran the release verbatim and even used one of the photos. It is impossible to calculate precisely the benefits that this article had, but it kept the telephone ringing steadily for two days! The handbag maker ordered reprints of the article and kept them at her booth when the trade show opened. Thus, she had fifty press kits (those reserved for the trade show) to give out to the media, as well as article reprints to hand out to prospects and browsers.

Between the customer interest in her reprints and the inquiries generated from the article based on the press release, and the goodwill derived from the professionally produced press kit, the handbag manufacturer's promotion paid for itself several times over. She generated about thirty sales leads, and immediate sales totaling almost $2,800. The manufacturer, though not especially diligent about tracking her response, knows that the promotion was a short-term success. She knows that the promotion may be even more valuable in the long run, as prospects become ongoing customers for her handbags.

Follow-up

You've sent your release, placed your ad, mailed your brochure. Leads are starting to flow in. What now? If you've prepared for the leads, you'll have established a mechanism for following them up. Once your prospect has replied he expects fast action.

If your objective was direct sales, make sure that whoever fills orders knows about your promotion, and that sufficient inventories are on hand to handle the maximum number of returns you expect.

If your main objective was to get leads for your salespeople, be sure there is a system for forwarding the leads to them.

All leads should be logged in so that information like cost per lead can be calculated. Also, you need to be in touch with your sales force to determine how many of the leads convert into sales.

There may be times when you follow up on a promotion by making telephone calls. By following up on a press release or an inquiry resulting from advertisements or direct mail, you can learn firsthand how your promotion was perceived. It also gives you an opportunity to use salesmanship to turn a no into a maybe and a maybe into a yes.

Your success at follow-up depends in large part upon the people you are calling. Are they "cold prospects," people who have expressed little interest in your product but who, for example, went so far as to ask to see a catalog? Or are they "hot leads," people who understand precisely what you are selling and seem to be ready to buy right now?

Your purpose for following up may differ from promotion to promotion. Following up leads resulting from direct mail may lead directly to business. Following up on a response to a press release will tell you how an editor viewed your story, and will teach you lessons about promoting yourself in the future. Following up on responses to an ad enhances your knowledge of the market and of your particular type of customer. Anything you can find out about who answered your ad and why will be valuable to you in every future promotion.

Naturally, time won't allow you to chat with everyone who expresses some interest in your product or service. It is not necessary to get on the telephone to quiz someone about why he or she was moved to send for your catalog. However, you may wish to follow up on a small *percentage* of the inquiries you generate. In this way, while you are attempting to make the sale (or sell an idea to an editor), you'll be giving yourself an opportunity to learn which elements of your promotion seemed to make the biggest impression on those who were exposed to it.

When you follow up by phone on inquiries from letters, ads, press releases, brochures, or flyers, here are a few things to keep in mind.

1. Follow up soon.

Don't think that your ad, letter, brochure, or press release will be remembered weeks after it arrives. Answer inquiries as quickly as possible. People who have received a mailing or who have made an initial response to an ad or flyer are *leads;* they expect you to follow up.

2. Determine if the answer to the inquiry was received.

Sometimes people don't respond to your follow-up because the material you've sent to them has gotten lost in the mail. Therefore, before launching into a sales pitch, first ask your prospect whether he's received what you've sent him.

3. Then ask the caller if he's had an opportunity to look at the material.

Don't make the assumption that just because you've responded quickly to a prospect's inquiry, your prospect will be in a hurry to respond to your sales solicitations. Some people take a while to get to their mail. So before jumping to the conclusion that a letter received is a letter read, ask if the person has had an opportunity to look at the material. It gives your prospect an easy out if he has shelved it. It also gives you an opportunity to say that you'll call again in a week or so.

4. Aim the conversation.

As a salesperson, you must guide the conversation toward a goal, and that goal is to move the prospect, at whatever speed, toward a sale. Your launching pad for the call is the prospect's initial interest. From there, you must find out whether this interest is sincere, and whether the prospect is in a position to act on his interests.

How to Test a Promotion Before You Use It

We test promotions in much the same way we test anything in life: by taking a consensus among a sampling of friends and strangers. We are in the habit of checking our actions and thoughts with others every day: "How did you like *E.T.?*" "How does my résumé look?" "Does this tie go with my blue blazer?" We do this because it is less costly to ask a question than to suffer the consequences inherent in presenting a sloppy résumé or a poorly planned outfit.

Even with the finest clothes, the sharpest résumé, or the best attitude, we may not achieve some of our goals, but at least we can help put the odds in our favor, and test out our ideas with a minimum of expense or embarrassment.

There is no need to complete an entire promotional project before judging its worthiness. An idea can be tested modestly before committing a great deal of time and money to it. One promotional idea that was ill conceived had to do with a letter sent to journalists telling them of a new perfume.

A perfume manufacturer in Northern California sent a promotional letter along with a photograph of the perfume to members of the American Society of Journalists and Authors (ASJA), reasoning that, as writers, some of them might wish to include the name of the perfume in an upcoming article.

This is fuzzy thinking. The members of the American Society of Journalists and Authors are diverse in their interests. There is a directory put out by the ASJA listing its members by their areas of specialization.

The perfume manufacturer might have been more successful if he had mailed his promotional package just to ASJA members who specialize in beauty, cosmetics, and fashion.

However, if the perfume manufacturer had spoken with a few members of the ASJA before sending his package, he would have discovered that:

1. The chances that a writer is currently working on an article about new perfumes is remote. Furthermore, it's unlikely that a writer would keep his press kit on file. Writers are always swimming in paper.

2. The package failed to offer any interesting angles to the story, leaving it to the writer to develop an angle to a story about a perfume he was only slightly familiar with.

3. The package did not indicate any particular care in its presentation. The letter is presented in its entirety below:

Dear Mr. Smith:

Please consider our perfume and cologne for mention in your next issue. The perfume has been market-tested from Northern California to New York (last at the Fashion Trade Show, May-June) with great success.

We hope you feel our product is worthy of favorable mention.

Although the letter was sent to professional journalists and authors, the person writing the letter seemed to assume that they were editors as well, hence the remark about "your next issue."

The person responsible for creating and distributing the release might have gotten more from his promotion if he had taken the time and trouble to call *ten writers* on his mailing list and try to feel out how they would respond to the material. In that way, he'd discover whether they were in a position to actually use the material or would just read it and throw it away. By sending the material to writers, the perfume manufacturer miscalculated. Even the most prolific magazine-article writers can use only a small fraction of the releases they receive. Few releases contain ideas worthy of stimulating a writer to generate an article. On the other hand, editors deal with hundreds of ideas. Beauty editors could easily file the release for use when an appropriate piece on perfumes was about to be written.

Testing Promotions: A Checklist

Testing any promotion requires great patience. Every time you ask for an opinion, you must be ready to adopt new ideas. That not only takes time and money, but a good solid ego. However, a first-rate promotion can declare a dividend each time you use it, so don't give up.

Here are a few questions to ask yourself:

1. How can you test a few people before many?

Simple. Do some market research. Survey a few of the people you're hoping to reach and ask them their reactions to your offering. Find out whether the people you are aiming to reach are the right people, the people who can make a purchasing decision.

If you're testing an ad, try it on your friends and family before placing it. Get feedback about the ad's general effectiveness. How about its typeface? Type size? Graphic look? Does it motivate you to take action?

Before you spend money on a big ad, try a little one. Before you go national or regional, test the ad in a local paper or magazine. Keep costs down. If the ad pulls, you can always be more adventurous.

2. How can you make sure that the elements of your package are compelling?

Creative people are always wavering between pride in their work and a healthy doubt that they've done the very best possible. It's very difficult to see your promotions with fresh eyes, but you must try to maintain a point of view characteristic of your customer. Try suddenly picking up what you've written and seeing if it catches your attention. Ask yourself if you've helped your customer visualize how he can make use of your service.

It's important to ask people you respect to review your ads or promotions. Also, it's valuable to have people who are completely outside your industry review it. Sometimes these people can see things that pros might miss. The first-blush reaction is a truer reaction than studied reaction: After all, your prospects will judge your promotion in a matter of seconds.

3. Can you change elements in a mailing or ad to see if that influences response?

Of course. It's wise to keep testing. Perhaps different copy, a larger typeface, a bigger ad, or a new graphic would increase response significantly. By experimenting with intrinsic elements such as copy, design, typeface, paper stock, and type size, you keep trying to find the perfect combination of elements to catch your prospect's attention.

4. What about extrinsic factors such as changing media, sending material to a new audience, or switching mailing lists?

All of these are reasonable options, especially if you feel that your promotion is not succeeding. You should examine the mailing list and think hard about the people on it: Are they the right audience? Are they geographically right? Are other demographics right for your business? The same thinking should go into a decision to switch media: Perhaps radio would have more impact than magazines, or a local newspaper might be better for you than a trade magazine.

Building a Prospect List

Whether your promotion consists of a press release, advertisement, flyer, or direct mail, you can take the inquiries which have been generated to build a prospect list.

The names of interested people are valuable because they provide a "data base" for future promotions. They help you get to know your audience and cater to it.

Names of prospects are so valuable that business people spend thousands of dollars trying to determine which groups of consumers will yield the greatest number of prospects for their products. There is one publisher in New York City who is in the habit of taking full-page ads in the *New York Times* in which he offers a lifetime subscription to his business magazine for less than $5.

The ad pulls thousands of replies. How can he make a profit? Simple. He takes the names and addresses of those who inquire about his publication and sells those names to people who want a mailing list of people who have responded to newspaper ads. In a sense, the publisher's profit comes from building and selling mailing lists of prospects.

The reasoning is clear. By taking the time and trouble to clip a coupon and send a check, the people who respond to the publisher's ad have "qualified" themselves. That is, they've set themselves apart from the rest of the *Times'* readers by showing the initiative to respond. People like this may well be open to responding to other newspaper solicitations.

In business, you will forever be uncovering prospects only to find that they either do business with you or may do business with you in the future. There will be many others that, after shopping around, may reject your product or service in favor of someone else's.

So, in order to keep neat, accurate records of your prospects, you should rely on some type of record-keeping system that allows you the flexibility for constant updating of your files. Any filing system that allows names to be quickly and neatly added or purged will allow you to keep current on prospects that are active or inactive.

Here are a few common systems for recording prospects and tracking them:

• *Rolodex.*™ This compact revolving card file has a capacity of more than 1,000 cards. The cards may be filed alphabetically or in any arrangement that is most convenient. It allows quick access and the ability to instantly purge the file of prospects that have become inactive, or those with whom you have followed up.

• *Pressure-sensitive labels.* If you rely on frequent direct mail, you may wish to keep lists of prospect names and addresses on pressure-sensitive labels. Once you have a typed master list of prospects, you can keep adding to it and deleting names. Meanwhile, you have the ability to photocopy your master list directly onto pressure-sensitive labels. The labels are then easily transferred to envelopes or self-mailers. Label masters save you the time of retyping mailing lists each time you wish to do a mailing.

• *Index cards.* When you wish to store additional data about each prospect, index cards afford you extra space on which to make notations. Available in a variety of sizes, index cards may be stored in inexpensive metal or plastic containers, and can be arranged in any pattern you wish: geographical, alphabetical, chronological, or by product.

• *Word processor.* A word processor can electronically store your prospect list and allow you to instantly update it. Once the information has been fed into the word processor, you can easily review your files, make changes, and, with a simple command, have the word processor type out letters or envelopes to each of your prospects. Word processors are rather expensive ($2,000–$3,000) but they can save a great deal of time for business people who have large mailing lists and who do repeated mailings.

• *Scriptomatic™ machine.* The Scriptomatic machine provides an addressing system that allows for great convenience. Scriptomatic cards prepared on an office typewriter become the basis of a filing system that allows you to keep a permanent record of a prospect while creating an addressed envelope. Changes and corrections are easy to make—just throw away the old card and slip in the new. Scriptomatic addressing machines address directly on your envelopes or other mailing materials without the need to attach labels. The key advantage of the Scriptomatic cards over label matrices is that Scriptomatic cards have room for additional information—a record of product purchases, a telephone number, and personal information. For more information about Scriptomatic machines, write Scriptomatic, Inc., 1 Scriptomatic Plaza, Philadelphia, PA 19131.

Classifying Prospects

One way to arrange prospects' names is according to their ability to become customers. We believe that the following classification describes the various "species" of prospects:

• *Hot prospect (hot sales lead).* This person responds to your promotion because he is shopping around and ready to buy. He will choose you or some other source.

• *Lukewarm lead.* This person is considering buying but may not be ready. He may seriously be seeking information now, and may buy in the future.

• *Qualified prospect.* He can afford to buy but he may not have even responded to your promotion. These are people you want to sell to but haven't as yet.

• *Brochure collector.* This person is not a qualified prospect but has responded to your promotion because he likes to receive free brochures, gifts, samples, etc. A real time-waster (includes competitors and just plain curious folk).

You can help qualify your prospects by asking questions: "Do you feel you may have an immediate need for my product?'' "Does the purchasing decision for my product or service have to be cleared with other people?'' "How are you currently filling this need?'' These questions and others like them will help you ferret out the few hot leads in a world of many non-prospects, shoppers, time-wasters, and competitors. And, after all, those hot leads are the people we've tried to help you reach during the past seventeen chapters.

Now it's up to you.

• • •

It is only by keeping accurate records of what works and what doesn't work that we progress as promoters. Just as the scientist learns from experiments that fail, we learn what to do right only by understanding what we have done wrong. There isn't much room in business for making the same costly advertising or public relations mistakes again and again. By facing the results of your promotional endeavors, you are forced to grow, to try new things. It is just this type of growth that adds vitality to new promotions. The challenge is clear: Keep expanding your horizons while holding on to those elements of your business promotions that have proved to be winners in the past.

• Appendix •

WHERE TO FIND MORE INFORMATION ON MANAGING, FINANCING, AND PROMOTING SMALL BUSINESS

Books

How to Promote Your Own Business deals with only one facet of running a small business—promotion. Small-business managers also need to know about such things as taxes, law, finance, human resources, management, marketing, and business start-up. The books listed below can provide you with much of the basics in these areas.

The Complete Legal Guide for Your Small Business, Paul Adams; John Wiley & Sons, 1982.

Running Your Own Show: Mastering the Basics of Small Business, Richard T. Curtin; John Wiley & Sons, 1982.

How to Start and Manage Your Own Business, Gardiner G. Greene; Mentor, 1975.

How to Finance Your Small Business with Government Money: SBA and Other Loans, Richard Stephen Hayes and John Cotton Howell; John Wiley & Sons, 1982.

Taxation for Small Business, Marc J. Lane; John Wiley & Sons, 1982.

Small Business Survival Guide, Joseph R. Mancuso; Spectrum, 1980.

People Management for Small Business, William Laird Siegel; John Wiley & Sons, 1978.

Insider's Guide to Small Business Resources, David E. Gumpert and Jeffrey A. Timmons; Doubleday, 1982.

Periodicals

There are three major magazines published specifically for small-business managers and entrepreneurs. These are:

Inc., 38 Commercial Wharf, Boston, MA 02110
Entrepreneur, 2311 Pontius, Los Angeles, CA 90064.
Venture, 35 West 45th St., New York, NY 10036.

Other publications of interest to small business include:
Business Ideas Newsletter, % Dan Newman Co., 930 Clifton Avenue, Clifton, NJ 07011.
New Ventures, 2430 Pennsylvania Avenue, Suite 106, Washington, DC 20037.

To keep up with the world of advertising and public relations, you can read any of the magazines listed below:
Advertising Age, 740 N. Rush St., Chicago, IL 60611.
Adweek, 820 Second Avenue, New York, NY 10017.
Media Decisions, 342 Madison Avenue, New York, NY 10017.
PR Journal, 845 Third Avenue, New York, NY 10022.

Finally, like all businesspeople, big and small, you'll want to keep up with the business world at large by reading *Forbes, Fortune, Business Week,* and, of course, *The Wall Street Journal.*

Reference Books

Here are some basic reference books that can help you in your business. Most are available at your local library.

Encyclopedia of Associations, Gale Research. Annual. Three volumes. Lists professional, trade, and other associations.
Bacon's Publicity Checker, Bacon's Publishing Company. Annual. Two volumes. Lists thousands of newspapers and magazines.

National Directory of Newsletters/Reporting Services, Gale
   Research. Four volumes.
Tax Guide for Small Business, Department of the Treasury,
   Internal Revenue Service. Publication No. 334.
O'Dwyer's Directory of Public Relations Firms, J.R. O'Dwyer
   Co. Lists 1,200 PR firms.
Standard Directory of Advertising Agencies, National Regis-
   ter Publishing Co. Semiannual.
Working Press of the Nation, National Research Bureau. Five
   volumes. Includes a listing of many free-lance writers as
   well as the topics they cover.
*Graphic Artists Guild Handbook: Pricing and Ethical Guide-
   lines*, Graphic Artists Guild, Inc., Robert M. Silver Associates. Outlines standard fees for a wide variety of graphic
   arts services.
Standard Rate and Data, Standard Rate and Data Service.
   The most comprehensive guide to all print and broadcast
   media.

Sources of Information on Small Business

1. *Small Business Administration* (SBA). The SBA offers
both free and low-cost pamphlets dealing with small-business
promotion, finance, management, and marketing. For a list of
free publications, write to Small Business Administration,
P.O. Box 15434, Fort Worth, TX 76119. Ask for form SBA
115A. To obtain a catalog of low-cost pamphlets, write to
Superintendent of Documents, Government Printing Office,
Washington, DC 20402. Request form SBA 115B.
2. *Small Business Reporter*. A series of booklets dealing
with all aspects of small business. Available from Small Business Reporter, Bank of America, Department 3401, P.O. Box
37000, San Francisco, CA 94137.
3. *SCORE* (Service Corps of Retired Executives). SCORE
is a volunteer force of more than 7,800 seasoned business
executives who offer their services without pay in all fifty
states. Check the phone book for the listing of your local
office. SCORE is sponsored by the government and under the
direction of the SBA.
4. *"Dun & Bradstreet's Management Source Publications*

for Small Business.'' This pamphlet lists publications of interest to small-business managers. Many of the publications are available at no charge; others can be borrowed from your local library.

INDEX